商务英语名品案例系列

国际市场投资高手案例分析

（英汉对照）

主　编：刘昕蓉
副主编：陈　媛
编　者：（按姓氏笔画排列）
　　　　王欣梅　王佳歆　李　伦　张春梅
　　　　袁建敏　董妍伽　葛瑞平

南开大学出版社
天津

图书在版编目（CIP）数据

国际市场投资高手案例分析：英汉对照／刘昕蓉主编.
天津：南开大学出版社，2008.4
（商务英语名品案例系列）
ISBN 978-7-310-02901-3

Ⅰ.国… Ⅱ.刘… Ⅲ.①英语－汉语－对照读物②投资－
案例－分析－世界 Ⅳ.H319.4:F

中国版本图书馆 CIP 数据核字（2008）第 044827 号

南开大学出版社出版发行

出版人：肖占鹏

地址：天津市南开区卫津路 94 号　　邮政编码：300071

营销部电话：(022)23508339　23500755

营销部传真：(022)23508542　　邮购部电话：(022)23502200

*

河北昌黎太阳红彩色印刷有限责任公司印刷

全国各地新华书店经销

*

2008 年 4 月第 1 版　　2008 年 4 月第 1 次印刷

787×960 毫米　16 开本　22.25 印张　407 千字

定价：35.00 元

如遇图书印装质量问题，请与本社营销部联系调换，电话：(022)23507125

前　言

近几年，投资方面的书籍总是引起那些极具聪明才智的人们的高度关注。但是要想找到一本涉及投资学理论及实践的入门教材，从中既可以纵观精彩纷呈的投资世界，又不会备感投资理论的艰涩，是很难的。

所以我们便策划和编著了这样一本书。在这个投资活动全球性扩张的时代，在这个信息技术爆炸式地增长的时代，我们想借助这本书的内容，把那些鲜活的投资案例和长盛不衰的投资学理论带入课堂，带进金融服务机构，带到商业企业乃至个人的投资经历中去。

几经筛选，我们选中了以《福布斯》杂志资深编辑 Richard Phalon 所著的《伟大的投资故事》中的案例为蓝本，保留了原文中逻辑性强、重点突出的部分，加上详细的语言及背景知识注释，强调系统的理论分析，又配以优美的译文。手捧此书，相信读者们会感到，在那个没有硝烟的战场上，历史和现实难免几度交汇，卓越与知识的魅力是那么持久和永恒。

本书共九章，每章分为四大部分。第一部分为英文原文的投资案例。读者可以读到原汁原味的精彩英文案例，生词和词组为读者学习提供了帮助，详细的注释介绍了案例中涉及的主要人物、公司及专业术语。第二部分为投资理论知识点。这部分简要归纳和介绍了与该案例内容相关的投资学理论要点，通读全书后，读者可以从中系统地学习到几经发展的投资学理论。第三部分为案例分析。这部分包括五至十个英文问题及答案，这些问题囊括了案例中的全部核心知识及主题。第四部分为案例的译文。在英汉对照的学习过程中，读者可以进一步地学习和欣赏优美的英文，更深刻地了解蕴含其中的那些在财富世界沉浮的人物的精彩人生和至理箴言。

本书所选的案例致力于客观还原投资世界的精彩与残酷，其分析部分旨在说明如何掌握这些投资学基本原则，并将其转化为现实投资问题的完备和实际的解决方案。本书的各个章节所覆盖的内容既有简单的概念，又有高深的公式。本书对各个案例的分析不仅用来说明人物的经历、介绍他们的洞见，同时也用来描述近半个世纪投资环境的特征及变化。

编写这本书的过程既艰辛又充满了乐趣，因为身边的同事、家人和朋友是那么无私地为该书的顺利完成提供了如此多的鼓励和帮助，尤其是我们这个编创团队，大家克服了种种困难，将智力和心力成功地"投资"到这本旨在成为伟大投资思想之传播工具的作品上。

深入研读本书，你将在投资及语言学习上获取更多更新的知识，你的思维方式及处事态度将会逐渐发生变化。过去的生活或许不会重演，更高的价值确实可以发现！

本书一至九章的编译负责人分别为：刘昕蓉、李伦、张春梅、王欣梅、陈媛、葛瑞平、王佳歆、董妍伽和袁建敏。全书的内容由刘昕蓉和陈媛进行修定和补充。匆忙之作，不足之处，敬请谅解。

编　者

目 录

Chapter One
Godfather of Modern Security—
Benjamin Graham

第一章
现代证券之父——本杰明·格雷厄姆

I. Case Study

Benjamin Graham's arrival on Wall Street in that summer of 1914 was not much more than a chance encounter, a light reconnaissance of the world of money. There were no telltales that Graham would live in that world for the next four decades, synthesize a dominant theory of value investing, and in the process create a class of thousands of superinvestors like himself. Among the chief disciples is one-time student and employee Warren Buffett, who graces Graham with the ultimate accolade. Graham, he says, had more influence on him than any man except his father.

Buffett underscored the link through his own son's middle name—Howard Graham Buffett. Among other expressions of filial gratitude, Buffett has unabashedly told fellow Berkshire Hathaway shareholders, "I benefited enormously from the intellectual generosity of Ben Graham, the greatest teacher in the history of finance."

Buffett doesn't burn incense at Graham's shrine simply because he was a nice guy. Graham has been dead for more than three decades now, but there are still uncanny touches of his style in the discipline that has made Buffett and dozens of other disciples very rich men.

What did Graham so lastingly teach this school of brilliant portfolio managers? The simple hardheaded principle that is at the heart of value investing: the need to cut through market prices to reality. When you buy a stock, you are not buying a piece of paper; you're buying part of a business. There is often a huge spread between the "intrinsic value" of the business and the price that a frequently manic stock market is putting on the paper. Buy a stock significantly above intrinsic value and you court a loss. Buy below intrinsic value and you have a good chance of making money over the long haul, with little risk of taking a permanent hit on your capital. The basic bet is that market value and intrinsic value will ultimately converge.

In one of a number of lead articles he wrote for *Forbes*, Graham thought of his strategy as "buying dollar bills for 50¢." It was a strategy that enabled him to survive the bad years of the 1929 crash while others were sinking and it brought him returns of 20 percent or more over many good years.

The touchstone is intrinsic value. How to establish it? Graham, an irrepressible polymath who loved puns, dancing at Fred Astaire studios (mainly for the pulchritude of the female instructors), and Latin verse, worked at refining his formula almost literally to his dying day in 1976 at age 82. First he concentrated on undervalued assets. Then he began working earnings and dividends into his risk/reward equations. His formula in its final form, a distillation to ten critical elements, took shape as Graham's "Last Will & Testament" in the Forbes of August 1, 1977 (see box).

Ten Points: Ben Graham's Last Will and Testament

In his last years, Ben Graham distilled six decades of experience into ten criteria that would help the intelligent investor pick value stocks from the chaff of the market.
The Ten:

1. An earnings-to-price yield of twice the triple-A bond yield. The earnings yield is the reciprocal of the price earnings ratio.

2. A price/earnings ratio down to four-tenths of the highest average P/E ratio the stock reached in the most recent five years. (Average P/E ratio is the average stock price for a year divided by the earnings for that year.)

3. A dividend yield of two-thirds of the triple-A bond yield.

4. A stock price down to two-thirds of tangible book value per share.

5. A stock price down to two-thirds of net current asset value—current assets less total debt.

6. Total debt less than tangible book value.

7. Current ratio (current assets divided by current liabilities) of two or more.

8. Total debt equal or less than twice the net quick liquidation value as defined in No.5.

9. Earnings growth over the most recent ten years of seven percent compounded—a doubling of earnings in a ten-year period.

10. Stability of growth in earnings—defined as no more than two declines of five percent or more in year-end earnings over the most recent ten years.

Together, Ben's ten points construct a formidable risk/reward barrier. The first five point to potential reward by pinpointing a low price in relation to such key operating results as earnings. The second five measure risk by measuring financial soundness and stability of earnings.
Backtesting has shown that concentrating on stocks that meet just two or three of these criteria can produce good results.

The refinements evolved out of his own experience in Wall Street, three decades of teaching at the Columbia Graduate School of Business, and the writing of his multiedition best-sellers, *Security Analysis* and *The Intelligent Investor*.

Graham had little time for the hype and hyperbole of Wall Street. Talking of growth stock fads and high-tech cults shortly before he died, Graham noted that the Bourbon Kings were said "to forget nothing and learn nothing." "Wall Street people," he added, "typically learn nothing and forget everything." It's fashionable in these high-flying days to dismiss Graham as irrelevant. If Graham is irrelevant, so is Warren Buffett.

The education of Ben Graham, Wall Streeter, began that summer in 1914. Graham was 20, a star young graduate and classics scholar who sometimes thought of himself as the wandering Ulysses.

Now, carrying a recommendation from Columbia Dean Frederick Keppel, Graham was pacing anxiously in front of Trinity Church, waiting for the hands on the steeple clock to creep to 3:10 PM. That was his cue to cut across the street to 100 Broadway and an after-the-market-close interview for a job as a junior bond salesman with the partners of the New York Stock Exchange firm of Newburger, Henderson & Loeb.

The reception was a bit starchy. Senior partner Alfred Newburger—"Mr. A.N." as he was known in the firm—seemed surprised that Graham, despite a fistful of distinctions in math, English lit, and philosophy, had dropped out of the only economics course he had taken. Graham had whizzed through Columbia on a scholarship in two and a half years, working the while at such odd jobs as a night shift manager for the U.S. Express Co. and peddling cut-rate photograph coupons door-to-door. Graham hurriedly told Mr. A.N. he just hadn't been able to reschedule the economics course, and then demonstrated his practical grasp of the subject by talking up the starting salary on his new job from $10 to $12 a week. "We always start our young men at $10 a week, but in view of your necessities we'll stretch a point and make it $12," Mr. A.N. told the new recruit.

He ended the interview, recalled Ben, with a warning. "If you speculate, young man, you'll lose your money. Always remember that." It was a warning that young Ben took to heart—but only after getting blind-sided a couple of times by his own enthusiasms. When he talked speculation, Mr. A.N. didn't mean the threat of a paper loss. He was talking about getting wiped out.

Learning the business from the ground up—matching buy and sell orders in the back office, swapping checks and stock certificates with other runners and went right on working two after-hours jobs. One of them was tutoring army officers' sons on Governors Island: the other teaching English to foreigners at night school.

Working his way out of backoffice chores to a slot in the Newburger bond department, Ben needed no repetition of Mr. A.N.'s warnings on the perils of speculation. He had learned of them at his mother's knee. Mrs. Grossbaum had a small margin account and, among other stocks, had been trading odd lots of U.S. Steel. As a small boy, recalled Ben, he had checked the financial pages to keep tabs on how the stock was doing—knowing just enough "to be glad when the price advanced, and sorry when it was down." His mother's account was wiped out in the panic of 1907, adding to the anxiety Graham often felt when Mrs. Grossbaum sent him to the bank to cash a personal check. "Is Mrs. Grossbaum good for five dollars?" the tellers would whisper.

At Newburger, Henderson & Loeb, Graham was beginning to formulate the crux of his theory of value investing. All investments are tinged with some element of speculation, he thought. The trick was to limit the level of risk. Always look for a margin of safety. Ben's theories did not spring full-blown, like Minerva from the brow of Jupiter. They grew by trial and error—some wins, some fearful losses—and maturation.

Did the family's business misfortunes help to forge Graham's conviction that the margin of safety was the supreme rule of the investment road? At age 20 he had already tasted what for many would have been a lifetime of exiguous bad luck—with plenty more to come.

Take the summer of 1910, spent after graduation from Boys High School in Brooklyn on a hard scrabble dairy farm in upstate New York. Ben was working a 60-hour week, pitching hay, slopping the pigs, mucking out stables. The pay: $10 a month and board. After chores at night, Ben was teaching himself ancient Greek by lantern light, certain that he had won a Pulitzer scholarship that would give him a full four-year ticket through Columbia.

Then came the devastating word. He thought he had sailed through a final interview only to be told that he had not made the cut after all. He drifted through a couple of monotonous assembly-line jobs, easing the tedium by reciting to himself passages from the Rubaiyat and the Aeneid.

Then came a stunning note from Columbia's Dean Keppel. Through some administrative mix-up, Ben's name had been confused with that of cousin, Louis Grossbaum, who already had a Pulitzer. "But I've lost a whole year," Ben told Dean Keppel. Then, characteristically, he set about cramming for placement exams that enabled him to catch up on lost time and then some.

Thus, by the time he had nodded acquiescence to Mr. A.N.'s caution on speculation two elements of young Ben's nascent theory of value investing were already in place: Anticipate the unexpected; prepare for it with rigorous study.

In spare moments at Newburger, Ben set about memorizing descriptions of the bonds on the firm's recommended list, jotting them down in a loose-leaf notebook.

He began looking for deeper patterns behind the raw numbers, a challenging task in a time when companies were only reluctantly beginning to disclose at least window dressing on their operations, and stock prices were more often as not a product of rumor and manipulation.

One of Ben's early reports—an analysis showing that Missouri Pacific Railroad bonds had slipped below investment grade—was so penetrating that it drew a job offer from a competing brokerage firm. Newburger preempted the bid by raising the upstart's pay from $12 to $18 a week. He was shifted out of bond sales (where he'd generated very little in commissions) and breveted the firm's first "statistician" (i.e., a security analyst).

At one point, he projected improving earnings for the Missouri, Kansas & Texas Railroad. The stock seemed cheap at $12 a share. Ben went into a joint account with one of Newburger's customers men on 100 shares and was showing a small profit when authority intervened in the person of Mr. A.N. ("He seemed to know everything about everybody in the firm," recalled Ben.) Newburger ordered Ben to unwind the deal and chewed him out.

"If you are going to speculate in something, you should have better sense than to pick a run-down, no good road like the M.K.T." It was another lesson in the need for rigorous analysis. Mr. A.N. had taken a hard look at the interest coverage on the road's bonds. Graham hadn't, distracted for the moment by what proved to be only a temporary (and suspiciously fortuitous) bulge in the M.K.T.'s profits.

In the end, Mr. A.N. was right, but so was Ben. The M.K.T. did indeed flounder into bankruptcy, but the Newburger firm made good money on a new piece of Graham analysis. On his suggestion, it bought stock at 50¢ a share that on the road's reorganization brought new stock worth twice as much.

The M.K.T. call launched Ben's career as a risk arbitrageur—a pursuit requiring a quick mathematical turn of mind, and an eye keen enough to distinguish two discrete bits of information: market price on the one hand and underlying value on the other.

Ben's first big such hit lay in the perception that the market was grossly underpricing the liquidation of the Guggenheim Exploration Company. It owned major interests in four Big Board-traded mining companies. As reconstructed by colleague (and fellow superinvestor) Irving Kahn in a study for the Financial Analysts Research Foundation, Guggenheim's going-out-of-business arithmetic looked like this: Each share of the holding company would receive .7277 shares of Kennecott Copper .1172 shares of Chino Copper; .0833 shares of American Smelting; and .185 shares of Ray Consolidated Copper.

All told, the package carried a market value of $76.23. Guggenheim

Exploration, on the other hand, was selling at a bargain $68.88. Ben recommended that Newburger simultaneously sell the pieces and buy Guggenheim for a clear gross profit of $7.35 a share.

The spread was there because of the risks: Shareholders might turn down the deal in the three months before it was scheduled to fall into place; the deal might get tied up in litigation or some regulatory hang-up; prices on the small pieces might rise sharply before they were distributed to Guggenheim holders, thereby wiping out the profit spread. Ben had assessed the dangers and decided they weren't substantial. Ben was right and won himself another raise. On the strength of the Guggenheim coup, he began to develop a personal following and a deepening sense of value investing: *When you spot intrinsic value at a discount, go for it!* Ben's margin of safety: the strong likelihood that Guggenheim would trade up to the value of the pieces.

Among his new followers was Algernon Tassin, one of Ben's favorite professors at Columbia. Tassin put his lifesaving—about $10,000 in blue-chip utility stocks—into a joint account. Ben would run the book; profits and losses would be split 50-50. Ben's reputation was anchored in the idea that he had tamed speculation. There was risk, but you weren't betting on some vague evanescent turn in the market to make you rich. You were buying a piece of hidden value the market would recognize soon or late and price accordingly.

The Tassin account was doing well, but much else was on the boil. The United States had entered World War I. Ben was financing a new venture of Leon's (he of the movie house failure). This involved the purchase of the Broadway Phonograph Shop, located uptown at Broadway & 98th St. The cost, about $7,000, had come out of Ben's share of the profits of the Tassin account. The record shop failed to live up to its promise. Unfortunately for Ben, its swan song coincided with a sharp peace scare sell-off in the stock market.

The peace scare—a flash that the Germans were about to surrender—was a hiccup typical of runaway bull markets. Traders glorying in war-driven prices had no confidence in the underlying economy.

In its full dimension, Ben's value theory holds that safety-minded investors (as distinguished from speculators) should shift proportionately more money out of stocks and into bonds as equity prices boom. The point is to be able to get back into stocks when bear market bargains reappear. Ordinarily, Ben would have been buying as peace scare prices fell. But with all his cash tied up in Broadway Phonograph and its Vocalion Brand record inventories, he was in a liquidity bind. He had no buying power. Worse yet, he couldn't meet margin calls on the money borrowed to leverage the Tassin account.

To cover the calls, he was forced to sell of some of his old professor's treasured blue chip, American Light & Traction stock.

In his memoirs, Graham recalls wandering the Financial District in bleak despair: "I had a debt to the account which I could not repay; what was worse... My management of Tassin's capital had failed abjectly."

The old tutor stuck with Ben, though it was almost two years before he was fully repaid at the rate of $60 a month—all Ben could afford. What comes around goes around. Tassin's continuing trust in Ben made him a rich man. And Ben, who subsequently bought a substantial piece of a bankrupt Aeolian Company preferred stock at distress prices, finally managed to squeeze a profit out of the record business. The Tassin failure burned, though. And while it made him much more conservative about borrowing money, Ben was about to get another lesson in humility that reinforced the innate caution of his still evolving market strategy.

A friend arranged for Ben to be let in on the ground floor of a heavily promoted new issue for an outfit called Savold Tire. The draw was high-tech stuff: Savold's revolutionary new process for retreading automobile tires. The stock opened at 10 and zipped to 35. Within a week, recalled Graham, his initial stake of $5,000 brought a check for three times that amount.

Graham clamored for more, getting himself and friends in for $20,000 on a Savold affiliate floated four weeks later. Inside price: $20. The stock opened at $50, and Graham celebrated his twenty-fifth birthday in a "blaze of excitement": a check for the original contribution, plus some 150 percent in profits.

Disappointingly, Graham and his friends were shut out of the next Savold offer. Sorry, just not enough stock to go 'round, Ben was told. Then came the good word— yet another affiliate was about to hit The Street. Last call! Graham quickly put together $60,000, half of it anted up by three friends, and got ready to pop the champagne on another smash debut.

The offering didn't go off as scheduled. Administrative delays, Ben was told. Anxious days went by. Then like a puff of smoke, bids on all the Savold companies totally disappeared in the raucous outcry of the old outdoor Curb Market.

Stunned by his own cupidity, Graham took the pledge. Moral: Late bull market IPOs are all part of the high-octane speculative environment. The game hasn't changed very much.

Ben, at least, had direct recourse. He ultimately collared the promoter and succeeded in squeezing out of him about 30¢ on every dollar that had been plunged on the last Savold offer. A chagrined Graham had done no homework on the issue— a lamentable breach of the advice handed down in a series of pamphlets ("Lessons for Investors") he had been writing for Newburger clients. Graham had put heavy emphasis in the pamphlets on the need to search for intrinsic value priced well below the market. Don't follow the crowd, he preached.

By 1926, Ben's reputation as a value player and the runaway bull market had brought new affluence to the young Grahams. There were three children now, and a spacious apartment at 86th St. and Riverside Drive, in a neighborhood that to Ben "spoke of financial success." The family summered in the carefully manicured enclave of Deal, on the New Jersey shore, and Ben began to take squash and golf lessons at the City Athletic Club.

The new affluence was a direct result of the under-valued situations Ben continued to dig up, sometimes almost by sixth sense. Working with $450,000 in capital now, much of it his own, Graham was winnowing through an Interstate Commerce Commission annual report on railroads one day when he did a double take on a footnote reference to a group of pipeline companies.

Graham was soon on a train to Washington, D.C. In the records room of the ICC, he requested documents he hadn't known existed before spotting the footnote reference in some of the pipeline financials.

Eight of these pipelines had come out of the breakup of the Standard Oil Company in 1911. Their job was to move crude oil from the wellheads to the refineries. Tankers had taken over much of their business and Wall Street was paying them little attention, as evidenced by the junk bond-like nine percent yield on Northern Pipeline Company common stock.

Dividend payout had already been cut some, and the yield was signaling that Wall Street expected still more trouble ahead. The mingy one-line income statement the pipelines made public did little to dispel this apprehension.

Shifting through the full balance sheets he found on file at the ICC—documents other "statisticians" had missed—Ben made a startling discovery. The pipelines were loaded with prime railroad bonds, which in the case of Northern Pipeline amounted to about $95 a share. The stock was selling at $65 and paying a $6 dividend. Ben began nibbling at the stock and slowly acquired 2,000 shares, making him and his partners in the Graham Joint Account the biggest holders of record after the Rockefeller Foundation.

Ben confronted the Standard Oil management with the unwelcome idea that all this surplus capital clearly not needed in the business ought to be distributed to shareholders. Not surprisingly, he was told to get lost and smothered in Robert's Rules of Order when he tried to make his point heard at an annual meeting.

Ben responded by buying up much more of Northern than his partnership could afford. He began lobbying other stockholders, and succeeded in getting himself elected to the board—something no outsider had ever managed to do before. It took two years, and some behind-the-scenes nudging by the puissant Rockefeller Foundation, but a restructuring finally brought Ben and his followers total value of about $110 on their shares. Ben's forte of rigorous research had once again carried the day. Ben didn't particularly like being portrayed as a self-serving outsider in the pipeline struggle—a "raider"—but he had learned another important lesson. It is one thing to perceive value; often another to capitalize on it.

The value of the Graham Joint Account was approaching $2.5 million, much of it reflecting Ben's reinvested profits. Some new money had come from fellow Boys High and Columbia grad Jerome Newman. Newman, a shrewd negotiator and businessman, was beginning to play Mr. Outside to Ben's cerebral Mr. Inside in a partnership destined to last more than 30 years.

Ben was sharing some of his investment ideas with Big Names. One of them was mover and shaker Bernard Baruch, who rather condescendingly (Ben thought) offered Graham a junior partnership. Ben was happy to be able to turn him down. The stocks that Baruch got aboard were typical Graham picks. They were rather stodgy solid franchises like Pepperell Manufacturing (sheets and pillowcases) and Heywood & Wakefield (baby carriages), selling well below going business value, ignored in the great bull market rush for glamour items like Radio Corporation.

Though still able to cherry pick values, Graham was certain a grossly overpriced market was riding for a fall—a point sounded often in the once-a-week, two-hour-long security analysis classes he had begun to teach at the Columbia Business School.

Ben had been talking about writing, a book on security analysis for some time now and thought that preparing a lecture series would help him put one together Ben's classes were liberally salted with Wall Street professionals, who happily swapped market tips. The classes focused on current market case studies (Pepperell Manufacturing, for one) and were wildly popular. As the market mounted to its 1929 peak, more than 150 students were absorbing the Graham keys to income statements and balance sheets, with particular emphasis on the ambiguities of corporate accounting practices.

It was 1929, and the excesses of the great bull market were coming home to roost. After a spectacular 1928 (up 60 percent versus 51 percent for the Dow Jones Industrials), Ben had come into 1929 with what he thought was a cautiously hedged position—about $2.5 million in convertible preferred stock offset by a short position in an equal amount of common stocks. If the market dropped, the common would fall faster than the preferred and Graham could close out the hedge with a profit.

In addition, he was carrying common stocks with a market value of about $ 4.5 million on borrowed money—margin of about $2 million. By the standards of the day (you could buy stock with as little as 10 percent down) Graham was looking at the world from behind what seemed to be a solid bulkhead. The painful memory of unmanageable debt in the Tassin account was never far from his mind. The waves of Black Tuesday, however (October 29, 1929), struck with unprecedented ferocity. Some $14 billion in market value got wiped out huge volume.

With the ticker running hours behind trades on the floor, prices were mainly guesswork. Exhausted clerks were catnapping nights in the office in a vain effort to keep the paperwork abreast of the flood. Peak to trough, the Dow Jones Industrials in 1929 sank from a wonderful nonsense 380 to under 200. Graham made money on the short side of the market, but still came out of the year with a 20 percent loss. The licking he took in 1930 was even worse—50 percent (versus 29 percent for the Dow Jones Industrials). Ben was struggling to pay down debt and at the same time hold on to stocks he saw as having solid potential.

By the end of 1932, the fund was down to less than 25 percent of the $2.5 million with which it had entered 1929. Fearful that the losses would never end, sick that he had failed friends and family, Ben wrote a poem that asked:

Where shall he sleep whose soul knows no rest
Poor hunted stag in wild woods of care?

Though haunted by uncertainty, Ben had actually done amazingly well. From the depths of the 50 percent loss in 1930, he was down only 16 percent in 1931 (versus minus 48 percent for the Dow Jones Industrials) and down only three percent (versus minus 17 percent DJIs) in 1932. Ben was battered but alive. If Graham had done as badly as the market as a whole, he would have been wiped out. His margin of safety: relatively conservative borrowing, a cautiously hedged position that produced major profits on the downside.

Still a lot better off than he had been 10 years before, Ben began to retrench "The crash reaffirmed parsimonious viewpoints and habits that had been ingrained in me by the tight financial situation of my early youth," he recalled in his memoirs.

Ben's intuitive sense of value right along had focused on such great finds as Guggenheim Exploration and Northern Pipeline—situations where he spotted underlying riches at well below market prices.

Graham had to work hard to dig up ten strikes like those. Now, suddenly, after the Great Crash that had put him in such hot water, value was everywhere and going begging. Ben set a cadre of his students to matching market prices and values for all 600 industrials listed on the New York Stock Exchange. This was foot slogging work in the pre-calculator, pre-computer age, but the results were startling. One out of every three of the 600 could be bought for less than net working capital. More than 50 were selling for less than the cash (and marketable securities) they had in the bank.

Montgomery Ward, for example, was trading for less than half of net quick assets. For $6.50 a share, you got $16 in working capital and the whole of this great retailing franchise—catalog business and all—for nothing. With issues like American Car & Foundry and Munsinger, $20 and $11 would bring $50 a share and $17 a share, respectively, in cash alone. The rest of the businesses—bricks, mortar, machinery, customers, and profits—was a free ride.

It was clear "that in the best judgement of Wall Street, these businesses are worth more dead than alive," Ben told *Forbes* readers. Liquidated in a private sale, they would at least fetch working capital, which was a lot more than what they were bringing on the floor of the New York Stock Exchange.

Yes, there was a bear market. Busted booms, continued Ben, always bring "unduly low prices." There had been a bear market in 1921, too, "but with respect to cash assets alone, present prices are relatively six time lower" than in the deep sell of eight years earlier.

Ben's students' research showed that corporate operating results were not "materially poorer, so why weren't investors stepping up to the plate on these bargains?" "50 Cents on the Dollar," read the Forbes headline. Why were they selling out for a fraction of such real values as cash in the till?

Good question. It is question—yet another of the many parallels in their lives—that Warren Buffett raised in *Forbes* 40 years later after go-go stocks cratered in the sell-off of 1973-1974. Prices were so low that Buffett felt "like an oversexed guy in a harem." "This is the time to start investing," he told *Forbes* readers. You had to be patient and wait for buying times like these, he added, echoing the value precepts of his mentor Ben Graham. "You're dealing with a lot of silly people in the marketplace; it's like a great big casino and everyone else is boozing. If you can stick with Pepsi, you should be OK."

Prices soon took off in one of the sharpest rallies ever, but Buffett was back in *Forbes* again five years later, preaching Grahamisms to pension managers in yet another sell-off. Why were they stampeding into bonds, asked Buffett, instead of bargain-basement equities "aggregating book value or less?"

His answer was not very different from Graham's take on the Great Crash 50 years earlier. Graham's diagnosis: The "new era madness" of 1928-1929 had brought deep psychological changes in the "proverbially weak" logic of Wall Street. Investors who used to routinely screen values in terms of balance sheet numbers had been carried away by the "excessive emphasis being laid" on reported or much ballyhooed anticipated earnings. Lost in the bull rush was the idea that rising earnings might be only a temporary one shot, or even deceptive.

As Buffett notes, Graham had no real intensity for money. Truly a classicist, his deepest satisfactions were intellectual—working the numbers, watching them come out.

He had married again (for the third time), started a new family, moved to Beverly Hills and began teaching at the UCLA Graduate School of Business in a tenure that lasted 15 years. He tinkered with inventing an improved version of the slide rule, translated a favorite novel from Spanish, and continued to refine his value strategies through successive editions of his books.

Ben began to focus more on earnings and dividends than assets. As published in *Forbes*, the new book was designed as a handy pocket tool for the average investor and produced superior results for five of the six ten-year market periods that Graham matched it against.

More recent—if limited—backtesting comes from Henry R. Oppen-heimer, professor of finance at the State University of New York, Binghampton. Tracking the years from 1974 to 1981 in an article for the *Financial Analysts Journal*, Oppenheimer found that stocks picked on the basis of two or three of Ben's criteria would have brought mean annual returns of at least 26 percent. That was double the 14 percent return on an index of Big Board and American Stock Exchange issues.

Graham's risk reward screens are so demanding it's often hard to find companies that meet more than a few of his criteria. Changes in business practices— a switch from high-dividend payouts to open market stock buy-backs, for example— have altered the relationship that Graham liked to see between stock and bond yields.

Other criteria have withstood the test of time. Minimum earnings growth and stability are certainly two of the hurdles any stock should clear before making the buy list. And while you may not be able to find any discounts at the moment, Graham's tests will help you determine whether the price you are being asked to pay is within reasonably conservative parameters or totally out of sight. As Mr. A.N. warned, "If you speculate, young man, you'll lose your money."

Graham himself thought all he had learned in six decades of tracking the market could be summed up in three words: margin of safety. The concept got lost— to considerable pain—in the super-heated environment of the last several years. Off-the-chart prices can be justified only if everything in an unpredictable future goes exactly right. By Graham's standards, the margin of safety on runaway stocks can be measured only in imaginary numbers.

The margin of safety is really a comfort factor—the idea is to cut some slack against such X-factors as bad judgement, bad luck, and the unpredictables always lurking around the corner. In an era of lower market multiples and interest rates, comfort factors were easier to come by. To cite one of Ben's examples, a more or less typical stock would be selling at an earnings yield of nine percent—the receiprocal of a price earnings ratio of 11. With high-quality bond yields at four percent, you had a margin of five percent going for you. Compounding the margin over a long-term investment in a company with reasonably predictably earning power, you would likely have no trouble sleeping nights.

This Grahamesque exercise remains a useful tool. It won't generate comfort levels of anything like five percent, but will nonetheless provide a realistic measure of the depth of the waters you're about to plunge into.

The touchstone is still intrinsic value—the discounted present value of the cash that can be taken out of a company over an investment period of a decade or so. Buy below intrinsic value, and you've got a margin of safety. Buy above it, and you may be looking for trouble.

In short, the margin of safety lies in minimizing business risk. For value players like O. Mason Hawkins and G. Staley Cates, chairman and president, respectively of the Memphis, Tennessee-based Longleaf Funds, that means looking for such competitive edges as low costs, entrenched brand names, and dominant market share.

You need to measure financial strength, too—low debt levels, limited liabilities, and plenty of free cash flow reinvested at high margins. The trick, of course, is to find at least some of these attributes in a package selling well under the market.

It can be done. In his noted essay on the "Superinvestors of Graham-and-Doddsville," commemorating the fiftieth anniversary of the publication of *Security Analysis*, Buffet cites the amazingly consistent performance of nine of Graham's former students and intellectual heirs. Their styles differ somewhat, but they all adhere to yet another of Ben Graham's tenets, a paraphrase of Spinoza: Value is best approached from the viewpoint of calamity.

Key Words and Expressions:

back office	内勤工作
balance sheet	资产负债表
bear market	熊市
Berkshire Hathaway Inc.	伯克希尔·哈撒韦公司
bond yield	债券市场利息率
book value	账面价值
bull market	牛市
chew out sb.	严厉责备某人
current ratio	流动比率
curb Market	股票证券场外交易市场

dividend payout	派息
dividend yield	股息生息率
earnings yield	收益率
free cash flow	自由现金流
GEICO	政府雇员保险公司
Guggenheim Exploration Company	古干海姆探测公司
interest coverage	利息保障倍数
interstate Commerce Commission	州际商务协会
IPO	首次公开募股
intrinsic value	内在价值
limited liability	有限债务责任
liquidation	n. 清算
litigation	n. 诉讼
Longleaf Funds	长叶基金
Minerva	密涅瓦，智慧、技术及工艺之神
Margin of Safety	安全边际
net current asset	流动资产净额
net quick liquidation	净清算价值
net working capital	净运营资本
Pepperell Manufacturing	佩博雷尔制造
pinpoint	vt. 查明
Phi Beta Kappa	美国大学优等生之荣誉学会
Rubaiyat	《鲁拜集》
runaway market	失去控制的市场
UCLA	加州大学洛杉矶分校
undervalued assets	低估资产
value investing	价值投资
value stocks	价值股
wiped out	adj. 精疲力竭的，资产被耗尽的，破产的

Notes:

1. Benjamin Graham 本杰明·格雷厄姆

本杰明·格雷厄姆（1894-1976）是华尔街的传奇人物，被称为"现代证券之父"，著有《证券分析》和《聪明的投资者》。他和戴维·多德合著的《证券分析》迄今已出版了第五版，有些学者将它奉为"华尔街圣经"。他的投资哲学——基本分析法和"风险缓冲带"为沃伦·巴菲特、马里奥·加贝利、约翰·奈夫、米歇尔·普赖斯、约翰·鲍戈尔等一大批顶尖证券投资专家所推崇。为了表彰他在证券分析领域的卓越建树，美国哥伦比亚大学商学院已设立了永久的"格雷厄姆/多德教授讲座"。

他不鼓励投资者短期的投机行为，而更注重企业内在价值的发现，并强调"对于理性投资，精神态度比技巧更重要"。这一理论可以概括为：当一个股票的价格远远低于其投资价值的时候，将会给投资者带来巨大的利润空间，而不是当股价被炒作起来时，愚蠢地去购买那些价格远远高于价值的股票。

2. Warren Buffett 沃伦·巴菲特

沃伦·巴菲特被喻为"当代最成功的投资者"。在历史上伟大的投资家中，巴菲特以他敏锐的业务评估技术而引人注目。他依靠在股票、外汇市场上的投资成为世界上数一数二的富翁。他是本杰明·格雷厄姆的学生，他所信奉和倡导的价值投资理论风靡世界。巴菲特曾将价值投资归结为三点：把股票看成许多微型的商业单元；把市场波动看作你的朋友而非敌人(利润有时候来自对朋友的愚忠)；购买股票的价格应低于你所能承受的价位。"从短期来看，市场是一架投票计算器。但从长期看，它是一架称重器"。

3. Berkshire Hathaway Inc. 伯克希尔·哈撒韦公司

伯克希尔·哈撒韦公司是一家拥有众多子公司的控股公司，在纽约证交所整体上市。旗下最主要的业务领域是财产保险及再保险。经营保险业务的公司主要包括政府雇员保险集团（GEICO）、通用再保险集团（General Re）、Berkshire Hathaway 再保险集团等。非保险活动则包括地毯制造、建筑材料、家具、服装、餐馆、媒体等多种领域。

巴菲特1965年收购该公司，原来主要经营纺织业，1967年进入保险业，2005年通过内部发展和收购，保费收入已经由1967年的2000万美元变为2005年的490亿美元。该公司不同业务单元的经营决策主要由各业务单元的管理层负责，而控股公司和子公司的投资决策和其他资本分配决策则主要由董事局主席巴菲特及副主席查尔斯·芒格（Charles Munger）共同决定。

4. GEICO 政府雇员保险公司

政府雇员保险公司，又称为"盖可"公司，是美国排名前 4 位的汽车保险公司，在私人汽车保险市场上的市场份额为 6.1%。创建于 1936 年，创建人古德温是一位保险会计师。公司的主要特色有二：第一，公司的客户是政府雇员，尽管汽车事故比较频繁，但政府雇员驾驶汽车出事的概率要比其他人低很多。第二，公司的产品直接通过邮寄直销而不是通过保险代理商来代理，这样可省保险费的 10%—25%。

1948 年，格雷厄姆的投资公司以 72 万美元的代价买下了盖可的 50% 股份。但美国证券交易委员会强迫格雷厄姆投资公司将持股比例减少 10%，因为这是《投资公司法》的规定。格雷厄姆只得把股份转让给雇员，后来，盖可发展成了一个拥有十几亿美元资产的公司时，那些员工都成了百万富翁。

5. IPO 首次公开募股

首次公开招股是指一家私人企业第一次将它的股份向公众出售。通常，上市公司的股份是根据向相应证监会出具的招股书或登记声明中约定的条款通过经纪商或做市商进行销售。一般来说，一旦首次公开上市完成后，这家公司就可以申请到证券交易所或报价系统挂牌交易。

6. Value Stocks 价值股

价值股是那些被投资者忽略但本身却隐藏扎实价值的股票。那些公司有可能因为某些不利事件的发生而得到不断的卖压，故股价持续下滑。但与此同时，公司的名称、名声、建筑物、固定资产、库存及子公司等皆具有一定的价值，而这些价值却因为种种原因而未能真实地反映在其股票的价格中。价值投资者寻找并购入那些被折价的股票，持有一段时间，希望有朝一日人们将认清那些价值股的内在价值，重新燃起对此类股票的投资热情，以便从中获利。

7. Value Investing 价值投资

在成熟的证券市场中，价值投资是与成长性投资相对应的一种投资理念，其核心思想是利用贴现现金流(DCF)等方法计算股票的内在价值，将之与股票的市价进行比较，从而决定相应的买卖策略。而后者侧重公司主营收入与利润的增长，购买股票的目的主要是获得价格差而非现金红利。

8. Margin of Safety 安全边际

"安全边际"被本杰明·格雷厄姆视为价值投资的核心概念，在整个价值投资的体系中，这一概念处于至高无上的地位。

安全边际的定义是：内在价值与价格的顺差。或者说，安全边际是价值与价格相比被低估的程度或幅度。根据定义，只有当价值被低估的时候才存在安全边际或安全边际为正（+），当价值与价格相当的时候安全边际为零，而当价值被高估的时候是不存在安全边际或安全边际为负（-）。价值投资者只对价值被低估特别是被严重低估的对象感兴趣。安全边际不保证能避免损失但能保证获利的机会比损失的机会更多。

II. Knowledge Points

1. Value investing

1) Definition and theory

Value investing is a style of investment strategy from the so called "Graham & Dodd" School. Followers of this style, known as value investors, generally buy companies whose shares appear underpriced by some forms of fundamental analysis; these may include shares that are trading at, for example, high dividend yields or low price-to-earning or price-to-book ratios.

The main proponents of value investing, such as Benjamin Graham and Warren .Buffett, have argued that the essence of value investing is buying stocks at less than their intrinsic value. The discount of the market price to the intrinsic value is what Benjamin Graham called the "margin of safety". The intrinsic value is the discounted value of all future distributions.

However, the future distributions and the appropriate discount rate can only be assumptions. Warren Buffett has taken the value investing concept even further as his thinking has evolved to where for the last 25 years or so his focus has been on "finding an outstanding company at a sensible price" rather than generic companies at a bargain price.

Value investing was established by Benjamin Graham and David Dodd, both professors at Columbia University and teachers of many famous investors. In Graham's book The Intelligent Investor, he advocated the important concept of margin of safety—first introduced in Security Analysis, a 1934 book he coauthored with David Dodd—which calls for a cautionary cautious approach to investing. In terms of picking stocks, he recommended defensive investment in stocks trading not far from below their tangible book value as a safeguard to adverse future developments often encountered in the stock market.

2) Value investing performance and value strategy

Value investing has proved to be a successful investment strategy. There are several ways to evaluate its success. One way is to examine the performance of simple value strategies, such as buying low PE ratio stocks, low price-to-cash-flow ratio stocks, or low price-to-book ratio stocks. Numerous academics have published studies investigating the effects of buying value stocks. These studies have consistently found that value stocks outperform growth stocks and the market as a whole. Buffett's conclusion is identical to that of the academic research on simple value investing strategies—value investing is, on average, successful in the long run.

2. Margin of safety

1) Definition

Margin of safety (safety margin) is the difference between the intrinsic value of a stock (i.e. value based on stock valuation and what the company is actually worth) and the price that the market sets on a stock (i.e. stock price is a matter of market participants' opinions and is different from the intrinsic value).

2) History

Benjamin Graham and David Dodd, founders of Value Investing, coined the term Margin of Safety in their seminal 1934 book, "Security Analysis." The term is also described in Graham's investment classic, "The Intelligent Investor." Graham said that "the margin of safety is always dependent on the price paid" (The Intelligent Investor, Benjamin Graham, HarperBusiness Essentials, 2003).

3) Application to investing

Using margin of safety principle, one should buy a stock when its worth is more than its price on the market. This is the central thesis of Value Investing philosophy which espouses preservation of capital as its first rule of investing. Benjamin Graham suggested to look at unpopular or neglected companies with low P/E and P/Book ratios. One should also analyze financial statements and footnotes to understand whether companies have hidden or unobvious assets (i.e. investments in other companies) that are potentially unnoticed by the market.

The margin of safety protects the investor from both poor decisions and downturns in the market. Because true value is difficult to accurately compute, the margin of safety gives the investor room to make a mistake.

Warren Buffett, possibly the most famous investor today, was Benjamin Graham's student at Columbia and once said that "the three most important words of investing are 'margin of safety'."

3. Stock valuation

There are several methods used to value companies and their stocks. They attempt to give an estimate of their fair value, by using fundamental economic criteria. This theoretical valuation has to be perfected with market criteria, as the final purpose is to determine potential market prices.

1) Fundamental criteria (fair value)

The most theoretically sound stock valuation method is called income valuation or the discounted cash flow (DCF) method, involving discounting the profits (dividends, earnings, or cash flows) the stock will bring to the stockholder in the foreseeable future, and a final value on disposition. The discount rate normally has to include a risk premium which is commonly based on the capital asset pricing model.

The Gordon model or Gordon's growth model is the best known of a class of discounted dividend models. It assumes that dividends will increase at a constant growth rate (less than the discount rate) forever. The valuation is given by the formula:

$$P = D \cdot \sum_{i=1}^{\infty} \left(\frac{1+g}{1+k} \right)^{i} = D \cdot \frac{1+g}{k-g}$$

and the following table defines each symbol:

Symbol	Meaning	Units
P	estimated stock price	$ or or pound
D	last dividend paid	$ or or pound
k	discount rate	%
g	the growth rate of the dividends	%

The P/E method is perhaps the most commonly used valuation method in the stock brokerage industry. By using comparison firms, a target price/earnings (or P/E) ratio is selected for the company, and then the future earnings of the company are estimated. The valuation's fair price is simply estimated earnings times target P/E. This model is essentially the same model as Gordon's model, if k-g is estimated as the dividend payout ratio (D/E) divided by the target P/E ratio.

2) Market criteria (potential price)

Some feel that if the stock is listed in a well organized stock market, with a large volume of transactions, the listed price will be close to the estimated fair value. This is called the efficient market hypothesis.

On the other hand, studies made in the field of behavioral finance tend to show that deviations from the fair price are rather common, and sometimes quite large.

Thus, in addition to fundamental economic criteria, market criteria also have to be taken into account market-based valuation. Valuing a stock is not only to estimate its fair value, but also to determine its potential price range, taking into account market behavior aspects. One of the behavioral valuation tools is the stock image, a coefficient that bridges the theoretical fair value and the market price and it is good for everyone.

4. Two analytical models

When the objective of the analysis is to determine what stock to buy and at what price, there are two basic methodologies.

1) Fundamental analysis

Fundamental analysis maintains that markets may misprice a security in the short run but that the "correct" price will eventually be reached. Profits can be made by trading the mispriced security and then waiting for the market to recognize its "mistake" and reprice the security.

Fundamental analysis of a business involves analyzing its income statement, financial statements and health, its management and competitive advantages, and its competitors and markets.

The analysis is performed on historical and present data, but with the goal to make financial projections. There are several possible objectives:

—to calculate a company's credit risk;

—to make projection on its business performance;

——to evaluate its management and make internal business decisions;

——to make the company's stock valuation and predict its probable price evolution.

2) Technical analysis

Technical analysis maintains that all information is reflected already in the stock price, so fundamental analysis is a waste of time. Trends "are your friend" and sentiment changes predate and predict trend changes. Investors' emotional responses to price movements lead to recognizable price chart patterns. Technical analysis does not care what the "value" of a stock is. Their price predictions are only extrapolations from historical price patterns.

Investors can use both these different but somewhat complementary methods for stock picking. Many fundamental investors use technicals for deciding entry and exit points. Many technical investors use fundamentals to limit their universe of possible stock to "good" companies.

The choice of stock analysis is determined by the investor's belief in the different paradigms for "how the stock market works".

5. Options

1) Definition

Options are financial instruments that convey the right, but not the obligation, to engage in a future transaction on some underlying security. For example, a call option provides the right to buy a specified amount of a security at a set strike price at some time on or before expiration, while a put option provides the right to sell. Upon the option holder's choice to exercise the option, the party that sold, or wrote, the option must fulfill the terms of the contract.

2) Option value

In finance, the value of an option consists of two components, its intrinsic value and its time value. Time value is simply the difference between option value and intrinsic value.

3) Intrinsic value

In finance, intrinsic value refers to the value of a security which is intrinsic to or contained in the security itself.

Intrinsic value is the difference between the exercise price of the option (strike price, K) and the current value of the underlying instrument (spot price, S). If the option does not have positive monetary value, it is referred to as out-the-money. If an option is out-the-money at expiration, its holder will simply "abandon the option" and it will expire worthless. Because the option owner will never choose to lose money by exercising, an option will never have a value less than zero.

For a call option: value = Max [(S − K), 0]

For a put option: value = Max [(K − S), 0]

4) Time value

Time value is, as above, the difference between option value and intrinsic value, i.e.

Time Value = Option Value − Intrinsic Value

More specifically, an option's time value captures the possibility, however remote, that the option may increase in value due to volatility in the underlying asset. Numerically, this value depends on the time until the expiration date and the volatility of the underlying instrument's price. The time value of an option is always positive and declines exponentially with time, reaching zero at the expiration date. At expiration, where the option value is simply its intrinsic value, time value is zero. Prior to expiration, the change in time value with time is non-linear, being a function of the option price.

III. Analyzing the Case

1. What did Graham lastingly teach those brilliant portfolio managers?

Graham taught them a simple hardheaded principle that is at the heart of value investing: the need to cut through market prices to reality.

When you buy a stock, you are not buying a piece of paper; you are buying part of a business. There is often a huge spread between the "intrinsic value" of the business and the price that a frequently manic stock market is putting on the paper. Buy a stock significantly above intrinsic value and you court a loss. Buy below intrinsic value and you have a good chance of making money over the long haul, with little risk of taking a permanent hit on your capital. The basic bet is that market value and intrinsic value will ultimately converge.

2. How did Graham establish the "intrinsic value", the touchstone of value investing? What's the relationship between the intrinsic value and margin of safety?

1) First, he concentrated on undervalued assets. Then he began working earnings and dividends into his risk/reward equations. His formula in its final form is distilled to ten critical elements. It took shape as Graham's "Last Will & Testament" in *Forbes* of August 1, 1977.

2) Margin of safety is a comfort factor—the idea is to cut some slack against such X-factors as bad judgment, bad luck, and the unpredictables always lurking around the corner.

3) Intrinsic value aims at that the discounted present value of the cash that can be taken out of a company over an investment period of a decade or so. Buy below intrinsic value, and you have got a margin of safety. Buy above it, and you may be looking for trouble.

3. How do you understand "Ben's Ten Points"?

Together, Ben's Ten Points construct a formidable risk/reward barrier. The first five point to potential reward by pinpointing a low price in relation to such key operating results as earnings. The second five measure risk by measuring financial soundness and stability of earnings.

4. What is Ben's first big success in identifying a value stock?

1) Ben's first big hit lay in the perception that the market was grossly underpricing the liquidation of the Guggenheim Exploration Company. It owned major interests in four Big Board-traded mining companies.

2) Guggenheim's going-out-of-business arithmetic looked like this: Each share of the holding company would receive .7277 shares of Kennecott Copper; .1172 shares of Chino Copper; .0833 shares of American Smelting; and .185 shares of Ray Consolidated Copper. So, the package carried a market value of $76.23. Guggenheim Exploration, on the other hand, was selling at a bargain $68.88. Ben recommended that Newbruger simultaneously sell the pieces and buy Guggenheim for a clear gross profit of $ 7.35 a share. Meanwhile, Ben had assessed the dangers and decided they weren't substantial. By doing this, Ben won himself another raise.

5. What trouble did Ben's management in the Tassin Account encounter during the "Peace Scare"?

1) The peace scare was a hiccup typical of runaway bull markets. Traders

glorying in war-driven prices had no confidence in the underlying economy.

2) In its full dimension, Ben's value theory holds that safety-minded investors should shift proportionately more money out of stocks and into bonds as equity prices boom. The point is to be able to get back into stocks when bear market bargains reappear.

3) Ordinarily, Ben would have been buying as peace scare prices fell. But with all his cash tied up in Broadway Phonograph and its Vocalion brand record inventories, he was in a liquidity bind. He had no buying power. Worse, he couldn't meet margin calls on the money borrowed to leverage the Tassin account. To cover the calls, he was forced to sell of some of his old professor's treasured blue chip, American Light & Traction stock.

6. What other elements of a business are also necessary to be considered and measured in order to achieve the margin of safety, which lies in minimizing business risk?

You need to measure financial strength, too-low debt levels, limited liabilities, and plenty of free cash flow reinvested at high margins. The trick, of course, is to find at least some of these attributes in a package selling well under the market.

IV. Translation of the Case

1914 年夏天，本杰明·格雷厄姆来到华尔街，这只是一次偶然的机遇，他对这个财富世界进行了一次小小的探索。没有人料到格雷厄姆会就此在这个世界里生活了四十余载，创造了一套极其卓越的价值投资理论，并在此期间创造了数位如他本人一样的超级投资家。沃伦·巴菲特是他的众多弟子之一，他曾是格雷厄姆的学生兼雇员，并对格雷厄姆极尽赞美之辞。他说，除了父亲，格雷厄姆是对他影响最深远的人。

巴菲特以自己儿子的第二个名——格雷厄姆（儿子的全名是哈佛·格雷厄姆·巴菲特）来强调他与格雷厄姆的密切关系。谈到格雷厄姆，巴菲特不仅以晚辈的口吻大发感激之辞，而且还直言不讳地告诉伯克希尔·哈撒韦公司的股东们："本杰明·格雷厄姆是金融历史上最伟大的导师，我从他的慷慨相授的睿智中获益良多。"

不仅仅因为格雷厄姆是个好人，巴菲特就会对他顶礼膜拜。格雷厄姆已经去世三十多年了，但是令人不可思议的是，他所创建的投资理论至今依然为他的弟子所沿袭。正是这一定律使巴菲特和格雷厄姆的其他弟子变得家财万贯。

格雷厄姆究竟用了什么经久不衰的法宝来指教这些杰出的证券投资组合的经理人呢？这就是价值投资理论的核心观点，也是一个简单且无懈可击的原则：把市场价格还原现实。当购买股票时，你买的不是一张纸，而是某个商家的一部分。然而，这个商家的"内在价值"和在狂燥的市场操纵下所体现的纸面价值之间有着相当大的差距。如果买进市场价格明显高于其内在价值的股票，那么你必然会遭遇投资失败；如果买进市场价值低于其内在价值的股票，那么从长远角度来看，你有很大的获利机会，这几乎不会使资金承担永久的风险。这一理论的基本策略就是，市场价值和内在价值将最终交会。

格雷厄姆为《福布斯》撰写过很多重要的文章，在其中一篇文章里，他把自己的策略描述成"用 50 美分购买 1 美元钞票"。在"1929 大崩盘"的几年中，其他人都一沉到底，而正是这一战略，帮助他奇迹般地渡过了难关，而且也为他在很多好年头中带来了至少 20% 的回报率。

内在价值才是试金石。那么，又该如何建立这套理论呢？格雷厄姆知识极其广博，他喜欢双关和拉丁诗文，还会在弗莱德·亚斯坦的舞蹈室里跳舞（主要是受到美丽的女舞蹈老师们的吸引）。他于 1976 年去世，享年 82 岁。直至去世的那一天，他还致力于精练自己所创建的公式。开始，他专注于价值被低估的资产；后期，他又开始把盈余、股息归入风险/回报等式。他最终版本的公式可以归结为 10 个要素。这一理论成型于他在 1977 年 8 月 1 日为《福布斯》撰写的"最后的遗愿与遗言"中（见下表）。

十大准则：本·格雷厄姆的遗愿和遗言

在本·格雷厄姆的最后几个年头中，他把自己六十多年的经验精炼成为十条准则，以帮助睿智的投资者在充斥着各种劣等股的市场中挑拣出价值股。

十条准则如下：

1. 盈余价格收益率达到 3A 级债券收益率的 2 倍。收益率是市盈率的倒数。
2. 市盈率降至该股近五年内市盈率最高平均值的 4/10（市盈率的平均值等于年平均股价/当年盈余。）
3. 股息生息率达到 3A 级债券收益率的 2/3。
4. 股价降到每股有形账面价值的 2/3。
5. 股价降到流动资产净值（即流动资产减去负债总额）的 2/3。
6. 负债总额少于有形资产账面价值。
7. 流动比率（流动资产/流动负债）大于等于 2。
8. 负债总额≤流动资产净值（其定义如第 5 条所示）的 2 倍。

9. 在最近十年内盈余增长超过每年 7%的复利（7%的复利可以在 10 年期内使收益增加 1 倍）。

10. 盈余增长的稳定性——最近十年内，年度盈余出现-5%以上的衰退记录不超过 2 次。

本的十点构建了一套稳固的风险/回报屏障。前五点通过盈余等重要经营结果找出相对的低价，来指出潜在的回报所在；后五点通过衡量财务的健全性和盈余的稳定性，来测试风险的大小。

事后验证，只要专注于符合上述 10 条标准中 2 到 3 条的股票，就能得到令人满意的收益。

这种精练源于他在华尔街的阅历，在哥伦比亚大学商学院三十年的教学经验，以及那两部多次再版的畅销著作——《证券分析》和《聪明的投资者》。

格雷厄姆无暇为华尔街做夸张渲染和大肆炒作。去世前不久，他还谈到人们对成长股票的狂热和对高科技股的追捧。他指出，有人说波旁王朝的国王们"什么也忘不了，什么也学不到"，又接着补充道，"华尔街的人却是典型的什么也学不到，什么都忘得了"。在这个充斥着野心的年代里，认为格雷厄姆的理论已经过时几乎成为一种时尚。如果格雷厄姆已经过时了，那么，沃伦·巴菲特则亦如此。

本·格雷厄姆，华尔街人，从 1914 年夏天起从事教育工作。那一年，20岁的他既是一个年轻的优秀毕业生，又是一位古典文学学者。他经常把自己比喻成"流浪的尤利西斯"。

现在，带着哥伦比亚大学商学院院长弗雷德里克·凯珀尔的推荐信，格雷厄姆焦虑地走到三一教堂门口，等待着尖塔上钟表的指针摆向下午三点十分的位置。那是他的开始。他穿过街道，来到百老汇 100 号参加一份工作的面试。工作职务是初级债券销售员，与纽泊格、亨德森和罗卜的纽约股票交易公司的职员共事。

接待显得有些刻板，高级搭档阿尔弗雷特·纽泊格（在公司中大家都称之为 A.N.先生），惊讶地发现格雷厄姆精通数学、英语文学、哲学，却放弃了唯一一门经济课程。在两年半的时间内，本在哥伦比亚大学取得了奖学金，与此同时，他还接了一些零散的工作，比如为美国快递公司做夜间值班经理、上门推销照片打折券。格雷厄姆匆忙地告知 A.N.先生，他无暇安排重修这门经济课程。接着，他说服老板将他的第一笔工资从每星期 10 美元提高到 12 美元，他也正是用这种方法向 A.N.先生证明，自己对这门功课有相当不错的实践能力。A.N.先生对这位新员工说："我们通常支付给新员工每星期 10 美元的酬劳，但是考虑到你的生活所需，我们将做一个变通，提高到每星期12美元。"

格雷厄姆后来回忆道，面试结束后，A.N.先生这样警告他："年轻人，如果你从事投机买卖，你会亏本的。一定要记住这一点。"对于这个警告，年轻的本一直铭记于心，但是有很多次，他也曾被热情冲昏了头，越发盲目之后才有所觉悟。A.N.先生所讲的投机买卖，并不是指一纸损失有多么可怕，而是指倾家荡产。

业务要从基础学起。比如，在幕后办公室把买卖单据整理平衡；与其他操作员交换支票和股票证书。下班后，他还要投入到其他两份工作中去。一份是给"总督岛"上军官的儿子们做家教，另一份是在一所夜校教外国人学英语。

后来，本离开了在内勤打杂的工作，来到纽泊格的债券部门工作。此时，对于他而言，已经无须再重复A.N.先生对他所谓投机冒险的警告了，毕竟当他嬉戏于母亲膝下的时候就早已对此耳濡目染。格罗斯保姆大人只有一笔很少的存款，除了其他几支股票外，他还零零散散地买了些美国钢铁股。本回忆说，当时他还是个小孩子，就要查看些财经方面的报道，并跟踪了解股票行情。"价格上涨，心情愉悦；价格下跌，情绪低落。"这是人之常情。母亲的积蓄在1907年的大萧条中损失殆尽，母亲经常让他到银行去兑换个人支票，这使他感到非常沮丧。出纳员总是低声耳语，"格罗斯保姆夫人的账户里还剩5美元了，她承受得了吗？"

在纽泊格、亨德森和罗卜的时代，格雷厄姆开始构筑其价值投资理论的关键环节。他认为，所有的投资都有投机的因素。而奥妙就在于如何限制风险和不懈地寻找安全边际。本的理论并没有迅速发展成熟，如同丘比特眉上的密涅瓦一般。他们也是在尝试与错误中发展起来的，有时成功，有时遭受可怕的损失，最终趋向成熟。

家族生意的没落是不是帮助格雷厄姆坚定了安全边际是投资道路的最高原则的信念呢？在他刚刚20岁的时候，就已经品尝了对很多人来说要用一生的时间去体验的厄运，而且这才仅仅是个开始。

1910年夏天，本从布鲁克林的男子高中毕业以后，来到了一个杂乱的、位于纽约偏远地区的牛奶场。他每周工作60个小时，打草、喂猪、清理马棚。待遇是：一个月10美元，提供住宿。夜里，打理好工作后，他就在灯笼的微光下自学古希腊语。他坚信，只要赢得普利策奖学金就等于买到了在哥伦比亚学院完成四年学业的通行证。

紧接着就传来了糟糕的消息。本原以为自己通过了最后的面试，没想到最后一关竟然没有通过。他此后从事了一些单调的装配线工作，平常阅读出自《鲁拜集》的文章和维吉尔所作的叙事诗，来打发这种乏味的生活。

接着，哥伦比亚商学院的院长凯伯尔带来了好消息。由于行政管理上的混乱，本的名字已和他的表兄，另一个普利策奖学金获得者路易斯·格罗思班的名字混在一起。本这样对院长凯伯尔说，"可我丢掉了整整一年的时间。"然后，为了补考，他进行了极具特色的填鸭式学习，以帮助自己追回丢掉的时间。

事实上，当年轻的本默许 A.N.先生那个关于投机的承诺时，他的价值投资理论的两个要素就已经成型，那就是：期待不可预计的；通过不懈的学习为之作好准备。

在纽泊格上班的闲暇时间，本开始记下公司推荐榜上关于债券的描述内容，然后把它们匆匆记在活页笔记本上。

他开始在这些原始数字背后寻找更有深度的模式，这在当时绝对是个有挑战性的任务，因为各个公司对于把他们运行的窗口公之于众的做法大都畏手畏脚，犹豫不决；而且，当时的股价并不像现在这样，是谣言和操作的衍生物。

在本早期的一篇报告中，他指出，密苏里太平洋铁路债券已经处于下滑状态，并已低于投资级别。他的分析显示了其超强的洞察力。因此，一家有竞争力的经纪人业务公司向他伸来了橄榄枝。纽泊格则先发制人，把这位新员工的工资在一周内从 12 美元提高到 18 美元。本也被调出了债券交易处（在这里，他收到的佣金微乎其微）。同时，他还被晋升为公司首位统计学家（级别相当于证券分析师）。

有一次，他规划着提高密苏里、堪萨斯和得克萨斯铁路股的收益，一股 12美元看起来很便宜。本就和纽泊格的一位顾客共同开启了一个 100 股的银行账户，而且还小赚了一笔。正当这时，当局开始干涉 A.N.先生（本回忆说："他看起来熟知公司中每个人的每件事。"）。纽泊格命令本就此住手，而且还严厉地训斥了他。

"如果真打算投机，你就应该具备较好的判断力，而不是去挑选一支没有前途的股票。再没有像密苏里、堪萨斯和得克萨斯铁路公司这样的好途径了。"这就为完成一份严谨的分析补充了一课。A.N.先生仔仔细细地了解了该债券的利息报道。而格雷厄姆却没有这样做，因为他当时已被证实仅仅是被临时的（被怀疑是偶然的）密苏里、堪萨斯和得克萨斯铁路的利润增长所迷惑。

结果表明，A.N.先生是正确的，然而，本也没错。密苏里、堪萨斯和得克萨斯铁路确实挣扎在破产的边缘，但是在格雷厄姆撰写的一篇最新的分析文章的帮助下，纽泊格公司也大赚一笔。在本的建议下，他们以每股 50 美分的价格引进，而后该铁路公司经过重组后，其股价翻了一倍。

密苏里、堪萨斯和得克萨斯铁路公司一举把本的职业生涯推为风险的套汇商——这需要具备灵活的数学转换思维和极其机敏的洞察力，以便区分两种不同的信息，一方面是市场价格，另一方面是潜伏在市场价格背后的内在价值。

在这方面，本的第一次大作为是，准确预期到市场已极大地低估了已停营清算的古干海姆探测公司的价值。这家公司在四大理事交易的矿物公司均占主要股份。他的一位同事欧文·卡恩，也是个超级投资者，在为金融分析研究协会撰写的一份分析报告中写到，古干海姆的商业外数学理论是这样的：持股公司每股将接收 0.7277 股的肯尼科特铜；0.1172 股的丝光斜纹棉布铜；0.0833 股的美国熔炼及 0.185 股的射线加固铜。

众所周知，这种持股组合占有 76.23 美元的市场价值；而另一方面，古干海姆探测公司却以每股 68.88 美元的低价卖出。本推荐纽泊格在抛售的同时，再以每股 7.35 美元的绝对毛利润买进古干海姆。

这种利润差额主要靠风险来实现，比如股东们可能在计划实践前三个月内拒绝交易，或是交易有可能会受刊诉讼或规章的限制，或是那些小额股份有可能在分到古干海姆股东手中之前就突然暴涨，从而断送了利润的差额。本早已提前预测到了这些风险，并断定它们并不会起到决定性的作用。本是正确的，并使自己再度向前迈进一步。借着古干海姆公司变动的时机，本又增加了一批追随者，并开始深入发展他的价值投资理论：如果你在一次折价中发现它的内在价值，抓住它！这就是本的安全边际：古干海姆公司非常可能重新实现它的真正价值。

阿尔杰农·塔森是他的新的搭伙人，也是本在哥伦比亚学院最喜欢的教授之一。塔森把他毕生的积蓄——大约 10,000 美元的蓝筹股放在了与本合开的账户里，并交由本来支配。赢亏均以 5-5 分成或担负。本当时已经以"驯服投机"的理念声名鹊起。风险确实存在，但你不应该把筹码赌在市场中那些模糊不清而又可能瞬间即逝的股票上，并以此幻想会使自己变得富有，你应该购买的是隐藏在市场背后的、迟早会被市场认可的内在价值及股票。

塔森的账户运转良好，但是很多人却挣扎在水深火热之中。美国当时已经卷入第一次世界大战。本开始对里昂音像店进行风险投资，此举包括购买位于百老汇第 98 街宅区的百老汇留声机店。这次投了约 7,000 美元，完全出自塔森账户中本的那份利润。然而，这家音像店没有达到预期的效果。对于本来说，不幸的是这次他遇上了一场和平恐慌所带来的大抛售。

这种因德国快要投降而起的和平恐慌，是导致牛市失控的主要原因。那些因战争催出的高价而沾沾自喜的商人们对于未来不定的经济形势毫无信心。

全面地讲，本的价值理论认为，倡导安全的投资者（他们与投机者不同）应当适当地从股票中移出部分资金，当证券价格上升时转投债券。关键是，当熊市低价再次出现时，能够将资金再次转入股票。通常情况下，当"和平恐慌"

导致价格下跌时，本是会持续购买的。但是，他的现金全部被百老汇留声机和"沃克里昂"牌的存货套住了，也就是说，本处于流动资金短缺的状况中，所以他没有购买力。更糟糕的是，他不能填补自己从塔森账户挪用的股款。

为了填补这笔股款，他被迫抛售了老教授珍藏的蓝筹股——美国轻型牵引股票。

在格雷厄姆的回忆录中，他回忆道，在极度抑郁的绝望中，他徘徊在金融区，"赊欠的那笔账，我偿付不了；更糟的是，我个人对塔森账户的管理以惨淡告终"。

这位年长的导师没有离开本，尽管几乎两年后他才以每个月 60 美金的利息得到偿还，好在本还担负得起。正所谓种什么因，得什么果，塔森一直非常信任本，这使他变成了一个十足的富人。随后，本以令人沮丧的价格购买了伊欧里斯这个破产公司的大量首选股，最终他还是从唱片行业中压榨出了利润。但是，塔森账户还是赔钱了。这使本今后在借钱方面显得更加保守。由此，本也谦虚地给自己上了一课，这使得他那本来就以严谨著称的市场战略更加严谨。

本的朋友安排他以最低价买进一支被热炒的名为萨沃德轮胎的机构股票。该机构所涉及的都是高科技内容，即萨沃德在轮胎自动补胎方面的革新。股票以 10 美元开盘，以 35 美元收盘。本回忆说，在一周的时间内，他那 5,000 美元的原始股为他带来了整整三倍的回报。

格雷厄姆急切地准备大量投入，四周后，萨沃德建立了一个分部，他与朋友们一起购入了 2 万美元的股票。内部价格为 20 美元。股票以 50 美元开盘，格雷厄姆用一张原始入股支票外加 150% 的利润，兴奋异常地为自己欢庆 25 岁的生日。

令人失望的是，在萨沃德下一次募股的时候，格雷厄姆和他的朋友却被拒之于门外。他们这样告知本："非常抱歉，没那么多股票了。"接着，好消息又接踵而至，又一个分部即将上市。最后的呼唤！格雷厄姆迅速凑齐 6 万美元（其中有一半是三个朋友筹集的），并准备为他们又一轮的"庆功宴"开香槟庆祝了。

然而，这次出盘并没有像预料的那样顺利。本被告知出现了"行政性延误"。他们焦虑着，日子一天天过去。接着，犹如突然迸发的烟雾，在古老的户外股票证券场外交易市场里沙哑的嘶叫声中，压在萨沃德公司上的所有资金都损失殆尽。

本惊讶于自己的贪心，并从此作了保证。从道德上来说，在牛市晚期进行首次公开募股是一种新颖的投机环境。游戏本身并没有改变。

本拥有直接追索权。他最终抓住了出资人，并成功地在萨沃德最后的出盘中以每美元 30 美分的利润获利。灰心的格雷厄姆在这个议题上没有做任何作业，这恰恰违反了他为纽泊格客户撰写的在一系列小册子（"为投资者上课"）中提出的很多建议。格雷厄姆在这些小册子中着重强调寻找隐匿在市场背后的内在价值的重要性。他讲道，不要随波逐流。

1926 年，本作为"价值"的奉行者已经声名在外，加上牛市已去的外在形势，年轻的格雷厄姆在当时已具有了新的影响力。那时的他已经有三个孩子，在华尔街 86 号及河畔路有宽敞的公寓，邻里都经常称赞本在"金融上获得巨大的成就"。夏天，他们一家人来到位于新泽西海岸的住处。本开始在城市运动俱乐部上壁球和高尔夫球课。

本不断挖掘这种被低估价值的行为，有时几乎是凭着自己的第六感。这也直接造就了他富足的生活。本在公司投入 45 万资金（大部分是归他个人所有）。一天，当他挑选洲际商务协会的年度报告关于铁路方面的股票时，突然发现他曾经在一组管道公司做过两次脚注。

很快，格雷厄姆乘火车赶往华盛顿。在国际计算中心的档案室里，他要求阅览一些资料。当年，在为那些管道公司做脚注时，他可不知道还有这些资料的存在。

在这些管道公司中，其中八家都是源自 1911 年标准石油公司分解后而产生的。他们的工作就是把原油从井口里送进炼油厂。在他们的商务中，油轮起着重要的作用，然而华尔街却并未对他们表示关注，北方管道公司的普通股只有9% 的投资收益，就如同垃圾债券般的普通股，由此可见一斑。

已经减少了部分派息，投资收益也发出了这样的信号：华尔街前方有更多的麻烦。而管道公司所公开的那微不足道的收入也无力驱除这种忧虑。

在国际计算中心找到的档案（其他统计学家所忽略的文件）中，本仔细彻底地查阅了其资产负债表的内容，结果得到了惊人的发现。这些"管道"里装着最好的铁路债券，北方管道公司的股票达到了每股 95 美元的价格。股票以 65美元售出，创造出 6 美元的红利。本开始一点点地研究这些股票并慢慢获得了2,000 股，这使他和格雷厄姆联合账户中的搭档们成为继洛克菲勒协会后最大的持股人。

现在，本向标准石油管理层提出了一个不受欢迎的观点。他指出，所有多余的、商业中确实不需要的资金应该发放到股东手里。不出所料，在他参加的一次年会上，他企图用自己的观点说服别人却遭遇失败，而且被罗伯特秩序条例逼得几乎窒息。

本用实际行动做出了自己的回答，他购买了大量的北方股票，这些已经远远超出其搭档可支付的能力。他开始游说其他股东，并成功入选董事会（过去可从没有外行人试图这样做过）。大约用了两年的时间，一些幕后故事也悄悄引起了强大的洛克菲勒协会的注意，但是公司的重组最终使本和他的追随者们的股份增值到大约 110 美元。本的这种充满活力的研究优势，就在那一天又得到了淋漓尽致的发挥。本非常不喜欢被别人评价为在管道奋斗中自我服务的外行人，或是个"侵入者"。但他却学到了非常重要的一课，即感知价值是一码事，但通常使之资本化又是另一码事！

格雷厄姆联合账户的价值已经达到了 250 万美元，其中很大部分都是本再投资的利润。很多新入资金来源于他的男子高中同学及哥伦比亚学院的校友杰罗姆·纽曼。纽曼是个精明的谈判者兼商人，在他和本的搭档过程中，开始从一个"外行人"向本那样的"内行人"转变，两个人的合作关系一直持续了 30 多年之久。

本开始和一些知名人士分享他的投资理念。其中一位是深具影响力的伯纳·巴鲁，他非常谦虚地（本认为）和本建立了初级合作伙伴关系。能够拉他入伙，本感到非常高兴。巴鲁在国外的那些股票是典型的格雷厄姆所挑选的，它们都是稳定的特许经营企业，如佩伯雷尔制造公司（Pepperell Manufacturing）（生产纸张和枕头套）和 Heywood & Wakefield 公司（制造婴儿车），这些股票的卖价要低于先行商业价值。这些产业在当时以追求光鲜产业（如收音机公司）为主的牛市大潮中是无人眷顾的。

格雷厄姆尽管仍然专注于挑选价值股，但是他也非常清楚一个要价过高的市场很快就会遭遇失败。他开始在哥伦比亚商学院进行每周一次的、每次长达两个小时的安全分析课程讲解。

自从本提及有意撰写一本关于证券分析的书籍，已经有一段时间了。他意图准备一个系列讲座，这样就可以和公众一起讨论学习。本的班级着重于智力的开拓。人群多是华尔街上的专家们，大家在一起开心地交换着市场消息。这些班级专注于当前市场的案例学习（佩伯雷尔制造是其中之一），并广受学生欢迎。当市场爬升至 1929 年顶峰的时候，150 多位学生吸取了格雷厄姆关于收入的观点和资产负债表的精华，尤其对公司会计操作不明朗的现象给予特别地关注。

1929 年，牛市的强势发展快走到尽头了。度过了一个轰轰烈烈的 1928 年（道琼斯工业指数从 51% 攀升至 60%），到了 1929 年，此时的形势是需要谨慎行事而又充满障碍的，因为本以约 250 万美元的可兑换首选股抵消了短期同等数量的普通股。如果股市下跌，普通股会比首选股跌得更快，这时格雷厄姆就会握住既得的利润，并隔绝这个障碍。

同时，他手头还留有用借来的钱申购的市场价值为 450 万美元的普通股，其利润约 200 万美元。根据日标准（即下降率仅为 10% 时，你方可购买），格雷厄姆正在洞察这个表面上看来坚不可摧的世界。对塔森账户因管理不当而造成的债务的痛苦依旧记忆犹新。然而，黑色星期二（1929 年 10 月 29 日）的旋风带着前所未有的残暴席卷而来。顷刻间，约 140 亿美元的市场价值被清扫一空。

　　时间一点点过去，交易还没有落实，价格依旧只是个猜测。疲惫的职员们夜晚在办公室里打着盹，他们想尽力完成大量的文书工作，却只是徒劳。当 1929 年到达波谷的时候，道琼斯工业指数从美妙到荒谬地步的 380 点狠跌到 200 点。格雷厄姆短期在市场挣了一些钱，但是到年终的时候还是有 20% 的损失。到了 1930 年，他更糟糕——（损失了了）50%（道琼斯工业指数当时是 29%）。本努力降低债务，与此同时他依旧保留了那些他认为有强劲潜力的股票。

　　到 1932 年底，250 万美元的基金总量已经下降到不足总额的 1/4，那笔钱是 1929 年入账的。担心损失还会继续，愧对朋友和家人，本写了一首诗，诗中问道：

　　一个灵魂不懂休憩的人，他该睡在哪里呢？
　　那只可怜的被擒的雄鹿会在森林中寻觅呵护吗？

　　尽管徘徊在这种不确定性的边缘，本实际上已经做到好得令人惊叹的地步了。自 1930 年 50% 的损失起，本在 1931 年仅仅下降了 16%（当时的道琼斯工业指数下跌了 48%）；1932 年仅仅下跌了 3%（当时的道琼斯工业指数至少下降了 17%）。本连连遭受重创却依旧存活。如果格雷厄姆的整体运作像这个市场一样糟糕的话，那么他必将遭受彻底的毁灭。他的安全边际是：相对保守的借入，在走下坡路时，需要采取谨慎屏蔽的态度，这样才会获得巨大利益。

　　尽管如此，本还是比十年前富裕很多，但是他也开始节省了。他在回忆录里这样写道："由于我青年时期的经济状况非常拮据，所以这场失败使我个人'吝啬'的观点和习惯更加根深蒂固。"

　　本对价值正确走向的直觉一直专注于如古干海姆探测公司和北部管道那样的伟大发现，在这种形势下，他总是可以洞察到隐匿在市场价格背后的真正财富。

　　本必须努力地工作，以便继续挖掘出像过去那样的优秀股票。现在，也就是在瞬息间大萧条把本推向水火之中，价值无处不在，只有祈求才能出现。本派他的一个学生把在纽约股票交易所的所有 600 个工业股的市场价格和真正价值一一匹配起来。这在一个计算器和计算机双双不存在的年代来说，可绝对堪称苦工，但是结果却异常惊人。600 个产业中，其中 1/3 可以以少于净运营资本的价格买下。超过 50 个工业股以低于银行现金（或有销路债券）的价格售出。

举例来说，蒙哥马利·沃德以少于速动资产净额/可兑换资产的一半进行交易。对于每股 6.50 美元的价格，你可以在运营资本和这场伟大的零售交易中不费劲地获得 16 美元（目录商业及其全部）。至于像美国汽车铸造（American Car & Foundry）和 Munsinger 公司，仅从现金角度来看，可以以 20 美元和 11 美元分别带来每股 50 美元和每股 17 美元的收益。至于商业的其他部分，像砖、水泥、机器、顾客和利润，则是可以自由驾驭的。

本这样对《福布斯》的读者说："对华尔街最精确的判断来看，这些商业奄奄一息,名存实亡。"但若是清算后进行私有买卖，他们至少可以赚回运营资本，这就已经比他们拿到纽约股票交易市场上的收益要多出不少。

是的，熊市出现了。本接着说，"急速繁荣通常会带来预料不到的低价"。1921 年也出现过一次熊市，"但是仅就现金资产来说，现在的价格比起 8 年前大抛售的时候低出了 6 倍"。

本的学生们的研究结果显示,公司的经营业绩并不是"实际上很差"，那么投资者们为什么要进一步与他们讨价还价呢？《福布斯》的头条写着"为 1 美元出价 50 美分"。他们又为什么要像抛售钱柜中的现金那样抛售这些实有价值的一部分呢？

问得好！这个问题（是他们生活中众多类似问题中的一个）是沃伦·巴菲特在 1973－1974 年间上等股票跌价 40 年后向《福布斯》提出的问题。价格太低了，巴菲特感觉自己"像在闺房中的一个性欲过剩的家伙"。他告诉读者说"是开始投资的时候了"。一定要有耐心，等待着这样的时机出现，他继续补充道："你要应对市场中很多愚昧的人；像是在一个大型的赌场里，其他每个人都在豪饮。如果你能坚持一直喝百事，那么你就绝对没问题。"他的言论简直与他的导师格雷厄姆的价值观念如出一辙。

一次极其明显的股市重振过后，价格很快又攀升上去了。但是巴菲特在 5 年后又重返《福布斯》了，他尝试规劝格雷厄姆，让他为经理们在下一次股票下跌的时候发放抚恤金。巴菲特问道，他们为什么顿足于债券而不留连于那些经讨价获得的"集合了账面价值或比之更少"的股本呢？

格雷厄姆的回答与他本人在 50 年前那次大萧条中的言论大同小异。格雷厄姆这样说，1928—1929 年那次"新世纪的疯狂"给华尔街"那无人不知的虚弱"的逻辑带来了沉重的心理打击。那些过去常根据资产负债表上的数字来例行筛选价值股的投资者已经因为过分注重并依赖"报道的或是大肆宣传的赢利而冲昏了头脑，最终被剔除出局。牛市中的失利，意味着提高赢利可能仅仅是昙花一现，甚至是带有欺骗性的"。

正如巴菲特记录的那样，格雷厄姆对于金钱没有真正的激情。他真的是个古典主义者，他所得到的最纯粹的满足是出于智力上的，比如研究数字、观察它们的结果。

他又结婚了，这已经是第三次，他建立了新家庭并移居到贝华利山，并开始在加州大学洛杉矶分校商业研究生院执教了至少 15 年。他不断地修改一本关于下跌法则的书，还翻译了一本他最喜欢的西班牙语小说，又通过不断出版不同版本的个人书籍，继续精炼他的价值战略。

比起资产研究，本现在更多地专注于赢利和股息的钻研。正如在《福布斯》发表的那样，这本新书被设计成为口袋工具，它为普通投资者服务，并且在五到六年的时间内在市场上产生了很好的反响。

再近些时候，来自宾厄姆顿纽约州立大学的金融学教授亨利·R.奥本海默进行了这样一个幕后检测。在金融分析杂志上发表的一篇文章（1974－1981 年）中，他发现凡是符合本的标准中的两到三个点的股票将会至少带来每年 26% 的收益，整整比大董事会和美国股票交易市场期刊发布的 14% 指数所显示的回报多了一倍。

格雷厄姆的风险报偿屏障非常苛刻，找出他所列标准符合其中几点的公司绝非易事。商业运作上发生了一些变化——从高红利的支出向开放性市场股票返销转变，举例来说，就是转变了格雷厄姆乐于看到的股票和债券利息率的关系。

其他的标准一直经得起时间的考验。在当时，在列出购买清单之前对任何股票都要弄清两个选股屏障，那就是最小的赢利增长额和稳定性。而且也许你在某一时刻没有发现任何折价，格雷厄姆的检测将会帮助你决策对方要求你偿付的价格是在合理的、保守的分寸之内还是完全没有前途。正如 A.N.先生警告的那样，"如果你投机，年轻人，你会亏本的"。

格雷厄姆本人认为，他六十年征战股市的经验可以总结为这几个字：安全边际。在近几年这个超级火热的环境里，这一观念已不再流行，这一点令人相当痛心。只有在不可预计的未来，当一切都进展顺利的情况下，不合理的价格才可能被合理化。从格雷厄姆的标准来看，只有在想象的数字中，才能衡量那些飚涨股的安全边际。

安全边际的确是个安慰因素——它可以抵消和对抗诸如错误的判断、不佳的运气以及伺机出动的不可预计性等未知因素。在市场本益比及利率较低的时期，安慰因素较容易获得。用格雷厄姆的一个例子来说，典型的股票价格盈余收益率约为 9%，即市盈率 11 的倒数；由于高品质债券的生息率是 4%，因此你等于拥有 5% 的安全边际，如果长期投资一家具有可以合理预测其盈余能力的公司，再加上5%的安全边际，你很可能就不会辗转难眠了。

格雷厄姆的这个计算公式仍然是一个有用的工具。它虽然很难提供 5%的安慰度，但却提供了一个切实可行的方法，让你在涉水之前先测量水的深度。

试金石依旧还是内在价值，即投资一家公司，大约十年时间可以从该公司取得现金的折现价值。购买低于内在价值的股票，你就获得了安全边际（或安全空间）；而购买高于内在价值的股票，则等于自找麻烦。

总之，安全边际就是要将企业的风险最小化。而对于霍金斯和凯茨等价值实践者来说，它的意义就是寻找竞争力优势，如低成本、根深蒂固的品牌，以及主导性的市场占有率等。霍金斯和凯茨是位于田纳西州孟菲斯的长叶基金公司的董事长和总裁。

投资人也必须衡量公司的财务实力，其中包括低负债水平、有限债务责任，以及大量的自由现金流可供再投资，以便获取高额利润。当然，诀窍就是在一个投资组合中，至少要同时包含几项上述特征，且价格要远远低于市场水平。

这确实办得到。为纪念《证券分析》出版五十周年，巴菲特发表了一篇题为"格雷厄姆和道得斯维乐旗下的超级投资家"的著名文章，用以表彰九位业绩持续惊人的格雷厄姆早先的学生和其知识的继承者。他们的投资风格虽略有不同，但都一致地信奉格雷厄姆改述自斯宾诺沙的另一个信条：从灾难的角度出发，是接近价值的最好方法。

Chapter Two
Vulture Investor —
Marty Whitman

第二章
秃鹰投资商——马蒂·惠特曼

I. Case Study

Marty Whitman, sometime "Vulture Investor," likes nothing better than combing the wreckage of the bankruptcy courts in search of the low-risk bargains that are his trademark.

"Of course I'm different. I know I'm different."

That's the combative Martin J. (for Jacob) Whitman speaking. As a guy who runs some $2 billion of other people's money with one of the most eclectic value strategies in the business, Whitman makes quite a point of differentiating himself from the Wall Street mainstream.

No Savile Row tailoring or maundering over efficient market theories here. This is the plain, unvarnished Marty Whitman. What you see is what you get. Slouched in an armchair, sneakered feet crossed on a glass-topped coffee table, Whitman is in his customary office casual—plaid flannel shirt open at the neck; blue, mail-order corduroy jeans just a few miles short of fraying at the knees.

Whitman's office overlooking Third Avenue is chock-a-block with such treasures as a bronzed bear copulating with a bull. Significantly, there is nowhere in sight that most common artifact of Wall Street environment, the manic flicker of a stock market monitor.

Whitman's laid-back air can be read as a political statement. It goes with his conviction that Wall Street fixation on such supposed predictive as the higher economics, investor psychology, and short-term earnings swings is just so much noise. "We don't carry a lot of excess baggage," he says in the flatted vowels of his native Bronx. "A lot of what Wall Street does has nothing to do with the underlying value of a business. We deal in probabilities, not predictions."

Like Warren Buffett and other spiritual heirs of Dr. Value himself, Benjamin Graham, Whitman aims to buy "safe and cheap." Basically, that means buying assets and earnings at a discount. Typically, value and growth stocks outrun the market at different phases of the economic cycle. Value stocks (think low prices to earnings and book value) tend to outperform in periods of no to slow expansion, Growth stocks (think fast rising earnings, high price earnings ratios) tend to outperform when the economy is on the move.

Whitman, in the main, breaks the mold. His Manhattan-based Third Avenue Fund did lag the market in the final stages of the now busted great growth stock craze, but over the last decade he nonetheless managed to crank out an average annual return of 19 percent—a point above the market, with a third less volatility.

The record entitles him to argue that "There are only two kinds of passive investing—value investing and speculative excess." "For the last two years, like 1928-1929 and 1972-1973," continues Whitman, "we've had nothing but speculative excess."

OK, so reports of the death of value are greatly exaggerated. What do you do if "safe and cheap" stocks are thin on the ground, as they were for much of the decade in which Whitman did so handily? Surprisingly, he pulled off deep bets against the market in bummed out high-tech stocks, mainly depressed chip equipment manufacturers. He burrowed away to the point where tech stocks got to be a third of his portfolio. "If you had told me seven years ago I would be so heavily involved as a value investor in small-cap high-tech plays, I would have said forget about it," says Whitman with a pleased grin. In the manic twists of the market, there are times— and prices—at which growth stocks become value stocks.

Whitman has also opportunistically been scouring the deep discount markets of Japan for "cheap and safe." In the larger strategic sense, he has been pushing an updated model of Ben Graham's value strategies into the far more complex world of latter-day financial engineering.

In Graham's pre-Internet time, you bought shares below what seemed to be a company's value as a going business, counted on a rising tide of earnings and dividends to bring the price up, and ultimately looked to open market sale to take you out at a profit.

Life is no longer that simple. Look at the long-term profits investors have pulled out of the now struggling AT&T. In the years since the company was broken up by an antitrust fiat, the big money has come not from the Grahamesque fundamentals of earnings and dividends, but from a dizzying and far less predictable succession of mergers, acquisitions, and spin-offs. What Graham thought of as "extraordinary events" have become the ordinary, and a major point of departure for Whitman's brand of value investing.

Over any three-to-five-year period, he says, most of the stocks in his biggest investment pool, the $1.8 billion open-end Third Avenue Value Fund, the biggest of his three funds, will be overrun by some major happening. The possibilities crackle of Whitman's tongue: "mergers and acquisitions, hostile takeovers, divestitures, spin-offs, refinancings, and going private."

Casting a mordant eye over 22 companies in which Third Avenue owned major positions lately, Whitman counts 13 in the throes of some sort of "resource conversion." The prospects go like this: two cash sales of control and one exchange of stock; three attempts at hostile takeovers; five acquisitions of smaller companies; one partial liquidation; one sale of a new issue of common stock.

All these deals were cooking at a premium above going market prices. Whitman typically tries to capitalize on such sleights of financial engineering by putting more emphasis on quality assets and less on operating earnings than Graham fundamentalists. These days, argues Whitman, management has to be appraised not only as operators of a going business, "but also as investors engaged in employing and redeploying assets."

This is in some ways an extension of Warren Buffett's dictum that "being a businessman makes me a better investor, and being an investor makes me a better businessman."

Whitman digs into personal experience to amplify the point. In the late 1980s, he helped put together a prepackaged bankruptcy for Nabors Industries, now one of the world's biggest and best capitalized oil drilling contractors. Whitman saw to it that Nabors came out of the reorganization debt free, with an all-equity base. When hard times hit the industry, Nabors had no difficulty raising the money it needed to buy up debt-ridden competitors at bargain prices. "Other industry participants did not have the financial wherewithal to bid against Nabors for those assets," notes Whitman.

The result was that Nabors was able to turn operating losses of more than $20 million into positive cash flow of better than $200 million. Among the beneficiaries of the move: longtime holder Whitman and his Third Avenue Value Fund. Whitman's point on the Nabors' success—one frequently ignored on Wall Street—is that shrewd analysis of balance sheet potential is a better tool for predicting future earning power than a study of fast earnings patterns.

As a long-term investor looking to a number of possible exit strategies, Whitman glories in the freedom to ignore near-term earnings predictions and results. Acidly, he argues that Wall Street spends far too much time "making predictions about unpredictable things."

His search is for companies backed by strong financials that will keep them going through hard times ("safe"), selling at a substantial discount below private business or takeover value ("cheap"). Buying quality assets cheap almost invariably means that the company's near-term results are rocky enough to have turned off Wall Street. "Markets are too efficient for me to hope that I'd be able to get high-quality resources without the trade-off the near-term outlook not being great," says Whitman. He chuckles and runs a hand through a fringe of white hair. "When the outlook stinks, you may not have to pay to play."

Whitman's penchant for seizing on opportunities left for dead by Wall Street has won him some celebrity as a "vulture investor." Whitman likes this journalistic tag line. "It's a lot better than being called an indexer or an asset allocator," he says, taking another poke at standard Wall Street dogma.

Whitman learned the dogma from the ground up. He started on Wall Street as an analyst in the late 1940s after a three-year hitch in World War II as a Navy Pharmacist's mate, and a post-graduate year in economics at Princeton. He says his education in distress merchandise didn't start until several years later when he began picking up retainers as an expert witness on valuation in bankruptcy cases. Whitman made his first big money in the early 1970s, buying up senior mortgage bonds of the busted Penn Central Railroad. "The bonds were cheap because not too many people realized they were safe," recalls Whitman.

Trolling troubled waters for bargains, Whitman offers a cheery insight into the limits of risk.

From the 1970s through the 1990s, he says severe recessions have whipped through a baker's dozen of industries without grossly affecting the economy as a whole. Among the victims: energy, banking, real estate, savings and loans, retail trade. Semiconductor equipment and other high-tech capital gods producers now crowd the casualty list. Typically, many stocks in these depressed industries trade down to ultra-cheap levels as Wall Street walks away from grim near-term prospects. It's a combination that brings out the vulture in Whitman.

He argues that scouting depressed industries is not a particularly dangerous way to live. Every investment, he contends, has something wrong with it. Whitman's job is to sniff out what is wrong, and figure out the trade-offs against what is right, particularly in terms of some form of potential asset conversion. Mutual fund management companies, for example, throw off huge amounts of cash, but because entry cost are low, they are vulnerable to new competition that keeps barging into the business. Capital intensive companies such as oil refiners, on the other hand, do not have to worry overmuch about new competition, but tend to take their lumps in the down end of the business cycle.

Among the most common wrongs Whitman tries to avoid:

• Attractive-seeming highly liquid cash positions that on inspection prove to be in the custody of managements too timid to put surplus assets to good use;

• Seductively high rates of return on equity that often signal a relatively small asset base;

• A combination of low returns on equity and high net asset value that may simply mean that asset values are overstated;

• High net asset values that may point to a potentially sizable increase in earnings, but which just as often point to swollen overhead.

Whitman's willingness to take on companies like the stereotypical "sick, lame, and lazy" he treated as a pharmacist's mate—the old salt, in Navy slang, still thinks of himself as having been a "pecker checker"—is not unalloyed. Buying seeming trouble at a discount, Whitman ignores market risk (current price swings). Whitman worries all the time, though, about investment risk (the possibility he may have misjudged a temporary illness that will prove terminal).

Two critical elements Whitman focuses on in weighing investment risk are the "quality and quantity of resources." The dynamics behind these seemingly bookeeperish abstractions show in the long run that Whitman has made at semiconductor equipment manufacturers. Outfits like Applied Materials, Electroglas, and KLA-Tencor produce the highly specialized tools needed to shape the ubiquitous microchip, increasingly embedded in everything from credit cards and greeting cards to telephones and toys. Despite its expansive reach, the chip business is highly cyclical for end producers and suppliers alike.

Whitman first started nibbling at the manufacturing stocks some five years ago at the beginning of an indeterminate down cycle he thought might last anywhere "from two quarters to three years, or maybe even longer." It was hard to get a handle on the negatives. Globle growth was slowing, the personal computer market for integrated circuits was approaching saturation, and business was demonstrably lousy.

To Whitman's great satisfaction, Wall Street took the customary short-term view and began dumping the stocks. That's when Whitman started his move, buying much of the time at less than a 50 percent premium over book value ("cheap"). He dove into the equipment producers rather than their customers, chip makers such as Intel, mainly because they were cheaper.

As smallish niche producers, often protected by proprietary techniques, the equipment manufacturers seemed less vulnerable to shake out, and had better "quality" assets. Unlike the far more capital-intensive chip makers, with their heavy investments in bricks and mortar, the equipment producers operate out of comparatively low-cost clean rooms, and buy, rather than make, most of their components. Research and development costs are high, but Whitman cannily focused on companies that expensed rather than capitalized them. Those running charges understated earnings, making them seem particularly weak in the down cycle. So much the worse for Wall Street.

Whitman was looking at hard book value (few intangibles) that gave him a high level of "quality" resources. He was unsettled for a bit when a minor bull market perversely erupted in the stocks, but his worst case estimate of how long the downturn would last proved to be bang on Major Third Avenue Value holdings like Electroglas were reporting straight-line quarterly sales and operating earnings declines of 60 percent or more. Predictably, the stocks continued south to the point where many plunged to well under book value.

Whitman continued to buy a cross section of equipment producers at quotes he regarded as "Better than even first stage venture capitalists have to pay, and for companies already public and very, very cash rich."

So Whitman's "cheap" stocks got even cheaper, but were they still "safe?" That question loomed ever larger as Whitman pushed his stake in the equipment producers to as high as 22 percent of Third Avenue Value's assets. Whitman was averaging down, a key part of his strategy, but anathema to Wall Street's momentum players.

Whitman was betting turnaround. The question was when it would materialize. He showed shareholders a stiff upper lip: "Explosive growth" lay ahead, thanks to expanding applications and basic advances in technology. "The use of smaller and smaller circuits to achieve increased density," Whitman expostulated, "will in and of itself result in semiconductor manufacturers having no choice but to replace equipment simply in order to remain competitive. They have to ante up for the latest tools as a cost of doing business."

That was Whitman, talking up the stocks for public consumption. Underneath the rhetoric, he was assessing values with his customary gimlet eye. Whitman spread some $300 million over a mix of close to a dozen equipment-makers, hardheadedly diversifying because it was clear that not all the smaller company stocks he had picked up would make it on their own. "Most," he thought, "ought to do okay and a few ought to be huge winners, but there would be a few strikeouts." The exit strategy for the strikeouts, in a consolidating industry, would almost certainly be acquisition.

Beyond diversification, Whitman protected himself by loading up on management that fit his two acid tests: good at day-to-day operations and equally good as asset managers. His biggest holdings were among the likes of Applied Materials, companies that had been riding high in the up cycle, and capitalized on their then popularity on Wall Street to sell stock.

"Lots of these guys were quite smart," says Whitman. "Even though they didn't need the cash at that time, when the market was terrific, they took advantage of the opportunity to raise a lot of money." Looking at stocks like Electroglas, with cash-to-asset ratios of 35 percent or more a share, Whitman felt well-fortified to ride out adversity. The one nagging question of course, was the "burn rate." Would the industry-wide depression go so deep and continue so long that much of the cash would he siphoned off by attrition? Operating losses were mounting as the big chip makers, fighting hard times of their own, were pressing on the prices of the limited amount of new equipment they were buying, and putting off orders on the next generation of tools the equipment-makers were spending so much money to develop.

The impasse prompted stomach-churning sell-offs of 40 percent or more in at least three of Whitman's equipment producers—Clare Corporation, FSI International and SpeedFam-IPEC. Two (FSI and SpeedFam) were sitting on extremely solid cash positions. Seemingly thriving on adversity, Whitman rated them (along with eight other portfolio issues down 25 percent or more) as either promising "very good operating results," or likely candidates for some form of financial engineering. And, in fact, that was exactly what happened. Several, including Whitman's biggest holding, Silicon Valley Group, were acquired at substantial premiums.

Once again scoffing at market risk, Whitman underlines the comforts of being cushioned by strong financials "When you're in well-capitalized companies, if they do start to dissipate, you get a chance to get out," "On the other hand," he continues, "when you're in poorly capitalized companies, you better watch the quarterly reports very closely."

As a buy-and-hold investor, with one of the lowest portfolio turnover rates in the business, Whitman is the first to admit that he is slow on the sell side. He is quick to unload obvious mistakes, but is often in a quandary with stocks that seem "grossly overpriced."

That's because he thinks in terms of multiple markets. What may seem to be a very rich price to an individual investor can be a perfectly reasonable one for control buyers looking to an acquisition. They can afford to stump up a premium because of the advantages control brings. Among them is the ability to finance a deal on easy terms with what Whitman calls "OPM" (Other People's Money) and "SOTT" (Something Off The Top) in the form of handsome salaries, options, and other goodies that come with general access to the corporate treasury.

Thus, through long experience, Whitman has decided that his analytical sense works better on the buy side than the sell side. "I've held securities for three years and sold them for a double only to see them triple over the subsequent six months," he says. Moral: "Just sitting around is a better way to make money." That conclusion helps to explain why so many of Whitman's exits are by acquisition rather than outright sale.

There is another angle to this. Whitman thinks of himself as being in the business of "creating wealth" rather than managing money as such. That means keeping as big a chunk of the profits at work for as long as you can. Whitman's waiting game and trademark low turnover, besides catching financial engineering premiums, help to keep tax liabilities down.

The waiting game certainly paid off with the chip equipment producers. The turnaround Whitman was looking for finally did materialize. Wall Street tastemakers like Morgan Stanley, in the Millennium, once again began posting "outperform" stickers on the stocks. Whitman once again laughed his contrarian way to the bank. His profits sweated out over several years, demonstrates the essence of the Whitman strategy—ignore market swings, except to average down; ignore Wall Street's accepted wisdom. Shop depressed industries for strong financials going cheap and hang on. By strong financials Whitman means companies with little or no debt and plenty of cash. What's cheap? No hard and fast rules. "Low prices in terms of the resources you get," he generalizes.

For industrial companies, Whitman tries to pay no more than 50 percent to 60 percent of takeover value. One value indicator is the multiple of price-to-book—stock price divided by book value. The lower the multiple, the better. Book value, of itself, doesn't tell the whole story, but as a best-case example, Whitman was more than happy averaging down on some of the chip equipment producers at as little as 40 percent of very hard book.

Some of his other pricing rules of thumb:

• For small cap, high-tech companies, a premium of no more than 60 percent over book—about what venture capitalists would pay on a first stage investment.

• For banks, Whitman's limit is no more than 80 percent of book value.

• For money managers, Whitman looks to assets under management (pay no more than 2 percent to 3 percent).

• For real estate companies, he zeros in on discounted appraised valued rather than book.

Whitman, thumbing his nose at convention, has clearly established himself as an outside force on Wall Street. Despite the philosophical linkage, he even backs off from identification with what he calls Graham & Dodd Fundamentalists. The basic similarities are striking: long-term horizons, a rigorous analytic approach to the meaning behind reported numbers, and an unshakeable belief that probabilities favor those who buy quality at the lowest possible price. Like Ben Graham, Whitman scoffs at the academicians who hold that stock prices are set by a truly knowledgeable and efficient market. Acknowledging his debt to Graham, Whitman argues that his calculated exploitation of exit strategies has added a new dimension to value investing. Graham, he insists, was far more preoccupied with market risk and macroeconomic factors that he simply ignores.

Give Whitman an edge. He has moved value investing into the new century, but in personal terms he is not as far from Graham as he contends. Like Graham, Whitman grew up in a family business. His parents, who emigrated from western Poland in 1920, made felt underbodies for women's hats. Whitman grew up in the middle-class enclave of the Grand Concourse in the Bronx, not far from Yankee Stadium. He helped with deliveries and did odd jobs, but was not particularly interested in the family shop. His passions were basketball and baseball. He was such an indifferent student in high school that his sister Phyllis, a Pennsylvania Superior Court Judge, at Whitman's seventy-fifth birthday party, reminded everyone of the family fear that he would never amount to much.

Whitman traces his value orientation in part to the windup of his father's business. "He liquidated and then did a lot of speculating." Recalls Whitman. "I couldn't see myself doing that, buying and selling all the time." Still ruminating, Whitman says, "I couldn't be a trader. I'm very slow with numbers. I have to understand what they mean."

Whitman sees value investing as a "good enough" business—no swinging for the fences. "It's the art of the possible," he says. "The aim is not to maximize profits, but to be consistent at low risk. I never mind leaving something on the table."

Out of the Navy, Whitman struggled through an early marriage that lasted only six months. He finished his undergraduate work at Syracuse with distinction in 1949 ("I guess I was finally maturing," he laughs), ran out the rest of his GI Bill eligibility with a graduate year at Princeton, and then gravitated to Wall Street. Much of the work he did on his first job as an analyst at Shearson Hayden Stone quickly festered into disenchantment with Wall Street's myopic view of value.

"It was ridiculous," recalls Whitman. "98 percent of the emphasis was on short-term earnings and the near-term outlook." "One company came my way," he continues, "a lumber company that had little or no visible earning power, but plenty of timber. I couldn't analyze it, so I know there had to be some other way of doing things."

Whitman's sense of something else—a long-term view and the assets side of a business as a store of value—sharpened when he moved on to the Rosenwald Foundation. That charitable repository, funded by a Sears, Roebuck founding family, held controlling interests in number of other companies, including Western Union. "That's when I began to get a glimmering that whatever you did, it was $10 million of your own money, and that it would be committed on a permanent or a semipermanent basis for a long time," recalls Whitman.

It was a vital part of Whitman's education. The virtues of buy and hold were beginning to crystallize. The distinction between market risk and investment risk was beginning to take on a new dimension, too. In yet another parallel with Ben Graham, Whitman began to pick up retainers as an expert witness, among other cases testifying for the government in an investigation of misdoing in the Teamsters Union investment practices. Whitman soon developed a reputation for smarts in stockholder litigation and bankruptcy cases. "The less respectable areas of corporate law," laughs Whitman. The key question in his work for bankruptcy trustees often centered on valuation. How to put a price on this security? What is this company worth?

"Preparation, preparation, preparation" for his stints in the courtroom gave Whitman an object lesson in how skewed market prices and their underlying asset values could become. Panicky creditors or bondholders, stampeding through a very narrow exit in anticipation of a bankruptcy, were truly at the peril of the market. Opportunists picking up the pieces at distress prices got the benefit. They were pretty well-insulated from market risk. How much further could prices drop? The monkey on their back was investment risk. Would their business plan work? Could they control a redistribution of assets that would turn their cheap paper into gold?

The rewards were persuasive enough to turn Whitman the theorist into an activist. Hired as an advisor by a group of creditors, Whitman in the early 1970s bought $100,000 of the egregiously busted Penn Central Railroad senior first mortgage bonds at a deep discount. He made five times his money when the fully secured paper was paid off at face value. It was a splendid opener for Whitman's advent as a vulture investor.

As an expert witness, Whitman had been getting a thorough grounding in utility finance. He testified as a rate expert in the Senate hearings on the breakup of AT&T, and subsequently served as financial adviser to the Presidential Commission named to investigate the near meltdown of the General Public Utilities Three Mile Island nuclear plant.

Whitman put the technical background to good use for clients of the newly established brokerage and advisory firm of M. J. Whitman & Company. The specicalty, of course, was distressed utility paper.

Working for partners like Citicorp, Whitman analyzed the prospect of bankruptcy workouts on such troubled nuclear power companies as the Michigan-based Consumers Power Company and the even more controversial Public Service Company of New Hampshire. Ecological problems and the heavy leverage of idle nuclear capacity hung over the securities of both companies like a mushroom cloud. Weighing the values, Whitman bought into the utilities' heavily sold mortgage bonds, calculating he could come out ahead even if the companies did go through the bankruptcy wringer.

In a cliffhanger, both companies scraped by—at least for the moment. In a little over two years, Whitman doubled his money, coming out with a gain of some $15 million. The profit was a gratifying testament to the distinction between market risk and investment risk. When the fix at Public Service of New Hampshire proved to be only temporary, Whitman went back for more. The second helping centered on third mortgage bonds trading at around 60¢ on the dollar and yielding around 13.75 percent.

Fronting for a major Citicorp investment, Whitman worked out and presented to creditors a well-publicized reorganization strategy: a consensual prepackaged bankruptcy that would permit the utility to shed debt in a quick turn through bankruptcy court. The plan had something for everybody except PSNH management.

Whitman and his clients had carefully assembled enough voting power to block any other reorganization plan put on the table, including one backed by management. Pressing heavily on a Nativist PR pedal, PSNH responded by picturing Whitman as plotting a "complete takeover by New York bankers for a whopping profit." Chivvied by dozens of other creditors, and denied a critical rate increase, the utility lurched into bankruptcy on its own. Three years and dozens of lawsuits later, the utility emerged with a huge rate increase and a merger bid from neighboring

Northeast Utilities Holding Company.

Acceptance of Whitman's consensual prepackage would have speeded the reorganization immeasurably, but he couldn't quarrel with the wrap-up. Citicorp and a number of Whitman appendages split an $80 million profit on a $100 million investment. Trophies all around! Whitman presented his partners with navy-blue caps sporting a vulture triumphantly perched on a nuclear cooling tower. Citicorp presented Whitman with his prized bronze of a bull fornicating with a bear.

Key Words and Expressions:

acquisition	n 收购
aggressive conservative investor	积极和谨慎的投资商
American online (AOL)	美国在线服务公司
as buy-and-hold investor	作为买入并持有的投资者
as vulture investor	秃鹰投资商
at the peril of	冒……的危险
bankruptcy	n. 破产
bankruptcy trustee	破产管财人
cheap and safe investment philosophy	廉价和安全的投资原则
cheap and safe investment	廉价安全的投资
chivvy	v. (使)烦扰, 耍花招
Citicorp	西特公司
custody	v. 收容
depressed stock prices	低迷的股票价格
divestiture	n. 剥夺（财产、权利等）
dogma	n. 定理,教条,武断的意见
effective market theory	有效市场理论
egregiously	adv. 惊人地,无比地,异乎寻常地
Electroglas	伊智公司
energy industry	能源工业
expostulate	vi. 劝诫, 忠告
financials	n. 财政
front for	主办
growth stocks	成长股

hitch	n.延迟，蹒跚，障碍
idle capacity	闲置生产能力，空闲容量
Japanese market	日本市场
litigation	n. 诉讼，起诉
margin of safety investment rule	安全系数投资规则
market risk	市场风险
Nabors Industries	石油钻探公司
nativist	n. 先天论者，本土主义者
nuclear power industry	核能公司
Penn Central Railroad bonds	佩恩中央铁路债券
pick up the pieces	（跌倒后）重新爬起来（对小孩讲的话）
power and light companies	能源和照明公司
price-to-book value	股价与股票账面值的比率
pricing of companies	公司的定价
Public Service Company of New Hampshire	美国新罕布什尔州公用事业公司
real estate	房地产
reorganization strategy	重组策略
repository	n. 贮藏室，智囊团，知识库，仓库，储存库
resource conversion	资源转换
retail industry	n. 零售业
risk limiting	风险限制
Rosenwald Foundation	罗森沃尔德基金会
savings and loan industry	储蓄和贷款业
selling of investments	投资出售
semiconductor equipment manufacturers	半导体设备制造商
semiconductor equipment	半导体设备
senior mortgage	优先抵押债务
short-term earning	短期收益
Swiss Bank Corporation	瑞士银行有限公司
the underlying value of a business	潜在的商业价值
Third Avenue Value Fund	第三大道基金公司

Tokyo Marine & Fire Insurance	东京海运和火灾保险
value investing	价值投资
value strategy	价值策略
Whitman Martin J.	马丁·J.惠特曼
Whitman's investments	惠特曼的投资
whopping	adj. 巨大的，庞大的
	adv. 非常地，异常地
wringer	n. 敲诈者

Notes:

1．AT&T 美国电话电报公司

美国电话电报公司（AT&T）是一家美国电信公司，创建于 1877 年，曾长期垄断美国长途和本地电话市场。AT&T 在近 20 年中，曾经过多次分拆和重组。目前，AT&T 是美国最大的本地和长途电话公司，总部位于得克萨斯州圣安东尼奥。

2．Applied Materials 应用材料公司

应用材料公司是全球最大的半导体生产设备和高科技技术服务企业，为财富 500 强全球化发展增长型企业之一，连续十几年在半导体生产设备领域独占鳌头。

3．FSI International Inc.　FSI 国际有限公司

30 多年以来，FSI 国际有限公司已经为创新的、可扩展的和灵活的表面处理清洗方案建立了标准；依托在 20 多个国家和地区的 200 多家微电子客户，公司的实践经验成为了工艺特性和生产能力的基准。FSI 总部位于美国明尼苏达州的 Chaska 市，公司多年来通过就近提供直接销售及服务的策略为全球客户提供支持；FSI 通过战略性的部署，在美国、欧洲、亚太地区的服务机构以及 mFSI (FSI 在日本的合资企业)提供服务。FSI 对客户的鼎力支持渗透到了客户服务的每一个细节，例如与 DHL 合作为客户提供的全球物流服务。

4．KLA-Tencor

KLA-Tencor 是为半导体行业提供工艺控制和成品率管理解决方案的领先供应商。

KLA-Tencor Corporation 和 ADE Corporation 联合宣布他们已签署了一份正式收购协议。根据该协议，KLA-Tencor 将在 2006 年 2 月 22 日股

票收市价格的基础上，以约 4.88 亿美元的股票市值收购 ADE。

5．American online 美国在线

美国在线（AOL）创立于 1985 年，是第一个网上消费服务项目。美国在线可向顾客提供即时咨讯、电子邮件，而且是首个服务于宽带用户的项目。大约 30 万人在世界各地期望自己成为美国在线的成员。在线成员积极支持和参与服务，每天发送大约 450 万封电子邮件、约 1.5 亿即时讯息。每天近 17 万人在聊天室享受开放式服务。

II. Knowledge Points

1. Market risk

Market risk is the risk that the value of an investment will decrease due to moves in market factors. The four standard market risk factors are:

Equity risk, or the risk that stock prices will change.

Equity risk is the risk that one's investments will depreciate because of stock market dynamics causing one to lose money.

The measure of risk used in the equity markets is typically the standard deviation of a security's price over a number of periods. The standard deviation will delineate the normal fluctuations one can expect in that particular security above and below the mean, or average. However, since most investors would not consider fluctuations above the average return as "risk", some economists prefer other means of measuring it.

Interest rate risk, or the risk that interest rates will change.

Interest rate risk is the risk that the relative value of a security, especially a bond, will worsen due to an interest rate increase. This risk is commonly measured by the bond's duration, the oldest of the many techniques now used to manage interest rate risk.

There are a number of standard calculations for measuring the impact of changing interest rates on a portfolio consisting of various assets and liabilities. The most common techniques include:

1) Marking to market, calculating the net market value of the assets and liabilities, sometimes called the "market value of portfolio equity".

2) Stress testing this market value by shifting the yield curve in a specific way.

Duration is a stress test where the yield curve shift is parallel.

3) Calculating the Value at Risk of the portfolio.

4) Calculating the multiperiod cash flow or financial accrual income and expense for N periods forward in a deterministic set of future yield curves.

5) Doing step 4 with random yield curve movements and measuring the probability distribution of cash flows and financial accrual income over time.

6) Measuring the mismatch of the interest sensitivity gap of assets and liabilities, by classifying each asset and liability by the timing of interest rate reset or maturity, whichever comes first.

Currency risk, or the risk that foreign exchange rates will change.

Currency risk is a form of risk that arises from the change in price of one currency against another. Whenever investors or companies have assets or business operations across national borders, they face currency risk if their positions are not hedged.

Transaction risk is the risk that exchange rates will change unfavorably over time. It can be hedged against using forward currency contracts.

Translation risk is an accounting risk, proportional to the amount of assets held in foreign currencies. Changes in the exchange rate over time will render a report inaccurate, and so assets are usually balanced by borrowings in that currency.

The exchange risk associated with a foreign denominated instrument is a key element in foreign investment. This risk flows from differential monetary policy and growth in real productivity, which results in differential inflation rates.

Commodity risk, or the risk that commodity prices (i.e. grains, metals, etc.) will change.

Commodity risk refers to the uncertainties of future market values and of the size of the future income, caused by the fluctuation in the prices of commodities. These commodities may be grains, metals, gas, electricity etc. A Commodity enterprise needs to deal with the following kinds of risks:

Price risk (Risk arising out of adverse movements in the world prices, exchange rates, basis between local and world prices)

Quantity risk

Cost risk (Input price risk)

Political risk

2. Assets

Intangible asset

Intangible asset is an asset that is not physical in nature. Corporate intellectual property (items such as patents, trademarks, copyrights, business methodologies), goodwill and brand recognition are all common intangible assets in today's marketplace. An intangible asset can be classified as either indefinite or definite depending on the specifics of that asset. A company brand name is considered to be an indefinite asset, as it stays with the company as long as the company continues operations. However, if a company enters a legal agreement to operate under another company's patent, with no plans of extending the agreement, it would have a limited life and would be classified as a definite asset.

While intangible assets don't have the obvious physical value of a factory or equipment, they can prove very valuable for a firm and can be critical to its long-term success or failure. For example, a company such as Coca-Cola wouldn't be nearly as successful were it not for the high value obtained through its brand-name recognition. Although brand recognition is not a physical asset you can see or touch, its positive effects on bottom-line profits can prove extremely valuable to firms such as Coca-Cola, whose brand strength drives global sales year after year.

Tangible asset

Tangible asset is an asset that has a physical form such as machinery, buildings and land.

This is the opposite of an intangible asset such as a patent or trademark. Whether an asset is tangible or intangible isn't inherently good or bad. For example, a well-known brand name can be very valuable to a company. On the other hand, if you produce a product solely for a trademark, at some point you need to have "real" physical assets to produce it.

Net tangible assets

Net tangible assets are calculated as the total assets of a company, minus any intangible assets such as goodwill, patents and trademarks, less all liabilities and the par value of preferred stock. It is also known as "net asset value" or "book value".

To calculate a company's net asset value on a per bond, or per share of preferred or common stock, divide the net tangible assets figure by the number of bonds, shares of preferred stock, or shares of common stock.

3. Book value

1) The value at which an asset is carried on a balance sheet. In other words, the cost of an asset minus accumulated depreciation.

2) The net asset value of a company, calculated by total assets minus intangible assets (patents, goodwill) and liabilities.

3) The initial outlay for an investment. This number may be net or gross of expenses such as trading costs, sales taxes, service charges and so on.

4) In the U.K., book value is known as "net asset value".

Book value is the accounting value of a firm. It has two main uses:

1) It is the total value of the company's assets that shareholders would theoretically receive if a company were liquidated.

2) By being compared to the company's market value, the book value can indicate whether a stock is under-or overpriced.

3) In personal finance, the book value of an investment is the price paid for a security or debt investment. When a stock is sold, the selling price less the book value is the capital gain (or loss) from the investment.

4. Price-to-Book Ratio - P/B Ratio

A ratio used to compare a stock's market value to its book value. It is calculated by dividing the current closing price of the stock by the latest quarter's book value per share.

Also known as the "price-equity ratio".

Calculated as:

$$\mathbf{P\,/\,B\ \ Ratio} = \frac{\textbf{Stock Price}}{\textbf{Total\ Assets - Intangible Assets and Liabilities}}$$

A lower P/B ratio could mean that the stock is undervalued. However, it could also mean that something is fundamentally wrong with the company. As with most ratios, be aware this varies by industry.

This ratio also gives some idea of whether you're paying too much for what would be left if the company went bankrupt immediately.

5. Price to Tangible Book Value - PTBV

A valuation ratio expressing the price of a security compared to its hard, or tangible, book value as reported in the company's balance sheet. The tangible book value number is equal to the company's total book value less the value of any intangible assets. Intangible assets can be such items as patents, intellectual property, goodwill etc. The ratio is calculated as:

$$PTBV = \frac{\textbf{Share Price}}{\textbf{Tangible Book Value per Share}}$$

In theory, a stock's tangible book value per share represents the amount of money an investor would receive for each share if a company were to cease operations and liquidate all of its assets at the value recorded on the company's accounting books. As a rule of thumb, stocks that trade at higher price to tangible book value ratios have the potential to leave investors with greater share price losses than those that trade at lower ratios, since the tangible book value per share can reasonably be viewed as about the lowest price a stock could realistically be expected to trade at.

6. Book Value of Equity Per Share – BVPS

A financial measure that represents a per share assessment of the minimum value of a company's equity. More specifically, this value is determined by relating the original value of a firm's common stock adjusted for any outflow (dividends and stock buybacks) and inflow (retained earnings) modifiers to the amount of shares outstanding.

Calculated as:

$$BVPS = \frac{\textbf{Value of Common Equity}}{\textbf{\# of Shares Outstanding}}$$

While book value of equity per share is one factor that investors can use to determine whether a stock is undervalued, this metric should not be used by itself as it only presents a very limited view of the firm's situation. BVPS provides a snap shot of a firm's current situation, but considerations of the firm's future are not included.

For example, XYZ Corp., a widget producing company, may have a share price that is currently lower than its BVPS. This may not indicate that the XYZ is undervalued, because looking ahead, the growth opportunities for the company are vastly limited as fewer and fewer people are buying widgets.

7. Book Value per Common Share

A measure used by owners of common shares in a firm to determine the level of safety associated with each individual share after all debts are paid accordingly.

Formula:

$$\text{Book Value per Share} = \frac{\text{Total Shareholder Equity - Preferred Equity}}{\text{Total Outstanding Shares}}$$

Should the company decide to dissolve, the book value per common indicates the dollar value remaining for common shareholders after all assets are liquidated and all debtors are paid.

In simple terms it would be the amount of money that a holder of a common share would get if a company were to liquidate.

III. Analyzing the Case

1. In what way is Martin J. Whitman similar to Benjamin Graham?

Like Benjamin Graham, Whitman aims to buy "safe and cheap," which means "Buying assets and earnings at a discount".

2. What is the relationship between value and growth stocks and the economic cycle?

Typically, value and growth stocks outrun the market at different phases of the economic cycle. Value stocks tend to outperform in periods of no to slow expansion, while Growth stocks tend to outperform when the economy is on the move.

3. What's Whitman's opinion about the management of a business?

Whitman thinks management has to be appraised not only as operators of a going business, but also as investors engaged in employing and redeploying assets.

4. What's the implied meaning of Whitman's sense of something else?

He actually thought of a new idea of a long-term view and the assets side of a business as a store of value.

5. Whitman actually benefited from the utilities' heavily sold mortgage bonds and gained $15 million. What does it prove?

The profit testified the distinction between market risk and investment risk.

6. What kind of strategy did Whitman work out for Citicorp investment?

Whitman worked out and presented to creditors a well-publicized reorganization strategy: a consensual prepackaged bankruptcy.

7. How do opportunists earn money from the stock market?

They picked up the pieces at distressed prices and get the benefit after the selling at much higher prices.

8. How does Whitman regard value investing?

He regards it as a good enough business.

9. Why did Whitman think himself couldn't become a trader?

Because he was very slow with numbers and couldn't understand the meaning of them.

10. What did his family think of him when he was young?

His family feared that he would never amount to much.

IV. Translation of the Case

马蒂·惠特曼，也被称为"秃鹰投资家"。他最喜欢的事情就是搜索破产法庭的剩余财产，借此寻找一些低风险的交易。这就是他的特征。

"当然，我知道我是与众不同的。"

这就是好胜的马蒂·雅戈布·惠特曼对自己的评价。他运用商业领域最折衷的价值策略之一，成功地运转了别人投资的 20 亿美元资本。作为这样一个人，他很重视把自己和华尔街的主流区分开来。

马蒂·惠特曼没有穿萨维尔街精心裁剪的西装，也没有喋喋不休地谈论有效市场理论。这就是普通而率真的马蒂·惠特曼，在这里你看到的就是最真实的情况。惠特曼懒散地坐在扶手椅上，双脚搭在玻璃咖啡桌上，脚上穿着一双运动鞋。他上身是一件平常的办公服装——一件随意的开领法兰绒花格衬衫；下面穿着蓝色的灯心绒牛仔裤，膝盖的地方有些磨损。

惠特曼的办公室俯瞰着第三大道，里面堆满了类似青铜熊和公牛嬉戏的宝贝东西。值得注意的是，在他的办公室里，我们看不到像华尔街这种环境下最常见的人工制品——不停闪动的股票市场监测器。

惠特曼回避的态度可以看作是一种政治立场。他确信华尔街对想象中的类似高效经济、投资者心理和短期收益波动的关注，只不过是些噪音罢了。"我们不承担过多的额外负担，"他的声音中夹杂着地道的布朗克斯口音，"华尔街的很多做法都与潜在的商业价值毫无联系。我们是凭借概率做生意，而不是凭借预言。"

像沃论·巴菲特和其他所谓的价值博士本杰明·格雷厄姆的精神继承人一样，惠特曼的目标是"安全又廉价"地买进。也就是说，折价购进资产和收益。一般说来，价值股和成长股在不同的经济周转阶段都会超越股市增长。价值股票（高股息收益及价值相对账面比率低）在不能阻止缓慢膨胀的阶段往往会超越大市。成长股（能很快聚集收益，有很高的市盈率）往往在经济高速发展时超越大市。

惠特曼彻底打破了固有的模式。他的总部设于曼哈顿的第三大道基金公司在形势一片大好的股市中往往总显得有些行动迟缓，但在过去的十年间他却成功地赢得了高达19%的年收益。在市场连续三年持续走低的情况下，这个数字已经是相当高了。

有了这样的记录，难怪他有资格说："只有2/3的被动买入、增值买入和投机盈余。"他接着又说："在最后两年中，比如从1928－1929年，以及从1972－1973年间，我们只从投机盈余中获利。"

所以所谓的不存在升值空间的报道是过度夸大了。如果你遇到惠特曼在十年前碰到的情形，也就是在市场中几乎找不到什么"安全又廉价"的股票，你会怎么做呢？要知道惠特曼在那段时间可是做得游刃有余呢。令人吃惊的是，他并不看好低价的高科技股，其主要依据是芯片生产商低迷的状态。当高科技股几乎占到他公司总业务值1/3的时候，他就抽身而退了。"如果你在七年前来告诉我，作为一名有眼光的投资人，应当加大对高科技股的投入，我可能会不予理解。"惠特曼笑了笑说道。如果市场处于狂热的状态，在某些时间和价位，成长股可能会变成增值股。

惠特曼也曾经在低迷的日本股市寻找"安全又廉价"的股票。从战略的角度，他实际上是把本·格雷厄姆十分时髦的价值战略模式应用到日本这个后来成为世界经济发动机的国家中去了。

在格雷厄姆的时代还没有电脑网络，你看准一家公司的股价低于其实际价值，便出手购进，期待着能有大幅的收益和红利，把股价推高，最后再找机会抛出，赚上一笔。

现在可没那么容易了。长线的投资者已经收手，不再为美国电话电报公司(AT&T)而奔波。自从公司因为一部反托拉斯法令的出台而破产之后，就很少再靠收益和红利这种格雷厄姆式的方式来赚大钱了，而是转向一系列并购、收购和回购，虽然这些方法显然有些让人茫然，也更不可预期。以前在格雷厄姆看来的"大事"早已变得司空见惯了，而且以这些"大事"为起点，将进一步偏离惠特曼标准性的增值买入。

惠特曼三家基金公司中第三大道增值基金公司，资产总额达 18 亿美元。他提出，每隔三到五年时间，该公司所持有的大多股票，就会因为一些"大事"的发生而变得一文不值。惠特曼就曾谈道："(包括)并购、恶意收购、回购、重新集资和私有化。"

在"第三大道"所有占据主要股份的 22 家公司中，有 13 家都是惠特曼在这些企业处于"资产转换"的关键时期将它们收入帐下的。收过来后，就会经历如下一些过程：两次以现金形式现销现售控股权；一次交易股票；三次被恶意收购的危险；五次收购比自己更小的公司；一次部分的清算；再加上一次售出新发行的普通股。

所有这些交易都是在超过市值的情况下进行的。惠特曼就是从这些金融的交易中牟利的。他的具体做法就是，更多地强调高质量的资产，不太重视运营收益，这与格雷厄姆固有的做法显然不同。在惠特曼看来，时下公司的管理层不应当只被看作企业的运营官，而应当是对企业资产进行使用并重新配置的投资人。

这种观点在一定程度上也可以说是将"股神"沃论·巴菲特的一句名言延伸了。这句名言大致的意思是："管理企业让我成了更好的投资人，而进行投资也使我在企业管理方面受益匪浅。"

惠特曼用自己的亲身经历充分证明了这句话。在 20 世纪 80 年代末，他帮助促成了石油钻探公司（现在最大的也是最盈利的石油钻探承包商之一）的预先包装的破产。正是惠特曼确保了石油钻探公司在完成重组后，没有背上任何债务，而且还拥有完整的股权权益基础。在石油产业遭遇困境时，石油钻探公司轻而易举地筹得了所需资金，以超低价将那些负债累累的竞争者买了过来。惠特曼说："其他从业者根本不具备相当的财力与石油钻探公司相抗衡，去争夺那些资产。"

结果，石油钻探公司成功地将原来 2,000 万美元的经营亏损，变成了超过 2 亿美元的正向现金流动。而这次行动的收益方之一就是：石油钻探公司的长期股东惠特曼和他的第三大道增值基金公司。惠特曼在石油钻探公司案中的成功之处，也往往为华尔街所忽视的，就是与一味地研究过去的盈利模式相比，对资产负债表进行敏锐的分析是更好的预测未来盈利潜能的方法。

作为一个寻求一系列合理的退出投资战略的长线投资商，惠特曼得意自己可以随意地忽略对短期盈利的预测和结果。具有讽刺意味的是，惠特曼却认为华尔街在预测那些难以预料的事情上花费了太多时间。

惠特曼的目的是搜寻那些可以凭借强大的财力后盾渡过难关（因为这样的公司比较安全）的公司，而这些公司正在以低于私人企业或收购价值（"便宜"）的价格出售。以低价收购上好的优质资源似乎一直就意味着，公司的近期收益足够稳固得使它完全可以离开华尔街。"市场对我来说效率太高了，我都不能指望我可以不通过协调和平衡近期不太乐观的市场状况而购得上好的资源。"他一边笑着说，一边用手捋一捋他的白发，"当市场状况糟透了的时候，你用不着花着钱在市场上进行争夺。"

惠特曼的嗜好就是利用一切华尔街留下的已经不值得考虑的机会，这使他赢得了"秃鹰投资家"的声望。惠特曼很喜欢媒体给他的这一绰号。他说这比叫他指数索引家或资产分配家要好得多。他这么说无疑义对标准的华尔街式教条戳了一鼻子。

虽说是教条，可惠特曼却是从零开始学起的。早先在二战期间他做了三年的海军药剂师，在普林斯顿大学读了一年的经济学硕士，然后在20世纪40年代到华尔街开始了他分析师的生涯。他说他在来到华尔街的几年后才学习了险境经营学，那时他开始作为一个内行进行破产评估并且赚了些钱。70年代他买了已经破产倒闭的佩恩中央铁路的房地产抵押高级债券，惠特曼也因此第一次赚得大笔的钱。惠特曼回忆说："当时没有多少人认为这债券是安全的，没什么人买，所以很便宜。"

说到交易的混乱时，惠特曼兴高采烈地谈了他关于风险的独到见解，他认为风险是有限度的。

他说，从70年代到90年代，经济的严重萧条使包括能源、银行业、房地产、储蓄和贷款、零售贸易在内的13个行业陷于瘫痪，但是没有影响整体经济。半导体设备生产商和高新技术资本货物生产商现在也成为其中的一员。通常，由于华尔街选择逃避这种暗淡的市场前景，涉及这些萧条产业贸易的很多股票都会很便宜。这就是为什么惠特曼会如此贪婪。

他认为寻找萧条的产业并不是一种尤其危险的生活方式。他觉得每笔投资都存在着一定的问题。惠特曼的任务就是要找出问题所在，并且指出如何与正确方面进行平衡，尤其在某些形式的潜能资产兑换上。比如，共同基金管理公司会投入大笔的现金，但是由于准入成本较低，他们会难以应对行业内不断产生的新的竞争。资金密集型公司，像炼油商就不必过多地担心新的竞争，但是在商业周期处于下跌的情况下，他们只能自认倒霉了。

惠特曼试图避免的最普通的问题包括：

• 看似极具吸引力的高流通性现金态势其实在严格的管理下显得毫无胆

识，不敢合理利用多余的资产。

- 股票诱人的高回报率通常只代表相对小的资产基础。
- 既有低股票回报又有高额净资产值仅仅意味着资产值被夸大了。
- 高额净资产值可能指潜在的、客观的收益的增长，但是却经常用来指膨
  胀了的管理费用。

惠特曼愿意接管这样的公司，就像他过去做药剂师时治疗虚弱的、瘫的、懒散的海军水手一样，这样他觉得他还是一位"精神理疗师"，但是这种意愿并非来得那么纯粹。以低价收购似乎总是伴有麻烦，因此惠特曼选择忽略市场风险（即当前的价格波动）。但是惠特曼一直在担心投资风险问题（拿疾病来打比方，即他误判为暂时性的疾病有可能已经到了晚期）。

在衡量投资风险时，惠特曼将焦点集中在两个关键因素上，即"资源的数量和质量"。这些看似老套的抽象概念背后的原动力从长远看来却恰恰被惠特曼应用在了半导体设备制造业方面。很多像 Applied Materials, Electroglas 和 KLA-Tencor 一样的商家都在生产高度专业性工具。这些工具是制造普遍使用的微型芯片所必需的，而这种芯片被广泛应用于信用卡、贺卡、电话以及玩具中。尽管用途广泛，芯片对于终端的生产商和供应商都同样具有可循环性。

惠特曼初次涉足制造业是在五年前，当时这一产业刚刚开始走下坡路，前途未卜。惠特曼认为制造业的颓势可能会持续两个季度到三年，甚至更长时间。很难逆转这种颓势，因为全球经济增长放缓，集成电路的个人电脑市场几近饱和，业务量也少得可怜。

华尔街又从短期利益出发，开始抛出股票。这却正中了惠特曼的下怀，于是他采取行动了，以低于账面价值 50%的价钱购进了大量股票。惠特曼之所以介入设备制造业，就是因为当时它的股票市值比起芯片制造业要低。

设备的生产商，由于受到独有技术的保护，不大容易为市场所淘汰，而且资产质量也更出色。资本密集型的芯片制造商将大笔资金投入厂房的建设，与之截然不同的是，设备制造商的生产地点则是在一些低成本的干净的房间内，而且其大多零部件也不是自己生产，而是从外面购进。研发的成本相对较高，但惠特曼精明地舍弃那些需要大笔投入，并将眼光集中在那些能给自己带来收益回报的公司。一些公司高额的研发费用远远超过了收益，使得它们在低迷的市场中更加一蹶不振。华尔街的情况就更糟了。

惠特曼正在关注一些能够给他带来"高质量"资产的账面价值。当股市小牛市出现了一些表现反常的股票时，他有些犹豫不决，但他对股市颓势持续时间长短的估计却得到了证实。第三大道增值基金公司所持的一些主要股票，比如工艺管理工具制造商，在每季的销售情况报告中显示运营收益降低了 60%甚

至更多。可以预见，股价会继续走低，直至低于账面价值。

惠特曼继续购进大量的设备制造企业，在他看来，这时的价格简直比一些冒险投机商要化的钱还要低。而对于那些已经上市的公司，就可赚取大笔的现金。

这样一来，惠特曼原本就廉价的股票变得更便宜了，但是这些股票是不是还"保险"呢？在惠特曼把第三大道增值基金公司超过22%的资本投入到设备制造公司后，这个问题就显得更为突出了。惠特曼本人不过是在贯彻他一贯的战略，但却并不为华尔街的操作者们所称道。

惠特曼认定一定会出现转机，只不过是时间早晚的问题。他对股东们显示了自己的乐观态度，他坚信因为应用范围的增大和技术革新，"暴涨"马上就会出现。惠特曼说："集成电路会越来越小，从而进一步增加密度。这样，半导体的制造商们没有别的办法，只有更换设备，以保持自己的竞争力。要想继续自己的业务，这些企业只有更换成最新的设备。"

在惠特曼对股票所有这些言论背后，其实他是在以睿智的眼光去评估价值。惠特曼将3亿美元分投在十几家设备制造企业。这种分散投资的做法显然十分明智，因为并非他选择的所有股票都一定会表现出色。惠特曼认为："大多数会表现不错，个别的还会大获成功，但也会有一些表现不佳的。"对设备制造这个正处于不断整合的产业来说，那些表现欠佳的企业的唯一出路就是，接受并购。

惠特曼自保的办法，除了分散投资外，还有一个就是加强管理。所谓加强管理，有两个标准：一是每天要有出色的表现；二是既要注重企业运营，也要善于资产管理。他持有最多的股票有像 Applied Materials 这样的公司，这些公司在股市的升势时，一直不断攀升，利用自己在华尔街的知名度赚取利润，再将股票抛出。

"许多这样的人都相当精明，"惠特曼说，"即使他们当时并不需要现金，在市场表现极佳时，他们也会充分利用机会，大赚一笔。"对于像 Electroglas 这样每股现金和资产比达到或超过35%的股票，惠特曼有把握它们会安然度过逆境。当然唯一令人头疼的问题就是"火险比率"。整个产业范围内的颓势会不会持续过久，将所有的现金都耗干呢？运营亏损的不断激增，大的芯片制造商难以为继，使得他们只能以相对低廉的价格购进数量有限的新设备，推后对更新设备的订单。而设备制造企业为研发这些新型设备却不惜重金。

这次困境促使他作出了痛苦艰难的抉择，卖掉了至少三家惠特曼旗下设备制造商的 40% 以上的股份，这三家设备制造商是 Clare 公司、FSI 国际和 SpeedFam-IPEC。其中两家，即 FSI 和 SpeedFam-IPEC 正处于赢利的大好形势中。表面上看来，这两家制造商仍然在窘境中创造着繁荣，但惠特曼这样评价它们（以及其他下跌 25%以上的组合投资）：他们要么会创造出良好的经营效果，要么会成为参与某种形式财务工程最可能的候选。事实上，惠特曼的这种估计也确实发生了。惠特曼旗下最大的控股公司硅谷集团以及其他若干家公司以可观的价格被收购了。

再次以嘲笑藐视的口吻谈及市场风险时，惠特曼强调了有强大的财力作铺垫所带来的那种欣慰感。他说："如果你在一家资金充裕的公司里，如果他们因此而开始挥霍浪费的话，那么你就有理由离开这家公司。另一方面，如果你所在的公司资金短缺，那么你就应该管好季度报告了。"

作为一个买入并持有的投资者，惠特曼第一次承认虽然他获得的投资组合周转率是最低的，但站在卖出方的角度来讲，他的行动却是迟缓的。他可以很快地改正明显的错误，但是持有定价极高的股票却时常使他陷入困惑，犹疑不决。

原因在于他是从倍数市场的角度来考虑问题的。个体投资者认为很荒谬的价格对于寻求收购的处于控制地位的买主来说却是一个颇好的合理的价格。虽然不情愿，但由于控制可以带来不少好处，所以他们还是可以负担这种溢价的。好处之一就是可以用惠特曼所谓的"别人的钱"和"二等之物"来为某个交易分期融资，这些资金通常以高薪水、买卖特权及公司金库存取权等形式出现。

因此，凭借长期积累的经验，惠特曼判定他的分析判断力更适用于一个买者而非卖者。他说："我以双倍的价格卖出买了三年的证券，但是在接下来的六个月中它们的价格却涨到了原来的三倍。"寓意："有时候坐以待毙是一种更好的赚钱方式。"这个结论可以很好地解释为什么有那么多惠特曼存在，而他们都是选择去收购而不是彻底地廉价出售。

对此还有另外一种观点。惠特曼认为自己不是在管理金钱而是在"创造财富"。意思是说在工作中尽可能多地保有利润，而且保有的时间越长越好。除了追求财务工程溢价外，惠特曼的这种等待、观望的游戏规则和他的低周转率使他的纳税保持在低水平状态。

等待、观望的游戏规则也的的确确凭借着几家芯片设备生产商获得了成功。惠特曼一直寻求的经营状况的好转也最终实现了。华尔街的领军人物们，像摩根·斯坦利，在新千年的时候又一度开始在股票上贴上"超越大市"的标签。惠特曼嘲笑自己的这种与银行背道而驰的做法。几年来，惠特曼一直保持着盈利，体现了惠特曼战略的真谛——除市场衰落外，忽视市场的摇摆不定；忽视公认的华尔街制规。由于雄厚的财务状况持续走低，因此商业削弱了工业。所谓雄厚的财务状况是指公司有很少的甚至没有债务，且拥有充足的现金——

惠特曼如是说。那么是什么变得廉价,持续走低了呢?不是严格的规则,"而是你所获得的资源的价格",惠特曼这样概括。

对于工业企业来说,惠特曼试图只付收购价值的 50%到 60%。其中一个价值指标就是股价与多重账面价值(即股价与账面价值的比)的倍数。倍数越小越好。账面价格本身并不能说明整体的状况,但确实可以作为解释最佳案例的例证。在计算出几家芯片制造商的股价下跌仅为硬账面价格的 40%时,惠特曼显得十分高兴。

以下是惠特曼其他的定价规则:

- 对小额资本的高新技术企业,溢价只能高出账面价格的 60%——这关系到风险投资家们在第一阶段的投资中会出什么价。
- 对银行,惠特曼定的限度是不超过账面价值的 80%。
- 对金钱管理者,惠特曼依靠管理资产额(不超过 2%到 3%)。
- 对房地产企业,惠特曼的目标是打了折扣的估价而非账面价值。

惠特曼显得并不在乎所谓的惯例,他把自己定位为华尔街的外来势力。尽管有着哲学上的关联,但他还是不愿承认他会认同格雷厄姆与 Dodd 是原教旨主义者。一些基本的相似之处十分明显,像对事物的远虑、对所报数字背后隐含的意义进行严格的分析以及坚信成功的可能性属于那些以低价购入的优质股。像本·格雷厄姆一样,惠特曼嘲讽那些学术界人士,这些人认为股票的价格是由信息灵通和有效的市场来决定的。虽然惠特曼承认格雷厄姆对他的影响,但他又称,他所研发和运用的撤出战略为价值投资开辟了一片新天地。惠特曼坚持认为格雷厄姆过于专注市场风险与宏观经济因素,而他却对此置之不理。

如果惠特曼占了优势,他将会把价值投资的理念带入新的世纪,但就个人而言,他并不像自己声称的那样与格雷厄姆相距甚远。像格雷厄姆一样,惠特曼在家族生意的环境下成大。1920 年,他的父母从波兰西部移居美国,颇感寄人篱下的滋味。惠特曼生长在一个中产阶级云集的高档居住区。这个名叫布朗克斯的地区距离新英格兰人的运动场不远。他帮助别人送货,做零工,但对于自家的买卖却丝毫没有兴趣。他的激情全部投入到了篮球和棒球运动上。上高中时,他是一个对学习丝毫不感兴趣的学生,以至于他的妹妹菲莉丝——宾夕法尼亚州高等法院法官,在惠特曼 75 岁的生日聚会上,回忆起当时家里人都担心他会永远没有出息。

惠特曼认为他的价值取向的形成是由于他父亲生意的终结。"他清理账目,然后做了很多的思考。"惠特曼回忆道:"我无法想象自己整天与买卖打交道。"惠特曼若有所思地说:"我无法成为一名商人。我对数字反应迟缓。我很难理解数字的含义。"

　　惠特曼认为，价值投资是一个"相当好"的生意——不会摇摆不定。"这是一种可能性的艺术，"他说道，"其目的不是为了赚取最大利润，而是要在低风险的状态下长期持有。我从来不介意保留一些股份。"

　　惠特曼从海军退役后，经历了他的第一次婚姻。这次婚姻只持续了六个月。惠特曼在锡拉库扎大学读完本科学业，1949 年以优异成绩毕业（"我想我终于成熟了"，他笑着说）。惠特曼竭尽全力读完了普林斯顿大学研究生的课程。然后来到了纽约的华尔街。他的第一份工作是在希尔森·海登斯通公司作分析师。该工作使他不久就对华尔街的短视价值观念不再抱有幻想。

　　"这是非常可笑的，"惠特曼回忆。"98%的工作重点放在短期收益和近期前景上"，"我遇到一家公司，"他继续说，"这是一家木材公司，没有或很少有明显的赚钱能力，但却有大量的木材。我无法对这家公司作出正确的分析。因此，我知道一定还有其他的做事方法。"

　　惠特曼感受到的新方法——一种从长远的角度将企业资产作为价值储蓄的方法——很快形成，这时他已调到罗森沃尔德基金公司工作。这是一家为慈善事业创办的基金公司，经费由西尔斯·罗巴克家族企业提供，拥有多家公司的控制权益，其中包括西联汇款。"那时我对自己所做的一切抱有一线希望。这属于自己的 1,000 万美元，将是永久性或非永久性投资的基础。"惠特曼回忆起当时的情景时这样说道。

　　这是惠特曼所接受的重要一课。购买和持有的益处开始显现。市场风险和投资风险的差别也开始有了新的意义。与本·格雷厄姆可以相提并论的另一方面是惠特曼也是由随从升为专家证人，除了参与一些其他案例外，还为政府调查卡车驾驶员工会在投资方面的错误做法提供证据。惠特曼很快在处理股东诉讼和破产案件方面建立了良好的声誉，"只是在不大受尊重的公司法的领域，"惠特曼笑着说道。他工作的关键问题在于为破产受托人进行财产评估。如何确定一个可靠的抵押价格？公司价值究竟是多少？

　　惠特曼从案例的准备工作中学到了很多实践经验，学会了如何在倾斜的市场价格背后正确估算潜在的资产价值。慌恐的债权人或债券持有人在预期破产的情况下争先恐后夺路而逃，这才是真正的市场危机，而机会主义者却振作精神起来，从低迷的价格中获得收益。这些人颇能规避市场的风险。价格还能降低多少？用他人的财产作抵押存在一定的投资风险，他们的业务计划是否可行？他们所控制的经过重新分配的资产是否能升值？

　　投资所得到的收益是最有说服力的，这使得惠特曼由一位理论家成为了成功的实践者。被很多债权人聘为顾问后，惠特曼在 20 世纪 70 年代初以 10 万美元超跌价格买下了佩恩铁路破产后的第一批优先抵押债券。当他的全额担保债券以面值赎回时，其价值翻了五倍。对于惠特曼来说，作为秃鹰投资者，这也是他辉煌时期的开始。

作为专家证人，惠特曼全面接管了公用事业的融资工作。作为估价专家，惠特曼出席了参议院就美国电话电报公司解体议案举行的听证会。后来出任总统委员会的财务顾问，该委员会专为调查近于崩溃的三哩岛核电厂的大众公共事业而成立。

惠特曼很好地利用了他的专业知识为 M.J.Whitman & Company 新成立的经纪和咨询事务所的客户服务。

在为西特公司这样的合伙人工作时，惠特曼对于那些问题颇多的核能公司进行了资产测算并对破产后的前景进行了分析。这些公司包括总部设在密执安州的消费者电力公司和更具争议性的公众服务的公司。生态问题和闲置核能力的严重影响像蘑菇云一层一样笼罩着这两家公司的证券。权衡价值后，惠特曼买入公用事业大量出售的抵押债券，计算出即使公司经历破产期间的敲诈勒索，自己也能够从中获益。

在这两家公司险被瓜分的两年多之后，惠特曼的资金翻了一倍，抛售收益约 1,500 万美元。可喜的利润再次证明市场风险和投资风险是有区别的。当新罕布什尔公共服务事业的固定资产被证明只是暂时性的时候，惠特曼再次购进争取更丰厚的收益。第二次购入的重点是第三期抵押债券，每份以约 60 美分成交，收益约为 13.75%。

主办西特公司的投资时,惠特曼拟定并提交给债权人一个广为宣传的重组策略：合意提前打包破产，这将使公用事业摆脱债务，快速地通过法庭宣告破产。该计划能够使除新罕布什尔公共服务事业管理层之外的每一个人获得利益。

惠特曼和他的客户在仔细收集了足够的投票权来阻止任何其他重组计划的实施，其中包括管理计划。新罕布什尔公共服务事业公司在对本地公关层面施加压力，说惠特曼"为了赚取高额利润，策划通过纽约银行家来完成收购"。后来公用事业公司在饱受几十个债权人的困扰，并否认了临界率增加的情况下，艰难地宣告破产来保护自己。在经历了三年时间和十几场官司之后，公用事业公司承受着巨额的债务与附近的东北公用事业控股公司合并。

假如该公司接受了惠特曼的合意提前打包破产计划，就会迅速实现重组，但后悔为时已晚。西特公司和若干惠特曼的附属公司从 100 万美元的投资中获得了高达 80 万美元的利润。四周都是战利品。惠特曼将一个海军蓝色头盔送给他的伙伴，头盔上面的核冷却塔上站着一只洋洋得意的秃鹫。西特集团颁发给惠特曼的是他的珍贵的青铜公牛与熊嬉戏的雕塑。

Chapter Three
Growth Master —
T. Rowe Price

第三章
成长投资大师——托马斯·罗·普里斯

I. Case Study

In his office high above the bustle of Baltimore Harbor, David Testa—chief investment officer of the $130 billion T. Rowe Price Mutual Fund group—is musing over the peculiar genius of his company's founder.

"The important thing to remember about Mr. Price is that most investment managers are like passengers on a ship," says Testa. "As long as the ship is going in the right direction, everything is fine. But when you get an unexpected change in direction, there's panic. Nobody has any idea of what to do next. With just one good idea about how to manage that change, you can make a brilliant career." Testa pauses and smiles. "Mr. Price had at least three good ideas."

Three brilliant ideas about critical changes in market direction and hundreds of smaller ones—all focussed on the growth stocks that were Price's ruling passion. A roll call of the companies Price turned up while developing his growth stock theory in the 1930s shows some amazingly prescient picks—perennials that have persisted on "Nifty Fifty" lists through nearly seven decades of good times and bad. Among them: Abbott Laboratories, Black & Decker, and GE.

There were some clunkers, of course. An insomniac—driven, competitive, autocratic—Price had few close friends, no small talk, and was as hard on himself as on his associates.

"Will I ever learn a few basic fundamentals?" Price railed in a diary entry after a too cautiously placed limit order forced him to pay up two points on a stock he had been following. "Buy and sell at the market," he admonished himself.

David Testa, as a young analyst, recalls Price poking his head in the door one day and demanding, "What's a growth stock?" The startled Testa stammered something about compounding earnings. "You haven't learned a thing!" snapped Price. A couple of days later, Testa found in the middle of his desk, underlined in red ink, the Full Monty from one of Price's pamphlets: "Growth stocks can be defined as shares in business enterprises which have demonstrated favorable underlying long-term growth in earnings and which after careful research study, give indications of continued secular growth in the future."

Growth stocks are so closely tied to the investment strategy Price pioneered that he often seems to have invented them. In fact, Price was not so much Edison as Henry Ford, systematizing bits and pieces of existing lore the way that Ford's idea of standardizing parts revolutionized the assembly line.

Price was the consummate pragmatist. He wrote often about his growth stock theory, but its essential points could be bulleted on the back of a post card. Price was not a theorist in the way that Ben Graham was. He liked to think of himself as relying on "what my grandmother called gumption, my father called horse sense, and most people call common sense."

Operating in the backwaters of Baltimore, deliberately aloof from the trendiness of Wall Street, Price loved going against the crowd. As his son Thomas Rowe Price, III, put it, "He would sometimes go the other way out of sheer obstinacy." Price pursued growth when mainstream investors were looking for safety; switched to small company growth when big company growth caught on; and when all kinds of growth got overpriced, he took to underpriced basics such as oil and timber. Like that other sage of Baltimore, the feisty editor-writer Henry L. Mencken, Price was an original.

Starting with a three-man shop in 1937, Price kept his strategy simple: Look for companies in "new and fertile fields," buy them in an early stage of growth, stick with them as long as earnings are demonstrably on the rise, and sell when the growth cycle begins to mature.

Price's theory, at bottom, is still the philosopher's stone. His long success helped create a school of thousands of mutual funds and investment advisers— followers who believe that exponential long-term earnings growth is the one sure way to outsized market gains.

As David Testa notes, Price had found way to master major changes in market direction. Most money managers in the 1930s were in shock over the combined impact of a bear market and the Great Depression. The old idea that Golconda lay in buying blue chips and simply tucking them into the strongbox had died of a thousand cuts. In a deflationary spiral, when high current income and safety were the rule, few were willing to hazard that corporate earnings would ever retrace the palmy levels of the 1920s.

Price offered a beguiling option. Yes, many of the old war horses like American Tobacco no longer had legs, he said, but plenty of other vibrant possibilities had gotten lost in the general disenchantment. Look at Monsanto. The $4.40 a share it earned in 1937 was more than double the $2 a share of boom year 1929, and there were solid reasons for thinking the company would remain on the upgrade.

In a series of articles in *Barrons*, Price postulated that corporations—like humans—have a distinct three-phase life cycle—"growth, maturity, and decadence." "Risks," argued Price, "increase when maturity is reached." The trick to maximizing profits and minimizing risk lay in "growth stocks" of the sort Price had been tinkering with since 1934.

Price's goals were modest enough in an investment world sick of get-rich-quick hyperbole: A 100-percent gain in earnings over 10 years suited him just fine. Along with a bump in capital, you could also look to a rising curve of dividends.

The weight of Price's seemingly simplistic approach is underscored by the wreckage of yet another get-rich-quick market. Wall Street is littered with dozens of now flattened non-dividend-paying dot-coms that went through the roof of "pro forma" reported earnings that were in fact losses. The important thing to remember is that through good markets and bad, Price's approach worked.

The experimental portfolio Price unveiled in *Barrons* ("an actual fund, not theoretical," he insisted) from 1935 through 1938 showed a capital gain of 76 percent compared with 49 percent for the Dow Jones Industrial averages. Dividend income was up striking 130 percent versus only 12 percent for the averages.

Price's main income producers included Coca-Cola, IBM, and Procter &

Gamble—low yielding outfits even today whose continuing growth translates into cumulatively fattening dividend checks. Price scratched some of the better yielding stocks of the day—tobaccos, for example, as slipping into maturity. By 1972, $100 in Price's model growth portfolio had increased to $ 7,400; the income from cash dividends from $3.30 to $92.

What made IBM a better buy than the equally well-established American Tobacoo? Price theorized that consistently higher earnings at each new peak in the business cycle was one of the tell tales. You had to check for new highs at the peaks to make sure you were looking at sustained underlying growth and not a mere cyclical recovery. Growth stocks would almost certainly suffer along with everything else in a market decline, but as long as the earnings trajectory held, lower prices just made growth a better buy.

It wasn't easy to determine when a company was about to tilt out of its growth phase into maturity and decay, said Price. You had to watch trends in sales, profit margins, and returns on invested capital, any of which could be affected by X-factors like new competition, patent expirations, management changes, or adverse legislation.

To see how some of these negatives could choke growth, you had to look no further than the power and light companies, Price wrote in *Barrons*. Their earnings climbed right through the 1929 Crash only to run headlong into the pieties of the New Deal. A change in the regulatory climate bit deeply into profit margins—and stock prices.

Thus, in the search for "new and fertile fields," it was important to bypass industries in which government spoke in a loud voice—rails and communications, for example. In this *Barrons* piece in 1939, Price presciently saw air conditioning, aviation, plastics, and television as good places to start the hunt. Divisions of old industries focussing on new products (office equipment from typewriters to business machines, for example) showed promise. So did specialty producers pushing into expanding markets (Coca-Cola and Minnesota Mining & Manufacturing, for example). Searching today, Price would probably be canvassing cutting-edge but profitable software possibilities such as Adobe Systems and Xilinx.

Unfortunately for them, as David Testa notes, most competing money managers did not get Price's message. In a diary he kept for four decades, Price wrote that he was banking heavily on his *Barrons* article to bring in business "We don't have enough money to pay the rent and the advertisement appearing in the *Sun* last month," he wrote, "It's not a very comfortable feeling to have paid out all you have borrowed and still have insufficient capital to pay salaries and bills each month. If this [the *Barrons* piece] doesn't put us on the road to success, I don't know what will."

That's Price, still struggling to get his fledgling advisory firm into the black two years after setting up shop at age 39 as an investment counselor in Wall Street's darkest days. "I may be a darn fool for taking this unnecessary risk, but I'm going to have the satisfaction of knowing that I tried," his diary says. "If I fail, I will have no regrets," Not till a decade later did T. Rowe Price Associates show a profit.

The first couple of years were especially rocky. Like Ben Graham, Price was crafting a new strategy for a devastated market. Price's take on growth seemed to carry a lot more risk than Graham's play on cheap assets, and it was consequently a much harder sell. Price made a couple of bad market calls, excoriating himself for "stubbornness" in bucking a sharp downturn in 1938. "I hereby resolve that in the future… I will not buy until it is established that the downward trend has been reversed," he wrote.

Looking for new ways to bring in business, Price mused that it might be a good idea to put in "a special powder room for the ladies, with such facilities as a telephone, writing desks, etc." "While lady clients are often difficult to handle," he reasoned, "there are certain advantages to be gained by catering to this class of business. A large percentage of accumulated wealth in stocks and bonds is held by women."

Price confessed he did not have the temperament "to spend the major part of (his) time listening and talking to fussy old ladies." It would pay, though, to do "the little things which create goodwill, which are keenly appreciated by the ladies, and which most other business organizations would not consider necessary."

In fact, without considerable help from one wealthy lady—his wife—T. Rowe Price Associates might not have made it through the early years.

Just before Christmas 1941, for example, finances were at a "distressing crisis." The firm's checking account showed a balance of exactly $11.07. Price had to plead with the bank to get his notes extended. He and his partners, meeting for lunch, could barely muster a total of $2 among them. Price's secretary, Marie Walper, had not been paid for a month, but gamely "offered to lend her Christmas club money to help out in an emergency."

Price worried a lot. A kind of Splengerian gloom permeates much of the diaries and almost all of his professional writings. He frets about the impact of long hours on his health, and professes from the warp of his "life cycle" theory that "after one reaches 40, he does slow down both mentally and physically." Price is so "mentally exhausted" after completing all but the finishing paragraph of a brochure titled "Change—The Investor's Only Certainty" that he asks a friend to write a "decent conclusion" for him.

This promotion piece, floated at the beginning of President Franklin Roosevelt's second term in 1937, is Price's big picture look at how the tax and regulatory policies of the New Deal were reshaping investment potentials. "The government," wrote Price, "by increasing taxes on the wealthy, is taking away from the Haves and giving to the Have Nots in one form or another—relief, bonuses, public works projects, agricultural payments, etc." Price reassuringly notes this was not an attempt to overthrow capitalism, but "part of a process of great change in the kind of capitalism." Labor "will receive a larger percentage of corporate income, increasing regulation will stunt profits in such basic industries as public utilities." Price's conclusion: Buckle your seat belts against raging inflation.

The fear of toxic inflation is a specter that haunts Price right through the dozen interviews and/or columns that ran in *Forbes* in the late 1970s. Ultimately, it is at the heart of his growth stock theory. The only way to beat inflation was to get spiel. This son of a country doctor conjures up the malady, and then pulls the cure out of his pocket. How to come out on top: Invest in "new and rapidly growing industries, employing relatively few people and less subject to governmental interference." That's all gospel now, but a break with convention when Price enunciated it.

So, scratch the dour Price and you find an optimist. And never more so than when he hung up his shingle as an independent investment adviser. He took some odd turns getting there. Some colleagues think Price was ticketed to Swarthmore College in 1915 with the idea he would soon take over his doctor father's general practice in the farm community of Glydon, Maryland.

Price loaded up on chemistry credits, but finessed medicine for a job at the laboratory bench of the Fort Pitt Stamping & Enameling Company. It didn't last very long. Price, years later, allowed that he was "green and inexperienced" and had taken the job because he liked the young Princeton graduate who hired me." Fort Pitt was not in great shape. There was a strike and the company went bust—an experience that stuck deep in Price's investment consciousness. Low labor costs and good labor relations were two of the items Price learned to look for when he was scouting a buy.

His sense of the need for both intensified when he was laid off in a company wide cutback after two years as a chemist at DuPont. Though still interested in the technology, Price's enthusiasm had begun to drift. "I found that I was spending my evenings reading financial magazines instead of learning more about the chemical industry," he recalled.

Price's personnel file shows he spent the next two years at two small brokerage firms—less than happy with the job of selling securities. He made some money playing the market, vacationed in Europe, and came back to find that the first firm had been shut down as a bucket shop—yet another step in the making of T. Rowe Price, securities analyst.

"I considered this experience costly but helpful," Price recalled acidly. "Two out of the first three firms with which I had been associated failed—one because of lack of experience, the other because of dishonesty. This taught me to be more critical and skeptical." An assessment of management quality—extracted from interviews with chief executives—went to the top of Price's analytical checklist.

Price was certain now that the investment research side of Wall Street was where he wanted to be. It took five years of dues paying as a broker at the Baltimore firm of Mackubin, Goodrich & Company before he got there.

As the firm's newly breveted head of investment management, the ever-contentious Price had his own ideas about how things should be run. Further, he was having his own personal problems with a killer market in 1931 that had just dropped to new lows. Price's boss. John Legg (the firm was a predecessor of the existing Legg, Mason & Company) urged Price to take his losses and get out of the market. "I cannot write a sell ticket on stocks after the decline they have had. My hand would become paralyzed," Price noted in his diary. He hustled up more margin rather than take an $11,000 loss that would strip him of collateral and leave him with an outstanding loan that would take years to repay "a few dollars at a time." "I am going to hang on," vowed Price.

He griped that the research he was asked to do ended all too frequently being harnessed to stock issues Mackubin was trying to sell. Price bridled at what he saw as a conflict between big producers' sales commissions and their clients' best interests. "The stocks and bonds which produced the biggest commissions for salesmen were often the least desirable for the client," goes one fretful diary entry.

Fighting to build an independent research group, Price was definitely not regarded as a team player. He was chastised for blowing up at an executive committee meeting, and variously described as being "unpleasant and unapproachable." "All in all," grumbled the nonconforming Price, "it seems that I am guilty of many misdeeds."

Worse yet, Price's investment management group was clearly not going to become a profit center any time soon. The "too idealistic, too impatient" Price just couldn't sell the idea that investment advice should be unbundled from the commission business and offered to clients on a fee basis. His growth stock theory was also plowing sterile ground in the Mackubin executive suite.

Price was 39. Time to go.

Price brought with him from Mackubin the indomitable Miss Walper and two other associates who shared his view that there was more to growth stocks than theory.

Price often worked from the top down, drawn to promising industries like chemicals or aviation by the voracious range of reading that soothed his insomniac hours. He often invested across the board at first, buying as many as a half dozen companies in an industry in small lots, and then winnowing as he and Kidd picked the best of the crop.

On at least one occasion, Price was incensed to learn that Kidd had beaten him to a punch. Price had been bullish on aviation for more than a half dozen years, seeing growth of major proportions ahead. He did well with the likes of Douglas Aircraft and then sold out, convinced by Kidd that the stocks had become overpriced. Aviation issues dipped and then soared, leaving Price "angry with myself for not having the courage of my convictions." "Kidd tells me that while I was away he bought Glenn Martin in the low thirties," reads the diary entry for February 24, 1939. "I have continuously talked to him since last fall about the purchase of Glenn Martin and asked his views as to when to buy. The stock sold at 39 today."

As David Testa describes a collaboration that lasted for some three decades, "Mr. Price would get these ideas and send Walter Kidd halfway around the U.S., by train, with his trunk, to check them out."

Price's legman clocked plenty of mileage. Kidd once calculated that he'd made 893 visits to 187 firms during his tenure as Price's research director. There were a lot of peripatetic payoffs. While calling on computer manufacturer Minneapolis Honeywell in 1939, bought the year before at around $3.80 a share a friend suggested that Kidd also go see the folks at Minnesota Mining & Manufacturing across town. Kidd flagged a taxi, got a look at the firm's work with adhesives and told Price the stock was a steal at $1 a share.

Charles Shaeffer was also on the road, trying to sell institutional investors on the virtues of growth stocks and at the same time prospecting for good buys. One of them turned out to be IBM. Price, always drawn to new technology, decided in 1940 to dip into slim resources for an IBM office system he hoped would save the firm $500 a year. Thus cued, Shaeffer talked his way into a promised "half hour" with IBM founder Thomas Watson, Sr. He got to spend most of the day with Watson and brought home another early portfolio win.

Price aimed to get at least three out of every four buys right. One miscalculation sealed his caveats about the workings of big government. Pursuing a favorite theme—growth spun off from old industries—Price put in a buy on International Nickel. Steel, he figured, even with rearmament orders pouring in, was over the hill as a growth candidate. But the industry's demand for alloys like nickel and molybdenum was heating up. Price's premise was right, but so were his forebodings about the dead hand of regulation. Federal price controls materialized soon after he bought the stock and put a lid on the rise in Inco profits he had looked for.

On the whole, T. Rowe Price & Associates was doing well by its clients, but there just weren't enough of them. Salaries were still going unpaid, and Price compensated his colleagues for their sweat equity by peeling off pieces of a still profitless partnership. "I let my associates write their own tickets and in every case offered more than they asked for," notes the diary entry for January 11,1941. "I would like them to have every advantage that is possible, under the circumstances, believing that in future years they will prove their appreciation."

The World War II years brought not very much more recognition to Price's growth stock theory, and only modest growth to the firm. One of Price's most notable purchases in the period may have been a 77-acre farm that he acquired some miles outside Baltimore. Price saw land as yet another buffer against inflation, of course, but associates joked that it was actually a hedge against the possibility of the Japanese winning the war.

"Everybody figured there would be no need for investment advisers and we could all go out and grow vegetables on Mr. Price's farm," laughs one associate. This was something of an in joke on Price. He grew roses (often wearing one in his lapel), but for all his interest in technology, was a dub when it came to the practicalities of working the farm. It became something of a late Friday afternoon hangout for the partners—a place to do a couple of beers, talk strategy, and work at cutting locust fence posts. Charles Shaeffer, who grew up poor on a farm in Lancaster, Pennsylvania, shakes his head at the memory and smiles. "Rowe never could get the rhythm of the two-man crosscut saw," he says.

This recollection from one of Price's few close friends is yet another index to the angularity of the personality. Shaeffer was Mr. Outside to Price's Mr. Inside for 40 years and succeeded him as president in 1963. Shaeffer says Price played some social golf and tennis mainly "because he thought it was good business for the firm." Price worked best alone. "He'd get an idea, he'd say 'I want to think about this' and close the door," concurs chairman George Roche.

What was the source of the stock-picking genius that flourished behind those closed doors? Go figure why Sammy Sosa hits all those home runs. A mix of preternatural skill and slavish work habits seem to be at least part of the answer. Price's perceptions were so sharply attuned that they sometimes seemed totally intuitive.

Take his hit on Magnavox, an early starter in the quality color TV market. Price woke at 2:00 A.M., two days before the president of the company was to make a pitch to security analysts, with a "premonition" he should buy the stock. On the phone at the first crack of business, he put in orders for his wife, the firm's trading account, and himself.

Next night, in the hours before dawn, "Magnavox was one of the chief thoughts again," and Price put a number of clients into the stock. He went to the security analysts meeting as scheduled, left before the Magnavox president finished his talk, and bought more stock—"for Eleanor, the firm, and me, and recommended it to others."

"God help me if I am wrong," Price told his diary, "but I still have a strong conviction that this company has sound management and that over a period of years, it would prove to be an outstanding 'growth' stock."

Magnavox went on to have a good run. The purchase was a perfect example of how Price was often driven by the white heat of his ideas, shooting first at some dimly sensed potential, and then filling in the details. It also shows how Price often bought first for his family accounts before putting clients into a stock, apparently wanting to scope the target before advising them to pull the trigger. It's always a good sign when a money manager eats his own cooking, but Price would never have been able to trade in that unbuttoned way in today's ethos. "The SEC would call it front running and throw him in the slammer," laughs chairman George Roche.

One administrative problem Price took behind the closed door was the question of how to bundle dozens of the small trust accounts that clients had been pressing him to open for children and grandchildren. Price was managing around $40 million in 1950 (up 38 percent from $28 million in 1945) and eager to put even marginal-seeming accounts on the books. Too small to be handled individually, these were rolled up into a totally new business—the T. Rowe Price Growth Stock Fund.

It opened Price's growth stock strategy for the first time to investors of modest means; unusual (for the time) in that it was a "no load" fund. There were no sales commissions, with a one percent redemption fee (payable to the fund) to encourage long-term holding. Price's distaste for the commission business, of course, was one of the elements that drew him to fee-based counseling. And in any event, he had neither the capital nor the distribution channels it would take to put a major marketing effort behind the fund.

Here was Price once again going against the trend in a revolutionary way. The great truth of the day was that "mutual funds are not bought, they're sold." In fact, as Price was about to prove, the reverse was true. Investors needed no intermediary hands to find their way to consistent performance. Other major fund groups soon hopped aboard the "no load" bandwagon, happy to wash their hands of the gathering scandal in high-pressure mutual fund sales. Among the legion of salesman cold calling prospects (at commissions that ate up 8 percent or more of capital) were plenty of former "tin men" who had cut their eyeteeth educating the hapless on the virtues of aluminum siding and phony oil leases.

There were other "growth" funds in the field, basically looking to growth of capital rather than to growth stocks in Price's single-minded sense of the term. The fund was run as an extension of the individual portfolios in-house, and Price was happy with the result. Assets climbed to over $1.2 million by the end of the first year, creating another modest layer of management fees that helped to build what Price called "the most successful year in my business career."

The Growth Stock Fund was something of a by-blow, serendipitous, but there was Price the innovator again, way out in front of a major marketing change. The Growth Stock Fund was an early model of the 3,000 or so mutual funds now pursuing the same objective with similar tactics.

It was positioned to benefit from a bull market that, with a few bumps in the road, ran for almost a decade. Stocks that Price had caught in their infancy began surging into brawling adolescence. By 1955, a $10,000 initial investment in the Growth Stock Fund had zipped to $27,300. Price tried to stay abreast of his own firm's growth by switching his three-man partnership to a corporation and adding staff, but he was still personally supervising more than 40 percent of the $150 million in assets on the books.

Stocks were getting "too high, too fast," he felt. When a break did come along in 1957, the sharpest in two years, Price was characteristically relieved. Price was thinking of a new category killer—emerging growth stocks "hundreds of companies in such 'new and fertile fields' as missiles, rocket propulsion, electronics, nuclear energy, and flight control systems." Especially, he was thinking of companies too young, too small, too risky, and too far down the food chain to excite the interest of rabid institutional investors. Price had actually been mulling such a strategy since 1935. The time had come to put this brainchild in motion. The result was the New Horizons Fund—a creation that once again put the protean Price out in front of a major change in market direction. Getting out front called for subtle changes in tactics. Many young companies just hadn't been around long enough to put together the long-term earnings history Price had insisted on in the past. Nor by force-feeding growth with retained earnings, were they likely to give off the rising stream of dividend income that Price had also counted on. The trading strategy was different, too. The market in small capitalization stocks was thin. They had to be nibbled at in small quantities on the buy side and were far more volatile than stocks further on in the growth cycle.

Price figured he could lower the risk profile by blending small growth with a mix of possibilities—older companies rejuvenated by new management or new profits, or relatively unknown family-owned businesses on a growth roll coming public. In a move with little precedent, he temporarily closed New Horizons entirely to new investments, and then reopened it only to shareholders already on the books. The decision cost the firm management fees on new money that was rolling in at the rate of about $10 million a month. The closing had a nice old-fashioned aura of rectitude about it. Better to forgo profits than to put shareholders at high risk by chasing overheated stocks selling well over Price's buy limits.

Price had begun to get leery at the runaway market in growth stocks as early as 1964. In the past, he had not worried much about rising prices as long as earnings were growing at a good clip. Now he'd begun to talk about "high" price earnings ratios; the need to look at "intrinsic investment values," a term he rarely used before; and the prudence of taking money off the table if earnings get "dangerously overvalued."

Ironically, Price was warning against excesses that had grown out of three decades of his own work. Price gloried in success, but was too wise a bird to believe in miracles. When prices got decoupled from demonstrated earning power, there was trouble ahead.

Sharp recession was in the wind. So was a blood-bath stock market. In the 1973-1974 crash, both the Growth Stock Fund and New Horizons took a terrible pasting. Over the two years, Growth Stock was off 25 percent and 33 percent; New Horizons 42 percent and 38 percent, respectively. The Growth Stock Fund's assets peaked at $1.4 billion in 1972 and didn't get back to that level for 17 long years.

New Horizons fared better. Even so, it was a half-dozen years before its assets climbed back to the 1972 peak. The pressure on prices was (and has been) extraordinary. At their 1972 peak, the likes of Coca-Cola, IBM, and Procter & Gamble were selling at an average of 43 times earnings—more than double the market as measured by the Standard & Poor's 500 stock index. The dividend yield, at 1.1 percent was less than half the market. Sound familiar? Of course, but few were looking at the market of the late 1990s with anything like Price's prescience, or even a sense of history. Price's point was for the ages: Crazily extrapolated earning growth focused on "one decision" stocks is folly in search of an accident.

Would future earnings growth justify buying these "one decision" stocks at any price? If you do overpay, will time bail you out? It will if you like odds of three to one—against. Wharton School professor Jeremy Siegel found that over the next quarter century fewer than one out of every three of the Nifties bought at the 1972 peak would have earned their keep. For every stock like Coca-Cola, which could have been bought for almost twice its 1972 P/E of 46 and still have matched the market in total return, there were three fumbles like Polaroid. At peak, the company sold at close to 100 times earnings. It then shuffled through a rocky earnings history that at best should have commanded no more than 16 times earnings. At this writing the stock is selling at close to an all-time low.

Still backtracking, Siegel figured that a buy of the whole Nifty Fifty at the 1972 peak would have brought an annualized return of 12.7 percent. Return for the market as a whole: 12.9 percent.

On his own, Price started nibbling at some of the old burned-out growth stocks that had begun to look cheap (Disney and Black & Decker among others). He sent on to Forbes his list of "Growth Stocks of the Future" (Viacom, for one). Bedridden and seriously ill, Price wouldn't quit. His last piece in *Forbes* ("Stocks for the Mid-Eighties") ran just 10 months before he died, and his old pals at Rowe Price Associates were among the first to learn that he'd just made a killing in gold.

Key Words and Expressions:

aerospace industry	航空航天工业
air reduction	空气还原
angularity	n. 有角的部分
aviation industry	航空工业
brevet	vt. 使名誉晋升
caveat	n. 中止诉讼手续的申请
clunker	n. 不值一文的东西
deflationary	adj. 通货紧缩的
dividend	n. 股息，红利
dot-com	n. 网络公司
expiration	n. 终结;期满
exponential	adj. 指数的
feisty	adj. 好争吵的，活跃的
forest products industry	林产工业
hyperbole	n. 夸张法
insomniac	n. 失眠症患者

General Electric	（美）通用电气
malaise	n. 不舒服;抑郁;心神不安
molybdenum	n. [化]钼（金属元素,符号 Mo,原子序号 42）
portfolio	n.（投资者持有的）全部有价证券，投资组合
serendipitous	adj. 善于作意外发现的;侥幸得到的
spiel	n. 招揽生意的言辞
tenure	n. 占有期;任期;占有条件
trajectory	n. [数] 轨线;常角轨道

Notes:

1．Nifty Fifty　漂亮 50

　　源于美国三十年前两份玩笑式的名单，三十年后，却成为了金融界和资本市场一个广为流传的神话。上世纪 70 年代美国《福布斯》杂志对其有新的脚注，此后成为"最值得拥有的股票"的代名词，并在此后三十年间为投资人提供了平均 13.13%的年回报率。

2．limit order　限价委托

　　指客户对于证券经纪人的买卖委托中设有低于市场价格的买进价格，或高于市场价格的卖出价格之指示。

3．growth stock　成长股

　　成长股是指这样一些公司所发行的股票，它们的销售额和利润额持续增长，而且其速度央于整个国家和本行业的增长。这些公司通常有宏图伟略，注重科研，留有大量利润作为再投资以促进其扩张。

4．blue chips　蓝筹股

　　"蓝筹"一词源于西方赌场，在西方赌场中，有三种颜色的筹码，其中蓝色筹码最为值钱。蓝筹股多指长期稳定增长的、大型的传统工业股及金融股。此类上市公司的特点是有着优良的业绩、收益稳定、股本规模大、红利优厚、股价走势稳健、市场形象良好。

5．Standard & Poor　标准普尔

　　标准普尔是国际上最重要的评级机构。标准普尔作为金融投资界的公认标准，提供被广泛认可的信用评级、独立分析研究、投资咨询等服务。

6．Henry Ford　亨利·福特

　　亨利·福特创立了全世界第一条汽车流水装配线。这种流水作业法后来被称为"福特制"，并在全世界广泛推广。他还利用花旗银行的资金扩大

再生产，使公司成为 20 世纪世界最大的汽车公司。福特本人也被称为"汽车大王"，其家族成为美国几个主要财阀之一。

7. cut one's eyeteeth

意思是获得智慧、变得善于人情世故。

8. Xeros 施乐

世界最大的复印机厂商。

9. Forbes 《福布斯》

福布斯集团（Forbes Inc.）作为全球著名的出版及媒体集团，首开美国商业新闻的先河。它成立于 1917 年，距今已有 91 年的历史。其旗舰刊物《福布斯》杂志，是美国最早的大型商业杂志，也是全球最为著名的财经出版物之一。

10. Viacom：维亚康姆

国际传媒巨头。《财富》杂志把维亚康姆公司的股票列为 21 世纪前十年中最值得购买的十大股票之一。这艘传媒娱乐航空母舰在创新、推进与传播娱乐、新闻、体育和音乐方面，一直走在世界的前列，为世界各地的广告商提供了第一大平台。

II. Knowledge Points

1. Growth investing

Growth investing is a style of investment strategy. Those who follow this style, known as growth investors, invest in companies that exhibit signs of above-average growth, even if the share price appears expensive in terms of metrics such as price-to-earning or price-to-book ratios. In typical usage, the term "growth investing" contrasts with the strategy known as value investing.

However, some notable investors such as Warren Buffett have stated that there is no theoretical difference between the concepts of value and growth ("Growth and Value Investing are joined at the hip"), in consideration of the concept of an asset's intrinsic value. In addition, when just investing in one style of stocks, diversification could be negatively impacted.

Growth at Reasonable Price

After the busting of the dotcom bubble, "growth at any price" has fallen from favour. Attaching a high price to a security in the hope of high growth may be risky, since if the growth rate fails to live up to expectations, the price of the security can plummet. It is often more fashionable now to seek out stocks with high growth rates that are trading at reasonable valuations.

Growth Investment Vehicles

There are many ways to execute a growth investment strategy. Some of these include:

Emerging markets

Recovery shares

Blue chips

Internet and technology stock

Smaller companies

Special situations

Second-hand life policies

2. Growth stocks

1) Definition and theory

Shares in a company whose earnings are expected to grow at an above average rate relative to the market. A growth stock usually does not pay a dividend, as the company would prefer to reinvest retained earnings in capital projects. Most technology companies are growth stocks. Note that a growth company's stock is not always classified as growth stock. In fact, a growth company's stock is often overvalued.

2) Characteristics

Growth stocks have some common characteristics, although individual investors may tweak the numbers for their own purposes. Here are some of the indicators:

- Strong growth rate—both historic and projected forward. Historically, you want to see smaller companies with a 10%+ growth rate for the past five years and larger companies with 5%—7%. You might want these same rates and more for projected five-year growth rates. Big companies will not grow as fast (normally) as small companies, so you need to make some accommodation.

- Strong Return on Equity. How does the company's return on equity (ROE) compare with the industry and its five-year average?

- What about earnings per share (EPS)? Especially look at pre-tax profit margins. Is the company translating sales into earnings? Is management controlling costs? Pre-tax margins should exceed the past five-year average and the industry average.
- What is the projected stock price? Can this stock double in price in five years? Analysts make these projections based on the business model and market position of the company.

A "growth investor" does not usually buy a company simply because it is overpriced, but will usually look at how fast it is growing and what is expected in the future.

3. Ford's idea of standardizing parts

Definition and theory

Henry Ford was born in 1863. In 1892 he created the Quadricycle, while working as an engineer for the Edison Company. With his invention he started his own company in 1903, the Ford Motor Company. Ford revolutionized the industry by coming up with the idea of the assembly line. In the assembly line each worker was responsible for putting one part, or doing a piece of work on each automobile. This allowed workers to perfect one area of building, and greatly reduced the production time of automobiles. He also came up with the idea of standardizing a single model of car. First he marketed Model-N which sold for $650.00 and was discontinued in 1907. The Model-T was invented in 1908, and changed the automobile industry forever.

4. Inflation

1) Definition and theory

Inflation is an increase in the price of a basket of goods and services that is representative of the economy as a whole. Inflation is an upward movement in the average level of prices. Its opposite is deflation, a downward movement in the average level of prices. The boundary between inflation and deflation is price stability. Because inflation is a rise in the general level of prices, it is intrinsically linked to money, as captured by the often heard refrain "Inflation is too many dollars chasing too few goods".

2) Phillips curve

The Phillips curve is a historical inverse relation and tradeoff between the rate of unemployment and the rate of inflation in an economy. Stated simply, the lower the unemployment in an economy, the higher the rate of change in wages paid to labour in that economy.

Alban William Phillips, a New Zealand-born economist, wrote a paper in 1958 titled "The relationship between unemployment and the rate of change of money wages in the United Kingdom 1861-1957", which was published in the quarterly journal Economica. In the paper Phillips describes how he observed an inverse relationship between money wage changes and unemployment in the British economy over the period examined. Similar patterns were found in other countries and in 1960 Paul Samuelson and Robert Solow took Phillips' work and made explicit the link between inflation and unemployment—when inflation was high, unemployment was low, and vice-versa.

In the 1920s an American economist Irving Fisher noted this kind of Phillips curve (PC) relationship. However, Phillips' original curve described the behavior of money wages. So some believe that the Phillips Curve should be called the "Fisher curve."

In the years following Phillips' 1958 paper, many economists in the advanced industrial countries believed that his results showed that there was a permanently stable relationship between inflation and unemployment. One implication of this for government policy was that governments could control unemployment and inflation within a Keynesian policy. They could tolerate a reasonably high rate of inflation as this would lead to lower unemployment—there would be a trade-off between inflation and unemployment. For example, monetary policy and/or fiscal policy (i.e., deficit spending) could be used to stimulate the economy, raising gross domestic product and lowering the unemployment rate. Moving along the Phillips curve, this would lead to a higher inflation rate, the cost of enjoying lower unemployment rates.

During the 1960s, a leftward movement along the PC described the path of the U.S. economy. This move was not a matter of deciding to achieve low unemployment as much as an unplanned side-effect of the Vietnam war. In other countries, the economic boom was more the result of conscious policies.

3) Stagflation

In the 1970s, many countries experienced high levels of both inflation and unemployment also known as stagflation. Theories based on the Phillips curve suggested that this could not happen, and the curve came under concerted attack from a group of economists headed by Milton Friedman—arguing that the demonstrable failure of the relationship demanded a return to non-interventionist, free market policies. The idea that there was a simple, predictable, and persistent relationship between inflation and unemployment was abandoned by most if not all macroeconomists.

NAIRU and rational expectations

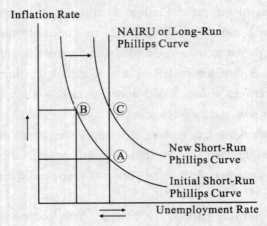

Short-Run Phillips Curve before and after Expansionary Policy, with Long-Run Phillips Curve (NAIRU)s

New theories, such as rational expectations and the NAIRU (non-accelerating inflation rate of unemployment) arose to explain how stagflation could occur. The latter theory, also known as the "natural rate of unemployment", distinguished between the "short-term" Phillips curve and the "long-term" one. The short-term PC looked like a normal PC but shifted in the long run as expectations changed. In the long run, only a single rate of unemployment (the NAIRU or "natural" rate) was consistent with a stable inflation rate. The long-run PC was thus vertical, so there was no trade-off between inflation and unemployment. Edmund Phelps won the Nobel Prize in Economics in 2006 for this.

In the diagram, the long-run Phillips curve is the vertical line. The NAIRU theory says that when unemployment is at the rate defined by this line, inflation will be stable. However, in the short-run policymakers will face an inflation-unemployment rate tradeoff marked by the "Initial Short-Run Phillips Curve" in the graph. Policymakers can therefore reduce the unemployment rate temporarily, moving from point A to point B through expansionary policy. However, according to the NAIRU, exploiting this short-run tradeoff will raise inflation expectations, shifting the short-run curve rightward to the "New Short-Run Phillips Curve" and moving the point of equilibrium from B to C. Thus the reduction in unemployment below the "Natural Rate" will be temporary, and lead only to higher inflation in the long run.

Since the short-run curve shifts outward due to the attempt to reduce unemployment, the expansionary policy ultimately worsens the exploitable tradeoff between unemployment and inflation. That is, it results in more inflation at each short-run unemployment rate. The name "NAIRU" arises because with actual unemployment below it, inflation accelerates, while with unemployment above it, inflation decelerates. With the actual rate equal to it, inflation is stable, neither accelerating nor decelerating. One practical use of this model was to provide an explanation for Stagflation, which confounded the traditional Phillips curve.

The rational expectations theory said that expectations of inflation were equal to what actually happened, with some minor and temporary errors. This in turn suggested that the short-run period was so short that it was non-existent: any effort to reduce unemployment below the NAIRU, for example, would immediately cause inflationary expectations to rise and thus imply that the policy would fail. Unemployment would never deviate from the NAIRU except due to random and transitory mistakes in developing expectations about future inflation rates. In this perspective, any deviation of the actual unemployment rate from the NAIRU was an illusion.

However, in the 1990s in the U.S., it became increasingly clear that the NAIRU did not have a unique equilibrium and could change in unpredictable ways. In the late 1990s, the actual unemployment rate fell below 4 % of the labor force, much lower than almost all estimates of the NAIRU. But inflation stayed very moderate rather than accelerating. So, just as the Phillips curve had become a subject of debate, so did the NAIRU.

Further, the concept of rational expectations had become subject to much doubt when it became clear that the main assumption of models based on it was that there exists a single (unique) equilibrium in the economy that is set ahead of time, determined independent of demand conditions. The experience of the 1990s suggests that this assumption cannot be sustained.

4) built-in inflation

The last reflects inflationary expectations and the price/wage spiral. Supply shocks and changes in built-in inflation are the main factors shifting the short-run PC and changing the trade-off. In this theory, it is not only inflationary expectations that can cause stagflation. For example, the steep climb of oil prices during the 1970s could have this result.

Changes in built-in inflation follow the partial-adjustment logic behind most theories of the NAIRU:

Low unemployment encourages high inflation, as with the simple Phillips curve. But if unemployment stays low and inflation stays high for a long time, as in the late 1960s in the U.S., both inflationary expectations and the price/wage spiral accelerate. This shifts the short-run Phillips curve upward and rightward, so that more inflation is seen at any given unemployment rate. (This is with shift B in the diagram.)

High unemployment encourages low inflation, again as with a simple Phillips curve. But if unemployment stays high and inflation stays low for a long time, as in the early 1980s in the U.S., both inflationary expectations and the price/wage spiral slow. This shifts the short-run Phillips curve downward and leftward, so that less inflation is seen at each unemployment rate.

In between these two lies the NAIRU, where the Phillips curve does not have any inherent tendency to shift, so that the inflation rate is stable. However, there seems to be a range in the middle between "high" and "low" where built-in inflation stays stable. The ends of this "non-accelerating inflation range of unemployment rates" change over time.

5. Deflationary spiral

Definition and theory

Deflationary spiral is a term from economics which describes the situation where decreases in price lead to lower production, which in turn leads to lower wages and demand, which leads to decreases in price. Since reductions in general price level are called deflation, a deflationary spiral is when reductions in price lead to a vicious circle, where a problem exacerbates its own cause. The Great Depression was regarded as a deflationary spiral.

6. Dow Jones Industrial Average

1) Definition and theory

The Dow Jones Industrial Average (NYSE: DJI, also called the DJIA, Dow 30, or informally the Dow industrials, the Dow Jones or The Dow) is one of several stock market indices created by Wall Street Journal editor and Dow Jones & Company co-founder Charles Dow. Dow compiled the index as a way to gauge the performance of the industrial component of America's stock markets. It is the oldest continuing U.S. market index, aside from the Dow Jones Transportation Average, which Dow also created.

Today, the average consists of 30 of the largest and most widely held public companies in the United States. The "industrial" portion of the name is largely historical—many of the 30 modern components have little to do with heavy industry. To compensate for the effects of stock splits and other adjustments, it is currently a scaled average, not the actual average of the prices of its component stocks—the sum of the component prices is divided by a divisor, which changes over time, to generate the value of the index.

2) Criticism

With the current inclusion of only 30 stocks, some argue the DJIA cannot function as an index of overall market performance even though it is the most cited and most widely recognized of the stock market indices. Historically, though, it has performed very much in line with the broader U.S. market.

Additionally, the DJIA is criticized for being a price-weighted average, which gives relatively higher-priced stocks more influence over the average than their lower-priced counterparts. For example, a $1 increase in a lower-priced stock can be negated by a $1 decrease in a much higher-priced stock, even though the first stock experienced a larger percentage change. Many critics of the DJIA recommend the float-adjusted market-value weighted S&P 500 or the Dow Jones Wilshire 5000, the latter of which includes all U.S. securities with readily available prices, as better indicators of the U.S. market.

Another issue with the Dow is that not all 30 components open at the same time in the morning. Only a few components open at the start and the posted opening price of the Dow is determined by the price of those few components that open first and the previous day's closing price of the remaining components that haven't opened yet; therefore, the posted opening price on the Dow will always be close to the previous day's closing price (which can be observed by looking at Dow price history) and will never accurately reflect the true opening prices of all its components. Thus, in terms of candlestick charting theory, the Dow's posted opening price cannot be used in determining the condition of the market.

Beginning at around 2pm EST on February 27, 2007, the DJIA began to experience a delay due to extremely heavy trading volume. Over the next hour, the reported value for the index diverged sharply from its true value. A backup system was brought online to correct the problem. The SEC is investigating the issue.

3) Components

The individual components of the DJIA are occasionally changed as market conditions warrant. They are selected by the editors of The Wall Street Journal. When companies are replaced, the scale factor used to calculate the index is also adjusted so that the value of the average is not directly affected by the change.

On November 1, 1999, Chevron, Goodyear Tire and Rubber Company, Sears Roebuck, and Union Carbide were removed from the DJIA and replaced by Intel, Microsoft, Home Depot, and SBC Communications. Intel and Microsoft became the first two companies traded on the NASDAQ exchange to be listed in the DJIA. On April 8, 2004, another change occurred as International Paper, AT&T, and Eastman Kodak were replaced with Pfizer, Verizon, and AIG. On December 1, 2005 AT&T's original T symbol returned to the DJIA as a result of the SBC Communications and AT&T merger.

The Dow Jones Industrial Average consists of the following 30 companies:

Company	Symbol	Industry
3M	(NYSE: MMM)	Diversified Industrials
Alcoa	(NYSE: AA)	Aluminum
Altria Group	(NYSE: MO)	Tobacco, foods
American Express	(NYSE: AXP)	Consumer Finance
American International Group	(NYSE: AIG)	Full Line Insurance
AT&T	(NYSE: T)	Telecoms

Company	Symbol	Industry
Boeing	(NYSE: BA)	Aerospace/Defense
Caterpillar	(NYSE: CAT)	Commercial Vehicles & Trucks
Citigroup	(NYSE: C)	Banks
Coca-Cola	(NYSE: KO)	Beverages
DuPont	(NYSE: DD)	Commodity Chemicals
ExxonMobil	(NYSE: XOM)	Integrated Oil & Gas
General Electric	(NYSE: GE)	Diversified Industrials
General Motors	(NYSE: GM)	Automobiles
Hewlett-Packard	(NYSE: HPQ)	Diversified Computer Systems
Home Depot	(NYSE: HD)	Home Improvement Retailers
Honeywell	(NYSE: HON)	Diversified Industrials
Intel	(NASDAQ: INTC)	Semiconductors
IBM	(NYSE: IBM)	Computer Services
Johnson & Johnson	(NYSE: JNJ)	Pharmaceuticals
JPMorgan Chase	(NYSE: JPM)	Banks
McDonald's	(NYSE: MCD)	Restaurants & Bars
Merck	(NYSE: MRK)	Pharmaceuticals
Microsoft	(NASDAQ: MSFT)	Software
Pfizer	(NYSE: PFE)	Pharmaceuticals
Procter & Gamble	(NYSE: PG)	Non-Durable Household Products
United Technologies Corporation	(NYSE: UTX)	Aerospace
Verizon Communications	(NYSE: VZ)	Telecoms
Wal-Mart	(NYSE: WMT)	Broadline Retailers

Company	Symbol	Industry
Walt Disney	(NYSE: DIS)	Broadcasting & Entertainment

4) Calculation

To calculate the DJIA, the sum of the prices of all 30 stocks is divided by a divisor. The divisor is adjusted in case of splits, spinoffs or similar structural changes, to ensure that such events do not in themselves alter the numerical value of the DJIA. The initial divisor was the number of component companies, so that the DJIA was at first a simple arithmetic average; the present divisor, after many adjustments, is less than one (meaning the index is actually larger than the sum of the prices of the components). That is:

$$DJIA = \frac{\sum p}{d}$$

where p are the prices of the component stocks and d is the Dow Divisor.

Events like stock splits or changes in the list of the companies composing the index alter the sum of the component prices. In these cases, in order to avoid discontinuity in the index, the Dow divisor is updated so that the quotations right before and after the events coincide:

$$DJIA = \frac{\sum p_{old}}{d_{old}} = \frac{\sum p_{new}}{d_{new}}$$

III. Analyzing the Case

1. In what way is T. Rowe Price superior to other investment managers according to Mr. Testa?

According to Mr. Testa when there is change in the investment market other investment managers have no more than one good idea, while Mr. Price have at least three good ideas in handling the change in market direction.

2. Why is T. Rowe Price more like Henry Ford than Edison?

Mr. Price so pioneers in the investment theory that it seems that he invents the growth stocks theory, but actually he just systematize the bits and pieces of the existing lore the way that Henry Ford did to standardize parts revolutionizing the assembly line.

3. What are the four stages in Price's investment theory?

1) To look for companies in "new and fertile field".

2) To buy them in an early stage of growth.

3) To stick with them as long as earnings are demonstrably on the rise.

4) To sell when the growth cycle begins to mature.

4. In what way are the corporations like humans according to Price?

Corporations—like humans—have a distinct three-phase life cycle-"growth, maturity, and decadence."

5. What good idea does Price have for the lady clients? And why?

His good idea for the lady clients is to put in a special powder room for the ladies, with such facilities as a telephone, writing desk, etc. Because there are certain advantages to be gained by catering to women clients, and a large percentage of accumulated wealth in stocks and bonds is held by women.

6. According to Price how to deal with inflation?

According to Price the only way to beat inflation is to get out in front of it: e.g. investing in "new and rapidly growing industries, employing relatively few people and less subject to governmental interference."

7. Why is T. Rowe Price Growth Stock Fund unique as a new outlet?

Because it opens Price's growth stock strategy for the first time to investors of modest means, for example, the small trust accounts open for children and grandchildren, and it is a "no load" fund.

8. Why does Price take on the high risk and volatility of growth stocks and give up the serene index mutual fund?

Because there is money to be made in growth stocks, but few of them are forever, which is the central point to Price's theory.

IV. Translation of the Case

在俯瞰喧嚣的巴尔的摩港的办公室里，大卫·泰斯塔——这位价值 1,300 亿美元的托马斯·罗·普里斯信托基金集团的首席投资主任——正在思考他的公司缔造者普里斯先生的独特天赋。

泰斯塔说："关于普里斯先生，重要的是要记住一点，那就是大部分投资经理就像船上的乘客，只要船是朝着正确的方向行驶，就万事大吉。但是当船在行驶过程中出现了出人意料的变化，他们就会惊慌。没人知道下一步该做什么。而这个时候，只要你能有一个应对这种变化的好点子，你就能拥有辉煌的事业。"泰斯塔停了停，微笑着说："普里斯先生至少有三个这样的好点子。"

这三个关于如何解决市场方向上的关键性变化以及千百个小变化的精彩点子都集中在普里斯的主要抱负——成长股上。20 世纪 30 年代普里斯在发展他的成长股理论时曾经列出了一些公司的名单，这张名单惊人地显示了有预见性的选择，因为名单上的公司无论世道好与坏都一直被列入"漂亮 50"的名单里。其中包括雅培实验室、百得和通用。

当然这也带来一些缺憾。由于压力、竞争、专制而失眠的普里斯几乎没有朋友，没有闲聊的机会，对他的同事和对他自己一样冷酷。

一次一个过于谨慎考虑过后的限价委托迫使他在他一直跟进的股票上损失了两点。之后他在自己的日记中写道："我怎么一点常识都没有啊？"他责备自己："不就是简单的股票市场上的买和卖吗！"

作为一个年轻的分析家，大卫·泰斯塔回忆：有一天，普里斯探头进来，问道："什么是成长股？"泰斯塔吓一跳，结结巴巴地说了些关于增加收益之类的话。普里斯厉声说："你什么都不懂！"过了一两天之后，泰斯塔在桌子正中发现了普里斯的一本小册子，上面用红笔勾出的地方写道："成长股是指这样一些公司所发行的股票，它们的销售额和利润额持续增长，而且其速度快于整个国家和本行业的增长。这些公司通常有宏图伟略，注重科研，留有大量利润作为再投资以促进其扩张。"

成长股与普里斯倡导的投资理论联系如此紧密，可以说是他发明了这个理论一样。和爱迪生相比，他更像亨利·福特。他将已有理论的星星点点系统化，就像福特标准化部件的点子革新了流水线一样。

普里斯是个完美的实用主义者。他经常写到他的成长股理论。但是理论的要点可以列在一张明信片的背面。他与本·格雷厄姆成为理论家的方式不同。事实上，他认为他是依靠了被他称作魄力的母亲和称为粗浅知识的父亲，以及被大多数人称之为常识的东西而取得成功的。

普里斯将办公地点选在巴尔的摩港逆流的地方，特意远离华尔街的时髦，因为他喜欢特立独行。他的儿子，小托马斯·罗·普里斯是这样说的："他只是有时候会与完全的固执行为背道而驰。"当主流的投资者在寻求稳定的时候，他会力求增长；而当大公司增长迅速的时候，他会转向小公司；当所有价格都增长过高的时候，他会转向一些价格增长不高的基础产品，比如石油、木材。像巴尔的摩的有识之士，编辑兼作家亨利·曼肯说的"普里斯是原创的"。

1937 年普里斯从一家仅有三个人的小店起家，到今天他一直保留着他的策略：在新的多产的领域寻找大公司，在它们成长的早期就购买，只要它们一直处在上升趋势就抓住不放等到增长期趋于成熟的时候就卖出。

普里斯的理论实际上仍然是点金之石。长期的成功使他拥有了一群信托基金和投资顾问——他们都相信收益在指数上的长期增长是获得特大市场收益的一个确定方式。

正如大卫·泰斯埃说过的，普里斯找到了掌握市场方向大的变化的方式。20世纪30年代的大多数投资经理都会对当时熊市与大萧条的综合效应感到震惊。认为购买蓝筹股，再把它们塞入保险箱就万事大吉的老观念已经不复存在了。在通货紧缩的循环里，当人们需要的是高收入和安全时，没有人愿意拿公司的收入去冒险来重新获得20年代的繁荣。

普里斯在《巴伦周刊》发表的一系列文章中指出，公司就像人一样有三个本能的生命周期阶段——成长、成熟、衰落。他认为当成熟期到来的时候风险就会增加。而使利润最大化、风险最小化的关键就在于他在1934年一直思索的成长股。

在厌倦暴富的投资世界里，普里斯的目标很适中。十年来百分之百的回报率对他来讲实至名归。

普里斯看似简单的方法由于另外一个暴富市场的失败而显得更加重要。华尔街有些毫无希望的无支付股利的网络公司虽然报道形式上有收益，但实际上是亏损的。重要的是，无论市场境况好坏，普里斯的方法是奏效的。

经实验，普里斯在《巴伦周刊》上揭示（他强调，是实际的基金，而非理论上的），从1935年到1938的资金收益达到76%，而道琼斯平均指数的收益只有49%。红利收益则惊人的高达130%，可平均指数的收益却只有12%。

普里斯的主要收入采自可口可乐公司、国际商用机器公司和宝洁公司，甚至今天这些公司还是低收益的公司，但其不断的增长转化为累计的丰厚的红利收入。他指出，今天一些收益更好的股票，比如烟草，已经进入成熟期。到1972年为止，普里斯公司每100典型投资组合已增长到7,400美元；而现金红利的收入由3.30美元增长到92美元。

是什么使国际商用机器公司与同样信誉卓著的美国烟草公司相比更值得购进呢？普里斯的理论认为，在每一个商业周期的高峰期，一贯的更高收益都是不可靠的。你得检查是否还有新的高度以确认你看到的是持续的、潜在的增长，而且不仅是周期性的反弹。和其他股票一样，在市场衰落期，成长股也会有损失，但只要收入轨道保持住，低价位会使购买成长股成为更佳的选择。

他认为很难判定什么时候一个公司将会结束增长期，进入成熟期和衰落期。你必须紧盯销售趋势、利润以及投资回报率，其中每一项都可能受到竞争、专利权终结、管理层的变化或不利的立法等不定因素的影响。

在《巴伦周刊》中，他写道：要看到这些负面因素如何抑制增长，你得比其他公司看得更远。因此，在寻找新的利润更丰厚的领域的时候，重要的是要越过政府大声疾呼的产业，比如铁路和电信。1939 年发表在《巴伦周刊》上的这篇文章中，他很有预见性地指出，空调业、飞机制造业、塑料及电视业是很好的投资领域。一些集中生产新产品的旧的产业部门（如打字机、商用机器等办公设备）前景看好。今天经过搜寻，普里斯可能会建议一些尖端但获利的软件如美国阿道比系统公司和商赛灵思公司。

大卫·泰斯塔指出，可惜的是大多数投资经理没有得到普里斯的信息。在一本大卫保留了 40 年的日记中，普里斯写道，他很期望他在《巴伦周刊》上的文章能够应用于商界。他说："我们没有足够的钱支付上月的租金和广告。每月已经花了所有借来的钱，仍然没有足够的资金发薪水和付账单，这种感觉可不舒服。如果这还不能让我们踏上成功之路，什么能呢？"

这就是普里斯，在华尔街最灰暗的日子里，39 岁的他在建立了公司之后仍然在奋斗，要把他的刚刚起步的咨询公司发展起来。在日记里他写道："我可能很愚蠢冒这个不必要的风险，但如果我失败了，我将不会有遗憾。"

头两年尤其困难重重。像本·格雷厄姆一样，普里斯正在为要垮掉的市场拟出一个策略。但他的启用成长股的策略要比本·格雷厄姆利用廉价资产的方式风险大得多。普里斯在 1938 年作出了错误的市场决定，他痛责自己固执的没有看清当时市场的急剧下滑。他写道，"我从中认识到，以后我会在确定下滑期已经扭转之后再买入。"

普里斯试图寻找能够带来业务的新方法，他觉得为女士增加一间特殊的化妆室也许是一个好主意，配上电话、写字台等设施。他解释说："女客户通常很难应付，而迎合这部分商业客户是有好处的。很大比例以股票和债券形式积累的财富是掌握在女性手中的。"

普里斯承认他没有心情花大部分时间去听那些"老女人"谈话，但是做一些让这些女士非常欣赏的善意的小事，是会得到报偿的。

事实上，如果没有一位富有的女士——也就是他的妻子的巨大帮助，早期的时候，他的公司可能无法坚持下来。

在 1941 年的圣诞节前，金融面临一场经济危机。公司的财务账面上实际盈余只有 11.07 美元。普里斯不得不恳求银行对贷款进行延期。他和他的合伙人在用午餐时才勉强凑得上 2 美元，而他的秘书玛丽已经有一个月没有领到薪水了，却果敢地从自己的圣诞储蓄金里拿出钱来帮公司解决燃眉之急。

普里斯非常焦急，在他的信件和日记里都体现出了其低落的情绪。他开始长时间地为自己的健康感到焦虑，在这种扭曲的心态中他总结出了自己的人生哲言:"当一个人活到 40 岁后,体力和脑力都开始下降",普里斯在完成几乎所有的工作后感到精疲力竭,他还有一本没有写完的书《变化——投资者的永恒》,不得不让他的朋友帮忙撰写总论。

这种情况一直延续到富兰克林总统执政的第二年——1937 年的年初,局面显示政府的税收和其他方面的新政正在改变潜在的投资环境。普里斯写道:"政府,提高富人的税收,通过救济、公益事业、农业支出等形式将财产从富人转给穷人。"普里斯指出这不是对资本主义的颠覆,而是一种资本主义的变通形式,劳动者会从分工合作中得到更大的回报。普里斯总结道:请在高速中系牢你的安全带。

在 1970 年末,对于恶性通货膨胀的恐惧一直萦绕在普里斯的心头。最终形成了他的成长股的核心理论,即"要击败通货膨胀的唯一办法就是从中跳出来并走在它的前面"。有时候毁灭理论是不容易从销售的高谈阔论中察觉到的。这个乡村医生的儿子使人们看到了疾患并从自己的口袋里拿出了解决的办法。如何尽快走出困境:投资于新的并且高速成长着的工业,雇用少量的员工并且顺应政府的主旨。这对大家确实是个福音,但也是对传统观念的挑战。

当你拨开乌云就可以看到阳光,由此普里斯成为了单独投资指导者。一些人认为他要在 1915 年云斯沃斯莫尔学院学习并且继承他父亲的工作。

普里斯修的是医药学课程并且在一家医药厂的实验室里工作,但这种情况并没有维持很长时间。一年后,由于药厂的本身问题再加上一场罢工的影响而逐渐走向破产。这次经历让普里斯明白了低劳动成本和良好的公司架构都是必需的,这也成为他投资的指导方向。

两年后当他在杜邦公司作为一名药剂师被解雇后,这种理念愈发地强烈。他的工作热情开始转移:"我把所有夜晚都用在阅读金融杂志上,而不再学习更多的化学药品工业方面的知识了。"普里斯说道。

普里斯的个人资料显示,他在接下来的两年时间里在两家经纪公司从事证券的销售工作。但当他从欧洲度假回来后发现,其中的一家已经倒闭,而他成为了一名证券分析师。

"我想这些经历对我有很大的帮助",普里斯说道,"在我工作过的三家公司里有两家我失败了,一家是因为经验不足而另一家是因为不诚实。从而,这使我以后的工作更加严格而谨慎。"

现在普里斯确信他的工作应该是在华尔街的投资领域,但在去那里之前,他作为一名股票证券师已在一家公司工作了五年。

当他晋升为投资部的主管后,爱争论的他对于如何运转业务有了自己的主见。在 1931 年金融市场出现了危机并且滑落到新低的时候,普里斯也遇到了自己的问题。普里斯的老板——约翰敦促他赔偿所造成的损失并且不允许他再进行证券交易工作。"我甚至连一张卖单都不能写，我的手都变得麻木而僵硬了。"普里斯在他的日记中写道。但他并没有屈服，他从其他渠道得到了一笔贷款，他没有将这笔钱用以偿还所造成的 11,000 美元损失，而是用它来尽可能地挣得利润。"在关键的时候我得到了一些钱，"普里斯说道："我必须得坚持下去。"

在工作中，普里斯看到了作为一名经纪人所赚取的佣金和客户所要求的利润最大化之间的冲突。"股票和基金可以给经纪人带来大额的佣金，可这也是客户所向往的。"在普里斯的日记里体现出了这种忧虑的情绪。

反对建立独立经纪人团体的普里斯被视为不是一个好的团队合作者，他的这种特立独行的方式遭到了很多人的责备，他被视为一个不易亲近的人。而普里斯也抱怨道："我好像是一个犯了罪的人"。

糟糕的是，普里斯的投资部已经不再是一个快速赚取利润的部门了，他的投资理念也贯彻不下去，反而被认为是过于理想主义。他的成长股理论也滑落至低潮。

普里斯 39 岁，时光流逝。普里斯同沃尔普小姐一同离开了公司，另外还有两个志同道合的伙伴，他们对其成长股概念的诠释并不仅限于理论。

普里斯夜以继日地工作着，在那些不眠的日夜里他贪婪地学习医药和航天航空领域的知识，并挑选了 6 家相关领域里的小型公司进行投资，然后他同沃尔特再从中进行筛选。

至少在一个争端上，普里斯发现沃尔特在用拳击打他。普里斯已经关注航天航空领域 6 年了，并且看到了其良好的发展前景。他在道格拉斯航空公司的投资就相当有成效，但沃尔特劝说他卖了手中的股票，因为它已经到了最高点。可航空公司的股票先是小幅下挫然后迅速上涨。普里斯非常后悔没能坚持自己的主见。"沃尔特告诉我说，在我离开时他以 30 美元的市值购买了马丁公司的股票。"普里斯 1939 年 2 月 24 日写道"我经常告诉他，上次马丁公司的股票下跌是在什么时候并且什么时候再次购进，今天这只股票卖到 39 美元。"

戴维这样描述："这种合作持续了 30 年，普里斯先生把他的主意传达给沃尔特，而他几乎跑遍了半个美国，或坐火车或开他的卡车。"

普里斯的外务员记录下了总的里程数。沃尔特作为投资顾问，在任期间总共对 187 家公司进行了 893 次拜访，但收效都不是很大。在 1939 年决定购买惠普公司的股票时，其市值为每股 3.8 美元。而一个朋友建议沃尔特去考察明尼苏达矿业公司，沃尔特租了一辆计程车前去考察后告诉普里斯，现在其股票的市值为每股 1 美元。

约翰依然在从事他的老本行，买卖业绩好的股票的同时在寻找新的股票购进。IBM 公司就是其中之一。普里斯总是在不断尝试新的东西，在 1940 年他决定探究如何为 IBM 公司削减办公系统从而为公司每年节省 500 美元。约翰把他的想法告诉了 IBM 公司的创始人托马斯先生，他经常同托马斯先生进行相关问题的讨论并把有关卷宗带回家研究。

　　普里斯在投资方面的 3/4 的选择都是正确的，但有一次却错误地判断了形势。普里斯认为老工业有成长的前景，他购买了国际镍铁公司的股票，经过测算他甚至追加了投资。但工业市场对镍及钼合金的需求持续疲软。普里斯的推断是正确的，但他对形势有不祥的预感。在他卖出股票后不久，国家政府开始调控原料价格，从而股票价格又开始上升。

　　总之，普里斯基金的运行还是可以的，但这还远远不够，薪水依然没有发放，同时他还要为其同事的成长付出代价。"我让每位同事自己填写卖单并尽可能做得更多，"普里斯在 1941 年 1 月 11 日的日记中写道，"我希望他们都能发挥自己的所长并在不久的将来取得很大的进步。"

　　在第二次世界大战期间，普里斯的生意不多，在此期间他收购了 77 英亩的农场。看着农场的土地，普里斯仿佛看到了加速缓冲器。当然，有的同事开玩笑说，他的这种无谓的收购所起到的作用比日本赢得这场战争还难。

　　"每个人都在想市场不再需要投资经纪人了，我们应该到普里斯的农场种蔬菜。"一个同事笑着说。普里斯在农场种起了玫瑰，但他的注意力依然放在了技术上。每周五的下午他都会同伙伴一起修剪篱笆、喝啤酒并讨论局势。查理晃着头笑着回忆道："他总是跟不上两个人拉锯修剪篱笆的节奏。"

　　这种情况只有普里斯几个最亲近的朋友才知道。作为他 40 多年的朋友，查理说普里斯经常喜欢打高尔夫和网球，"因为这是对公司业务有益的活动"，普里斯喜欢单独思考问题，他经常关上办公室的门而苦思冥想某个问题。

　　是什么令这个天才在门后手舞足蹈呢？最基本的答案就是超常的技巧和对市场规则的对立统一，普里斯的直觉经常和所有人得出的总论合拍。

　　普里斯是早期进入彩电市场的投资人。他在凌晨两点钟醒来，两天前彩电公司的董事长组织安全质量分析专家进行了一次野营。直觉告诉普里斯他应该买这个公司的股票。于是他在第一时间通过电话为他的妻子、公司财务主管和他自己购入了股票。转天晚上，他参加了正在举行的安全质量会议，并且在公司董事长的发言没有结束时就离开了。他购买了更多的这家公司的股票并且还推荐给别人。

　　"上帝，请帮助我，如果我是错的，"普里斯在日记中写道。但他对自己的判断依然很有信心，"用不了几年，这家公司就会成为快速成长的绩优股。"

　　果然这家公司的运转十分出色，这次购买也显示了普里斯的投资理念，在事情不是特别清晰前就要判断出其走势并采取行动。这同时显示普里斯经常先用自己的资金去尝试购买股票，然后再劝说客户购买，这种行为对客户来讲也是个良好的信号，一个投资者可以用自己的资金挣到钱。但他的这种行为在当今的社会是不能实现的，"国家安全局会将他叫来并把他投入监狱"，基金会主席乔治笑着说。

另一个困扰普里斯的问题是如何把众多小的客户资金聚集到一起。1950年，他把很多小的资金聚集起来组建了新的基金会——普里斯成长股基金，总额达到 4,000 万美元。当时普里斯的成长股战略的独特销售方式体现在：它是非贷款基金，没有投资佣金，只需付给基金会 1% 的费用即可，用以鼓励投资者长期持有。普里斯取消了佣金业务，取而代之的是付给基金会基本的费用。事实上，他既没有资金也没有销售渠道，但他以基金会的方式给大家提供了一个交易平台。

这又是普里斯进行的一场革命性的举措，事实证明共有基金不是被买的而是被卖的，当普里斯不断提高时，越发能够证明，投资者不再需要中间环节去维持其连续经营。其他基金组织很快效仿，使"无贷款"基金成为当时的一种潮流。

在这一领域中还有其他的成长基金，普里斯觉得资本的增长比股票的增长更加实际。普里斯十分满意他取得的成果，第一年末他的资产已经达到了 120万美元，这一年被普里斯称为他职业生涯中最为成功的一年。

成长股基金也会受到间接的冲击，但普里斯都会在市场变化前采取相应的措施进行调整。在这一领域里有 3,000 多家基金会追随成长股基金会的策略。

虽然过程时有坎坷，但从牛市中获取利润几乎持续了 10 年时间。普里斯抓住了股市从萌芽到成熟期的机遇。到 1955 年，成长股基金从最初投资 10,000美元上涨到 27,300 美元。普里斯想扩大公司的规模并且招聘新的员工，但他个人仍持有超过 40% 的公司股份。

普里斯感到股市涨得过高过快了，1957 年股市迎来了大幅下调，而且在两年内都保持熊市，普里斯借机也得到了调整放松。普里斯正在考虑新的经营模式——对成长股进行组合，在新的有活力的领域如导弹制造、火箭助推、电力、原子能和航空控制系统中涉及几百家公司。他尤其关注的是非常年轻、非常小、有很大风险的公司，这些公司往往不能引起国际大投资集团的注意。他从 1935年就开始构思这种战略，现在是将其独创的理论付诸实施的时候了。他建立了新的基金会用以应对市场的变化，通过精妙的战略而走在变化的前面。很多年轻的公司没有足够的时间聚合在一起赚取利润，每个公司放弃各自的理想状态而组合到一起，当然贸易战略也是有区别的。市场上适合小规模股本的较少，他们只有用少量的资金逐步地运作，等待爆发性地循环增长。

　　普里斯指出，也可以通过新老企业的相互融合从而降低市场风险，使老企业增加活力，使家庭企业走向社会化。有别于惯例的是，普里斯有时会暂时关闭基金会而转向新的投资，当重新开放时只对在册的股东开放。通过这种管理方式每月可以吸引 1,000 万美元的资金。暂时关闭基金有其积极的一面，通过适度限制交易的方式可以减少股东所面临的风险。

　　1964 年，普里斯在快速增长的股市里变得越发谨慎了。过去他很少担心随着股价的上涨，所赚取的利润的增长是否在合理的点上。现在他开始考虑投资回报率，需要考核内在投资价值和投资面临的实际风险。

　　普里斯警告在过云的 30 年里股价的增长是不可想象的，他无疑是成功的，但每个人不能总期盼奇迹的发生。当价格走低的时候，麻烦也随之而来了。

　　20 世纪 70 年代，由于严重的经济衰退，股票市场死伤惨重。1973 年到 1974年之间成长股基金和新视野都很艰难。在这两年里，成长股 1973 年跌了 25%，1974 年是 33%，而新视野分别跌了 42% 和 38%。1972 年成长股基金的资产达到了最高点 14 亿美元，而在其后的 17 年里再没有达到过这个高度。

　　新视野境况好一些，只用了六七年的时间其资产总额就恢复到了 1972 年的高度。价格的压力非常大。1972 年高峰期的时候，像可口可乐、IBM、宝洁这些股份以 43 倍的收益价格售出，这是美国标普 500 股指数的两倍。而红利受益只有 1.1%，低于市场上的大部分公司。听起来熟悉吗？当然熟悉，但是几乎没有人会看到 20 世纪 90 年代的市场有任何地方与普里斯的预言是相似的。几十年来普里斯的观点是：经一次决定集中购买的股份，其收益增长如果疯狂地外推出来将是很愚蠢的行为，一定会的。

　　未来的收益增长会给购买这些一次决定的股份带来充足的理由吗？如果你的确付了过高的价格，时间会不会帮你解决问题呢？这种比例大约是 3:1。沃顿商学院的教授杰里米·西格尔发现，在接下来的 25 年里，1972 年高峰期购买的"漂亮 50"中的股票，每三种股票只有不到一种能够勉强维持。像可口可乐这样的股份回报率仍然与市场持平。但也有像宝丽来这样的经营不善的公司，高峰期的时候公司以将近 100 倍的收益出售股份，但随后公司经历了重重的困难，收益降到了最多 16 倍。而在笔者写这篇文章的时候，该股票正在以历史上的最低价格出售。

　　据杰里米·西格尔计算，购入 1972 年"漂亮 50"的所有股票所获得的年收益是 12.7%，而当时整个市场的回报率是 12.9%。

　　购入风险高、易变、收益又低的成长股而抛掉指数稳定的信托基金的道理何在呢？

成长股是能赚钱的，但是几乎没有哪个股票是永远赚钱的。这一点就是托马斯·罗·普里斯理论的核心。

普里斯已经开始慢慢抛掉一些旧的变得廉价的成长股（其中包括迪斯尼和百得）。他给《福布斯》送去了一份列出了 20 个未来成长股的名单（如维亚康姆）。虽然卧病在床，病得严重，但普里斯不会放弃。临终前的 10 个月，他在《福布斯》上发表了他的最后一篇文章《80 年代中期的股票》。他在普里斯联合公司的老朋友是第一个获悉他是在短期内已经大获成功的人。

Chapter Four
Extending the Growth Culture—
Tom Bailey

第四章
延伸成长投资文化——汤姆·贝雷

I. Case Study

In 1984, when the deficit-ridden Kansas City Southern Railway laid out $25 million for an 83 percent stake in Janus Capital Corporation, the New Economy had not yet been invented. Diversification was nice, but what exactly did a venerable old hauler of coal and wheat know about sophisticated soft goods like mutual funds?

That management of the $400 million assets open-end Janus Fund was best left in the hands of its founder, the then 47-year-old Thomas H. Bailey. Bailey had been running money for more than two decades, picking up on early growth trends like bowling and discount department stores.

He brought to research the same doggedness he displayed in school years on the hockey rink. His watchwords: "Every stock blows up sometime. You can't take anything for granted." It was a mindset Bailey shared with the progenitor of growth stock theory, T. Rowe Price—a theory Bailey, over the next couple of decades, was to raise to new levels. Unlike Price, Bailey had no Man Friday to pack a steamer trunk and do his leg work for him, so he spent a lot of time on the road himself grilling management on earnings prospects and the basics of the business. Getting behind the income statements wasn't enough. Bailey talked to salesmen, customers, and competitors. By Bailey's lights, the nexus was simple: Tough-minded research meant investment performance; investment performance brought in more net assets to manage.

That proved to be such a winning formula that the KCS parent, Kansas City Southern Industries, soon became the caboose, and Janus the locomotive. From the KCS deal to 1997, Janus Fund assets alone grew almost five times to $19.3 billion, and from 1997 to more than $46 billion. Janus subsequently hived off at least 14 other brand-name funds, with total assets that peaked at more than $300 billion and then slipped to around $200 million. Most of the slippage was due to sharply declining market prices rather than wholesale shareholder liquidations.

Even top-notch research can take you only so far along the line of probability. Volatile issues like Cisco Systems and Sun Microsystems had practically become a Janus trademark. Bailey has paid the price—temporarily, sticking with them. Long-term shareholders who'd hung in with Bailey for three years or so, however, were still ahead of the game. In the case of his two oldest and biggest domestic funds—the big company-oriented Janus and Janus 20—they were looking at average total returns of twice the market.

No one, least of all the pragmatic Tom Bailey, thought gains of that magnitude sustainable through every phase of the market. That was scant consolation to unwary investors who jumped in at the peak of the tech mania, but they can't say they weren't warned.

Bailey hedged against the turn when he began shutting down eight of his most popular funds to new investors well before the market hit the wall. The shutdown cost Janus billions in what would have been easily harvested assets and was unprecedented in magnitude. Bailey was unmistakably signaling that too much money was chasing too few stocks. Shades of growth guru T. Rowe Price and his prescient call on the great break of 1972-1974! The same old signs of excess were flashing, but few were picking them up. Wasn't this the New Paradigm?

Déjà vu all over again.

Targeting the long haul, Bailey made it clear he was not going to trim his aggressive style to what he saw as a short-term change in the weather. Janus would go right on doing what it had been doing—pursuing the typically higher multiple "best business and financial models we can find." "Over a long period of time," insisted Bailey, "You're gonna make a ton of money."

As one of the U.S. top growth managers, Janus itself meets every test of the classic growth stock definition. Among the earmarks: consistently expanding earnings; whacking operating profit margins of better than 45 percent; a growing share of a growing market (at the expense of entrenched leaders like the Fidelity and Vanguard groups); and proven top-flight management in the person of Bailey. Bailey cannot be weighted too heavily in this equation. Now 64, he is one of those rare founders who has created a culture in which young people thrive, and who knows when to keep his hands off.

Although his mother owned "very minor" amounts of General Motors and AT&T, both parents "had come out of the Depression" and stocks were "not the stuff of dinner-table conversation." Born in Pittsburgh, Bailey grew up in Leamington, Ontario, where his father helped manage a tomato farm for RJ Heinz & Company. Bailey did his undergraduate work at Michigan State, where his main enthusiasms were "girls, sports, and skylarking." Bailey finished an MBA in finance in 1962 at the University of Western Ontario, and in the spirit of the times, headed for Denver and the Rockies. "I liked to ski Aspen, and was at peace in the mountains," recalls Bailey.

Bailey also cottoned to the Wall Street lore he picked up at grad school. "Classes were small and I had some great professors," he recalls. He talks about how he began to trade odd lots—"five shares of this, or fifteen shares of that"—while working at a stopgap job selling mimeograph machines. He did not buy on whim, "doing the numbers" with a slide rule. "It was the kind of thing that all the geeks at school would run around with sticking out of their shirt pockets," laughs Bailey. The mimeograph machines he was selling were old timey, too, "the kind that made your hands dirty when you worked with them." They sold briskly, though, briskly enough to leave Bailey with plenty of leisure so that it was "easy to be free by noon, and you could spend the rest of the day lying around the pool with airline stewardesses."

Bailey's first step to Wall Street—and ultimately to Janus—was the New York outpost of Boettcher and Company, an old-time Denver regional brokerage firm. Dipping into Wall Street argot for an easy mark, Bailey describes himself as a "mullet," the bait fish replacement New York manager Fred Larkin needed to speed his own return to Denver. Larkin subsequently left the business and gained solid recognition as a photographer. Bailey recalls Larkin as unstintingly generous in teaching him the ropes. "If anyone ever had any influence on me, it was certainly

Fred Larkin," says Bailey.

The influence was a lasting one. Bailey himself has similarly mentored Janus chief financial officer James Craig, leading him through Bailey recalls that Larkin had him look "at a lot of companies and exposed me to a lot of people. I enjoyed selling, absolutely. The whole organization was about selling, and you had to do it. But I was more interested in the why," recalls Bailey.

Bailey isn't exactly sure why the research side of the business appealed most. "It wasn't rocket science," he says. "All it took was a sense of curiosity and some competitive fire." In the high-momentum markets of the 1960s—not unlike those of the 1990s—basic analysis took a backseat to hype. Under the Larkin tutelage, Bailey did traditional grunt work. He learned to figure out why the gross margins on a department store in Kansas City might be twice those in one in New York City, and still not be a great buy. "In those days, all you had to do was study the prospectus and the footnotes," says Bailey, "and you had a competitive advantage." "These days," he continues, "computers do the modeling and everybody is looking for an edge. I never had the pressure these kids have today. I'm not sure I'd get hired today."

Bailey liked the work. Surprisingly, he liked New York, too. Bailey married and was happy except for one thing. He was desperate to take the step up from research to actually running money. In the evolution of growth stock investing, it was another turn of mind that Bailey shared with T. Rowe Price. Both responded with virtuosity to major changes in the direction of the market, and adjusted style accordingly. Bailey got his first chance to build a portfolio in 1967 when a group of a half dozen friends put together $150,000.

Deciding that his status as a greenhorn with no long-term experience running money would make it difficult to reenergize a sales force, Bailey revamped the fund as a no-load. Out of her interest in mythology, his wife, Jeanne (the couple divorced in 1990), christened the fund Janus for the Roman god of new beginnings. Bailey was off as a one-man research team—a conservative one, with sometimes as much as 80 percent of his assets in cash. Working on his own gave Bailey a keen sense of responsibility. "You," he says, underscoring the pronoun, "are buying the stock. You've got to do the numbers yourself."

Bailey is describing another piece of personal experience that has become part of the Janus culture—large measures of autonomy for portfolio managers, combined with strict accountability. It was a personal code that helped Bailey grow through the 1970s, a period of "massive change, including the high cost of paying for the Vietnam War, inflation, and price controls." "I love change," continues Bailey. "You have to keep reinventing yourself."

With growth stocks, explains Bailey, you always have to look five to ten years out. "You know that many of these companies are going to be merged out. They'll be gone." Bailey has casualties like the once-promising Levitz Furniture in mind. "Change is the one constant, the unexpected, and I love it," he says.

Bailey's adaptability is one of the keys to his success. Although Janus is now practically a synonym for the likes of network hardware producer Cisco and mobilephone innovator Nokia, Bailey takes a lot of kidding about a study he did a number of years ago lambasting high-tech stocks. "If you can't wear it and you can't eat it, don't buy it" was his advice.

Bailey admits to having missed some bets along the way. He lost money in the 1973-1974 crash that brought about the downfall of "Nifty Fifty" one-decision stocks like Xerox and Polaroid. That debacle set off a bear market that really didn't lift for a decade. Bailey's consistent long-term results kept him afloat: up 15 percent in 1970; 40 percent in 1971; 35 percent in 1972. He beat the averages in 10 of the 16 years that he ran the Janus Fund.

Janus Fund, Bailey's baby, had prospered by concentrating on large, well-established companies. He began tutoring a new hire, young James Porter Craig, in the fine art of legwork, much as he had been. Alabama-born Craig, 27, had been working as an analyst for the Trust Company of the West. The graduate degree in finance he had picked up at the Wharton School hadn't prepared Craig for quite so demanding a life on the road. Visits to as many as 13 companies in four days, half of them with Bailey, weren't unusual. "If you keep asking the right questions, you can learn any business," insists Bailey.

It took three years of seasoning for Craig to win his spurs. Bailey took hands off and the Janus Fund became Craig's baby. He poached portfolio manager Tom Marsico, then 31, one portfolio manager notes, Bailey likes to lead "with a velvet touch," but when the chips are down he is quick to act.

The newly launched Janus Value Fund was floundering. Marsico, with two years at Janus under his belt, was assigned to redesign it. The portfolio was stripped to concentrate on a more limited number of stocks and renamed the Janus 20. Now, with better than $30 billion in assets, it is second in size only to the Janus Fund. With returns approaching 50 percent at Janus and better than 50 percent at the more aggressively styled Janus 20 in 1989 and 1991, billions in new assets rolled in. Equally significant, both funds held up well in 1990, a bad year for most competing funds.

Yet another imperative pushing for a lift in performance was the paradox of how to deal with the penalties of success. So much new money was pouring in that the funds were becoming increasingly difficult to manage. Size is a mixed blessing in the fund business. It generates more management fees, but compromises the ability to take sizable positions that will have a measurable impact on performance. Big money demands high liquidity—issues with enough floating shares available to minimize the price impact of major buys and sells. The universe is a limited one. Driven by the huge sums increasingly devil-may-care investors were shoveling into the market, money managers crowded into many of the same high-tech names. As liquidity tightened, price swings widened, multiples tore through the roof, and so did risk levels. Chief investment officer Jim Craig was getting gun-sky.

Rising valuations aside, Craig was deeply skeptical of the technology stocks that had been catching fire. As he told *Kiplinger's Personal Finance Magazine* as early as 1993, "I'm thoroughly convinced there's no franchise to these businesses. Product cycles are so fast that it's difficult for them to make money." "There's no barrier to new competitors," continued Craig. "A couple of engineers in their garage can make a super-computer. Even IBM has finally fallen. They all will."

The volatility of a few bad buys deepened Craig's skepticism. He was getting ready to sell a slug of Electronic Data Services only to see it drop 20 percent in a single day on a bum earnings report before he could kick the stuff out the door.

Time for some soul searching. Thanks to the wide grant of autonomy Bailey has instilled in the Janus culture, at least two other managers were approaching the market with a more aggressive tilt than Craig. Scott Schoezel, for one. Seconded out of Janus Olympus to replace the departed Marsico, Schoezel gave Janus 20 a thorough housecleaning. He cut the number of stocks in the portfolio for a sharper focus, dumped a number of cyclical stocks that had been in the fund for ballast, and brought in such new economy names as AOL.

Other more conservative managers began drifting in the same direction. In the end, so did Craig. He decided that he was trying to run big money the way he had run small money. "I was too reactive," he says, "too cautious to realize that Janus was in the midst of an unbelievable, unpredictable, inexplicable bull market where the rules and regulations regarding valuation parameters were being busted left and right."

Tech stocks Craig had viewed as struggling for franchise values a few years earlier were suddenly a lot easier to identify. Companies like Intel, Microsoft, AOL, and Cisco had all crushed their competitors to emerge as top dogs. Craig stopped looking at price multiples as a major determinant, and focused more on cash flow and return on equity. "If they're increasing," he says, "I'm not that concerned about the P/E relative to the growth rate. I've recognized that valuable companies making themselves more valuable deserve a premium."

In short, GARP (Growth At A Reasonable Price) was out. A once useful analytical tool was downplayed in an investment environment demanding immediate result—or else. Craig had decided to ride the tiger.

It was a radical change. In the new philosophy, paying 200 times earnings for a company like AOL would not be too much. As Janus Mercury manager Warren Lammert told *Forbes*, "Companies can grow into a valuation if they deliver on earnings. The reverse isn't true. Reasonable price won't protect you from nonperformance."

Focus was very much part of the new look. Craig more than halved the number of stocks in his portfolio from 140 to 65, allowing that "diversification led to mediocrity." Tech names such as Cadence Design Systems, Maxim Integrated Products, and Texas Instruments quickly mounted to 25 percent of Janus Fund assets; the top ten stocks to some 40 percent of assets.

The change in style quickly percolated through the rest of the funds. Even the conservatively run Equity-Income Fund was soon showing chunks of Microsoft and Cisco Systems. The generally good performance elicited a wariness from some fund analysts. "I was skeptical hearing about these changes, thinking it was late in the game to decide to go with the flow a little more," said Christine Benz of Morning-star, Incorporated, the Chicago-based fund rating outfit.

The pay-off was immediate. In the two years following the strategy lift, Janus and Janus 20 handily beat the market and most competitors by double digits. As a group in 1999, Janus 15 equity funds according to Morning Star, generated an average return of 76 percent—almost twice as much as the second best complex, the

AIM family of funds. As ever, new cash followed performance. Assets swelled 130 percent to $249 billion, making Janus the United States' fifth largest fund manager. Three years earlier, the group ran twelfth, with assets of $68 billion.

Tom Bailey tended to emphasize performance rather than the asset growth that was compounding Janus advisory profits. "This is not about asset growth," he told reporters. "If it was about asset growth, we wouldn't have closed half the funds." "If it was about asset growth," continued Bailey, "we'd be opening five funds a year, and I'd be hiring portfolio managers all over the place. That's not what we're about. We're about trying to get to that area roughly around first quartile performance, and add value to shareholders. That's the sole focus of the firm."

Still, Bailey's unquenchable competitive fire was compounding the higher risk levels he had taken on in the switch from the old standard of growth at a reasonable price.

As a business decision, the shift in emphasis could not be faulted. Bailey and Craig had got the temper of the times right. Sharper performance brought in so much more new money that Janus vaulted to a remarkable number three (behind Fidelity and Vanguard) among direct sellers of funds. Soon, 28¢ out of every dollar invested in mutual funds was being ticketed to Janus, and the group was so swamped that eight of the biggest funds were closed to new money.

The risks of *not* cranking up the strategy could be seen in the slowed headway of the T. Rowe Price group, the gilt-edged pioneer name of growth stock funds. As wary of runaway valuations as the converted Jim Craig had been earlier, the Price funds stuck to the traditional strategy of growth at a reasonable price. Performance slipped, redemptions rose, and the management company's own stock price fell to the point where Price began to be mentioned as a takeover candidate. It was an ironic riff on founder T. Rowe Price's urging colleagues to get out of growth stocks before the 1973-1974 crash.

Bailey had been hurt in 1973-1974, too, but was not haunted by history. By the end of fiscal 1999, big winners like Sun Microsystems, Cisco, and Nokia were beginning to pop up in almost all of the Janus major funds.

Comcast, Sun, and Cisco alone, for example, accounted for about 15 percent of Janus Fund's $35.8 billion in assets. The latter two stocks made up 12 percent of Janus 20's $28.7 billion in assets. More broadly, there were 17 overlaps among the 10 top holdings of Janus Fund, Janus 20, Worldwide, and Mercury. Most prominent among the common holdings: AOL Time Warner, Cisco, AOL, Nokia, Sprint, EMC, and AT&T Liberty. Even the conservatively run Balanced Fund was holding goodly chunks of cable outfits like Comcast and Viacom.

The concentration was an inevitable result of Janus' decision to go where the growth was, but the overlapping big bets on so many volatile high-tech names worried some analysts. Morningstar's Christine Benz, for one, argued that the core holdings tended to make "the funds act a lot alike," so that owning more than one of them could increase risk rather than provide the higher level of diversification conservative investors might be looking for.

Predictably, when tech stocks got clocked big time, concentration in them left Bailey particularly vulnerable. Most of the Janus Funds fell faster than the market as a whole. Top holdings like AOL Time Warner and Cisco Systems were off 50 percent or more. Janus 20, in a whirl-wind 60 days, lost 20 percent of its value.

It's not as if the Janus portfolio managers were caught flat-footed. A half dozen had moved defensively into cash positions as uncharacteristically high as 17 percent of assets.

Though some of the managers agreed on many of the major holdings spread across the funds, you can see their autonomy at work in a comparison of Bailey's two biggies, Janus 20 and Janus. Janus 20's Scott Schoezel, for example, for three years hands running, had been warning investors that "outsize returns were not sustainable." He was among those who upped his cash position, but otherwise made few concessions to the prospect of a major sell-off. He even eased low-risk standards like Fannie Mae and Wal-Mart out of the portfolio in favor of more adventurous names like Network Solutions and Aether Systems, soon hammered to well under their highs.

The range of strategic shifts showed that adversity had not chilled the Bailey doctrine of letting a thousand flowers bloom among his portfolio managers. Some seemed to be edging out of tech to a broader reach of core holdings in pharmaceutical and energy stocks. Others remained convinced that a lot of still-promising tech stocks had been thrown out with the bath water. They unswervingly continued buying into suddenly unhot stocks like radio broadcast behemoth Clear Channels Communications and cable big Comcast Corporation. Multiples on many such stocks had dropped so far so fast that Janus could almost argue it was once again edging into the comfort zone of growth at a reasonable price.

Sticking to its guns, Janus was taking long bets on the quality of its own research. In general, Bailey was holding and/or adding to a core of familiar tech names—Nokia, GE, Comcast, AOL Time Warner—that had done so well on the upside. Some were now down 60 percent or more from their highs, dizzying descents that in Warren Lammert's view discounted a lot of bad news. The now winnowed group might ship still more water short term, went the rationale, but the long-term payoff was still there. "I have tried to maintain a core of holdings in technology that I think will be marketshare winners as we go through a very difficult economic environment," said Warren Lammert.

More reassuring than the portent of purely statistical past performance was a continuing show of self-questioning and fierce internal debate. They demonstrate that Janus' biggest asset—its culture—is still alive and well. Thus, Janus managers are not coming on as high-tech hotshots glorying in past successes. Persevere in hard times, counsels Bailey "We're going to go on doing exactly what we're doing today," he says, "Doing work on the companies, the competitors, and the supplier because in the end, what you're buying is a business, living breathing things run by people."

So, why didn't Tom Bailey take a leaf from old, T. Rowe Price's book and preserve his gains by shifting to a more conservative stance? Would Janus have done better if it had diversified more broadly and retreated to its more traditional strategy of growth at a reasonable price? Short term, yes. Janus 20, for example, sold off far more sharply than the more cautious Rowe Price Growth Stock Fund. Some of Bailey's glory day gains were wiped out, but over the last five years (at this writing) Janus 20 still trumps the average Rowe Price return to shareholders by more than 25 percent. Risk does have its rewards.

Still, the magnitude of Janus lost values is a sharp reminder that risk and volatility are the price of admission to aggressive growth investing. Growth is a revolving door. Does that mean that the conservative investors should stick with value—that it's safer to waltz with Ben Graham and Marty Whitman than to swing with T. Rowe Price and Tom Bailey? Nope, it just means that both schools take on different coloration in different phases of the market.

Key Words and Expressions:

accountability	n. 责任，义务
ballast	n. 压舱物，稳定力量
christen	vt. 命名
debacle	n. 崩溃
diversification	n. 分散风险
downplay	vt. 贬低，低估
franchise	n. 特权
hype	n. 大肆宣传，炒作
greenhorn	n. 生手，缺乏经验的人
liquidation	n. 停止营业
liquidity	n. 流动性，偿债能力
no-load	n. 资产净值
open-end	n. 开放基金
progenitor	n. 先辈
portfolio	n. 证券投资组合
stopgap	adj. 暂时的，权宜之计的
sustainable	adj. 可持续的
underscore	vt. 强调
virtuosity	n. 精湛技巧，高超
volatility	n. 挥发性，反复无常

Notes:

1. T.Rowe Price　普里斯金融集团

1937 年创立，管理资产为 2,937 亿美元，是全球第二大上市资产管理公司。

2. AOL-Time Warner　美国时代华纳

全球媒体巨无霸，拥有 7.9 万名雇员，2000 年收入 318 亿美元，在各个传媒领域均有佳绩。

3. Sun Microsystems　太阳微系统公司

Sun 起初由包括 Scott McNealy（现任 Sun 公司首席执行官）等 4 名在 Stanford 大学和加州大学 Berkeley 分校上学的研究生创建，1982 年 2 月正式注册，先以工作站的设计制作为业务重点，6 个月后开始创收盈利。Sun

公司的名称，实际为 Stanford University Network 3 个英文单词首字母之缩写，中文意为：斯坦福大学网络，而跟太阳没有任何关系。

4．one-decision stock 一锤定音股

人们认为任何时候购买都不会错的已经被历史证实的成长股。

5．Fidelity: 富达国际创业投资有限公司，投资领域在 IT 和医疗行业。

6．mutual fund 共同基金

汇集许多小钱凑成大钱，交给专人或专业机构操作管理以获取利润的一种集资式的投资工具。

7．GE 通用电气公司

世界上最大的多元化服务性公司，同时也是高质量、高科技工业和消费产品的提供者。GE 在全世界 100 多个国家开展业务，在全球拥有员工近 313,000 人。GE 所有的业务集团在中国都已开展业务活动，在华建立了 30 家合资企业和独资企业，员工人数达 9,000 名。

8．Morningstar 著名基金评级公司，在美国颇受一般投资者欢迎。

II. Knowledge Points

1. Mutual Fund

1) Definition and theory

People invest money in the hope their wealth will grow over time. Some have financial advisers make their investments for them. But even people without very much money can invest. Of course, there are no guarantees. So one way investors try to limit their risk is to buy shares in a mutual fund. A mutual fund is a collection of different financial securities. A mutual fund is a form of collective investments that pools money from many investors and invests their money in stocks, bonds, short-term money market instruments, and/or other securities. In a mutual fund, the fund manager who is also known as the portfolio manager, trades the fund's underlying securities, realizing capital gains or losses, and collects the dividend or interest income. The investment proceeds are then passed along to the individual investors. The value of a share of the mutual fund, known as the net asset value per share (NAV), is calculated daily based on the total value of the fund divided by the number of shares currently issued and outstanding.

Legally known as an "open-end company" under the Investment Company Act of 1940 (the primary regulatory statute governing investment companies), a mutual fund is one of three basic types of investment companies available in the United States. Outside of the United States (with the exception of Canada, which follows the U.S. model), mutual fund is a generic term for various types of collective investment vehicle. In the United Kingdom and western Europe (including offshore jurisdictions), other forms of collective investment vehicle are prevalent, including unit trusts, open-ended investment companies (OEICs), SICAVs and unitized insurance funds.

In Australia the term "mutual fund" is generally not used; the name "managed fund" is used instead. However, "managed fund" is somewhat generic as the definition of a managed fund in Australia is any vehicle in which investors' money is managed by a third party (NB: usually an investment professional or organization). Most managed funds are open-ended (i.e., there is no established maximum number of shares that can be issued); however, this need not be the case. Additionally the Australian government introduced a compulsory superannuation/pension scheme which, although strictly speaking a managed fund, is rarely identified by this term and is instead called a "superannuation fund" because of its special tax concessions and restrictions on when money invested in it can be accessed.

2) Usage

Mutual funds can invest in many different kinds of securities. The most common are cash, stock, and bonds, but there are hundreds of sub-categories. Stock funds, for instance, can invest primarily in the shares of a particular industry, such as technology or utilities. These are known as sector funds. Bond funds can vary according to risk (e.g., high-yield or junk bonds, investment-grade corporate bonds), type of issuers (e.g., government agencies, corporations, or municipalities), or maturity of the bonds (short- or long-term). Both stock and bond funds can invest in primarily U.S. securities (domestic funds), both U.S. and foreign securities (global funds), or primarily foreign securities (international funds).

Most mutual funds' investment portfolios are continually adjusted under the supervision of a professional manager, who forecasts the future performance of investments appropriate for the fund and chooses those which he or she believes will most closely match the fund's stated investment objective. A mutual fund is administered through a parent management company, which may hire or fire fund managers.

Mutual funds are liable to a special set of regulatory, accounting, and tax rules. Unlike most other types of business entities, they are not taxed on their income as long as they distribute substantially all of it to their shareholders. Also, the type of income they earn is often unchanged as it passes through to the shareholders. Mutual fund distributions of tax-free municipal bond income are also tax-free to the shareholder. Taxable distributions can be either ordinary income or capital gains, depending on how the fund earned those distributions.

3) Net asset value

The net asset value, or NAV, is the current market value of a fund's holdings, usually expressed as a per-share amount. For most funds, the NAV is determined daily, after the close of trading on some specified financial exchange, but some funds update their NAV multiple times during the trading day. Open-end funds sell and redeem their shares at the NAV, and so process orders only after the NAV is determined. Closed-end funds (the shares of which are traded by investors) may trade at a higher or lower price than their NAV; this is known as a premium or discount, respectively. If a fund is divided into multiple classes of shares, each class will typically have its own NAV, reflecting differences in fees and expenses paid by the different classes.

Some mutual funds own securities which are not regularly traded on any formal exchange. These may be shares in very small or bankrupt companies; they may be derivatives; or they may be private investments in unregistered financial instruments (such as stock in a non-public company). In the absence of a public market for these securities, it is the responsibility of the fund manager to form an estimate of their value when computing the NAV. How much of a fund's assets may be invested in such securities is stated in the fund's prospectus.

4) Turnover

Turnover is a measure of the fund's securities transactions, usually calculated over a year's time, and usually expressed as a percentage of net asset value.

This value is usually calculated as the value of all transactions (buying, selling) divided by 2 divided by the fund's total holdings; i.e., the fund counts one security sold and another one bought as one "turnover". Thus turnover measures the replacement of holdings.

In Canada, under NI 81-106 (required disclosure for investment funds) turnover ratio is calculated based on the lesser of purchases or sales divided by the average size of the portfolio (including cash).

Turnover generally has tax consequences for a fund, which are passed through to investors. In particular, when selling an investment from its portfolio, a fund may realize a capital gain, which will ultimately be distributed to investors as taxable income. The process of buying and selling securities also has its own costs, such as brokerage commissions, which are borne by the fund's shareholders.

5) Expenses and TER'S

Mutual funds bear expenses similar to other companies. The fee structure of a mutual fund can be divided into two or three main components: management fee, nonmanagement expense, and 12b-1/non-12b-1 fees. All expenses are expressed as a percentage of the average daily net assets of the fund.

Management Fees

The management fee for the fund is usually synonymous with the contractual investment advisory fee charged for the management of a fund's investments. However, as many fund companies include administrative fees in the advisory fee component, when attempting to compare the total management expenses of different funds, it is helpful to define management fee as equal to the contractual advisory fee + the contractual administrator fee. This "levels the playing field" when comparing management fee components across multiple funds.

Contractual advisory fees may be structured as "flat-rate" fees, i.e., a single fee charged to the fund, regardless of the asset size of the fund. However, many funds have contractual fees which include breakpoints, so that as the value of a fund's assets increases, the advisory fee paid decreases. Another way in which the advisory fees remain competitive is by structuring the fee so that it is based on the value of all of the assets of a group or a complex of funds rather than those of a single fund.

Non-management Expenses

Apart from the management fee, there are certain non-management expenses which most funds must pay. Some of the more significant (in terms of amount) non-management expenses are: transfer agent expenses (this is usually the person you get on the other end of the phone line when you want to purchase/sell shares of a fund), custodian expense (the fund's assets are kept in custody by a bank which charges a custody fee), legal/audit expense, fund accounting expense, registration expense (the SEC charges a registration fee when funds file registration statements with it), board of directors/trustees expense (the disinterested members of the board who oversee the fund are usually paid a fee for their time spent at board meetings), and printing and postage expense (incurred when printing and delivering shareholder reports).

12b-1/Non-12b-1 Service Fees

12b-1 service fees/shareholder servicing fees are contractual fees which a fund may charge to cover the marketing expenses of the fund. Non-12b-1 service fees are marketing/shareholder servicing fees which do not fall under SEC rule 12b-1. While funds do not have to charge the full contractual 12b-1 fee, they often do. When investing in a front-end load or no-load fund, the 12b-1 fees for the fund are usually .250% (or 25 basis points). The 12b-1 fees for back-end and level-load share classes are usually between 50 and 75 basis points but may be as much as 100 basis points. While funds are often marketed as "no-load" funds, this does not mean they do not charge a distribution expense through a different mechanism. It is expected that a fund listed on an online brokerage site will be paying for the "shelf-space" in a different manner even if not directly through a 12b-1 fee. Fees and Expenses Borne by the Investor (not the Fund)

Fees and expenses borne by the investor vary based on the arrangement made with the investor's broker. Sales loads (or contingent deferred sales loads (CDSL)) are not included in the fund's total expense ratio (TER) because they do not pass through the statement of operations for the fund. Additionally, funds may charge early redemption fees to discourage investors from swapping money into and out of the fund quickly, which may force the fund to make bad trades to obtain the necessary liquidity. For example, Fidelity Diversified International Fund (FDIVX) charges a 1 percent fee on money removed from the fund in less than 30 days.[edit] Brokerage Commissions

An additional expense which does not pass through the statement of operations and cannot be controlled by the investor is brokerage commissions. Brokerage commissions are incorporated into the price of the fund and are reported usually 3 months after the fund's annual report in the statement of additional information. Brokerage commissions are directly related to portfolio turnover (portfolio turnover refers to the number of times the fund's assets are bought and sold over the course of a year). Usually the higher the rate of the portfolio turnover, the higher the brokerage commissions. The advisors of mutual fund companies are required to achieve "best execution" through brokerage arrangements so that the commissions charged to the fund will not be excessive.

6) Types of mutual funds

Open-end fund

The term mutual fund is the common name for an open-end investment company. Being open-ended means that, at the end of every day, the fund issues new shares to investors and buys back shares from investors wishing to leave the fund.

Mutual funds may be legally structured as corporations or business trusts but in either instance are classed as open-end investment companies by the SEC.

Other funds have a limited number of shares; these are either closed-end funds or unit investment trusts, neither of which is a mutual fund.

Exchange-traded funds

A relatively new innovation, the exchange traded fund (ETF), is often formulated as an open-end investment company. ETFs combine characteristics of both mutual funds and closed-end funds. An ETF usually tracks a stock index (see Index funds). Shares are issued or redeemed by institutional investors in large blocks (typically of 50,000). Investors typically purchase shares in small quantities through brokers at a small premium or discount to the net asset value; this is how the institutional investor makes its profit. Because the institutional investors handle the majority of trades, ETFs are more efficient than traditional mutual funds (which are continuously issuing new securities and redeeming old ones, keeping detailed records of such issuance and redemption transactions, and, to effect such transactions, continually buying and selling securities and maintaining liquidity position) and therefore tend to have lower expenses. ETFs are traded throughout the day on a stock exchange, just like closed-end funds.

Exchange traded funds are also valuable for foreign investors who are often able to buy and sell securities traded on a stock market, but who, for regulatory reasons, are unable to participate in traditional US mutual funds.

Equity funds

Equity funds, which consist mainly of stock investments, are the most common type of mutual fund. Equity funds hold 50 percent of all amounts invested in mutual funds in the United States. Often equity funds focus investments on particular strategies and certain types of issuers.

Bond funds

Bond funds account for 18% of mutual fund assets. Types of bond funds include term funds, which have a fixed set of time (short-, medium-, or long-term) before they mature. Municipal bond funds generally have lower returns, but have tax advantages and lower risk. High-yield bond funds invest in corporate bonds, including high-yield or junk bonds. With the potential for high yield, these bonds also come with greater risk.

Money market funds

Money market funds hold 26% of mutual fund assets in the United States. Money market funds entail the least risk, as well as lower rates of return. Unlike certificates of deposit (CDs), money market shares are liquid and redeemable at any time. The interest rate quoted by money market funds is known as the 7 Day SEC Yield.

Funds of funds

Funds of funds (FoF) are mutual funds which invest in other underlying mutual funds (i.e., they are funds comprised of other funds). The funds at the underlying level are typically funds which an investor can invest in individually. A fund of funds will typically charge a management fee which is smaller than that of a normal fund because it is considered a fee charged for asset allocation services. The fees charged at the underlying fund level do not pass through the statement of operations, but are usually disclosed in the fund's annual report, prospectus, or statement of additional information. The fund should be evaluated on the combination of the fund-level expenses and underlying fund expenses, as these both reduce the return to the investor.

Most FoFs invest in affiliated funds (i.e., mutual funds managed by the same advisor), although some invest in funds managed by other (unaffiliated) advisors. The cost associated with investing in an unaffiliated underlying fund is most often higher than investing in an affiliated underlying because of the investment management research involved in investing in fund advised by a different advisor. Recently, FoFs have been classified into those that are actively managed (in which the investment advisor reallocates frequently among the underlying funds in order to adjust to changing market conditions) and those that are passively managed (the investment advisor allocates assets on the basis of on an allocation model which is rebalanced on a regular basis).

The design of FoFs is structured in such a way as to provide a ready mix of mutual funds for investors who are unable to or unwilling to determine their own asset allocation model. Fund companies such as TIAA-CREF, Vanguard, and Fidelity have also entered this market to provide investors with these options and take the "guess work" out of selecting funds. The allocation mixes usually vary by the time the investor would like to retire: 2020, 2030, 2050, etc. The more distant the target retirement date, the more aggressive the asset mix.

Hedge funds

Hedge funds in the United States are pooled investment funds with loose SEC regulation and should not be confused with mutual funds. Certain hedge funds are required to register with SEC as investment advisers under the Investment Advisers Act. The Act does not require an adviser to follow or avoid any particular investment strategies, nor does it require or prohibit specific investments. Hedge funds typically charge a management fee of 1% or more, plus a "performance fee" of 20% of the hedge fund's profit. There may be a "lock-up" period, during which an investor cannot cash in shares.

No-load fund

No-load fund is a mutual fund that does not assess a sales commission or sales charge when shares are initially purchased in the fund.

Balanced Fund

Balanced fund is a mutual fund that invests its assets into the money market, bonds, preferred stock, and common stock with the intention to provide both growth and income. Also known as an "asset allocation fund".A balanced fund is geared towards investors looking for a mixture of safety, income, and capital appreciation. The amount the mutual fund invests into each asset class usually must remain within a set minimum and maximum.

2. New Economy

1) Definition and theory

New Economy was a term coined in late 1990s by pundits to describe what some thought was an evolution of the United States and other developed countries from an industrial/manufacturing-based wealth producing economy into a service sector asset based economy from globalization and currency manipulation by governments and their central banks. At the time, some analysts claimed that this change in the economic structure of the United States had created a state of permanent steady growth, low unemployment, and immunity to boom and bust macroeconomic cycles. Furthermore, they believed that the change rendered obsolete many business practices. When the stock market bubble burst, analysts soon realized they had been wrong. While many of the more exuberant predictions proved to be wrong, some pundits continue to use the term New Economy to describe contemporary developments in business and the economy.

In the financial markets, the term has been associated with the Dot-com boom. This included the emergence of the NASDAQ as a rival to the New York Stock Exchange, a high rate of IPOs, the rise of Dot-com stocks over established firms, and the prevalent use of such tools as stock options. In the wider economy the term has been associated with practices such as outsourcing, business process outsourcing and business process re-engineering.

General idea is that a business should focus on those areas of its operation which are critical to its success and where it has a competitive advantage. Other areas of its operation should be outsourced, typically using technology as the facilitator. In a developed economy, the critical success factors to a leading business are likely to be intellectual things such as brands, products specifications and technical capabilities. Many routine business functions (such as manufacturing and customer service desks) may be outsourced.

2) Background

Around 1995, U.S. economic growth accelerated, driven by faster productivity growth. Since the early 1970s, labour productivity growth had only averaged around 1-1.5 percent per year, but since 1995, growth has been much faster: 2-2.5 percent. In addition, unemployment rates were lower than they had been in years and inflation stayed low as well. Already in 1995, Newsweek coined the phrase "New Economy" to refer to this happy state. According to many commentators in the late 1990s, investment in Information technology (ICT) had eliminated economic fluctuations and ushered in a golden age of economic prosperity. The economist Robert J. Gordon referred to it as the Goldilocks Economy.

As with many things that seem too good to last, the recession of 2001 discredited many of the more extreme predictions made during the boom years. However, subsequent research strongly suggests that productivity growth has been stimulated by heavy investment in ICT. Furthermore, continuing strong productivity growth since the 2001 recession make it likely that some of the gains of the late 1990s may endure.

3) Technology sector

At the same time, there was a lot of investment in the companies of the technology sector. Stock shares rose dramatically. A lot of start-ups were created and the stock value was very high where floated. Newspapers and business leaders were starting to talk of new business models. Some even claimed that the old laws of economics did not apply anymore and that new laws had taken their place. They also claimed that the improvements in computer hardware and software would dramatically change the future, and that information is the most important value in the New Economy.

4) Investment

Some, such as Joseph Stiglitz, have suggested that a lot of investment in Information technology, especially in software and unused fibre optics, was useless. However, this may be too harsh a judgement, given that U.S. investment in Information technology has remained relatively strong since 2002. While there may have been some overinvestment, productivity research shows that much of the investment has been useful in raising output.

3. T. Rowe Price (NASDAQ: TROW)

Definition and theory

T. Rowe Price (NASDAQ: TROW) is an independent global investment management firm and mutual fund manager based in Baltimore, Maryland. It was founded in 1937 by Thomas Rowe Price, Jr.T. Rowe Price provides a broad array of mutual funds, sub-advisory services, and separate account management for individual and institutional investors, retirement plans, and financial intermediaries. The firm also offers a variety of sophisticated investment planning and guidance tools.

4. Return on Equity: ROE

1) Definition and theory

Return on Equity (ROE, Return on average common equity, return on net worth) measures the rate of return on the ownership interest (shareholders' equity) of the common stock owners. ROE is viewed as one of the most important financial ratios. It measures a firm's efficiency at generating profits from every dollar of net assets, and shows how well a company uses investment dollars to generate earnings growth. ROE is equal to a fiscal year's net income (after preferred stock dividends but before common stock dividends) divided by total equity (excluding preferred shares), expressed as a percentage.

$$ROE = \frac{Net\ Income}{Average\ stockholders'\ equity}$$

But not all high-ROE companies make good investments. Some industries have high ROE because they require no assets, such as consulting firms. Other industries require large infrastructure builds before they generate a penny of profit, such as oil refiners. You cannot conclude that consulting firms are better investments than refiners just because of their ROE. Generally, capital-intensive businesses have high barriers to entry, which limit competition. But high-ROE firms with small asset bases have lower barriers to entry. Thus, such firms face more business risk because competitors can replicate their success without having to obtain much outside funding. As with many financial ratios, ROE is best used to compare companies in the same industry.

High ROE yields no immediate benefit. Since stock prices are most strongly determined by earnings per share (EPS), you will be paying twice as much (in Price/Book terms) for a 20% ROE Company as for a 10% ROE company. The benefit comes from the earnings reinvested in the company at a high ROE rate, which in turn gives the company a high growth rate.

ROE is irrelevant if the earnings are not reinvested.

The sustainable growth model shows us that when firms pay dividends, earnings growth lowers. If the dividend payout is 20%, the growth expected will be only 80% of the ROE rate.

The growth rate will be lower if the earnings are used to buy back shares. If the shares are bought at a multiple of book value (say 3 times book), the incremental earnings returns will be only "that fraction" of ROE (ROE/3).

New investments may not be as profitable as the existing business. Ask "what is the company doing with its earnings?"

Remember that ROE is calculated from the company's perspective, on the company as a whole. Since much financial manipulation is accomplished with new share issues and buyback, always redo the calculation on a "per share" basis. EPS/book.

2) The DuPont Formula

The DuPont formula, also known as the strategic profit model, is a common way to break down ROE into three important components. Essentially, ROE will equal net margin multiplied by asset turnover multiplied by financial leverage. Splitting return on equity into three parts makes it easier to understand changes in ROE over time. For example, if the net margin increases, every sale brings in more money, resulting in a higher overall ROE. Similarly, if the asset turnover increases, the firm generates more sales for every dollar of assets owned, again resulting in a higher overall ROE. Finally, increasing financial leverage means that the firm uses more debt financing relative to equity financing. Interest payments to creditors are tax deductible, but dividend payments to shareholders are not. Thus, a higher proportion of debt in the firm's capital structure leads to higher ROE. Financial leverage benefits diminish as the risk of defaulting on interest payments increases. So if the firm takes on too much debt, the cost of debt rises as creditors demand a higher risk premium, and ROE decreases. Increased debt will make a positive contribution to a firm's ROE only if the firms ROA exceeds the interest rate on the debt.

$$ROE = \frac{Net\ Income}{Sales} \times \frac{Sales}{Total\ Assets} \times \frac{Total\ Assets}{Average\ stockholders\ equity}$$

III. Analyzing the Case

1. What are Bailey's watchwords?

His watchwords: Every stock blows up sometime. You can't take anything for granted.

2. What's Bailey's first step to Wall Street—and ultimately to Janus?

It was the New York outpost of Boettcher and Company, an old-line Denver regional brokerage firm.

3. Who had influence on Bailey?

Fred Larkin.

4. Bailey married and was happy except one thing. What's that?

He was desperate to take the step up from research to actually running money.

5. What's Bailey's first chance to build a portfolio?

A group of a half dozen friends put together $150,000.

6. Why did Bailey's wife, Jeanne, christen the fund Janus?

Because she's interested in mythology. Janus is the Roman god of new beginnings.

7. What's Bailey's another piece of personal experience that has become part of the Janus culture?

Large measures of autonomy for portfolio managers, combined with strict accountability.

8. What's one of the keys of Bailey's success?

Adaptability.

9. Bailey took hands off and the Janus Fund became whose baby?

Craig's baby.

10. Sticking to its guns, what was Janus taking long bets on?

The quality of its own research.

IV. Translation of the Case

1984 年，负有赤字的肯萨斯市南方铁路公司投资 2,500 万美元，占其股本的 83%，在购买杰纳斯基金公司基金的时候，新经济模式还未形成。多种投资、分散风险是正确的，可是一个令人尊敬的致力于煤炭和小麦的老牌公司对复杂的软产品，如共同基金又了解多少呢？

拥有 4 亿美元资产的开放基金——杰纳斯基金最好是由杰纳斯的创始人，当时 47 岁的托马斯·H. 贝雷来进行。贝雷运作资金已有 20 多年了，挑选了一些有早期增长趋势的行业，如保龄球和折扣商店。

他把学生时代在曲棍球场上的执著带到了对股票的研究上。他的口号是："每支股票都会有暴涨的时候。你不能认为这一切是理所应当的。"这是贝雷与增长型股票理论的前辈——托马斯·罗·普里斯所共有的思想。在后来的几十年中，贝雷把这个理论提升到一个新的高度。与普里斯不同的是，贝雷没有得力助手奔波于各地的船上，替他跑腿，所以他自己要在路上花很多时间，加强对收益前景和业务基础的管理。只处在损益表后是不够的，贝雷亲自和销售人员、顾客，甚至竞争对手交谈。以贝雷的眼光看，这种关系是简单的：实际的研究意味着投资业绩，投资业绩带来更多的可管理的净资产。

事实证明这个获胜的方案使得母公司肯萨斯市南方工业公司很快成为了

车尾，而杰纳斯成了车头。从与肯萨斯市南方工业公司的交易到 1997 年，杰纳斯基金的资产增长了几乎 5 倍，达到 193 亿美元，从 1997 年至今达到了 460 亿美元。杰纳斯随后推出了至少 14 种品牌基金，全部资产最高达到超过 3,000 亿美元，然后下滑到大约 2 亿美元。大部分下滑是由于市场价格的急剧下跌，而不是大批股东的波产。

即使是一流的研究迄今为止也只能告诉你各种可能性。像思科和太阳电脑这样不稳定的股票，实际上已成为杰纳斯的商标了。贝雷为此已付出了代价——暂时的，他愿意坚持下去。然而，追随贝雷三年左右的长期股东仍然处在赢家的地位。就贝雷创建时间最长和规模最大的国内基金而言——面向大公司的杰纳斯和杰纳斯 20——它们看到的是平均为市场两倍的总回报。

尤其是，除了讲求实际的贝雷之外，没有人想到收益的多少和持续性是要通过市场的各个阶段来确定的。对于在热衷科技股的高峰时期投入的不谨慎的投资者而言，那是不足以安慰他们的，但他们不能说他们没有受到警告。

在市场受挫之前，贝雷开始对新投资者关闭了 8 种最受欢迎的基金，这时他对市场的转折已有防备。这次关闭损失了杰纳斯几十亿美元，这原本是可以轻易收获的资产，并且在数量上是前所未有的。贝雷明明白白地发出信号：太多的钱在追捧极少数的股票。这是增长型股票的领袖托马斯·罗·普里斯以及他对 1972－1974 年大跌有先见之明的预测的影子。对股市过度增长的同样的老信号在闪烁，但很少有人理解。这是不是新的经典范例呢？

以长期的结果为目标，贝雷表明不会因为他所看到的短期的变化而改变他敢想敢干的风格。杰纳斯会继续一如既往，追求典型的更高复合型的"我们能发现的最佳业务和金融模式"。贝雷坚持说："经过一段较长的时期，你会赚到大钱的。"

作为美国一流的增长型管理公司之一，杰纳斯遇到了典型的增长型股票定义中的各种考验。存在于如下特征中：连续增长的收益；削减超过 45% 的营业利润率；增长的市场中增长的股票（使像富达和先锋集团这样的地位巩固的领头企业付出了一定的代价）；证明了贝雷有资格做到一流的管理。在这种均衡中贝雷并没有负重过多。他现年 64 岁，属于那种不多见的创始人之一，他创造了一种文化，在这种文化中，年轻人的事业兴旺发达，同时他也知道何时不应插手、不应干涉。

尽管他母亲拥有很少量的通用汽车和世讯的股票，但他的父母都经历过大萧条，而且也从不在餐桌上谈股票。贝雷出生在匹兹堡，成长于安大略州的利明顿，他父亲在那里帮助别人为 DJ 亨氏公司管理一个种植番茄的农场。贝雷在密西根州上完大学，不过在那里他的主要热情在于"女生、体育和玩笑"。1962

年贝雷在西安大略大学获得金融专业的 MBA 学位，按照当时时代的潮流，他去了丹佛和落基。贝雷回忆说："我喜欢在阿斯盘山上滑雪，感受山脉的宁静。"

贝雷也喜欢他在学校学到的华尔街的知识。他回忆说："班级不大，但教授很棒。"他谈论他如何交易一些零星股票——"5 股这种股票，15 股那种股票"——同时在做一份卖油印机的临时工作。他不是心血来潮地买入，而是用计算尺"做数据"。贝雷笑着说："这是学校里的怪人才会做的事，他们衬衣口袋向外翻着，四处奔波。"他卖的油印机太老式了，"是那种你用它干活就会把你的手弄脏的油印机"。尽管这样，它们卖得很兴旺，兴旺得使贝雷有充足的休闲时间，以至于"到中午就闲下来了，你可以在剩下的时间里躺在游泳池周围，和空姐们在一起"。

贝雷进入华尔街的第一步——基本上是进入杰纳斯的第一步——就是波特歇尔公司在纽约的前哨阵地，历史悠久的丹佛区域经纪代理公司。初涉华尔街，易于受人利用，贝雷描述自己为一条鲻鱼，是纽约分部经理福莱德·拉汀所需要的如鱼饵般的替代品，这样可以使他尽快返回丹佛。拉汀后来离开了商界，成为一个颇受认可的摄影师。贝雷回忆拉汀毫无保留地教他熟悉情况。贝雷说："如果有谁对我有所影响的话，那肯定是福莱德·拉汀。"

这种影响是持久的。贝雷自己同样指导杰纳斯的首席财务官詹姆斯·克雷格，按照类似他自己的学徒经历引领着克雷格。这是个要求很高的工作。贝雷回忆说，拉汀让他"看了许多公司，并接触了许多人。我确实喜欢销售，整个机构都是关于销售的，你必须做这个工作，但我对为什么这样做的原因更感兴趣"。

贝雷并不十分确定为什么对这个行业的研究非常有吸引力。他说："这不是火箭科学，它所需要的是好奇心和某种竞争热情。"在 60 年代势头强劲的市场中——类似 90 年代的市场——相对于炒作，基本分析占次要地位。贝雷做了传统的工作。他学会了理解为什么堪萨斯市的百货公司的毛利是纽约的百货公司的两倍，而这却仍然不是最好的买入。贝雷说："在那些天，你必须做的就是研究招股书和附注，并且你有竞争优势。"他继续说："现在，计算机做出模式图，人人都在找优势条件。我从来没有今天这些年轻人的压力，我不知道在当今时代我能否找到工作。"

贝雷喜欢工作。出人意料的是，他还喜欢纽约。贝雷结婚了，很幸福，除了一件事外。他极想从研究迈步到实际运作资金。在增长型股票投资的发展中，贝雷和托马斯·罗·普里斯都有另一个思想上的转变。他们都以高超的技巧对市场方向上的主要变化作出反应，并作出相应的调整。1967 年，当 6 个朋友凑了 15 万美元的时候，贝雷第一次有机会构建了一个证券投资组合。

　　由于贝雷认为自己是个没有长期管理资金经验的新手，而这一点对加强销售力量是有一定困难的，所以他把基金改进为免佣基金。他妻子詹妮（于1990年离异）出于对神话的兴趣，把基金命名为掌管新起点的罗马门神杰纳斯。贝雷是以只有一个人的研究团队开始的——一个保守的团队，有时多达80%的资产是现金。独自工作赋予了他强烈的责任感。他特别强调着代词"你"说："你，正在买股票，你，必须自己作数据。"

　　贝雷描述了另外一段个人经历，而这已成为杰纳斯文化的一部分——给证券组合投资经理们以较大程度的自主性，同时又结合其所承担的责任。这是一个帮助贝雷在70年代成长起来的个人法则。70年代是有巨大变化的时代，包括为越南战争、通货膨胀和价格管制付出的高昂代价。贝雷继续说："我喜欢变化，但你必须一直要彻底改造自己。"

　　贝雷解释说："对于增长型股票，你必须看5年到10年那么远。你知道这些公司中有许多将被吞并。它们将消失。"贝雷记得像曾经看好的拉维兹家具给他带来的损失，他说："变化是持续和出乎意料的，但我喜欢。"

　　贝雷的适应性是他成功的关键之一。虽然现在杰纳斯实际上是网络硬件制造商思科和手机革新者诺基亚这一类型的同义词，但贝雷在几年前所作的研究中痛斥高科技股票，他对此开了许多玩笑。他的建议曾经是："如果这个东西你吃不了，也穿不了，就别买它。"

　　贝雷承认曾经错过了一些该下注的机会。他在1973—1974年的暴跌中损失了钱。这次暴跌导致了"俏皮的50大型股"、一锤定音股富士施乐和宝力丽莱的衰落。那次崩溃开始了10年没有复苏的熊市。贝雷始终坚持的长期结果使他渡过了难关：1970年上升15%，1971年上升40%，1972年上升35%。在他管理基金的16年中有10年高于平均涨幅。

　　杰纳斯基金，像贝雷的孩子一样，是通过把业务集中在大型、固定的公司而成功的。他开始指导新雇员，年轻的詹姆斯·鲍特·克雷格，和贝雷一样善于做跑腿的工作。出生在阿拉巴马州的27岁的克雷格，曾一直在西部信托公司作分析员。在沃顿学院获得的金融学位并没有使克雷格对如此多的要求在路上奔波做好准备。他在4天内拜访了13个公司是很平常的，其中一半是和贝雷一起去的。贝雷坚持说：'如果你不断地提问恰当的问题，你就能学到各项业务。"

　　克雷格用了三年的适应时间赢得了鼓励，贝雷放手了，杰纳斯基金成了克雷格的孩子。他还挖走了当时31岁的负责投资组合的经理汤姆·马斯克。正如一位证券投资组合经理所注意到的那样，贝雷喜欢以"温和的接触方式"来领导，但关键时刻，他会迅速出击。

　　新创建的杰纳斯价值基金在挣扎中前进。马斯克在杰纳斯已两年了，他被指派重新设计这支基金。这个证券投资组合被削减，为了集中在更有限数量的股票上，便更名为杰纳斯 20。现在，杰纳斯 20 的资产超过 300 亿美元，在规模上仅次于杰纳斯基金，处于第二位。在 1989 年和 1991 年，杰纳斯基金的回报接近 50%，更积极进取的杰纳斯 20 基金的回报超过 50%，数十亿的新资产涌入进来。同样意义重大的是，在 1990 年，两支基金都很坚挺，而对大多数参与竞争的基金来说那是糟糕的一年。

　　然而，另一个为了提升业绩急需推行的是如何处理对成功的处罚这样一个反论。由于有太多的新资金一下子注入到公司中，以至于对资金的管理变得越来越困难。规模在基金业是毁誉参半的事。规模大就产生更多的管理费用，但对大规模资金的管理能力的下降会对业绩产生一定的影响。大额资金需要较高的流动性——即有足够的可流动性的部分用于最大程度上减低价格对买进和卖出的影响。这个空间是有限的，受到不断增加的盲目的投资者进入市场所带来的大额资金的影响，资金管理经理们在许多相同的高科技股票中扎堆。随着流动性变差，价格浮动增加，成倍增长超过一定的限度，风险也超过了一定的限度。投资总负责人克雷格变得有所顾忌。

　　撇开增长了的价值不谈，克雷格深深地怀疑一直火爆的高科技股票。早在1993 年，他就曾在基普棱格个人金融杂志上说：“我完全确信这些行业是没有优势的，产品的周期太快，所以不好赚钱。”他继续说：“新的竞争对手很容易进入，没有障碍，几个工程师在车库里就可以制造出超级电脑。甚至 IBM 公司最终也会衰落，这行中所有的公司都会这样。”

　　几次暂时的失败的买进加深了克雷格的怀疑。他开始要卖掉一部分电子数据服务公司的股票，只是因为他看到一份没有什么价值的收入报告上显示这支股票在一天内跌了 20%，他就把这支股票踢出门外。

　　这也是一些人在探索的时期。由于贝雷在杰纳斯基金文化中所注入的广泛的自主性，至少还有两名经理是以比克雷格更积极的倾斜政策打入市场的。斯克特·叟载尔就是其中一个。在支持奥林匹斯基金来代替已经过时的马斯克基金的同时，叟载尔对杰纳斯 20 进行了彻底的改革。他把证券投资组合中的股票数量按更鲜明的重点进行消减，抛弃了一些曾经是在基金中压仓底的周期性股票，增加了诸如美国在线等新公司的股票。

　　其他更为保守的经理开始朝同样的方向转变。最终，克雷格也这样做了。他决定要以运作小额资金的方式运作大额资金。他说：“我太敏感、太谨慎以至于没有认识到杰纳斯正处于令人难以置信又费解的不可预测的熊市中，在这个市场中关于价值参数的规则正在破裂。”

　　克雷格在几年前看到的为特许权价值而努力的科技股突然很容易识别。像英特尔、微软、美国在线和思科都挤垮了对手，以优胜者的姿态出现。克雷格不再把价格乘数作为主要的决定因素，而是集中于现金流量和股本收益率。他说："如果它们在增长，我不关心与增长率相关的市盈率，我已承认那些使自己更值钱的有价值的公司应当是有溢价的。"

简言之，合理价格内的增长已经过时了。一个曾经有用的分析工具在一个直接要求结果或别的东西的投资环境中是不予重视的。克雷格决定冒险骑上虎背。

这是个根本的改变。在新哲学中，为像美国在线这样的公司支付 200 倍的收益不算太多。正如杰纳斯墨丘利基金经理沃任·莱沫特对福布斯杂志所说的那样："如果公司提供收益，对它的估定价值就增长了。反之则不对。合理的价格不能保护你免受不履行合同的风险。"

侧重点是新态度中非常重要的部分。克雷格把投资组合中的股票数量减了一多半，从 140 减到 65，考虑到分散风险导致平庸投资。科技股如卡德斯设计公司、美信集成产品公司、得克萨斯设备公司迅速占据了杰纳斯基金资产的 25%；前 10 位股票大约占资产的 40%。

风格上的迅速改变渗透到其他的基金上。甚至被保守运作的价值型股票基金也很快展示出其大部分为微软和思科。总体良好的业绩引起了一些股票分析家的注意。晨星公司，一个以芝加哥为基地的基金等级评定组织，这个公司的克瑞斯汀·班茨说："我怀疑所听到的变化，我认为在这个游戏中过多地随着潮流而动有些为时过晚。"

回报是立竿见影的。在随后策略提升的两年中，杰纳斯和杰纳斯 20 这两支基金以双倍的数字击败了大多数的竞争对手。根据晨星公司的分析，总的来说，1999 年杰纳斯 19 投票基金产生了平均 76%的回报——几乎是位于第二位的最佳组合产品——AIM 基金家庭的两倍。新的资金依旧按照业绩而注入。资产增长了 130%，达到了 2,490 亿美元，使杰纳斯成为美国第五大基金管理公司。三年前，这个集团排名第十二，拥有资产 680 亿美元。

汤姆·贝雷倾向于强调业绩而不是构成杰纳斯咨询利润的资产增长。他告诉记者说："我们要的不是资产增长。如果我们要资产增长的话，我们就不会关闭一半的基金。如果我们要资产增长的话，我们就会一年开 5 个基金，我会在各地雇用投资组合经理。那不是我们要做的。我们要努力使这一区域粗略达到第一个四位数的业绩，为股东增加价值，那是本公司唯一的侧重点。"

然而，在从合理价格增长的旧标准的转变中，贝雷不可遏制的如火的竞争力也造成了他承担更高的风险水平。

作为一个商业决定，在重点上的转移是无可挑剔的，贝雷和克雷格正确掌握了时代的特征。更鲜明的业绩吸引了很多新资金，使杰纳斯在基金的直接销售中引人注目地排名第三（在富达和先锋之后），很快投资在公共基金的每一美元中有 28 美分购买的是杰纳斯，这个集团拥有的资金量太大，以至于 8 个最大的基金对新资金已不接纳了。

没有为策略做好准备的风险可以在托马斯·罗·普里斯集团的放慢的进展速度中看出，它是顶尖的增长型股票基金。如同已改变观念的克雷格以前一样，普里斯基金对不易控制的估价小心谨慎，它坚持传统策略，即在合理价格内的增长。业绩下滑，基金赎回上升，管理公司自己的股票价格跌至普里斯开始被提及为接收候选人的点位。这是一个讽刺的重现，即增长型股票的创始人托马斯·罗·普里斯催促同事在 1973－1974 年的股市大跌之前脱手增长型股票基金。

贝雷在 1973－1974 年也受到了损失，但没有被历史所缠住。到 1999 年财政年底，像太阳计算机、思科和诺基亚开始突然出现在杰纳斯几乎所有的主要基金中。

仅以康卡斯特、太阳和思科为例，它们占到杰纳斯基金 358 亿美元的资产的 15%。后两种股票构成杰纳斯 20 基金的 287 亿美元资产的 12%。在大体上，在前十位的杰纳斯基金、杰纳斯 20、全球基金、墨丘利基金中持有的股票有 17 个是重叠的。在普通股中，最突出的是在线时代华纳、思科、美国在线、诺基亚、SPRINT、易安信、世讯自由。甚至保守运作的平衡型基金也持有相当一部分有线设备股，像康卡斯特和维亚康姆。

如此集中是杰纳斯紧随增长率的决定的不可避免的结果，但是大额资金过分重叠下注在这样多的风雨难测的高科技股上令一些分析家担忧。晨星公司的克瑞斯汀·班茨就是其中的一个，他认为，这些核心股票易于使"基金表现雷同"，结果是拥有不止一支这样的基金会增加风险，而不是提供给保守的投资者所期待的高水平的分散风险。

正如所预料的一样，当科技股到关键时刻，集中于科技股使贝雷相当脆弱。大部分的杰纳斯基金比市场整体跌得更快，像在线时代华纳和思科这样排名第一的股票下跌了 50%或更多。杰纳斯 20 在旋风般的 60 天就丧失了 20%的价值。

杰纳斯的投资组合经理们并不是没有准备的，其中 6 个人防御性地转向现金头寸，轻易地达到了资产的 17%。

虽然一些经理赞同分布在基金中许多主要股票，但是与贝雷的两支主要基金杰纳斯 20 和杰纳斯相比，你能看到他们的自主权。举例说，负责杰纳斯 20 的斯克特·叟载尔连续 3 年警告投资者"超大的回报是不能持久的。"他提高了现金头寸，但在其他方面他几乎不认为会有股市大跌的可能。他甚至把像范妮梅和沃尔玛这样的低风险标准的股票从投资组合中去掉，为了支持像 NSI 和 AETH 这样更冒险的股票，很快在高价位出手了。

策略转移的范围显示出逆境没有打消贝雷让投资组合经理们百花齐放的方针。一些经理似乎将核心股从科技股中逐渐退出，更广泛地集中到医药和能源股上。另外一些经理依然相信许多仍具有潜力的科技股是被不分好坏地一概摒弃的。他们继续坚定地买入一些突然变冷的股票，如无线电广播巨头克莱尔频道和有线巨头康卡其特。许多这样的股票的乘数迄今为止下降得很快，以至于杰纳斯几乎认为它再一次步入了合理价格增长的最佳空间。

杰纳斯保持着它积极进取的风格，尽管有出乎意料的令人不快的收益，还是继续买入，但对所承担的风险谨慎了。表面廉价的不一定便宜。关键是区分出是由于恐慌卖出造成的影响还是潜在基本因素的改变。那些胆气豪壮的实行反向策略的人也许认为以 18 的价位买入思科（从 82 的高位跌下来的）是很棒的，但是贝雷的经理们把这个公司的股票砍掉了超过 1/3——从 1.8 亿股（2.5% 为拖欠的）到不足 1 亿股。半导体制造商德州仪器、光纤设备供应商 JDS 单相公司和其他不再受宠的股票中的大部分也被抛了出去。管理杰纳斯·墨丘利基金的沃任·莱沫特对晨星公司的高级分析员说："我已经不像以前那样关注明显的收益，而是关心基本的走势。"

杰纳斯坚持自己的观点，他长期将重点放在自己研究的质量上。总体上，贝雷持有或是在熟悉的核心技术股上添加了诺基亚、通用、康卡斯特、在线时代华纳，它们在前期表现良好。现在其中一些从高位跌了 60% 甚至更多，尽管下跌得令人头晕目眩，但以沃任·莱沫特的观点，却对许多坏消息并不在意。现在这个经过筛选的组合在短期内还要承担更多的损失，但就基本理论而言，仍然有长期的成果。沃任·莱沫特说："我努力将技术股保留为核心股，我想当我们度过了很困难的经济环境之后，我们就是股市的赢家。"

继续显示出的自我反省和热烈的内部讨论比按照纯粹数据上的过去业绩作出的预示更让人放心。他们展示了杰纳斯最大的资产——它的文化——现在依然存在。因此，杰纳斯的管理者们不是作为操作高科技股的能手出现的，那是过去的辉煌。贝雷奉劝在艰难时光要不屈不挠。他说："我们将继续作我们现在做的事，在公司方面、在竞争对手方面、在供应商方面做工作。因为最终，我们所买进的是一项业务，是由人操作的活生生的事物。"

为什么汤姆·贝雷不效仿旧时的普里斯，以更为保守的策略维持他的收益呢？如果杰纳斯基金更广泛地分散风险，退回到以合理价格增长的传统战略中，它是否会表现更好呢？短期内是的。举例说，杰纳斯 20 基金比谨慎的普里斯增长型股票基金更央比销售一空。虽然贝雷的辉煌时期的一些收益已不复存在了，但是在最近 5 年（到写这篇文章为止），杰纳斯 20 基金仍然以多于 25%超过了普里斯给股东的平均回报。风险确实带来回报。

然而，杰纳斯损失的价值数量也深深提醒我们：风险和易变状态是进入进取型增长投资的代价。增长如同一扇旋转门。这是否意味着保守型的投资者应该坚守价值原则——追随于本·格雷厄姆和马蒂·惠特曼进行投资比跟着普里斯和汤姆·贝雷更安全呢？不，这只意味着两个流派在市场的不同阶段呈现出不同的风格。

Chapter Five
A Bussinessman or a Swindler?— Anthony DeAnglis

第五章
亦商亦盗? ——安东尼·安吉列斯

I. Case Study

In reach and consequences, it was the swindle of the century. The first faint intimation of havoc came in a sparse two-line statement from the New York Stock Exchange.

Gathering momentum like an avalanche the con would cost panicky investors millions in market losses; bust two old-line brokerage firms and a clutch of commodity exporters; and relieve some of the United States' smartest financial names, in current terms, of an embarrassing $2.5 billion.

Unfolding, as yet unrecognized, was a morality play full of enduring lessons for investors. Among them: markets almost always overreact and panics are almost always a buy; almost all major fraud feeds on phony assets; accountants and securities analysts almost never get it straight; greed is almost always a more disorienting drive than sex or the political itch.

The Exchange itself had no sense of the carnage to come behind the simple statement that it was auditing two member firms because a big commodities customer had run into "serious financial difficulties."

Neither the firms nor the customer was identified. For the moment it seemed only that the Exchange was dealing with an unusual but not alarming set of circumstances.

The customer unaccountably had failed to come up to scratch on margin— money borrowed against commodity futures he was trading in big volume through the firms. They, in turn, had borrowed heavily from the banks on their own to cover for him and had slipped slightly below the minimum capital they were required to keep on hand.

Taking a quick pass at the numbers, the Exchange did not see a serious enough impairment to suspend the two well-established firms, Ira Haupt & Company and J. R. Williston & Beane.

Beyond the seeming calm at the Stock Exchange, there was yet another hint of calamity. For the second successive day, soybean oil futures on the Chicago Board of Trade and cottonseed oil contracts on the New York Produce Exchange were being routed in unprecedented volume by speculators betting on a major drop in prices.

Across the Hudson River in Newark, New Jersey, there was yet another unrecognized portent. Allied Crude Vegetable Oil Refining Company, the biggest vendor of commodity oils in the U.S. Food For Peace program was filing a bankruptcy petition showing some $200 million in liabilities.

In nearby Bayonne, New Jersey, yet another mysterious strand was being teased into place. Hurriedly assigned surveyors prowled in confusion the surreal limits of the sprawling storage tank farm that was Allied Crude's headquarters.

Wayward clouds of steam from the tanks heating units drifted erratically around the surveyors and oil-saturated mud sucked at their boots as they searched for the 160 million pounds of soybean oil Bunge Corporation had asked them to make sure was in place.

Stored in four specifically designated tanks, the stuff was worth about $15 million. Bunge had been stuck with some bounced checks. Worried about the solidity of Allied Crude's finances, the exporter wanted to make doubly sure that its oil was on tap.

Making their way through a maze of undifferentiated tanks, the surveyors first reported that all was well. Ordered to take a second look, they came back with hardly credible intelligence. The calibrations now showed that only one of the Bunge tanks was full to its floating top with what appeared to be soybean oil. Two were empty and one was half full.

Pandemonium!

Where was the missing oil? Could 160 million pounds of it, in the space of four short hours, somehow been siphoned into the interconnected tanks on the now suspect Allied Crude's backlot? To move that much oil in that little time was a physical impossibility.

The uproar spread from the Bunge surveyors to employees of American Express Warehousing, a subsidiary of the American Express Company. Its task, as independent custodian of the farm, was to measure and certify the amount of oil Allied had sequestered in its own and customers' tanks.

The certification was crucial. Allied, backed by the blue-chip name, financed its own business by borrowing against warehouse receipts issued by the Amexco subsidiary. The paper was collateralized by the oil Allied held in its tanks—a long-established practice in the commodities trade. With American Express on the job as a third-party cop, the banks and exporters that had been routinely lending Allied in the tens of millions on warehouse paper had nothing to worry about. Or did they? Where was the missing Bunge oil?

What missing oil? Rasped the Amexco custodians. They had released it to Allied two days ago on signed Bunge orders.

Into the midst of this peevish dialogue at the tank farm plunged bankruptcy court-appointed attorneys also in search of oil. It was their job to nail down Allied Crude assets of any kind, and pay off creditors whose own lawyers over the next several days began to show up outside the tank farm like suppliant depositors in a 1930s bank run.

Yet another pose of lawyers was milling about in the Haupt conference room in New York. They were trying to learn why a series of Haupt checks, mounting in the millions, had bounced—dead on arrival—in the cashiers' cages of such top banks as Chase Manhattan and Morgan Guaranty. Except for the prospect that thousands of innocent investors might get hurt if Haupt or Williston went bust, the imbroglio was beginning to take on the dimensions of farce.

Lawyers were running around everywhere. As one frustrated attorney in the clamoring mob in the Haupt conference room put it, "The most difficult thing is to find anyone who knows what the problem is."

The Produce Exchange, panicked by runaway selling, offered no better insight than anyone else in the commodity trade. It peremptorily decided to shut down trading for a day. It ordered the liquidation of cottonseed oil contracts at settlement prices that added heavily to the brokerage firms' woes.

Every one had a piece of the puzzle; no one could put it together. Bunge, in hot pursuit of its missing oil, charged American Express with abdicating its custodial obligations. The missing oil, the exporter contended in a New Jersey state court, had been released to Allied on forged orders and surreptiously pumped into adjoining tanks. Bunge wasn't talking missing oil: it was talking stolen oil.

Were the warehouse subsidiary's troubles serious enough to endanger its blue-chip parent? Howard Clark, the can-do president of American Express, was off on a field trip to Bayonne. After climbing to the summit of several 42-foot-high tanks and peering through hatch covers, he talked to newsmen. He assured them that the mystery of the missing oil would soon be resolved. Of course, hedged Clark, "There's quite a lot of confusion out there, as you can imagine."

Some of the confusion was already reflected in the price of American Express stock. There was no telling what kind of liabilities the warehouse subsidiary was facing, with every likelihood the parent would have to pick up the tab. This became all too clear when American Express Warehousing filed a bankruptcy petition showing liabilities of $144 million against assets of only $363,683.

Thanks partly to Clark's field trip, the confusion at Haupt was deepening into despair. American Express, sensing deep trouble, disavowed the $18.5 million in warehouse receipts the brokerage firm was holding against loans to Allied Crude as out and out forgeries. Forgeries? Who was the forger?

Stock Exchange auditors, beginning to sense the full dimensions of the brokerage firms' troubles, suspended both Haupt and Williston for being unable to meet current obligations. It was only the second time in its long history that the Exchange had shut down a member firm for insolvency. The sense of crisis sharpened as investors who attempted to close out accounts were turned away and some banks refused to honor Haupt checks. To some, it smelled of 1929, but the circumstances could not have been more different. Profits were up, interest rates stable, and the economy moving, but psychology once again trumped reason. Ancient flawed memories of The Great Crash brought heavy selling into the market, even as the Big Board managed to get Williston & Beane back into business with a bridge loan of less than a million.

The Exchange then turned to the far more intractable issue of a rescue plan for Haupt. The Exchange was fearful that the heavy press notice stirred by the plight of Haupt's locked-in customers would continue to hang over the market and trigger a run on other member firms.

Haupt's condition was far worse than originally thought. It had gone to the banks to cover Allied Crude's unmet margin calls, and owed more than a dozen of them well over $35 million. It was on the hook for who knew how much more in apparently phony warehouse receipts. Then there was the $100 million or so in securities Haupt clients had bought on margin. These, too, in the ordinary course of business, had been pledged with banks.

The Haupt partners, young men predominantly in their 30s, their personal resources at risk, had long since run out of credit. There was no standby mechanism the Exchange could call up to get the firm out of hock. Any one of the Haupt bank creditors could push the firm into bankruptcy. This very real threat could tie up Haupt's clients for years, and make hash of the Big Board's costly promotional efforts to bring "Wall Street to Main Street."

The much-feared possibility of a run on Wall Street was hardening into reality at the Bayonne tank farm. Rumors that the amount of collateralized oil in storage fell many millions short of the warehouse receipts outstanding were sweeping the trade. Traffic jammed the narrow approach roads to the farm as representatives of creditors as far afield as Rotterdam and Zurich were in search of not just vegetable oils, but such other pledged odements as tallow and fish oil.

The lenders fared no better in getting their assets released than the beleaguered investors at Haupt. Nathan Ravin, the short, snappish chief of the bankruptcy court-appointed lawyers, was badgered by so many conflicting claims that he got a writ banning withdrawals of any kind from the farm. Nothing was going out pending yet another survey of the tanks and the warehouse receipts behind them.

The reports were not encouraging. At least two of Bunge's supposedly segregated tanks were now found to contain not soybean oil, but gasoline. Others were loaded with sludge and sea water. More confounding still, missing oil seemed to correlate with a whole series of tanks that could not be found in the confines of one of Allied's related entities, Harbor Tank Storage Company. It, too, had generated a spate of warehouse receipt.

It wasn't just missing oil and missing tanks. There was quite a lot of cash missing, too, as a read of Allied Crude's bank accounts showed. Shortages of one kind or other might mean that Wall Street and as many as 50 banks were out as much as $200 million. Allied Crude lead bankruptcy attorney Nathan Ravin kept his. He called in the FBI. Then real panic struck. It was November 22, 1963.

At 1:33 P.M. the grim news became official: "President John Kennedy died at approximately 1:00 P.M. Central Standard time today here in Dallas. He died of a gunshot wound in the brain."

What's the lesson that runs from the Allied Crude swindle market to today? Fear drives all such surges. Behavioral psychologists talk of "thought contagion," a herd instinct that propels selling (or buying) frenzies simply because others are doing so. Call it the Hula Hoop or Tulip Bulb phenomenon. The tendency is exacerbated these days by delusion spread through the instant communication of the Internet.

If you are holding some really long gains, it's probably prudent to take some money off the table from time to time.

A time of seemingly acute trouble is not a time to sell. It's often a time to buy. If the market is climbing a wall of worry—inflation, declining profits, a war scare—wait to see what happens. Better to make a rational decision than to be swept along with the crowd. Many who sold into the Kennedy-salad oil swindle break paid a sizable premium to get back into the market.

The turnaround in the market generally, as it usually does, came from a return to basics. There was also a big push from the good news that the Exchange over the weekend had worked out a plan to free up the Haupt accounts and make sure that customers would not be out of pocket. The key was an unparalleled assessment against other member firms.

The Haupt rescue did nothing to resolve the unknowns that set it in motion. Missing oil, missing storage tanks, missing money. Also conspicuously missing was the one person who might have all of the pieces to the puzzle up his sleeve—Anthony DeAngelis president and chief shareholder of Allied Crude.

High School dropout and one of an immigrant rail worker's five children, DeAngelis was very much the self-made man. In a few short years, he had become Mr. Vegetable Oil, making big money out of a strategy that put Allied Crude at the hub of a thriving export trade.

He was prospering with a major assist from the heavily subsidized U.S. Food

For Peace program Supervised by the Agriculture Department, the program provided edible oils and other commodities on the cheap to hungry nations abroad. The humanitarian aim of feeding a less favored world not coincidentally helped to keep domestic farm prices high (and farm state legislators happy) by shunting surpluses off market.

DeAngelis, whose early ventures had been in the meat and tallow trade, saw an opportunity in middleman's role—buy soybean oil and cottonseed oil from crushers in the Midwest, refine the product in the East, sell to exporters at water's edge. Logistically, the Bayonne tank farm fit DeAngelis' specifications like a glove. It had good rail, barge, and deep-water connections, and the bulk space he needed to hold processed oil for such well-established exporters as Bunge Corporation and Continental Grain Company.

Starting with $500,000 in capital, DeAngelis whipped the tank farm, long a petroleum storage area, into shape. In a major coup, he persuaded American Express Warehousing to take over as custodian. The connection enabled DeAngelis to bootstrap his thin financials by borrowing against inventory certified by Amexco and its eminently negotiable warehouse receipts. In the same way, he took on additional loans at premium rates from his pleased export clients to build the newest and most efficient refinery in the trade.

Newsmen fired those questions at DeAngelis as he finally surfaced in response to a subpoena eight harrowing days after he put Allied Crude into bankruptcy. "Why was he hiding out? Why had Allied Crude so suddenly gone down the tubes?"

DeAngelis had not come alone. Convoying him through the crowd of newsmen was the well-connected criminal lawyer Walter D. Van Riper, a former judge and State Attorney General.

Q: What is your official position with Allied Crude Vegetable Oil Refining?

A: I respectfully decline to answer because to do so would tend to incriminate me.

Elucidating the now obvious, Van Riper intoned that DeAngelis, "for now," will refuse to answer all further questions.

Newsmen probing the silent DeAngelis' background found that paying to make business scrapes go away was a way of life with him.

More serious still was a wrangle with the Securities Exchange Commission. The SEC charged that DeAngelis had understated losses in a publicly owned meatpacker he took over. Creditors subsequently forced the firm, the Adolph Gobel Company, into bankruptcy. Yet another SEC charge grew out of the Gobel case The allegation was that DeAngelis had talked a witness into recanting damaging testimony that Tino had been borrowing money against phantom lard inventories.

In the early stages, the suspicion that Tino DeAngelis might be hanging paper, too, was little heard.

Much of the background on DeAngelis was spelled out in routine credit reports, but none of the questions raised hurt him in the trade. Business is business. DeAngelis was selling oil at sharply competitive prices. With only rare protest, he paid high interest rates on the increasing amount of borrowed money piggybacking into Allied Crude on warehouse receipts.

Though very much the rising tycoon, Tino was not for the high life. "I've had only one ambition in life, success," he said in his grandiloquent way. "Even as a kid, work came first. I partook very little of the gay life." On rare occasions DeAngelis could be spotted in an out-of-the-way saloon in Greenwich Village, quietly watching television with his companion, Lillian Pascarelli, the smartly turned out divorceé who was on the Allied Crude payroll as a "social hostess."

DeAngelis had anted the $40,000 down payment on the roomy Pascarelli home in suburban Tenafly, New Jersey, a few miles from the George Washington Bridge, on the pleasingly green reverse slope of the Palisades.

Tino's estranged wife lived in Tenafly, too, not far from the others in Tino's set. They included Leo Bracconeri, Tino's brother-in-law and Allied's plant manager; Ben Rotello, Allied's controller; and George Bitter, one of Allied's chief commodity traders. Foreign buyers were sometimes entertained at the Pascarelli home, and in summer the Allied Crude crowd enjoyed one another's company at backyard barbecues.

DeAngelis' suburban cronies were the nucleus of a tight-knit group of 20 or so that kept the Bayonne plant humming. There were a number of DeAngelis cousins on the payroll, all in a family circle where Tino often rewarded good work with handsome cash bonuses and the occasional gift of a Cadillac.

In a quickie second appearance in bankruptcy court, DeAngelis again took the Fifth. Attorney Walter Van Riper argued his client had no alternative, considering the volume of press coverage "alleging gross improprieties on his part."

Hailed before a federal judge on a contempt charge, DeAngelis altered his strategy. He agreed to answer more than 40 of the 60 questions he had finessed in bankruptcy court, with the proviso that the federal court would rule question-by-question on any other queries he chose not to answer.

Back to the bankruptcy court, then, where DeAngelis continued to obfuscate, well aware that he was now also the target of a federal grand jury investigation.

Two days before Christmas, the grand jury charged DeAngelis with 18 counts of moving $39.4 million in forged warehouse receipts in interstate commerce Theoretical maximum penalty: 180 years in jail and a $180,000 fine.

Courthouse buffs were betting that more indictments were in the works.

However noncommunicative in court, DeAngelis was now on a first name basis with the gaggle of reporters following in his wake. "Powerful forces have teamed with the federal government to put the little fellow out of business," Tino told at one impromptu press conference. All he had tried to do was expand the export trade so soybean growers "could get another 25¢ a bushel and the powerful interests didn't like it."

Like the chimes of the Jersey City church and the Jewish Home for the Aged, the farmers of the Midwest were suddenly part of the DeAngelis benefice. Tino's canonical mood was shattered by the equally sudden invocation of an obscure scrap of New Jersey law. Rarely invoked, it provides that defendants in a civil suit can be made to post bonds equal to the damages sought, or go to jail.

This arcane threat of debtors prison was draped over the now visibly troubled DeAngelis by Joseph M. Nolan, bankruptcy trustee for yet another of the Bayonne causalities, Harbor Tank Storage Company.

The one-time treasury agent's brief, field in a state court in Jersey City, succeeded in getting what none of the hundreds of other lawyers working on the cases had seemed possible—a warrant for DeAngelis' arrest.

Nolan's complaint: DeAngelis had hatched a "devious, complicated, and sinister plan" that resulted in Harbor Tank Storage floating $46.5 million in phony warehouse receipts. DeAngelis had been aided by a crony, Joseph Lomuscio, the Harbor Tank Storage custodian.

It was getting on dinner time of a Friday evening when Judge Robert A. Matthews called a temporary halt. He rescheduled the hearing for Monday morning and set interim bail of $150,000 for DeAngelis ($100,000 for Lomuscio). Then came the real sting: Both men would have to testify before the judge would fix permanent bail.

The ruling threatened to put a crimp in Tino's Fifth Amendment defense, and to throw embarrassing light on the state of his finances. If Tino could afford the $6,000 a weekend worth bail would cost, he would be playing into the general suspicion that plenty of coconuts were stashed away some place. For the moment, Tino had run out of options. He chose to weekend in the Hudson County jail .

DeAngelis came back into court Monday morning with his customary air of aggrieved innocence and a list. Ticking off the numbers with one of his ever handy pens, DeAngelis testified that he was $27 million in hock. Most of the liabilities were personal guarantees against Allied Crude debt. On the asset side, he could count only $140,000—mainly in loans due from Allied Crude's in-group. All told, DeAngelis poor-mouthed his liquid assets to less than $5,000, including "maybe six or seven suits."

This woebegone tale was catnip to the waiting Nolan, who had been feeding on DeAngelis personal bank statements. What about the $8,800 check drawn to Thomas Clarkin, one of Allied's messengers?

Tino rambled on with a story of yet another benefaction. Clarkin, he testified, was a long-time Allied employee, working two jobs to buy a home. Tino was touched by Clarkin's industriousness. "To the best of my knowledge, I gave him funds to put a down payment on or buy a home. I believe I gave it to him, not expecting to get it back."

An incredulous Nolan pursued DeAngelis when he subsequently changed his testimony to say the $8,800 had, in fact been paid back. Yes, there was also a $3,000 check made out to his codefendant Joseph Lomuscio, but DeAngelis couldn't remember why.

The level of transparency got no better when Nolan brought up the $63,500 that had come out of DeAngelis' account in checks payable to cash. The questions cracked like pistol fire: Why didn't you pay these people by check? Why would you take out $10,000 in cash and pay these obligations? You gave people cash, didn't you? And you can't remember who you gave it to?

Then Tino went on the offensive. He succeeded in getting an order that enabled him to reassign his assets from the custody of the bankruptcy court to Judge Matthews' Superior Court. That satisfied the judge. The bail Joseph Nolan was demanding had been mooted because "Mr. DeAngelis has in effect pauperized himself."

With several different sets of investigators tripping over one another in the effort to crack the mystery of missing assets, the initiative was still very much with DeAngelis. He showed that when he let the Allied bankruptcy trustee in on a little secret. There was, Tino just remembered, some $500,000 of Allied Crude money tucked away in a numbered account in the Union Bank of Switzerland. In the rush to get the Allied bankruptcy petition filed, said Tino, he'd forgotten totally about the cach in Geneva.

The voluntary disclosure of the Swiss accounts, however tardy, was yet another sign of his good faith, argued DeAngelis. "No one ever got a single penny. I would never allow anyone to take a penny," he said grandly.

Nolan demanded that DeAngelis be cited for criminal contempt. It was an open and shut case, he argued. Less than a month ago in this very court DeAngelis had denied under oath having a foreign bank account. And now this $500,000 providentially arrived in bankruptcy court from Geneva. What more needed to be said?

DeAngelis pleaded that life was too short for him ever to lie. He'd told the truth —literally. It wasn't his account. Never had been. The money belonged to Allied.

Judge Matthews wasn't buying, "My conclusion is that when asked about his personal assets, DeAngelis lied to this court," said the judge, and sentenced Tino to four months in jail. Out on $10,000 bail, DeAngelis appealed—and won. There was "no incontrovertible evidence" DeAngelis lied, ruled a three-judge appellate bench. Further, since he'd helped expedite repatriation of the money, DeAngelis could not be charged with obstructing justice.

More vexing still, there was no definitive explanation of the two critical elements—missing oil and supposedly forged warehouse receipts. The federal grand jury had come down with a second indictment, but with no proof showing other than an assertion that DeAngelis had circulated $100 million in phony American Express Warehouse receipts.

Tino was busily cultivating pals in the Ministry of Supply, and finally came up with a real showstopper—a huge contract for 275 million pounds of soybean oil worth around $36.5 million.

This was big money for Allied. DeAngelis did not have in storage anything like the amount of oil he needed to cover the contract. In standard business practice, he went into the futures market to nail down his supply.

Then came the body blow. The Spaniards abruptly cancelled, with no explanation. DeAngelis knew why. His American competitors, the Midwest crushers, had got to Opus Dei, the conservative Catholic faction with a lot of clout in the upper reaches of government.

DeAngelis gave the bankruptcy court a long tale of how he had been jobbed. Here he was "a man who had come up the hard way, without any lobby, without any politics, without any help." The crushers wanted him out of the way so they could grab the businesses for themselves.

Conniving through the shadowy mechanism of Opus Dei, they succeeded in pushing allied out of the running. Blustering, DeAngelis told the court that if "somebody sabotages you, you either have one thing to do or the other—fight, or throw in the towel."

Instead of unwinding his commitments in the futures market at some reasonably sustainable loss, DeAngelis elected to fight. He hung onto his contracts, running the risk that he might have to swallow delivery on as much as $20 million worth of soybean oil, with no big buyers in sight.

DeAngelis took the gamble. He bought ever more deeply into the futures market.

Much of the trading was funneled through dummy accounts, many of them opened in the names of Tino's tank farm operatives. One member of the network was a poultryman whose account was run under the name of his chicken farm. The terms were standard—an even split on profits; Allied Crude to swallow the losses.

The sweetheart deals were a sign of how hard DeAngelis had to work to keep prices up. The Agriculture Department export estimates he had been banking on proved grossly optimistic. DeAngelis kept rolling over futures at increasing losses, gambling that a couple of big deals would come along to bail him out.

Allied was now generating as much as 90 percent of the cottonseed oil buying on the Produce Exchange, and probably 50 percent of the volume in soybean oil on the much broader Board of Trade. The scale of Tino's action drew only modest regulatory response. The Board of Trade slapped him on the wrist with a 30-day suspension for fictitious trades, and the Agriculture Department made a warning pass at some of his dummy accounts.

DeAngelis' buying was reaching manic proportions, but who was going to quarrel with prosperity? DeAngelis was booking more than $100,000 a month in commissions with Produce Exchange brokers alone. Market manipulation? No way. It didn't take a genius to see that export markets were going to boom again.

The brokerage looked especially good to the young, aggressive partners—new names—who had just come into Ira Haupt & Company. Older heads at the firm first vetoed DeAngelis as a client because of his checkered past.

DeAngelis swept away the last of the reservations at Haupt by leading a tour of the Bayonne plant. It was the most efficient processor in the business, he bragged, run 24 hours around the clock, with only seven or eight men per shift.

Haupt did not learn that many of these $400-a-week shift workers were the dummy names fronting for some of the trading accounts the firm was so eager to land.

The expansion-minded partners at Haupt saw only opportunity and eagerly took on a $30 million sheaf of warehouse receipts. They were immediately pledged with big-name lenders like the Continental Illinois National Bank & Trust Company. Haupt itself was now holding for DeAngelis futures contracts with a value of more than $100 million—a huge potential burden if the market broke.

A drop of just a penny a pound in soybean oil would mean margin calls of some $13 million. DeAngelis had one slim hope going for him: rumors that Russia was on the brink of a big buy.

The design was simple: All he had to do was keep Amexco convinced he had more than enough oil to cover the receipts it was cranking out.

Many of Amexco's assistant custodians were hired right off Tino's payroll when Amexco's warehouse company took over the Allied account. The head custodian was buddy-buddy with Michael DeAngelis, one of Tino's many cousins, and shared an office with him. The custodian's chief assistant was a brother-in-law of Tino's secretary, and so it went—one big happy family at work and play on both sides of the custodial fence.

On inventory Fridays, Allied and Amexco workers deployed in two-man teams. The Allied member called off liquid measurements from the top of the tanks; remarkably uninquisitive Amexco workers jotted down the numbers. "They never checked on any of us who was gauging," testified one Allied hand. If the Amexco teams knew they were taking down phony numbers, "they kept it to themselves."

Sea water-loaded tanks were topped with a layer of oil.

He pleaded guilty to a conspiracy charge and bargained from eighteen to three the charges of circulating forged warehouse receipts he had been indicted on. The plea cut the maximum jail time he might face from 135 years to 35 years and a $35,000 fine.

DeAngelis came before Federal Judge Reynier D. Wortendyke for sentencing. Wortendyke sentenced him provisionally to 10 years, pending deeper psychological study of his motives at the Lewisburg, Pennsylvania federal penitentiary.

Expecting no more than the provisional 10 years he had been handed initially, DeAngelis was jolted when Wortendyke upped the ante to 20 year—10 years consecutively on two warehouse receipts charges, to run concurrently with the other two charges he had pleaded to.

Why the stiff double in the sentence? Had the shrinks brought to the judge's attention something darker in the DeAngelis psyche than mere entrepreneurial waywardness? In fact, a certain amount of judicial confusion had creeped into the proceedings. Under the little used law he had invoked, the judge had to sentence DeAngelis to a minimum of 10 years to get the psychological study he wanted done. But 20 it was, making DeAngelis eligible for parole in six years and eight months "I don't want DeAngelis loose on society in less than six years," Wortendyke told a reporter. "He might get into another scrape."

The recidivism should have surprised no one who had ever heard of Philip Musica or Billie Sol Estes. DeAngelis was running true to type. The itch to succeed never lets up. DeAngelis wasn't much of a businessman, and in the end, not much of a swindler either.

Key Words and Expressions:

bank run	银行挤兑
board of trade	同业公会，经济部
bounced check	空头支票
brokerage	n. 经纪人之业务，回扣
Chicago Board of Trade.	芝加哥交易所
collateralize	v. 以……作抵押
commodity futures	期货交易
Commodities Futures Exchange	商品期货交易所

criminal contempt	n. [律] 严重之藐视法庭行为
come up the hard way	通过艰苦努力而达到目前的地位
creditor	n. 债权人
credit report	信用报告
custodian	n. 管理人
down payment	预付定金
due from	应收
Futures Exchange	期货交易所
futures trading	期货交易
field trip	n.（学生）实地考察旅行
fifth amendment	[法] 第五条修正案
hatch cover	装货仓盖
hang paper	[美俚] 假造支票
heavy selling	抛售
insolvency	n. 无力偿还，破产
liquidation	n.清算
locked-in	牢固的，不上市证券的
member firm	美国证券交易所的成员行号
New York Produce Exchange	纽约物品交易所
on margin	凭保证金额购买证券
on tap	可随时使用
pandemonium	n. 喧嚣；大混乱；大吵大闹
pick up the tab	替人付账
produce exchange	物产交易所
settlement price	结算价
sequester	adv. 幽静的，隐蔽的
	vt. 使隐退, 使隔绝, 扣押, 没收
speculator	n. 投机者
standby	n. 可以信任的人，使船待命的信息，备用
in hock	在典当中，在坐牢，负债
inventory	n. 详细目录，存货，财产清册，总量
liquidate	v. 清算
ministry of supply	陆军供应部

numbered account	账号
obligations	n. 待付款
personal guarantee	个人担保
piggybacking	n. 载搭，捎带，指借助别人的道路进入的行为
premium	n. 额外费用，奖金，奖赏，保险费
premium rate	n. 保险费率
proviso	n. 限制性条款，附文，附带条件

Notes:

1. New York Stock Exchange—NYSE 纽约证券/股票交易所

纽约证券交易所是美国和世界上最大的证券交易市场。1792 年 5 月 17 日，24 个从事股票交易的经纪人在华尔街一棵树下集会，宣告了纽约股票交易所的诞生。1863 年改为现名，直到 1865 年交易所才拥有自己的大楼。坐落在纽约市华尔街 11 号的大楼是 1903 年启用的。交易所内设有主厅、蓝厅、"车房"等 3 个股票交易厅和 1 个债券交易厅，是证券经纪人聚集和互相交易的场所，共设有 16 个交易亭，每个交易亭有 16～20 个交易柜台，均装备有现代化办公设备和通讯设施。交易所经营对象主要为股票，其次为各种国内外债券。除节假日外，交易时间每周 5 天，每天 5 小时。自 20 世纪 20 年代起，它一直是国际金融中心，这里股票行市的暴涨与暴跌，都会在其他资本主义国家的股票市场产生连锁反应，引起波动。现在它还是纽约市最受欢迎的旅游名胜之一。

2. Chicago Board of Trade 芝加哥交易所

芝加哥商业交易所与芝加哥期货交易所分别创立于 1898 年和 1848 年，早期均从事与农产品相关的期货交易。出于地理上的便利条件，双方的合并计划早在上世纪七十年代中期就开始酝酿，其间共经历了 30 多年。合并的努力至少有三次，但均以失败告终。

据当事者回忆，合并道路之所以困难重重，主要由于双方企业文化之间的巨大差异，企业未上市前定价困难，以及历史留存的不信任因素。

至九十年代末期，芝加哥商业交易所抓住了电子交易时代对金融衍生商品交易的巨大需求这一良机，在短短的几年内，交易量连续超越纽约和伦敦，成为全球最大的金融衍生商品交易市场。2002 年 12 月，商业交易所公开发行股票上市，而期货交易所也在 2005 年 10 月上市。上市为两家交易所顺利合并奠定了基础。

3. New York Produce Exchange　纽约商品交易所

纽约商品交易所（COMEX）地处纽约曼哈顿金融中心，与纽约证券交易所相邻。它的交易主要涉及能源和稀有金属两大类产品，但能源产品交易大大超过其他产品的交易。交易所的交易方式主要是期货和期权交易，到目前为止，期货交易量远远超过期权交易量。

2003 年，纽约商品交易所能源期货合同交易量超过 8,700 万手，日均交易量超过 35 万手。在所有能源期货合同中，原油、天然气、汽油和取暖油四类产品的比重超过 98％。

4. bounced check　空头支票

空头支票是指支票持有人请求付款时，出票人在付款人处实有的存款不足以支付票据金额的支票。

票据法规定，支票出票人所签发的支票金额不得超过其在付款人处实有的存款金额，即不得签发空头支票，这就要求出票人自出票日起至支付完毕止，保证其在付款人处的存款账户中有足以支付支票金额的资金。对签发空头支票骗取财物的，要依法追究刑事责任。如果签发空头支票骗取财物的行为情节轻微，不构成犯罪，票据法规定要依照国家有关规定给予行政处罚。

5. Chase Manhattan Bank　大通曼哈顿银行

一般简称为大通银行。也有被称为蔡斯曼哈顿银行的说法。美国金融业巨头之一，大型商业银行。既是大通曼哈顿（持股）公司（Chase Manhattan Corp.，1969 年建立）的主要企业，又是洛克菲勒财团的金融中心。大通银行成立于 1799 年。1955 年由大通银行和曼哈顿银行公司合并而成。总部位于纽约。1972 年在莫斯科开设银行业务办事处（这是 1920 年后在前苏联设立分支机构的第一家美国银行）。1980 年 11 月 24 日在北京设立代表处。

大通曼哈顿银行在石油、金属、矿产、电子和农业部门有较大利益。一贯注重国际业务，在西欧和亚非拉地区有大量资本输出，不断向国外扩张势力。60 年代曾大力向拉丁美洲和欧洲发展业务，收买巴西、委内瑞拉、荷兰、洪都拉斯、比利时、爱尔兰等国银行的股份；70 年代同加拿大皇家银行、联邦德国地方储蓄银行、英国国民威斯敏斯特银行、日本三菱银行、意大利信贷银行组织了一个国际财团，共同经营国际银行业务，对各国政府和私营公司发放贷款。

6. Bridge Loan　过桥贷款

过桥贷款又称搭桥贷款，是一种过渡性的贷款，通常是指中介公司在安排中长期融资前，为其服务公司的正常运营而提供所需资金的短期融资。在国内，多应用于券商担保项下的预上市公司或上市公司流动资金贷款以及企业兼并、重组中的短期贷款等。

7. The Fifth Amendment 美国宪法第五修正案

美国宪法第五修正案规定，政府不得强迫当事人作不利于自己的证词，即任何人不得被迫自证其罪。

8. bank run 银行挤兑

银行挤兑指大量银行客户在同一时间要求提取银行存款，而银行的储备不足以应付提款。

9. settlement price 当日结算价

当日结算价是指某一期货合约最后一小时成交量的加权平均价。最后一小时无成交且价格在涨/跌停板上的，取停板价格作为当日结算价。最后一小时无成交且价格不在涨/跌停板上的，取前一小时成交量加权平均价。该时段仍无成交的，则再往前推一小时，以此类推。交易时间不足一小时的，则取全时段成交量加权平均价。

10. future exchange 期货交易

期货交易是一种集中交易标准化远期合约的交易形式。即交易双方在期货交易所通过买卖期货合约并根据合约规定的条款约定在未来某一特定时间和地点，以某一特定价格买卖某一特定数量和质量的商品的交易行为。期货交易的最终目的并不是商品所有权的转移，而是通过买卖期货合约，回避现货价格风险。

期货交易与现货交易相比，有以下几个重要特征：（1）期货合约是由交易所制定的、在期货交易所内进行交易的合约。（2）期货合约是标准化的合约。合约中的各项条款，如商品数量、商品质量、保证金比率、交割地点以及交易方式等都是标准化的，合约中只有价格一项是通过市场竞价交易形成的自由价格。（3）实物交割率低。期货合约的了结并不一定必须履行实际交货的义务，买卖期货合约者在规定的交割日期前任何时候都可以通过数量相同、方向相反的交易将持有的合约相互抵消，无需再履行实际交货的义务。因此，期货交易中实物交割量占交易量的比重很小，一般小于5%。（4）期货交易实行保证金制度。交易者不需付出与合约金额数量相等的全额货款，只需付3%～15%的履约保证金。（5）期货交易所为交易双方提供结算交割业务和履约担保，实行严格的结算交割制度，违约的风险很小。

II. Knowledge Points

1. Margin

1) Definition and theory

An amount in money, or represented by securities, deposited by a customer with a broker as a provision against loss on transactions made on account.

In finance, a margin is collateral that the holder of a position in securities, options, or futures contracts has to deposit to cover the credit risk of his counterparty. This risk can arise if the holder has done any of the following:

i. borrowed cash from the counterparty to buy securities or options,

ii. sold securities or options short, or

iii. entered into a futures contract.

The collateral can be in the form of cash or securities, and it is deposited in a margin account. On U.S. futures exchanges, margin is formally called performance bond.

2) Margin buying

Margin buying is buying securities with some of one's own cash together with cash borrowed from a broker. This has the effect of magnifying any profit or loss made on the securities. The securities serve as collateral for the loan. The net value, i.e. the difference between the value of the securities and the loan, is initially equal to the own cash used. This difference has to stay above a minimum margin requirement. This is to protect the broker against a fall in the value of the securities to the point that they no longer cover the loan.

In the 1920s, margin requirements were loose. In other words, brokers required investors to put in very little of their own money. When stock markets plummeted, the net value of the positions rapidly fell below the minimum margin requirements, forcing investors to sell their positions. This was one important factor contributing to the Stock Market Crash of 1929, which in turn contributed to the Great Depression.

3) Types of margin requirements

Current liquidating margin

The current liquidating margin is the value of a securities position if the position would be liquidated now. In other words, if the holder has a short position, this is the money needed to buy back, if he is long it is the money he can raise by selling it.

Variation margin

The variation margin or maintenance margin is not collateral, but a daily offsetting of profits and losses. Futures are marked-to-market every day, so the current price is compared to the previous day's price. The profit or loss on the day of a position is then paid to or debited from the holder by the futures exchange. This is possible, because the exchange is the central counterparty to all contracts, and the number of long contracts equals the number of short contracts. Certain other exchange traded derivatives, such as options on futures contracts, are marked-to-market in the same way.

Premium margin

The seller of an option has the obligation to deliver the underlying of the option if it is exercised. To ensure he can fulfil this obligation, he has to deposit collateral. This premium margin is equal to the premium that he would need to pay to buy back the option and close out his position.

Additional margin is intended to cover a potential fall in the value of the position on the following trading day. This is calculated as the potential loss in a worst-case scenario.

Minimum margin requirement

The minimum margin requirement is now the sum of these different types of margin requirements. The margin (collateral) deposited in the margin account has to be at least equal to this minimum. If the investor has many positions with the exchange, these margin requirements can simply be netted.

Example 1

An investor sells a call option, where the buyer has the right to buy 100 shares in Universal Widgets S.A. at 90¢. He receives an option premium of 14¢. The value of the option is 14¢, so this is the premium margin. The exchange has calculated, using historical prices, that the option value won't go above 17¢ the next day, with 99% certainty. Therefore, the additional margin requirement is set at 3¢, and the investor has to post at least 14¢ + 3¢ = 17¢ in his margin account as collateral.

Example 2

Futures contracts on sweet crude oil closed the day at $65. The exchange sets the additional margin requirement at $2, which the holder of a long position pays as collateral in his margin account. A day later, the futures close at $66. The exchange now pays the profit of $1 in the mark-to-market to the holder. The margin account still holds only the $2.

Example 3

An investor is long 50 shares in Universal Widgets Ltd, trading at 120 pence (£1.20) each. The broker sets an additional margin requirement of 20 pence per share, so £10 for the total position. The current liquidating margin is currently £60 in favour of the investor. The minimum margin requirement is now -(!)£60 + £10 = -£50. In other words, the investor can run a deficit of £50 in his margin account and still fulfil his margin obligations. This is the same as saying he can borrow up to £50 from the broker.

4) Margin call

When the margin posted in the margin account is below the minimum margin requirement, the broker or exchange issues a margin call. The investor now either has to increase the margin that he has deposited, or he can close out his position. He can do this by selling the securities, options or futures if he is long and by buying them back if he is short.

5) Margin-equity ratio

Margin-equity ratio is a term used by speculators, representing the amount of their trading capital that is being held as margin at any particular time. Traders would rarely (and unadvisedly) hold 100% of their capital as margin. The probability of losing their entire capital at some point would be high. By contrast, if the margin-equity ratio is so low as to make the trader's capital equal to the value of the futures contract itself, then they would not profit from the inherent leverage implicit in futures trading. A conservative trader might hold a margin-equity ratio of 15%, while a more aggressive trader might hold 40%.

6) Return on margin

Return on margin (ROM) is often used to judge performance because it represents the net gain or net loss compared to the exchange's perceived risk as reflected in required margin. ROM may be calculated (realized return) / (initial margin). The annualized ROM is equal to

(ROM + 1)(year/trade_duration) − 1

For example if a trader earns 10% on margin in two months, that would be about 77% annualized.

Sometimes, Return on Margin will also take into account peripheral charges such as brokerage fees and interest paid on the sum borrowed.

2. Locked in

Definition and theory

When an investor is unable to take advantage of preferential tax treatment because of time remaining on a required holding period. Also, a commodities position in which the market has a limit up or limit down day and investors are unable to move into or out of the market.

3. Warehouse Receipt

1) Definition and theory

A receipt used in futures markets to guarantee the quantity and quality of a particular commodity being stored within an approved facility.

Rather than delivering the actual commodity, warehouse receipts are used to settle expiring futures contracts. Also referred to as a vault receipt, they are most often used when settling futures contracts that have precious metals as their underlying commodities.

2) History

Warehouse receipts became a very successful form of representative money in ancient Egypt during the reign of the Ptolemies around 330 BC. Farmers deposited their surplus food grains for safe-keeping in royal or private warehouses and received in exchange written receipts for specific quantities of grain. The receipts were backed and redeemable for a usable commodity. Being much easier to carry, store and exchange than bags of grain, they were accepted in trade as a secure and more convenient form of payment, acting as a symbolic substitute for the quantities of food grain they represented. The warehouse receipt itself had no inherent value. It was only a symbol for something of value.

The invention of representative money had profound effect on the evolution of both money and society. It directly led to the creation of a new social organization, banking. The network of royal and private banks that were created during the reign of the Ptolemies constituted a national grain or giro-banking system. Grains were deposited in "banks" for safekeeping. Warehouse receipts were accepted as form of symbol money because they were fully "backed" by the grains in the warehouse.

More important but less obvious, the introduction of banking by the pharaohs made possible the creation of money. Until then new money could be grown as a crop, raised as an animal or discovered as metal in the earth. Now it could simply be created by writing a warehouse receipt. At first these receipts were issued only when additional grain was deposited and cancelled whenever the grain was withdrawn from the warehouse. But it required only a small step in imagination for the bankers to realize that they could also create new grain receipts on other occasions. If someone applied to the bank for financial assistance, the bank need not provide it in the form of grain. It could simply create and give to the borrower a new warehouse receipt that was indistinguishable from those issued when grain was deposited. Although the new receipts were not backed by addition deposits of grain, they were still backed by the total value of grain on deposit at the warehouse and, therefore, readily accepted in the market as a medium of exchange, so long as the public had trust and confidence in the overall financial strength of the grain bank.

This stage marks a crucial transition from money as a thing to money as a symbol of trust. In the case of commodity money, trust was placed in the inherent value of the metal or grain which constituted the form of payment. In the case of the warehouse receipt, trust was extended from the commodity to the social organization that held the grain and issued the receipts. This shift required a psychological willingness on the part of the individual to accept a symbol in place of a physical object and a social willingness on the part of the collective to evolve organizations and systems of account that could gain and hold the public trust. The invention of a new social organization was based on emergence of a new consciousness in society.

These ancient girobanks went even further. They introduced standardized accounting methods and bank accounts for their depositors. Deposits could be recorded as numerical entries in their books of account. Large transfers of money from one account holder to another could be done without even exchanging warehouse receipts, simply by changing the account balances in the bank's record books. The number in the record book became a symbolic form of representative money, an ancient forerunner of modern electronic forms of money.

4. Piggybacking

1) Definition and theory

A broker who is trading stocks, bonds or commodities in a personal account following a trade just made for a customer. The broker assumes that the customer is making the trade on valuable inside information.

A seasoned trade line (also called Piggybacking) is a method of allowing strangers with bad credit to become authorized users on a credit card account of someone with good credit, for a fee. (Disambiguation: Mortgage lenders may refer to seasoned trade lines as well, but this means lines of credit which the borrower has had for a long period of time—usually at least 2 years—to indicate that the potential borrower is credtworthy by consistantly paying bills on time, and is different than "piggybacking").

The benefit to the person with bad credit that they now have an account with excellent credit history listed on their credit report, thus raising their credit score. This may cost from $500 to $2,000 depending on the credit history of the new account.

The person with the good credit receives from $100 to $150 for this, with the rest of the money going to the middleman.

The risk to the "donor" is that the other person may actually charge the credit card account, and not pay it back. The brokers who provide the service claim that they never provide the entire account number to the recipient, however they may find it out anyway because this number may appear on some credit reports.

2) Legality

FTC spokesman Frank Dorman said: "What I've gathered from attorneys here is that it appears to be legal technically, however, the agency is not saying that it is legal."

However the practice can be fraudulent if, as required by the contract, a borrower does not disclose pertinent facts relating to his ability to pay back a loan.

3) Industry effects

Fair Isaac creator of the widely used FICO score has announced that they will no longer take into account Authorized Users in determining a credit score.

This will stop the practice of seasoned trade lines, but it will negatively affect students who use their parents cards and spouses with little credit history of their own.

Because of the Fair Credit Reporting Act and privacy laws there is no way for a lender to be able to tell who the other party of an authorized account is, and thus no way to distinguish legitimate use from fraud.

5. Herd instinct

1) Definition and theory

Some investors buy shares when they see hectic buying in the market by other investors, i.e., chasing the price of the stock up.

Psychological and economic research has identified herd behavior in humans to explain the phenomena of large numbers of people acting in the same way at the same time. The British surgeon Wilfred Trotter popularized the "herd behavior" phrase in his book, Instincts of the Herd in Peace and War (1914). In The Theory of the Leisure Class, Thorstein Veblen explained economic behavior in terms of social influences such as "emulation," where some members of a group mimic other members of higher status. In "The Metropolis and Mental Life" (1903), early sociologist George Simmel referred to the "impulse to sociability in man," and sought to describe "the forms of association by which a mere sum of separate individuals are made into a 'society.'" Other social scientists explored behaviors related to herding, such as Freud (crowd psychology), Carl Jung (collective unconscious), and Gustave Le Bon (the popular mind).

2) Stock market bubbles

Large stock market trends often begin and end with periods of frenzied buying (bubbles) or selling (crashes). Many observers cite these episodes as clear examples of herding behavior that is irrational and driven by emotion—greed in the bubbles, fear in the crashes. Individual investors join the crowd of others in a rush to get in or out of the market.

Some followers of the technical analysis school of investing see the herding behavior of investors as an example of extreme market sentiment. The academic study of behavioral finance has identified herding in the collective irrationality of investors, particularly the work of Robert Shiller, and Nobel laureates Vernon Smith, Amos Tversky, and Daniel Kahneman.

6. Inventory

1) Definition and theory

Inventory can be either raw materials, finished items already available for sale, or goods in the process of being manufactured. Inventory is recorded as an asset on a company's balance sheet.

High inventory isn't a good sign because there is a cost associated with storing the extra inventory.

Inventory is a list of goods and materials, or those goods and materials themselves, held available in stock by a business. Inventory are held in order to manage and hide from the customer the fact that manufacture/supply delay is longer than delivery delay, and also to ease the effect of imperfections in the manufacturing process that lower production efficiencies if production capacity stands idle for lack of materials.

2) Business inventory

The reasons for keeping stock.

All these stock reasons can apply to any owner or product stage.

Buffer stock is held in individual workstations against the possibility that the upstream workstation may be a little delayed in providing the next item for processing. Whilst some processes carry very large buffer stocks, Toyota moved to one (or a few items) and has now moved to eliminate this stock type.

Safety stock is held against process or machine failure in the hope/belief that the failure can be repaired before the stock runs out. This type of stock can be eliminated by programmes like Total Productive Maintenance.

Overproduction is held because the forecast and the actual sales did not match. Making to order and JIT eliminates this stock type. .

Lot delay stock is held because a part of the process is designed to work on a batch basis whilst only processing items individually. Therefore each item of the lot must wait for the whole lot to be processed before moving to the next workstation. This can be eliminated by single piece working or a lot size of one.

Demand fluctuation stock is held where production capacity is unable to flex with demand. Therefore a stock is built in times of lower utilisation to be supplied to customers when demand exceeds production capacity. This can be eliminated by increasing the flexibility and capacity of a production line or reduced by moving to item level load balancing.

Line balance stock is held because different sub-processes in a line work at different rates. Therefore stock will accumulate after a fast sub-process or before a large lot size sub-process. Line balancing will eliminate this stock type.

Changeover stock is held after a sub-process that has a long setup or change-over time. This stock is then used while that change-over is happening. This stock can be eliminated by tools like SMED.

These classifications apply along the whole supply chain not just within a facility or plant.

Where these stocks contain the same or similar items it is often the work practise to hold all these stocks mixed together before or after the sub-process to which they relate. This "reduces" costs. Because they are mixed-up together there is no visual reminder to operators of the adjacent sub-processes or line management of the stock which is due to a particular cause and should be a particular individual's responsibility with inevitable consequences. Some plants have centralised stock holding across sub-processes which makes the situation even more acute.

3) Special terms used in dealing with inventory

Stock Keeping Unit (SKU) is a unique combination of all the components that are assembled into the purchasable item. Therefore any change in the packaging or product is a new SKU. This level of detailed specification assists in managing inventory.

Stockout means running out of the inventory of an SKU.

"New old stock" (sometimes abbreviated NOS) is a term used in business to refer to merchandise being offered for sale which was manufactured long ago but that has never been used. Such merchandise may not be produced any more, and the new old stock may represent the only market source of a particular item at the present time.

4) The basis of inventory accounting

Inventory needs to be accounted where it is held across accounting period boundaries since generally expenses should be matched against the results of that expense within the same period. When processes were simple and short then inventories were small but with more complex processes then inventories became larger and significant valued items on the balance sheet. This need to value unsold and incomplete goods has driven many new behaviours into management practise. Perhaps most significant of these are the complexities of fixed cost recovery, transfer pricing, and the separation of direct from indirect costs. This, supposedly, precluded "anticipating income" or "declaring dividends out of capital". It is one of the intangible benefits of Lean and the TPS that process times shorten and stock levels decline to the point where the importance of this activity is hugely reduced and therefore effort, especially managerial, to achieve it can be minimised.

7. Premium rate

Definition and theory

The premium rate is calculated by multiplying the current interest rate on the loan with the appropriate factor from the "Premiums on Prepayment" schedule in the Loan Agreement. The premium rate so computed is then applied to the appropriate maturity to arrive at the prepayment premium for that maturity. Premia computed for all maturities being prepaid are added together to arrive at the prepayment premium for the loan.

III. Analyzing the Case

1. What is the lesson that runs from the Allied Crude swindle market to today?

Fear drives all such surges. Behavioral psychologist's talk of "thought contagion," a herd instinct that propels selling (or buying) frenzies simply because others are doing so. The tendency is exacerbated these days by delusion spread through the instant communication of the internet.

If you are holding some really long gains, it's probably prudent to take some money off the table.

A time of seemingly acute trouble is not a time to sell. It is a time to buy.

2. Starting with $ 500,000, how can TINO make Bayonne a success?

Starting with $ 500,000, DeAngelis whipped the tank farm, long a petroleum storage area into shape. In a major coup, he persuaded American Express Warehousing to take over as custodian. The connection enabled DeAngelis to bootstrap his thin financials by borrowing against inventory certified by Amexco and its eminently negotiable warehouse receipts. In the same way, he took on additional loans at premium rates from his pleased exported clients to build the newest and most efficient refinery in the trade.

3. What kept the Bayonne plant humming?

DeAngelis suburban cronies were the nucleus of a tight-knit group of 20 or so that kept the plant humming. There were a number of DeAngelis Cousins on the payroll, all in a family circle where Tino often rewarded good work with handsome cash bonuses and the occasional gift of a Cadillac.

4. What did the stock exchange do after they sensed the brokerage firms' troubles?

Stock Exchange auditors beginning to sense the full dimensions of the brokerage firms' troubles suspended both Haupt and Williston for being unable to meet current obligations. It was only the second time in its history that the Exchange had shut down a member firm for insolvency. The sense of crisis sharpened as investors who attempted to close out accounts were turned away and some banks refused to honor Haupt checks. To some, it smelled of the 1929, but the circumstances could not have been more different. Profits were up, interest rates stable, and the economy moving, but psychology once again trumped reason. Ancient flawed memories of the Great Crash brought heavy selling into the market, even as the Big Board managed to get Williston & Beane back into business with a bridge loan of less than a million.

5. What is the Haupt's condition after the Stock Exchange suspended it?

Haupt's condition was far worse than originally thought. It had gone to the bank to cover Allied Crude's unmet margin calls, and owed more than a dozen of them well over $35 million. It was on the hook for who knew how much more in apparently phony warehouse receipts. Then there was the $100 million or so in securities Haupt clients had bought on margin. These, too, in the ordinary course of business, had been pledged with banks.

IV. Translation of the Case

就其波及范围和造成的后果而言，那绝对是个世纪性的大骗局。显示这场危机即将到来的第一个迹象来自纽约股票交易所的两行寥寥数语的声明。

危机如雪崩般势不可挡。这场骗局会让那些恐慌的投资者损失几百万，也会让两家历史悠久的经济公司和众多商品出口商破产。其间许多美国国内精明的投资者也会因此而失去 2.5 亿美元，这会让他们颜面扫地。

对于投资者而言，市场永远是一场道德剧，给人寓意深刻的教训。这些训诫往往不过如此：市场总是在危机时刻反应激烈，恐慌总是应运而生；所有的骗局总以伪造资产出台；会计和股票分析师也无法分清是非；在这里，贪欲远比性欲和政治欲望更让人迷失方向。

尽管纽约股票交易市场的人声称由于某个大型商品企业陷入财政困难，他们正在对两家成员公司进行查账，但他们也未觉察到在这份声明后将要到来的灾难。

声明中并没有指名道姓到底是哪家商品企业和哪两家成员公司。似乎股票交易所只不过是在处理一些特殊却不让人担忧的情况而已。

这家商品企业就莫名其妙地无法达到凭保证金额度购买期货证券的标准。这家公司通过两家交易所的成员公司做经纪人，借钱做大宗期货生意。而这两家成员公司又以银行贷款为其作掩护，最终他们手中的钱也无法达到购买期货证券的标准。

交易所只是飞快地浏览了一下有关数字，他们没有预计到危机的严重性，所以他们并没有终止这两家有口皆碑的公司业务。

交易所貌似平静，而股票市场还曾出现过危机到来前的另一个征兆：转过天来，芝加哥交易所的豆油期货和纽约商品交易所的棉籽油合约出现了前所未有的巨大成交量。这是因为投机者认定棉籽油的价格会暴跌。

而另外一个不为人知的征兆则出现在哈得逊河对面的尼瓦克市（新泽西州）。美国粮食换食品计划中最大的商品油供应商——联合菜油加工公司申请破产，负债达 2 亿美元。

同样在临近的贝永市，出现了一队人马。他们是火速派来的审计人员。面对眼前胡乱堆放的储油罐，他们吃惊不已。这难道就是联合菜油公司的总部？

应出口商伯格公司的要求，这些审计人员要确认伯格名下的 1.6 亿磅豆油是否还在此存放。在满是储油罐电器元件散发出的蒸汽中，在脚下满是浸满油污的粘脚泥巴里，他们开始了寻找工作。

豆油存放在四个特殊设计的油罐中，价值 1,500 万美元。出口商伯格公司手中只有联合菜油公司的几张空头支票，这让他们很质疑联合菜油公司财政的可靠性，他们希望进一步确定自己的油是否可以随时取用。

审计人员在油罐迷宫中穿行，油罐从外表上看着都一样。他们在开始的报告中称一切正常。但再次被要求去现场查看后，他们带回了令人难以置信的消息：油罐标度显示，伯格公司手下的四个油罐里，只有一个似乎是装满了油样物质，另外一个是半罐，其余的两个是空罐。

天下大乱！

油去哪了？在这令人生疑的联合菜油储油厂里，那 1.6 亿磅菜油怎么能通过相连的管道悄无声息地被抽走？而这么短的时间里弄走这么多油简直是天方夜谭。

这场喧嚣很快从伯格公司监管人传到美国运通仓储公司——美国捷运公司的子公司。作为联合菜油公司储油场的独立监管人，运通公司负责测量和出具证明联合菜油公司的油罐和其他公司名下的油罐中的储油量。

运通公司出具的证明书对联合菜油公司而言颇为重要。有运通的强大后备力量，联合菜油公司通过运通公司出具的仓储收据可以向银行贷款用以资助自己的生意。根据商品行业的例行规程，证明书以联合菜油公司名下的油罐储油量作担保。有了运通公司作为第三方监管，银行和出口商已经定期给联合菜油公司几千万的贷款。他们没有什么可担心的。可伯格出口公司的油在哪儿？

丢什么油？捷运公司的担保人厉声质问。两天前，按照伯格公司的签署命令，捷运公司已经把油运到了联合菜油总部。

同时，在现场寻找豆油的还有法庭指定负责联合菜油公司破产调查的律师。他们也愤怒地质问联合菜油公司的人油在哪。他们此行的目的是确认联合菜油公司的资产，用以偿还债务。这几天，债主聘请的律师一直在公司外等候，那场景和30年代银行挤兑时门外都是可怜巴巴的存款人的情景别无二致。

远在霍普顿公司的会议室里，还有一批律师，他们正设法弄清霍普顿公司数额高达几百万美元的若干支票，为什么会在银行出纳手中成为一堆空头支票。要知道那些银行可是数一数二的大通曼哈顿银行和摩根财团，一旦霍普顿和威利斯敦两家公司破产，数千名无辜的投资者将会损失惨重，而相应带来的纠纷也会变为闹剧。

律师们跑遍霍普顿公司的各个角落。身处霍普顿公司喧闹的会议室中，一位烦躁不安的律师说："现在最难的是找到一个知情人。"

物品交易所的人们也搞不懂其中的缘由，市场中疯狂的抛售场面令他们恐慌。于是他们紧急叫停交易一天，并要求棉籽油的价格以当日结算价格为准。对于期货经纪公司而言，这简直是雪上加霜。

每个人都有各自的疑问，没有人将这些问题通盘考虑。伯格公司心急火燎地要找到丢失的油，它指控美国运通公司放弃监管职责。在新泽西州法庭，运通公司声称遵照伪造的伯格公司的命令，它已经把油运到储油场并秘密地输送到相互连接的油罐当中。伯格公司所说的不是丢失的油。它说的是被偷的油。

作为美国捷运公司的子公司——运通公司的麻烦会不会伤及它颇负盛名的总公司呢？霍华德·克拉克，作为美国捷运公司的总裁，亲自到贝永进行实地考察。他爬上几个高达42英尺的储油罐，通过装货仓盖向里面看了看。然后，对记者发表讲话。他保证这起神秘的豆油失踪案会水落石出。为了避免正面回答一些问题，他还说："正如你们所想，现在还有很多疑点。"

很多疑点早已显示在运通仓储公司的股票价格上。人们无从知晓运通将会面临怎样的负债，是否它的总公司有可能会为它买单，承担负债。当运通公司提出破产申请时，一切大白于天下，运通的资产只有363,683美元，负债额却高达144,000,000美元。

随着克拉克的实地调查，霍普顿公司一下子从混乱不堪坠入绝望的深渊。预感到大事不妙，捷运公司否认经纪公司持有的捷运公司的货舱收据，认定百分之百是联合菜油公司伪造的。伪造？那么是谁伪造了这些收据？

股票交易所的审计员意识到经纪公司所处的困境。考虑到他们无法偿还债务，审计员叫停了霍普顿和威利斯敦两家公司的业务。有史以来，股票交易所第二次以破产名义关闭其成员行号。交易所拒绝了许多投资者关闭账户的请求。银行也拒绝兑现霍普顿公司开具的支票。危机愈演愈烈。对很多人来说，他们似乎再一次感受到 1929 年危机时的紧张气氛。相比之下，这次的情况好不了哪儿去。利润上涨，利息平稳，经济状况良好，但人们的情感再次战胜了理智。尽管大盘设法以不足 100 万美元的过桥贷款方式让威利斯敦和 BEANE 公司重返市场，1929 年大崩盘时的痛苦回忆还是迫使人们在市场大量抛售。

此后该如何拯救霍普顿公司是交易所面临的更棘手的问题。交易所担心的是，霍普顿公司被套牢的客户所引发的新闻报道会持续影响交易市场，那会导致其他成员公司的抛售。

霍普顿公司的境况比预想的还要糟糕。它已经去银行交纳了联合菜油公司未偿付的保证金，欠银行共计 3,500 万美元。作为伪造仓储收据的显而易见的知情人，它的境况不妙。并且霍普顿的客户曾以保证金额度购买了一亿美金的期货合约。当然，这些股票是按照惯例从银行抵押购买的。

霍普顿公司的合作伙伴，大多数是 30 多岁的年轻人，他们的个人财产危在旦夕，早已超过了信用额度。股票交易所没有备用机制用以解救霍普顿公司，此时霍普顿的任何一家银行债权人都能让它顷刻间倒闭。如果这样，霍普顿公司客户的资金会被冻结多年，而大盘也会随之陷入混乱——它煞费苦心地将华尔街推向公众的努力也会受到重挫。

最令华尔街担心的情况在贝永油罐存放场里已成为铁的事实。缺少未偿付的货舱收据，抵押的豆油储量少了几百万吨的谣言四起，传遍整个业界。远在鹿特丹和苏黎世的债权人也纷纷派出代表赶往贝永储油场，他们拥堵在储油场的通道上。他们此行的目的不仅要找到菜油，也要找到抵押的残余品如动物油脂和鱼油。

债权人的恐慌程度绝不亚于那些焦头烂额的霍普顿公司的投资者。内森·拉文是法庭指定的首席律师，他个头矮小，性格急躁，面对多方自相矛盾的索赔要求，他吐露了实情。他说他手中有一份正式文件禁止从储油场以任何形式提货。就在事情还是一团乱麻的情况下，针对储油罐和仓储收据又开始了调查。

而调查报告并不激励人心。伯格公司名下的至少两个储油罐里都是石油而不是豆油。其他的油罐则装满了污泥和海水。令人困惑的是，许多本应存放豆油的储油罐也没了踪迹。人们在联合菜油公司的任何一家实体公司中也找不到这些油罐。其中，海港储油公司也持有大量仓储收据，却提供不出相应的豆油。

丢失的岂止是油和储油罐。看过联合菜油公司的账目，人们发现许多资金也不翼而飞。无论丢失其中的哪一种，都会让华尔街和 50 多家银行损失 2 亿美元。内森·拉文保持头脑冷静，他叫来了美国联邦调查局（FBI）的人员。此后，发生了一件大事，那才是真正的大恐慌。那是 1963 年 11 月 22 日。

下午 1:33，政府公布了一则令人悲痛的消息："约翰·肯尼迪于今天中央标准时间下午 1:00 去世，头部中枪死亡。"

我们又能从中吸取什么教训呢？恐慌导致心理波动，行为心理学家称之为"思想传染"——羊群效应——看到其他投资者在市场上追购或抛售股票，也不甘心落后的跟着买进或卖出。这也被称为呼啦圈式或郁金香球茎现象。现在，随着网络信息的快速传播，羊群效应会愈演愈烈。

如果你持有长期受益股，最好要不时地从中取走收益。

遇到危急时刻，也不应该抛售股票，而应买入。一旦市场面临通货膨胀、利润下滑、战争恐慌等不测，也应静观其变，不要随波逐流，保持清醒，作出权宜之计。在这场豆油骗局中，许多人抛售股票，导致市场价格暴跌，而为了重返市场这些人又不得不支付高额的贴水。

从哪里跌倒就要从哪里爬起来，市场的恢复也是如此。在过去的一周中，股票交易市场已做好计划解冻霍普顿的账户，并确保其客户不会损失一分钱。这个好消息产生了良好的市场推动力。问题的关键是其他的会员行号会分摊损失。在股票交易史上，这种做法可是前所未有。

即使让霍普顿摆脱困境的做法也不会揭开骗局中的种种疑团：失踪的油去哪了？油罐呢？钱呢？安东尼·安吉列斯也消失了踪影。身为联合菜油公司的总裁和最大的股东，他是揭开所有谜团的关键人物。

安吉列斯来自一个移民家庭，父亲是一名铁路工，家里有五个孩子。他中学时就辍学了。此后他白手起家，经过短短几年的努力，在蓬勃发展的出口业中，联合菜油公司占据了主导地位，生意兴隆，财源滚滚。安吉列斯成为"植物油老大"。

安吉列斯的成功得益于国家重点资助的美国"粮食换和平计划"。在农业部的监督之下，"粮食换和平计划"把食用油和其他产品以低价卖给那些遭受饥荒的国家。这个计划的初衷是善意的：人道主义援助那些贫穷的国家，同时也能减少国内商品市场过剩的局面。但即便如此，美国国内的农产品价格还是上涨，仍没能取悦那些以农业为主的州的立法委员。

　　早期从事肉类加工和动物油贸易的安吉列斯，看准了时机——作中间商。从中西部购买来豆油和棉籽油，在东部提炼，然后将提炼好的油卖给沿海的出口商。算来算去，贝永储油公司最合心意。贝永坐拥铁路、船舶及深水港码头便捷的交通网，拥有庞大的储藏空间。这样一来，历史悠久的出口公司伯格公司和大陆谷物公司就能在此储备加工好的油。

　　安吉列斯投入了 50 万美元资金，这使得曾是石油储藏地的贝永变成了颇具规模的食用油储藏场。后来，安吉列斯又出人意料地让美国运通仓储公司作为托管人，接管了贝永。这种业务关系使得安吉列斯在自己手头没多少资金的情况下，能通过运通公司出具的账目清单和可转让仓单向银行贷款。以同样的方式，安吉列斯用保险费率从他的出口商手中得到了附加贷款，这样他就可以建造本行业中高新高效的炼油场。

　　安吉列斯宣布联合菜油公司破产后，经历了 8 天痛苦的煎熬。他接到了法庭的传票，并首次在法庭露面。记者们连连向他发问："你为什么要藏起来？联合菜油公司何以倒闭？"

　　安吉列斯并没有一个人前往法庭，陪伴他的是出身名门的刑事辩护律师华特德·范·里泊。他曾任法官和司法部长。

　　（庭审问题如下：）

　　问：你在联合菜油公司担任何职？

　　答：尊敬的法官，我拒绝回答，如果回答，那样会暗示我有罪。

　　为了使"现在"这个词听得更清楚，范·里泊吟咏般地宣布，现在，安吉列斯拒绝回答任何问题。

　　而记者们调查安吉列斯的背景时发现，花钱消灾是他惯用的伎俩。

　　其中曾有一件让安吉列斯颇为头疼的事是他与美国证券交易委员会的纠葛。委员会指控安吉列斯低报了他所接管的一家公有制的肉类加工厂的亏损额。债权人逼迫阿尔道夫·格贝尔公司倒闭。另外的一项指控也和格贝尔案件有牵连。委员会声称安吉列斯劝诱一名证人撤回伤害性证词，该证词是关于蒂诺曾以伪造的猪油存货量贷款。

　　然而一开始的时候，人们很少听到有关安吉列斯伪造支票的传言。

　　人们可以从安吉列斯日常的信用报告中了解他的一些背景，但没有人怀疑他的生意会有什么问题。公事公办似乎是他的做事风格。他出售食用油的价格极具竞争力。在他人没有异议的情况下，安吉列斯以高额的贷款利率凭借仓储收据将银行的贷款间接地吸纳到联合菜油公司。

　　身为行业巨头，安吉列斯并不喜欢上流社会的生活。他曾夸大其词地说："我一生只有一个梦想——事业有成。还是小孩时，工作就是第一位。我很少享受幸福生活。"人们的确很少看到他出入社交场合，仅有的几次是由丽莲·帕斯卡瑞里陪着他出席。丽莲是一个离婚的女士，做派潇洒，安吉列斯是她的老板，付给她薪水，而她则充当安吉列斯的社交场合中的女主人。

在新泽西州郊区天纳福来市的帕瑟得，安吉列斯为帕斯卡瑞里买下了一处宽敞的住所，房子坐落在一块绿油油的反坡上，已经支付了 4 万美元的预付款。这离乔治·华盛顿桥只有几英里的路程。

蒂诺的妻子也住在这个城市，离蒂诺家不远。安吉列斯的小舅子 Leo Bracconeri 担任联合菜油公司的经理，BenRotello 担任联合菜油公司的会计主管，George Bitter 则是安吉列斯的主要商品交易商。帕斯卡瑞里的家主要用来款待海外的商户。每年夏天，联合菜油公司的人们都要来这里参加在后花园举办的野餐会，尽情地享乐。

安吉列斯乡下的这些 20 多个亲戚朋友成为联合菜油公司的核心力量，他们之间的关系牢不可破。正是因为这样的裙带关系，贝永的生意也随之蒸蒸日上。安吉列斯的几个表兄也在联合菜油公司工作，如果工作出色，他们会得到丰厚的奖金，偶尔也会得到一辆凯迪拉克。

第二次破产庭审的时候，安吉列斯短暂露面。依据宪法第五条修正案，他拒绝回答任何问题。律师华特德·范·里泊解释说，考虑到众多报道都是"断言安吉列斯的个人行为有问题"，他的当事人别无选择，只能保持沉默。

联邦法官指控安吉列斯蔑视法庭，对此安吉列斯改变了策略。60 个庭审问题，他同意回答 40 个。但附加条件是就一些有疑问的问题他有权拒绝回答。而在第一次庭审时，安吉列斯一个问题也没回答。

庭审时，安吉列斯继续混淆视听，他明白他仍是联邦大陪审团的调查目标。

圣诞节前两天，大陪审团指控安吉列斯在国内交易中，共计 18 次用伪造仓储收据的方式挪用款项达 3,900 万美元。按照法律，他应接受的最严厉的惩罚是坐牢 180 年，罚款 180 万美元。

那些关注法庭裁决的人打赌说还有许多裁决书尚未出炉。

法庭没有任何消息传出。安吉列斯这段时间却和记者们混得很熟，"大财团和政府狼狈为奸要将小人物踢出局"。在一次新闻发布会上，他即席发言。而他安吉列斯所能做的就是扩大出口业务，让豆农"每英斗大豆赚 25 美分，而大财团可不希望是这样"。

安吉列斯曾把一座钟捐给泽西市教堂，也曾在海外为犹太人建立了犹太人之家。而当他说上述那些话的时候，西部的农民也成了他恩泽的对象。然而来自新泽西州的一个法律条文却让安吉列斯的神圣想法落空。这款条文很少有人引用，它规定民事诉讼的被告应赔偿所有与损失同等的保证金或坐牢。

约瑟夫·诺兰是贝永案的另一个受害者——海港储油公司的破产代理人，是他让焦头烂额的安吉列斯又陷入坐牢的恐慌中。

诺兰曾经担任美国财政部弹劾特派员，他来到新泽西州法庭，没多久就拿到了逮捕安吉列斯的逮捕证。对于其他律师而言，这种可能性只有几百分之一。

诺兰指控安吉列斯精心策划了一切，他以伪造仓储收据的方式导致海港储油公司的在途资金达 4,650 万美元。这个阴谋的帮凶是安吉列斯的亲信约瑟夫·卢莫斯科，他担任海港储油公司的托管人。

快到周五晚餐的时候，大法官罗伯特·马修斯宣布暂时休庭。他安排周一早晨举行听证会，并规定安吉列斯要交纳 15 万美元的保证金，卢莫斯科交 10 万美元。最具杀伤力的是他要求这两个人必须在法官面前确定临时性的保释金。

这一要求颇具威力，安吉列斯拒绝回答问题的伎俩再不能得逞了。这也有助于查明安吉列斯的财产状况。如果他能担负周末 6,000 美元的保释金，人们就会认为他把钱放在别处了。这时，安吉列斯别无选择，他只能去哈得逊监狱度周末。

周一的早晨，安吉列斯回到法庭，还是那副受了委屈、清白无辜的表情。这次他带来了公司的账目。他用那只不离身的钢笔在账目上边打勾、边证明他现在负债 2,700 万美元。这其中大多是个人担保的形式，用以偿还联合菜油公司的债务。其中只有 1,400 万美元是联合菜油公司应赔偿的。坦白一切后，安吉列斯哭穷道，包括六七件衣服在内，他的现金不足 5,000 美元。

安吉列斯悲惨的现状的叙述，让一旁的诺兰很感兴趣。他一直在翻阅安吉列斯的个人银行结算单。他问道，开给安吉列斯的信使托马斯·克拉金的那笔 8,800 美元支票是怎么回事？

借此问题，安吉列斯又扯出他的另一个善举。他证明，克拉金是联合菜油公司的长期雇员，为了买房，他兼了两份职。蒂诺被他的勤奋打动，"就我所知，我给了他一笔钱让他交押金或买房。我自认为这钱给了他，也没指望他还给我"。

诺兰不相信安吉列斯的话，他继续追问。安吉列斯后来改了口，说那笔钱已经回来了。他也承认给约瑟夫·卢莫斯科 3,000 美元，但忘记为什么给他这笔钱了。

当诺兰提到安吉列斯曾给他人 63,500 美元时，整个案件还是扑朔迷离。诺兰咄咄逼人地连连发问：为什么给这些人现金？为什么用 10,000 美元支付待付款？你给他们现金吗？想不起来给过谁吗？

蒂诺继续他的攻势，他获准重新指定人选来保管他的财产。由原来的破产法庭转交到罗伯特·马修斯的最高法院保管。马修斯法官对这一做法很满意。鉴于蒂诺在哭穷，约瑟夫·马修斯提出重新讨论保释金问题。

　　几队人马都试图揭开资产的谜团，但都没有任何进展。主动权还在安吉列斯的手中。他表示他会让联合菜油公司破产托管人知晓内情。同时他也想起来，大约有50万美元藏在瑞士联邦银行的账号上。当时为了尽快提出破产申请，他都忘了还有一笔钱在日内瓦。

　　安吉列斯为自己辩解说，尽管这么晚才主动交待，起码表明了他的诚意。他还自负地说："没人能得到一分钱。我也绝不让任何人拿到一分钱。"

　　诺兰要求法庭援引安吉列斯的说法作为他蔑视刑事法庭的证据。诺兰认为这个案子并不棘手。因为不到一个月前，在破产法庭上，安吉列斯还曾宣誓否认拥有境外银行账户，而现在上天保佑他竟然有了日内瓦的50万美元，这还不足以说明一切吗？

　　安吉列斯托辞说生命短暂，没有机会说谎，他所说的都是真的。那笔钱不是他的，从来都不是。这笔钱属于联合菜油公司。

　　与修斯法官不相信这些，他说："我认定当问到安吉列斯的个人财产时，他对法庭撒了谎。"他判定安吉列斯入狱4个月，缴纳1万美元的保释金。安吉列斯出狱后，提起上诉，并胜诉。由三个法官构成的上诉法庭裁定："没有确凿的证据表明安吉列斯撒了谎。"他们同时认定，既然安吉列斯已经帮忙尽快将藏匿的钱汇回美国，法庭就不能指控安吉列斯妨碍司法公正。

　　但失踪的油和伪造的仓储收据这两个问题依旧悬而未决，让人百思不得其解。联邦大陪审团又提出第二项指控，安吉列斯以伪造美国运通公司仓储收据的方式挪用了1,000万美元。

　　蒂诺在西班牙销售豆油时，曾一直忙于同陆军供应部的人搞好关系。功夫不负有心人，他们得到了一个大订单——求购价值3,650万美元的2.75亿磅豆油。

　　对于联合菜油公司而言，这可是笔大数目的订单。但安吉列斯手中没有所承诺的豆油储量。按照标准交易流程，他进入期货市场确定货源。

　　然而这一切都落空了。西班牙人不经解释单方终止了合同，安吉列斯明白其中的缘由，原来安吉列斯的国内竞争对手——中西部的榨油公司已经和西班牙的主业社团有所接触，而后者在西班牙的上流社会颇具影响力。

　　上面就是安吉列斯给破产法庭讲的一个漫长的故事，也就是他怎么被欺骗的过程。他说到没有上下疏通关系，没有耍弄权术，没有他人的帮助，他完全是通过个人奋斗才在社会上出人头地，而那些榨油商就是想让他滚蛋，要把他的生意抢走。

　　有了西班牙主业社团的帮助，中西部榨油公司成功地将联合菜油公司踢出局。安吉列斯愤愤不平地对法庭说："有人蓄意破坏时，只有两条路可走——反抗或认输。"

安吉列斯并没有以可以接受的损失进行斩仓，而是选择了反击。他没有卖掉合约。这样一来，一旦找不到大买家，他将面临平仓的危险，承担 2,000 万美元的豆油期货。

安吉列斯非要赌一把。他买入过多的期货，面临巨大风险。

安吉列斯的这些期货交易大都通过伪造账户进行，合约的开户人都是蒂诺储油场的合伙人。其中一人是家禽商，他将账户开在他的鸡场名下。安吉列斯同这些开户人签订了合约，合约条款规定——开户人可获得盈利，损失由联合菜油公司自己负担。

这种私下签订的合约表明安吉列斯在尽力提高豆油价格。他期望人们对农业部的出口商品持乐观态度，但是事与愿违，他的损失越来越大。但他还心存侥幸，认为会有几个大买家出现能救他于水火之中。

联合菜油公司带动了物产交易所 90% 的棉籽油买入交易。这只给市场带来调节性反应。经济部象征性地惩罚了安吉列斯。鉴于进行虚假交易，安吉列斯必须中止交易 30 天，并且农业部还警告性地终止了他的几个账户。

安吉列斯以疯狂的比例买进，但没有人不喜欢繁荣市场。仅一个月，安吉列斯要付给物产交易所经纪人的佣金就高达 10 万美元。市场操纵？不可能。任何人都看得出出口市场再次火爆。

对于那些年轻气盛的合作者而言，这些佣金相当有吸引力。他们是艾拉·霍普顿公司的新人。对于元老级人物而言，他们不看好安吉列斯的原因是因为他的曲折经历。

安吉列斯安排霍普顿公司的人去贝永储油场走了一趟，这打消了他们的疑虑。安吉列斯向这些人夸赞自己的公司是行业中最高效的炼油厂，24 小时轮流上班，每次轮班的人数只有七八个。

霍普顿公司并不知道许多周薪 400 美元的工人都是用以充当开户人的假名字。

霍普顿公司那些期望扩大业务的合作者只看到了机会。他们迫切地想要拿到价值 3,000 万美元的仓储收据。因此，很快向大陆伊利诺伊国民银行和信托公司抵押。到此为止，霍普顿公司手中的期货合约已达 1 亿美元。——旦市场突变，他们将面临巨大的损失。

如果豆油价格下跌 1 美分，安吉列斯就会接到 1,300 万美元的补仓通知。安吉列斯只有一线希望，传闻俄国将要大量买进豆油期货。

现在安吉列斯所能做的就是让美国捷运公司相信他拥有仓储收据中所证明的豆油储量。而这些收据都是他伪造的。

当初美国捷运接管联合菜油公司账目时，蒂诺雇用了许多捷运公司的托管人，但这些人的名字并不在联合菜油公司的工资单中体现。并且托管主管是安吉列斯的兄弟——蒂诺的表兄，他们共用办公室。主管助理是蒂诺秘书的小叔子。这样一来，就成了一个在一起工作的其乐融融的大家庭，他们玩弄捷运公司于股掌之间。

每周五，联合菜油公司和捷运公司的人两个人一组检查油罐储量。联合菜油公司的人站在油罐顶部读取数据，捷运人员则理所当然地记下数据。"捷运公司从来不检查读取数据的人是谁。"联合菜油公司的职员这样说："如果他们知道记录的数据都是假的，他们肯定会亲历亲为。"

许多储油罐里都是海水，只不过上面漂浮了一层油。

安吉列斯向法庭认罪，承认犯有同谋罪和使用伪造仓储收据罪。主动认罪的行为让安吉列斯的刑期减少了许多，从最高135年减少到35年，并缴纳35,000美元的罚金。

联邦大法官瑞尼奥·D. 沃登迪克宣布对安吉列斯的判决，入狱10年，这只是临时判决。路易斯镇宾夕法尼亚联邦监狱首先要对安吉列斯进行犯罪动机心理研究之后，才会有最终的判决。最初安吉列斯并没有料到会有10年的监禁，所以当沃登迪克把刑期增到20年的时候，安吉列斯极度震惊。

刑期为什么会翻倍？难道法官注意到这场骗局并非是安吉列斯肆意行为而是出于内心的黑暗？事实上，司法混乱破坏了司法程序。根据法律规定，要想对安吉列斯进行心理分析必须对他判决最多10年的刑罚。但是20年的监禁又能使安吉列斯获得六年零八个月的假释。"至少6年里，我不想让安吉列斯在社会上肆意任为。"沃登迪克说"他会引发另一场灾难。"

（此后，安吉列斯出狱后，连续因伪造支票信用凭据而被判入狱20年和21个月。）

听到菲利浦·莫塞卡或比利·索伊斯特重新犯罪的消息，人们会坦然接受不会吃惊。安吉列斯和他们是一丘之貉，成功的渴望总是刺激他们一次又一次地铤而走险。安吉列斯不算个商人，最终也说不上是个骗子。

Chapter Six
Perfect Traps on the Sheets

第六章
完美的账目陷阱

I. Case Study

Whether you are a value investor, trust your instincts. If the story behind a stock looks too good to be true, it probably is. Despite SEC watchdogs and the billions industry spends on outside accountants, somebody may be cooking the books. Exhibit A: the astounding case of HFS and CUC International.

It starts with two centimillionaires, and you'd be hard put to find two more disparate personalities than Henry R. Silverman and Walter A. Forbes. Silverman, 61, thinks of himself as a "neurotic workaholic," a "perfectionist with no tolerance for people who are not as stressed out as I am." Forbes, on the other hand, comes on as a laid-back visionary, said to pad about the office in sneakers and jeans, snacking on saltines, often playing softball or flag football on weekends with his staff.

They sure sell in the stock market, though. Digging deep into the financial engineering kit, Silverman and Forbes flashed reported earnings growth of better than 25 percent a year, mainly by acquisition, and generally to raves on Wall Street. The securities analyst cheering squad, coupled with the impact of aggressive merger accounting helped to boost Silverman's and Forbes' multiples to as high as 50 times earnings. Thanks to the mysteries of purchase accounting they enabled Silverman and Forbes to post reported earning growth far in excess of real internal growth. In 1996, for example, Silverman's HFS told shareholders earnings were up 75 percent.

If you x-ed out the acquisition for that year, you could see that the real gain was closer to 20 percent. And much of the 20 percent, of course, in endless regress, was due to earlier acquisitions.

They raised to high art the quite legal technique of using the virtual currency of inflated stock to buy real assets. Inevitably the art brought the two together in a megamerger with still more hosannas from Wall Street. Against all predictions, the combination quickly disintegrated into one of the great financial disasters of the century, costing unwary investors billions.

It didn't have to happen. There were early warning signs that alert shareholders could have picked up. Some did. Most, victimized with a major assist by complacent accountants and securities analysts, took a shellacking. The story of Silverman and Forbes is worth looking at in detail. It is a cautionary tale and a survival guide in a time when reported earnings are almost never quite what they seem.

By the early 1980s, Silverman was in a leveraged buyout. He bought Days Inn successfully twice. His strategy of providing a centralized reservation and marketing system against a slice of the revenues was tailored to the leveraged buyout ideal. The aim was to invest in high margin situations that require minimal capital expenditures and generate enough cash flow to quickly pay down acquisition debt.

By 1996, Silverman was fronting eight national hotel-motel chains. Recorded earnings had spurted from $21 million to $80 million, and Wall Street hailed Hospitality Franchise, now renamed HFS, as a great new growth story. Growth fueled the market price, which made acquisitions cheap; cheap acquisitions helped keep the growth rate up. So the strategy went, propelling Silverman down the diversification path into other fragmented brand-name franchise fields, like real estate brokerage and auto rentals. The focus was unchanged: Keep HFS a virtual company by acquiring only the franchise. The purchases, first of Century 21, and then Coldwell Banker, made Silverman a major player in the residential brokerage and relocation business.

Walter Forbes, Chairman of CUC International, in just under a quarter century, had nursed CUC from its larval stage into the United States' biggest purveyor of discount membership buying services with sales of $2.3 billion. In 1984, after more than a decade of trying, Forbes seemed to be on his way to a storeless society. His strategy called for adding more discount services (dining and travel, for instance), building a broad base of membership that he could cross sell. Forbes' cross-selling effort resembled nothing so much as the links Henry Silverman was trying to cinch into place at HFS: The hotel franchises would tout guests into the recently purchased Avis auto rentals, and both companies would nudge househunters onto Century 21 real estate brokers.

Both were virtual entities—no inventory, with little use for hard assets, and every prospect of rich cash flow. Analysts at Morgan Stanley (Forbes' underwriter) were hailing CUC as a top-flight emerging growth company. Sales between 1985 and 1988 climbed from $87.5 million to $271.8 million. CUC was on its way to becoming the fifth largest holding of the 66 mutual funds specializing in small companies. The multiples generated by its demand (as they did with Henry Silverman) made CUC stock a super merger currency. He and Henry Silverman were strategic clones—merger equaled growth, equaled multiples, equaled merger, equaled…

By the time CUC's sales approached $2 billion in 1996, Forbes had engineered at least 25 acquisitions. Purchase accounting made CUC's numbers somewhat opaque. Few Wall Street analysts made much of an effort to look behind them, but as early as 1991 *Forbes'* (the magazine) Michael Ozanian began to question the aggressive accounting that was helping to propel CUC's seeming straight-line growth. Cutting through the Wall Street complacency, Ozanian found a cluster of early warning signs:

• CUC was finding it increasingly difficult to line up new members;

• Nearly one-third of those who did sign up were canceling their memberships at the end of the first year;

• The idea of cross-selling members multiple services was not panning out;

• Cash flow was being squeezed by marketing expenses, a dynamic masked by the company's accounting massage.

An SEC challenge to CUC's accounting practices deepened the unease among some analysts, yet Wall Street continued to put CUC common right up there with glamour multiples. Those multiples kept Forbes in the acquisition game. Reported sales and earnings continued their almost metronomic growth and led inevitably to one triumphal possibility: What about a combination of two great virtual companies —CUC and HFS? Walter Forbes and Henry Silverman needed one another. There were other question marks dangling over the $11 billion HFS-CUC combination as the merger talks moved to fruition. Among them were the sharply distinct personalities of the principals.

The signals on leadership were also decidedly mixed. Who would run the show? From the effective date of the merger (December, 1997) to January 1,2000, Silverman was to be president/CEO, with Forbes as chairman. After that date, the two would switch — Silverman to chairman; Forbes to CEO. The table of organization carried eight vice-chairmen (four from either side) and 28 directors (14 from each side). A number of directors had close enough outside business ties with the new company to raise obvious questions about their independence. Few mainstream analysts even hinted at these glaring drawbacks.

Whatever long-term promise the merger held for shareholders, there were immediate benefits for the brass. Forbes' base pay, premerger, was a little over $780,000 with a bonus of the same amount. His new scale went to a base of $1.25 million. His new bonus: The lesser of 100 percent of base pay, or 0.75 percent (from the first dollar rather than some performance bogey) of earnings before taxes and other costs.

Though the deal was billed as a merger of equals, it was clear that Silverman was more equal. His base pay: $1.5 million plus a bonus of the lesser of 150 percent of base pay, or 0.75 percent of earnings before taxes and other costs from the first dollar. This cornucopia—bigger base pay, bigger bonuses, bigger option grants, and easy vesting—trickled down from Silverman and Forbes through the rest of senior management. Silverman and Forbes were patting themselves on the back for having found one another.

With the two companies now united as Cendant, Silverman barnstormed many of CUC's subsidiaries for a firsthand look. His auditors had been given only limited access to CUC's nonpublic files. CUC was worried about giving away competitive information if the merger did not gel. He was edgy, though, about the amount of detail and timeliness with which CUC corporate results were reaching his desk. Silverman told Forbes he wanted division reporting switched from a two-step path through a CUC intermediary directly to one of his own people, chief accounting officer Scott Forbes (no relation to Walter).

Walter Forbes agreed, but asked to delay the change for a month until the close of the first quarter. An impatient Silverman agreed, but a week later abruptly changed his mind. He wanted CUC's reports forthwith. Scott Forbes met with E. Kirk Shelton, former CUC president and new Cendant vice chairman, to iron out the details. Four other CUC executives in the accounting loop sat in on the meeting.

Scott Forbes remembers that Shelton gave him a cash flow spreadsheet and asked him to help the CUC side to be "creative" for the new fiscal year in moving $165 million from merger reserves into income. The schedule Forbes was handed in fact shows that CUC was budgeting a total of $202 million in "revenue adjustments" for a couple of its divisions. The cash would come from reversing some of the $550 million the new company had charged against operations to cover such anticipated merger expenses as severance payments, litigation, plant closings, and other restructuring costs.

CUC seemed to be talking an aggressive push on audit standards, the so-called "big bath" accounting common enough in the great megamerger boom. Jamming what may turn out to be several years expenses into a "one-time charge" rather than stretching them out as the money is actually spent guarantees that future earnings will look better. In cases like CUC (and HFS), the compounding effect of multi-year mergers makes it difficult for outsiders to get a good picture of operating earnings. Overestimate the merger expenses, and you can then tap the excess to smooth out what might otherwise be a bumpy earnings curve. Scott Forbes did not like the tone of what he was hearing. True, Ernst & Young, the big five accounting firm that had been auditing CUC since the company went public in 1983, had signed off on the numbers.

How much of CUC's rising sales and earnings had come from operations, and how much of it had been hyped with nonrecurring items HFS had somehow failed to catch? Told that $144 million of CUC's 1997 net income had come from nonoperating sources, Silverman hit the roof. He was doubly vexed to learn that his CUC "equals" needed to pull as much as $200 million out of reserves to meet the proposed operating budget for 1998. He flatly told Walter Forbes that he wanted vice-chairman Shelton and chief financial officer Cosmo Corigliano out of the company, pronto! The resignations were glossed over in a press release that gave not a hint of the turmoil behind the scenes.

Even as Silverman poured soothing syrup over Wall Street in a conference call, accounting chief Scott Forbes was getting an earful at Cendant's Parsippany, New Jersey, headquarters. Still bird-dogging accounting chicanery, he sat down with old CUC hand Casper Sabatino. Sabatino told a flabbergasted Forbes that in the first three quarters of 1997 he had made a series of "topside" adjustments to sales and expenses that inflated CUC's reported earnings by about $176 million. The manufactured numbers were injected into consolidated numbers at the corporate level, but not into any of the operating unit's books. Laying out the detail for Forbes and chief financial officer Michael Monaco, who joined the meeting later, Sabatino said that he had then dressed up fourth quarter earnings by $93 million from reserves "without factual substantiation or support."

Basically, confessed Sabatino, the numbers were pulled out of thin air by higher-ups such as the departed CFO Corigliano to meet the earnings targets promised Wall Street. Predictable earnings growth—no downside surprises thank you—is the key to the megamergers game and momentum investing. Forget about basics. As long as there appears to be earnings growth, no price is too high to pay.

What the whistle-blowing Scoot Forbes and Monaco were hearing from Sabatino was an exercise in self-preservation. With Corigliano exiting, they did not want to take the rap for the book cooking he and senior vice president of finance Anne Pember had supposedly ordered. Other subalterns in the accounting loop at the division level had also been ordered to make "adjustments," either by helping with the booking of fictitious "topside" numbers, or with a grab on reserves. It was a classic example of how easy it is for aggressive accounting to jump the tracks.

The bad news quickly found its way into yet another press release—and less publicly to the SEC and the U.S. Attorney in Newark, New Jersey. The discovery of "potential" accounting irregularities at CUC might force Cendant to lop $100 to $15 million off the $872 million profit (before restructuring costs) it had reported for 1997. Earlier reported earnings on the CUC side might have to be restated as well.

Wall Street reacted savagely, whacking on extremely heavy volume almost 50 percent off the stock.

The first of more than 70 stockholder suits against Cendant, Silverman and Forbes and, alleging major disclosure breaches of the securities laws, was already on its way up the courthouse steps. Among the complaints: that Forbes and Silverman had benefited by selling between them a total of more than $70 million in Cendant stock in the months before word of the accounting debacle broke.

On the defensive, both Forbes and Silverman denied any prior knowledge of the doctored books.

Much of Silverman's rage was directed at his equal and clone, Walter A. Forbes. How could Forbes and Shelton—let alone the accountants at Ernst & Young—not have picked up the fraud? A trenchant question. Silverman felt he had been betrayed. So did Forbes. He wasn't told about the Sabatino whistle-blowing until five days after the event. "I should have known the second Henry Silverman knew," complained Forbes. Silverman retorted that Forbes had been kept in the dark because he (Silverman) "did not know who was complicit. It was in that poisoned atmosphere that Silverman began trying to elbow Forbes out of the company. The cumbersome governance structure Silverman had agreed to, though—a board divided equally between the two companies—tied his hands. Like many megamergers, Cendant was a house built on sand.

The impasse, reflected in Cendant's still sinking stock, was broken when forensic accountants at Arthur Anderson produced a preliminary report indicating the damages were far worse than the original estimates. An additional $200 million in "accounting errors"—accelerated revenues, deferred expenses—had been uncovered. CUC had been booking phony revenues for at least three years, and Cendant would have to cut its 1997 result by as much as $240 million—more than twice the first projections. The new numbers suggested that something like one-third of CUC's 1997 reported revenues were thin air.

Further, the auditors tweaked out some $2 million in questionable expenses Forbes had run up between 1995 and 1997. They included $1 million in undocumented cash advances and American Express charges, and almost $600,000 in private jet charges. The expense report Forbes signed for the plane charges noted that they were to be charged to the all-accommodating Cendant merger reserve. One easy inference was that the loose financial controls at CUC extended to the very top.

Forbes finally elected to jump before he was pushed. His resignation, he said, was "in the best interests of our shareholders and employees to resolve this uncertainty."

There were huge incentives for Forbes to bow out. Since he was resigning "without cause," Cendant had to stump up the severance stipulated in his employment contract. It was quite a package: $35 million in cash, some $22 million in fully vested options (on 1.3-million shares at $17, close to the then market), and a $2.1 million in escrowed life insurance premiums.

The full Arthur Anderson report was out now. Between 1995 and 1997, "irregular" accounting had inflated CUC earnings before charges by $500 million; accounting "errors" had overstated earnings by another $200 million. Stripped of the fictions, CUC now looked like a slow to no-growth hulk.

Building on the original whistle-blowing charges, the report cited innumerable phony entries on revenues, expenses and merger reserves by a score of people in an accounting loop traduced by orders from above. Their commands were handed down, the lower ranks contended, by executive vice president Cosmo Corigliano, CUC controller Anne Pember, and accounting chief Casper Sabatino. The objective: to pump up quarterly earnings by "the amount needed to bring CUC's results into line with Wall Street earnings expectations." "If actual income in a particular quarter was 10¢ per share and consensus analysts expectations were 18¢ a share," the report continued, "then adjustments of approximately 8¢ were made, without support, to increase earnings."

Ernst & Young had been auditing CUC for 15 years. Where were the accountants? At least four of CUC's top accounting people—including Corigliano and Pember—had worked at E & Y before joining CUC. So, they were certainly familiar with the firm's audit patterns. The Arthur Anderson report pieced together "a carefully planned exercise" in which operating, marketing, and administrative expense ratios were painstakingly kept consistent from quarter to quarter.

E & Y had signed off without qualification on CUC's books before the merger and like almost everyone else involved, became the target of several stockholders suits. Cendant also went on the attack. Rather than expose the fraud, Ernst & Young chose to facilitate it and continue to reap millions of dollars in fees," complained Cendant.

Ernst & Young, without admitting any wrongdoing, settled the Cendant stockholders suit for some $335 million, one of the largest such settlements ever.

The Arthur Anderson report cited several warning signs that E & Y might have picked up, but its main thrust was on the workings of Corigliano, Pember, and Sabatino. The report left hanging an obvious question: Why would the three have such an unfettered interest in running the risk of criminal charges in keeping CUC's earnings (and multiples) on the growth track?

Corigliano held options on more than 800,000 shares of CUC. He was making about $300,000 a year, including a $100,000 bonus, before he was fired, but did not seem to enjoy an exalted lifestyle. Home was a pleasant suburban enclave in Connecticut with a couple of Toyotas in the driveway. Was Corigliano the ringleader, subverting the entire accounting group on his own, or was he—like his underlings—

just following orders?

The Arthur Anderson report stopped at Corigliano and his cronies. None of the 80 witnesses interviewed directly implicated Forbes or Shelton. The directors on Cendant's audit committee, in their report to the full board, went no further than the general statement that both men were "among those who must bear responsibility for what occurred." They failed "to create an environment in which it was clear that inaccurate financial reporting would not be tolerated." Corigliano quickly copped a plea in Newark, New Jersey Federal Court to one count of conspiracy to commit false statements and one count of wire fraud. Pember pleaded guilty to a single conspiracy count and Sabatino to one count of aiding and abetting wire fraud.

Corigliano said flatly that "my superiors were encouraging me." CUC's free and easy culture, continued Corigliano, "had been developed over many years" and "was ingrained by our superiors."

Reporters didn't need an organization chart to tell that Corigliano's only superiors were Walter Forbes and E. Kirk Shelton. U.S. Attorney Cleary pointedly told newsmen he would "follow the evidence wherever it takes us." Henry Silverman had no doubts about where the evidence would lead. "Obviously," he told reporters, "only a very few" knew about the fraud and "at the end were Shelton and Forbes."

A sitting grand jury indicted Forbes and Shelton on conspiracy and wire fraud charges going back more than a decade. Both men denied any wrongdoing but were also faced with an SEC civil suit demanding they "disgorge profits on the CUC shares they sold while the supposed scheme was afoot."

There are hints, suggested the magazine *CFO*, that Silverman relied on the due diligence not to avoid risk, but to justify it. "You want to win, so you take some informed risks," Cendant vice-chairman Michael Monaco told *CFO*. Silverman was willing to take some risk, because he needed CUC to keep his own growth scenario going. Such calculated risks are typical of the megamerger boom. The mortality rate among combinations that look good on paper but can't cut it in the real world is very high. The temptation to push the accounting envelope to meet Wall Street's all-compelling expectations (ah, those options!) is often irresistible. Cendant is not an isolated instance.

Are executives so driven by the need to meet Wall Street numbers (ah, those options!) that they are willing to risk jail time? Typically, as appears to be the case in

Cendant, the chicanery starts small, with the need to smooth out a bumpy quarter. What looks like a "temporary" problem is still unfixed, so you have to grab more revenue next quarter to keep the treadmill rolling.

Where are the accountants as smoke billows into meltdown? It's a question the SEC has been raising for years. The culture of the accounting profession itself has undergone a major change. As what used to be the "Big Eight" coalesced into what is now the "Big Five," competition sharpened. One solution was to diversify out of the labor-intensive business of bookkeeping into the much higher margin line of "consulting" on items like management, technology, and recruiting. Consulting has boomed to the point where traditional audit fees now account for only 30 percent of Big Five revenues. Some of the cross-selling is done by regular line bean counters who have no wish to irritate the clients they are hoping to upgrade. How tough will the accountants hang in areas of judgment against an executive determined to make his numbers, no matter what? Warren Buffett highlighted this dilemma in letter to his Berkshire Hathaway shareholders. "The attitude of disrespect many executives have for accurate reporting is a business disgrace," said Buffett. "For their part," he continued, "auditors have done little on the positive side, though auditors should regard the investing public as their client, they tend instead to kowtow to the managers who choose them and dole out their pay."

The SEC, stung by the doubts over the quality of the numbers on which investors are basing their decisions, has tried to get accountants out of the consulting business. Some firms have already done so, others are duking it out.

What's to be learned from the Cendant debacle? Are some of today's hot stocks just smoke and mirrors like CUC? Are some apparent value stocks actually lousy value because the assets are overstated? You can almost bet on it. Not so easy, though, is detection.

Picking up internal fraud is beyond the reach of the armchair analyst. But as investment advisor Robert Renck showed in his early contrary opinions on CUC, early recognition of the illusions of aggressive accounting is a primary line of defense. His digging showed that Walter Forbes was hyping his cash flow by low-balling the reserves he should have been setting up for rising membership cancellations. Pulling on that thread, Renck was among the few Wall Streeters to conclude that Forbes' reported earnings were all smoke and mirrors.

Aggressive accounting, totally out of control at CUC, is usually legal enough because of the many grey areas pasted over the supposed Bible of Generally Accepted Accounting Principles. Like the Holy Bible, GAAP is subject to broad interpretation. Hence the abuse of the merger reserves that were recycled into earnings at CUC.

Manipulating merger reserves is a common enough practice. How to detect it? Check the footnotes in the annual report. They should spell out the size of the reserve, how it is being spent (severance pay, for example), and how much (if any) is filtering back into earnings. Reserves don't last forever. If they account for half of the $1 a share profit a company is reporting, for example, and the stock is selling at $20, it's trading not at a notional 20 times earnings but at 40 times earnings. Is the stock really worth that much?

Yet another front-loaded charge that distorts true earnings is the broadening trend for an acquiring company to take as big a write-off as possible on its new partner's research and development "in process."

The theory is that none of this R&D, underway but not yet at a commercial stage, may never pan out. The incentive to chalk up as many billions as possible to R&D is that they can be written off at once, making later earnings (presumably enhanced by maturing R&D) look good by comparison. The R&D write-off also tends to reduce the drag of "goodwill"—the premium the acquirer paid over book value. Since goodwill is depreciated and impacts earnings over many years, the aim is to keep it to a minimum.

Yet another merger wrinkle to check out is pooling of interest accounting, which permits the partners to combine their assets at book value. Doing so eliminates the whole nasty question of depreciating goodwill and hypes earnings for years to come. The hurdles for doing pooling are high. Poolings are supposed to meet a dozen accounting criteria, but the number of such deals has been increasing almost geometrically since the start of the great bull market in 1990. One other pleasing effect of pooling: It makes it easier for management to bury the premium it paid for a combination that may not work out.

Some other soft spots to check include: cash flow versus reported earnings. Cash flow (revenue minus all costs) is probably the truest measure of how well a company is doing. If reported earnings are growing faster than cash flow, the incremental difference has to be coming from somewhere. Hope that the source is not "topside" adjustments like the flummery at CUC.

Another potential danger is stock buybacks. There's nothing wrong with buybacks perse. If a company's stock is cheap in the market, a buyback can be a good use of excess cash. But watch out for buybacks financed with debt; this is simply a way to goose earnings by substituting debt for equity and can leave a company ill-equipped to handle a downturn in its business or the economy. This is fairly easy to detect: Go back a few years in the corporate history. Is the equity portion of capital shrinking while the debt portion is rising—along with growing earnings? Be skeptical of the growth. You can find the relevant historical numbers in Value Line's excellent industry reports.

Also take a hard look at the impact of management stock options on reported earnings. Though widely touted as an incentive to keep management hustling, options are in fact a two-edged sword. Although truly a labor cost, they are not stated as an expense, but capitalized. Thus, options have the effect of understating costs and overstating earnings, often by 30 percent or more.

The dilutive effect comes from the increase in the number of shares outstanding —the divisor used to calculate profits per share. The arithmetic is inexorable. If the number of shares outstanding increases by 10 percent without a corresponding increase in earnings, you are looking at a dilution of 10 percent. A 20 percent increase in profits against that dilutive factor would net to an increase of only 9 percent in earnings per share. The option effect has to be seen as a mortgage on the future. Assess it before you buy a stock with yet another foray into the footnotes of the annual report. Good luck. The rules are so ambiguous you can't be sure that any two companies value their options in the same way.

Options, not surprisingly, have been a major source of controversy at Cendant. So what about Henry Silverman and his discredited stock? As Silverman beavers away at repairing the damage, some of the skeptics are turning bullish on Cendant. "We don't need capital," Silverman recently told reporters. "We need credibility." Credibility, once shattered, is not easily rebuilt.

There is a moral here, more easily stated than applied: Don't take the reported numbers at face value. Do the homework it takes to get behind the numbers. And above all, remember this: If the "story" behind a stock seems too good to be true, it probably is.

Key Words and Expressions:

acquiring company	购入其他公司股权的公司
base pay	基本工资
bow out	退休；告老；辞职；不做（某事）
cash advance	现金垫款
civil suit	民事诉讼
cook the books	伪造或篡改财务报表，造假账
cop a plea	避重就轻地认罪
gloss over	辩解；掩饰
hit the roof	勃然大怒
leveraged buyout	融通债务,利用要收购的公司的资产价值来负担或融通收购过程中所负债务
multiple	n. 市盈率
pan out	成功
purveyor	n. 承办商
receivership	n. 破产管理，破产清算
severance payment	解雇费
underling	n. 部下
unload	v. 抛售
weather eye	密切注视，保持警惕
write-off	n. 销账,勾销,账面价值的削减, 不再有任何价值的东西
x out:	清除，取消，删除

Notes:

1. Cendant Corporation

　　Cendant 公司是一家以纽约为基地的业务和消费服务的供应商，主要从事房地产和旅游业。虽然公司以纽约城为基地，但是 Cendant 总部雇员多数都在位于新泽西的帕斯巴尼-特洛伊山。Cendant 最后一任首席执行官是亨利·西尔沃曼。

　　1997 年，CUC 国际和 HFS 合并为 Cendant 公司后，1998 年公司被指控犯有诈骗罪。同时，公司副主席 E. 柯克·希尔顿三年里虚报公司收入 5

亿美元。当消息公布的时候，因为市场价值导致公司的损失大约为 140 亿美元，公司股票交易也从高达 41 美元下降到了差不多 12 美元。这场惨败是美国历史上最大的会计诈骗案。希尔顿目前在监狱服刑（10 年）。

2. United States Securities and Exchange Commission (SEC) 美国证券交易委员会

美国证券交易委员会（SEC）属于美国政府机构，负责执行联邦证券法以及规范证券业/股票市场。

3. Ernst & Young 安永

安永是全世界最大的职业服务事务所之一，也是四大审计机构之一，与普华永道（PWC）、德勤（Deloitte）和毕马威齐名。安永是一家拥有许多成员事务所的全球性机构。

安永国际以英国伦敦为基地。其在美国的总部位于纽约时代广场 5 号。

4. cash flow 现金流量

现金流量是指在特定的一段时间内来自一项或数项财产，扣除税收和其他支付金额外所得的现金收入或净收入，常用来衡量公司的价值。

5. Option 期权

期权是指在规定时间内的以固定价格买卖特定的债券或商品的权利。

II. Knowledge Points

1. Cash flow

1) Definition and theory

The amount of cash a company generates and uses during a period, calculated by adding non-cash charges (such as depreciation) to the net income after taxes. Cash flow can be used as an Cash flow is an accounting term that refers to the amounts of cash being received and spent by a business during a defined period of time, sometimes tied to a specific project. Measurement of cash flow can be used:

i. To evaluate the state or performance of a business or project.

ii. To determine problems with liquidity. Being profitable does not necessarily mean being liquid. A company can fail because of a shortage of cash, even while profitable.

iii. To generate project rate of returns. The time of cash flows into and out of projects are used as inputs to financial models such as internal rate of return, and net present value.

iv. To examine income or growth of a business when it is believed that accrual accounting concepts do not represent economic realities. Alternately, cash flow can be used to "validate" the net income generated by accrual accounting.

Cash flow as a generic term may be used differently depending on context, and certain cash flow definitions may be adapted by analysts and users for their own uses. Common terms (with relatively standardized definitions) include operating cash flow and free cash flow.

2) Classification

Cash flows can be classified into:

i. Operational cash flows: Cash received or expended as a result of the company's core business activities.

ii. Investment cash flows: Cash received or expended through capital expenditure, investments or acquisitions.

iii. Financing cash flows: Cash received or expended as a result of financial activities, such as receiving or paying loans, issuing or repurchasing stock, and paying dividends.

All three together are necessary to reconcile the beginning cash balance to the ending cash balance.

3) Benefits from using cash flow

The cash flow statement is one of the four main financial statements of a company. The cash flow statement can be examined to determine the short-term sustainability of a company. If cash is increasing (and operational cash flow is positive), then a company will often be deemed to be healthy in the short-term. Increasing or stable cash balances suggest that a company is able to meet its cash needs, and remain solvent. This information cannot always be seen in the income statement or the balance sheet of a company. For instance, a company may be generating profit, but still have difficulty in remaining solvent.

The cash flow statement breaks the sources of cash generation into three sections: operational cash flows, investing and financing. This breakdown allows the user of financial statements to determine where the company is deriving its cash for operations. For example, a company may be notionally profitable but generating little operational cash (as may be the case for a company that barters its products rather than selling for cash). In such a case, the company may be deriving additional operating cash by issuing shares, or raising additional debt finance.

Companies that have announced significant writedowns of assets, particularly goodwill, may have substantially higher cash flows than the announced earnings would indicate. For example, telecoms firms that paid substantial sums for 3G licenses or for acquisitions have subsequently had to write-off goodwill, that is, indicate that these investments were now worth much less. These write-downs have frequently resulted in large announced annual losses, such as Vodafone's announcement in May 2006 that it had lost £21.9 billion due to a writedown of its German acquisition, Mannesmann, one of the largest annual losses in European history. Despite this large "loss", which represented a sunk cost, Vodafone's operating cash flows were solid: "Strong cash flow is one of the most attractive aspects of the cellphone business, allowing operators like Vodafone to return money to shareholders even as they rack up huge paper losses."

In certain cases, cash flow statements may allow careful analysts to detect problems that would not be evident from the other financial statements alone. For example, WorldCom committed an accounting fraud that was discovered in 2002; the fraud consisted primarily of treating ongoing expenses as capital investments, thereby fraudulently boosting net income. Use of one measure of cash flow (free cash flow) would potentially have detected that there was no change in overall cash flow (including capital investments).

4) Operating cash flow as proxy for income

Many investors have lost faith in the value of published income statements. One way to by-pass them is to use cash flows instead. The feeling is that:

Cash flows cannot be forged. This presumption may be inaccurate.

Cash liquidity is necessary for survival. This is true, and even more true for businesses with limited access to financing.

Cash is tangible proof of income.

5) Dangers of isolating operating cash flow

When analysts and the media refer to "cash flow", they are most likely referring to "Operating Cash Flow". This is only one of the three types of cash flows. There are adherent problems in isolating only this type of flows, because business can easily manipulate the classification.

Common methods of distorting the results include:

Sales—Sell the receivables to a factor for instant cash. (leading)

Inventory—Don't pay your suppliers for an additional few weeks at period end. (lagging)

Sales Commissions—Management can form a separate (but unrelated) company act as its agent. The book of business can then be purchased quarterly as an investment.

Wages—Remunerate with stock options.

Maintenance—Contract with the predecessor company that you prepay five years worth for them to continue doing the work.

Equipment Leases—Buy it.

Rent—Buy the property (sale and lease back, for example).

Oil Exploration costs—Replace reserves by buying another company's.

Research & Development—Wait for the product to be proven by a start-up lab; then buy the lab.

Consulting Fees—Pay in shares from treasury since usually to related parties.

Interest—Issue convertible debt where the conversion rate changes with the unpaid interest.

Taxes—Buy shelf companies with TaxLossCarryForward's. Or gussy up the purchase by buying a lab or O&G explore co. with the same TLCF.

Example of a positive $40 cash flow

Transaction	In (Debit)	Out (Credit)
Incoming Loan	+$50.00	
Sales (which were paid for in cash)	+$30.00	
Materials		-$10.00
Labor		-$10.00
Purchased Capital		-$10.00
Loan Repayment		-$5.00
Taxes		-$5.00
Total...	.......+$40.00.......	

In this example the following types of flows are included:

Incoming loan: financial flow

Sales: operational flow

Materials: operational flow

Labor: operational flow

Purchased Capital: Investment flow

Loan Repayment: financial flow

Taxes: financial flow

Let us, for example, compare two companies using only total cash flow and then separate cash flow streams. The last three years show the following total cash flows:

Company A:

Year 1: cash flow of +10M

Year 2: cash flow of +11M

Year 3: cash flow of +12M

Company B:

Year 1: cash flow of +15M

Year 2: cash flow of +16M

Year 3: cash flow of +17M

Company B has a higher yearly cash flow and looks like a better one in which to invest. Now let us see how their cash flows are made up:

Company A:

Year 1: OC: +20M FC: +5M IC: -15M = +10M

Year 2: OC: +21M FC: +5M IC: -15M = +11M

Year 3: OC: +22M FC: +5M IC: -15M = +12M

Company B:

Year 1: OC: +10M FC: +5M IC: 0 = +15M

Year 2: OC: +11M FC: +5M IC: 0 = +16M

Year 3: OC: +12M FC: +5M IC: 0 = +17M

OC = Operational Cash, FC = Financial Cash, IC = Investment Cash

Now it seems that Company A is actually earning more cash by its core activities and has already spent 45M in long term investments, of which the revenues will only show up after three years. When comparing investments using cash flows always make sure to use the same cash flow layout.

2. Equity

Definition and theory

Equity is a term whose meaning depends very much on the context. In general, you can think of equity as ownership in any asset after all debts associated with that asset are paid off. For example, a car or house with no outstanding debt is considered the owner's equity since he or she can readily sell the items for cash. Stocks are equity because they represent ownership of a company, whereas bonds are classified as debt because they represent an obligation to pay and not ownership of assets.

3. Option

Definition and theory

Options are financial instruments that convey the right, but not the obligation, to engage in a future transaction on some underlying security. For example, a call option provides the right to buy a specified amount of a security at a set strike price at some time on or before expiration, while a put option provides the right to sell. Upon the option holder's choice to exercise the option, the party that sold, or wrote, the option must fulfill the terms of the contract.

The theoretical value of an option can be determined by a variety of techniques, including the use of sophisticated option valuation models. These models can also predict how the value of the option will change in the face of changing conditions. Hence, the risks associated with trading and owning options can be understood and managed with some degree of precision.

Exchange-traded options form an important class of options which have standardized contract features and trade on public exchanges, facilitating trading among independent parties. Over-the-counter options are traded between private parties, often well-capitalized institutions, that have negotiated separate trading and clearing arrangements with each other. Another important class of options, particularly in the U.S., are employee stock options, which are awarded by a company to their employees as a form of incentive compensation.

Other types of options exist in many financial contracts, for example real estate options are often used to assemble large parcels of land, and prepayment options are usually included in mortgage loans. However, many of the valuation and risk management principles apply across all financial options.

4. Purchase accounting

Definition and theory

Method of accounting for a merger that treats the acquirer as having purchased the assets and assumed the liabilities of the acquiree, which are then written up or down to their respective fair market values. The difference between the purchase price and the net assets acquired is attributed to goodwill.

5. Goodwill

Definition and theory

Goodwill is an accounting term used to reflect the portion of the market value of a business entity not directly attributable to its assets and liabilities; it normally arises only in case of an acquisition. It reflects the ability of the entity to make a higher profit than would be derived from selling the tangible assets. Goodwill is also known as an intangible asset.

6. Multiple

1) Definition and theory

Another term for price/earnings ratio (P/E ratio or PE)—a measure of the value of a company's stock determined by its current share price divided by its current annual earnings per share (EPS).

The term multiple is used because the P/E shows how much investors are willing to pay per dollar of earnings. For example, a stock with $2 of EPS that is trading at $20 has a P/E of 10. This means investors are willing to pay 10 times the current EPS for the stock.

The P/E ratio (price-to-earnings ratio) of a stock (also called its "earnings multiple", or simply "multiple", "P/E", or "PE") is a measure of the price paid for a share relative to the income or profit earned by the firm per share. A higher P/E ratio means that investors are paying more for each unit of income. It is a valuation ratio included in other financial ratios. The reciprocal of the P/E ratio is known as the earnings yield.

$$P/E \text{ ratio} = \frac{\text{Price per Share}}{\text{Earnings per Share}}$$

The price per share (numerator) is the market price of a single share of the stock. The earnings per share (denominator) is the net income of the company for the most recent 12 month period, divided by number of shares outstanding. The earnings per share (EPS) used can also be the "diluted EPS" or the "comprehensive EPS".

For example, if stock A is trading at $24 and the earnings per share for the most recent 12 month period is $3, then stock A has a P/E ratio of 24/3 or 8. Put another way, the purchaser of stock A is paying $8 for every dollar of earnings. Companies with losses (negative earnings) or no profit have an undefined P/E ratio (usually shown as Not applicable or "N/A"); sometimes, however, a negative P/E ratio may be shown.

By relating price and earnings per share for a company, one can analyze the market's stock valuation of a company and its shares relative to the income the company is actually generating. Investors can use the P/E ratio to compare the value of stocks: if one stock has a P/E twice that of another stock, all things being equal, it is a less attractive investment. Companies are rarely equal, however, and comparisons between industries, countries, and time periods may be misleading.

2) Usage: determining share prices

Share prices in a publicly traded company are determined by market supply and demand, and thus depend upon the expectations of buyers and sellers. Among these are:

i.   The company's future and recent performance, including potential growth;

ii. Perceived risk, including risk due to high leverage;

iii. Prospects for companies of this type, the "market sector".

By dividing the price of one share in a company by the profits earned by the company per share, you arrive at the P/E ratio. If earnings move up in line with share prices (or vice versa) the ratio stays the same. But if stock prices gain in value and earnings remain the same or go down, the P/E rises.

The price used to calculate a P/E ratio is usually the most recent price. The earnings figure used is the most recently available, although this figure may be out of date and may not necessarily reflect the current position of the company. This is often referred to as a trailing P/E, because it involves taking earnings from the last four quarters; the "forward P/E" (or current price compared to estimated earnings going forward twelve months) is also used.

3) Interpretation

The average U.S. equity P/E ratio from 1900 to 2005 is 14 (or 16, depending on whether the geometric mean or the arithmetic mean is used to average). An oversimplified interpretation would conclude that it takes about 14 years to recoup the price paid for a stock [not including any income from the reinvestment of dividends].

Normally, stocks with high earning growth are traded at higher P/E values. For example, stock A may be expected to earn $6 per share the next year. Then the forward P/E ratio is $24/6 = 4. So, you are paying $4 for every one dollar of earnings, which makes the stock more attractive than it was the previous year.

The P/E ratio implicitly incorporates the perceived riskiness of a given company's future earnings. For a stock purchaser, this risk includes the possibility of bankruptcy. For companies with high leverage (that is, high levels of debt), the risk of bankruptcy will be higher than for other companies. Assuming the effect of leverage is positive, the earnings for a highly-leveraged company will also be higher. In principle, the P/E ratio incorporates this information, and different P/E ratios may reflect the structure of the balance sheet.

Variations on the standard trailing and forward P/E ratios are common. Generally, alternative P/E measures substitute different measures of earnings, such as rolling averages over longer periods of time (to "smooth" volatile earnings, for example), or "corrected" earnings figures that exclude certain extraordinary events or one-off gains or losses. The definitions may not be standardized.

Various interpretations of a particular P/E ratio are possible, and the historical table below is just indicative and cannot be a guide, as current P/E ratios should be compared to current real interest rates:

N/A	A company with no earnings has an undefined P/E ratio. By convention, companies with losses (negative earnings) are usually treated as having an undefined P/E ratio, although a negative P/E ratio can be mathematically determined.
0-10	Either the stock is undervalued or the company's earnings are thought to be in decline. Alternatively, current earnings may be substantially above historic trends.
10-17	For many companies a P/E ratio in this range may be considered fair value.
17-25	Either the stock is overvalued or the company's earnings have increased since the last earnings figure was published. The stock may also be a growth stock with earnings expected to increase substantially in future.

25+	A company whose shares have a very high P/E may have high expected future growth in earnings or the stock may be the subject of a speculative bubble.

It is usually not enough to look at the P/E ratio of one company and determine its status. Usually, an analyst will look at a company's P/E ratio compared to the industry the company is in, the sector the company is in, as well as the overall market (for example the S&P 500 if it is listed in a US exchange). Sites such as Reuters offer these comparisons in one table. Example of RHAT. Often, comparisons will also be made between quarterly and annual data. Only after a comparison with the industry, sector, and market can an analyst determine whether a P/E ratio is high or low with the above-mentioned distinctions (i.e., undervaluation, over valuation, fair valuation, etc).

4) The Market P/E

To calculate the P/E ratio of a market index such as the S&P 500, it is not accurate to take the "simple average" of the P/Es of all stock constituents. The preferred and accurate method is to calculate the weighted average. In this case, each stock's underlying market cap (price multiplied by number of shares in issue) is summed to give the total value in terms of market capitalization for the whole market index. The same method is computed for each stock's underlying net earnings (earnings per share multiplied by number of shares in issue). In this case, the total of all net earnings is computed and this gives the total earnings for the whole market index. The final stage is to divide the total market capitalization by the total earnings to give the market P/E ratio. The reason for using the weighted average method rather than "simple" average can best be described by the fact that the smaller constituents have less of an impact on the overall market index. For example, if a market index is composed of companies X and Y, both of which have the same P/E ratio (which causes the market index to have the same ratio as well) but X has a 9 times greater market cap than Y, then a percentage drop in earnings per share in Y should yield a much smaller affect in the market index than the same percentage drop in earnings per share in X.

An example

An easy and perhaps intuitive way to understand the concept is with an analogy:

Let's say, I offer you a privilege to collect a dollar every year from me forever.

How much are you willing to pay for that privilege now? Let's say, you are only willing to pay me 50 cents, because you may think that paying for that privilege coming from me could be risky. On the other hand, suppose that the offer came from Bill Gates, how much would you be willing to pay him? Perhaps, your answer would be at least more than 50 cents, let's say, $20. Well, the price earnings ratio or sometimes known as earnings multiple is nothing more than the number of dollars the market is willing to pay for a privilege to be able to earn a dollar forever in perpetuity. Bill Gates's P/E ratio is 20 and my P/E ratio is 0.5.

Now view it this way: The P/E ratio also tells you how long it will take before you can recover your investment (ignoring of course the time value of money). Had you invested in Bill Gates, it would have taken you at least 20 years, while investing in me could have taken you less than a year, that is, only 6 months.

If a stock has a relatively high P/E ratio, let's say, 100 (which Google exceeded during the summer of 2005), what does this tell you? The answer is that it depends. A few reasons a stock might have a high P/E ratio are:

i. The market expects the earnings to rise rapidly in the future. For example a gold mining company which has just begun to mine may not have made any money yet but next quarter it will most likely find the gold and make a lot of money. The same applies to pharmaceutical companies — often a large amount of their revenue comes from their best few patented products, so when a promising new product is approved, investors may buy up the stock.

ii. The company was previously making a lot of money, but in the last year or quarter it had a special one time expense (called a "charge"), which lowered the earnings significantly. Stockholders, understanding (possibly incorrectly) that this was a one time issue, will still buy stock at the same price as before, and only sell it at least at that same price.

iii. Hype for the stock has caused people to buy the stock for a higher price than they normally would. This is called a bubble. One of the most important uses for the P/E metric is to decide whether a stock is undergoing a bubble or an anti-bubble by comparing its P/E to other similar companies. Historically, bubbles have been followed by crashes. As such, prudent investors try to stay out of them.

iv. The company has some sort of business advantage which seems to ensure that it will continue making money for a long time with very little risk. Thus investors are willing to buy the stock even at a high price for the peace of mind that they will not lose their money.

v. A large amount of money has been inserted into the stock market, out of proportion with the growth of companies across the same time period. Since there are only a limited amount of stocks to buy, supply and demand dictate that the prices of stocks must go up. This factor can make comparing P/E ratios over time difficult.

vi. Likewise, a specific stock may have a temporarily high price when, for whatever reason, there has been high demand for it. This demand may have nothing to do with the company itself, but may rather relate to, for example, an institutional investor trying to diversify out risk.

5) The P/E concept in business culture

The P/E ratio of a company is a significant focus for management in many companies and industries. This is because management is primarily paid with their company's stock (a form of payment that is supposed to align the interests of management with the interests of other stock holders), in order to increase the stock price. The stock price can increase in one of two ways: either through improved earnings or through an improved multiple that the market assigns to those earnings. As mentioned earlier, a higher P/E ratio is the result of a sustainable advantage that allows a company to grow earnings over time (i.e., investors are paying for their peace of mind). Efforts by management to convince investors that their companies do have a sustainable advantage have had profound effects on business:

i. The primary motivation for building conglomerates is to diversify earnings so that they go up steadily over time.

ii. The choice of businesses which are enhanced or closed down or sold within these conglomerates is often made based on their perceived volatility, regardless of the absolute level of profits or profit margins.

iii. One of the main genres of financial fraud, "slush fund accounting" (hiding excess earnings in good years to cover for losses in lean years), is designed to create the image that the company always slowly but steadily increases profits, with the goal to increase the P/E ratio.

These and many other actions used by companies to structure themselves to be perceived as commanding a higher P/E ratio can seem counterintuitive to some, because while they may decrease the absolute level of profits they are designed to increase the stock price. Thus, in this situation, maximizing the stock price acts as a perverse incentive.

7. Mergers and acquisition

1) Definition and theory

The phrase mergers and acquisitions (abbreviated M&A) refers to the aspect of corporate strategy, corporate finance and management dealing with the buying, selling and combining of different companies that can aid, finance, or help a growing company in a given industry grow rapidly without having to create another business entity.

2) History

Merger

Merger is a tool used by companies for the purpose of expanding their operations often aiming at an increase of their long term profitability. Evidence on the success of M&A however is mixed: 50~75% of all M&A deals are found to fail in their aim of adding value.

Usually mergers occur in a consensual (occurring by mutual consent) setting where executives from the target company help those from the purchaser in a due diligence process to ensure that the deal is beneficial to both parties. Acquisitions can also happen through a hostile takeover by purchasing the majority of outstanding shares of a company in the open market against the wishes of the target's board. In the United States, business laws vary from state to state whereby some companies have limited protection against hostile takeovers. One form of protection against a hostile takeover is the shareholder rights plan, otherwise known as the "poison pill".

Historically, mergers have often failed to add significantly to the value of the acquiring firm's shares (King, et al., 2004). Corporate mergers may be aimed at reducing market competition, cutting costs (for example, laying off employees, operating at a more technologically efficient scale, etc.), reducing taxes, removing management, "empire building" by the acquiring managers, or other purposes which may or may not be consistent with public policy or public welfare. Thus they can be heavily regulated, for example, in the U.S. requiring approval by both the Federal Trade Commission and the Department of Justice.

The U.S. began their regulation on mergers in 1890 with the implementation of the Sherman Act. It was meant to prevent any attempt to monopolize or to conspire to restrict trade. However, based on the loose interpretation of the standard "Rule of

Reason", it was up to the judges in the U.S. Supreme Court whether to rule leniently (as with U.S. Steel in 1920) or strictly (as with Alcoa in 1945).

Acquisition

An acquisition, also known as a takeover, is the buying of one company (the "target") by another. An acquisition may be friendly or hostile. In the former case, the companies cooperate in negotiations; in the latter case, the takeover target is unwilling to be bought or the target's board has no prior knowledge of the offer. Acquisition usually refers to a purchase of a smaller firm by a larger one. Sometimes, however, a smaller firm will acquire management control of a larger or longer established company and keep its name for the combined entity. This is known as a reverse takeover.

3) Types of acquisition and mergers

i. The buyer buys the shares(and in effect the assets or whole company out right), and therefore control, of the target company being purchased. In effect this creates something that has higher growth rate in the given market.

ii. The buyer buys the assets of the target. This type of transaction leaves the target company as an empty shell, if the buyer buys out the entire assets. The cash the target receives from the sell-off is paid back to its shareholders by dividend or through liquidation. A buyer executes asset purchase, often to "cherry-pick" the assets that it wants and leaves out the assets and liabilities that it does not.

The terms "demerger", "spin-off" and "spin-out" are sometimes used to indicate a situation where one company splits into two, generating a second company separately listed on a stock exchange.

In business or economics a merger is a combination of two companies into one larger company. Such actions are commonly voluntary and involve stock swap or cash payment to the target. Stock swap is often used as it allows the shareholders of the two companies to share the risk involved in the deal. A merger can resemble a takeover but result in a new company name (often combining the names of the original companies) and in new branding; in some cases, terming the combination a "merger" rather than an acquisition is done purely for political or marketing reasons.

Classifications of mergers:

i. Horizontal mergers take place where the two merging companies produce similar product in the same industry.

ii. Vertical mergers occur when two firms, each working at different stages in the production of the same good, combine.

iii. Conglomerate mergers take place when the two firms operate in different industries.

A unique type of merger called a reverse merger is used as a way of going public without the expense and time required by an IPO.

The contract vehicle for achieving a merger is a "merger sub".

The occurrence of a merger often raises concerns in antitrust circles. Devices such as the Herfindahl index can analyze the impact of a merger on a market and what, if any, action could prevent it. Regulatory bodies such as the European Commission and the United States Department of Justice may investigate anti-trust cases for monopolies dangers, and have the power to block mergers.

Accretive mergers are those in which an acquiring company's earnings per share (EPS) increase. An alternative way of calculating this is if a company with a high price to earnings ratio (P/E) acquires one with a low P/E.

Dilutive mergers are the opposite of above, whereby a company's EPS decreases. The company will be one with a low P/E acquiring one with a high P/E.

The completion of a merger does not ensure the success of the resulting organization; indeed, many mergers (in some industries, the majority) result in a net loss of value due to problems. Correcting problems caused by incompatibility—whether of technology, equipment, or corporate culture— diverts resources away from new investment, and these problems may be exacerbated by inadequate research or by concealment of losses or liabilities by one of the partners. Overlapping subsidiaries or redundant staff may be allowed to continue, creating inefficiency, and conversely the new management may cut too many operations or personnel, losing expertise and disrupting employee culture. These problems are similar to those encountered in takeovers. For the merger not to be considered a failure, it must increase shareholder value faster than if the companies were separate, or prevent the deterioration of shareholder value more than if the companies were separate.

4) Financing M&A

Mergers are generally differentiated from acquisitions partly by the way in which they are financed and partly by the relative size of the companies. Various methods of financing an M&A deal exist:

Cash

Payment by cash. Such transactions are usually termed acquisitions rather than mergers because the shareholders of the target company are removed from the picture and the target comes under the (indirect) control of the bidder's shareholders alone.

Financing

Financing cash can be borrowed from a bank, or raised by an issue of bonds. Acquisitions financed through debt are known as leveraged buyouts, and the debt will often be moved down onto the balance sheet of the acquired company.

A cash deal would make more sense during a downward trend in the interest rates. Another advantage of using cash for an acquisition is that there tends to lesser chances of EPS dilution for the acquiring company. But a caveat in using cash is that it places constraints on the cash flow of the company.

Hybrids

An acquisition can involve a combination of cash and debt, or a combination of cash and stock of the purchasing entity.

5) Motives behind M&A

These motives are considered to add shareholder value:

i. Economies of scale: This refers to the fact that the combined company can often reduce duplicate departments or operations, lowering the costs of the company relative to the same revenue stream, thus increasing profit.

ii. Increased revenue/Increased Market Share: This motive assumes that the company will be absorbing a major competitor and thus increase its power (by capturing increased market share) to set prices.

iii. Cross selling: For example, a bank buying a stock broker could then sell its banking products to the stock broker's customers, while the broker can sign up the bank's customers for brokerage accounts. Or, a manufacturer can acquire and sell complementary products.

iv. Synergy: Better use of complementary resources.

v. Taxes: A profitable company can buy a loss maker to use the target's loss as their advantage by reducing their tax liability. In the United States and many other countries, rules are in place to limit the ability of profitable companies to "shop" for loss making companies, limiting the tax motive of an acquiring company.

vi. Geographical or other diversification: This is designed to smooth the earnings results of a company, which over the long term smoothens the stock price of a company, giving conservative investors more confidence in investing in the company. However, this does not always deliver value to shareholders (see below).

vii. Resource transfer: Resources are unevenly distributed across firms (Barney, 1991) and the interaction of target and acquiring firm resources can create value through either overcoming information asymmetry or by combining scarce resources.

viii. Vertical integration: Companies acquire part of a supply chain and benefit from the resources.

ix. Increased Market share, which can increase Market power: In an oligopoly market, increased market share generally allows companies to raise prices. Note that while this may be in the shareholders' interest, it often raises antitrust concerns, and may not be in the public interest.

These motives are considered to not add shareholder value:

i. Diversification: While this may hedge a company against a downturn in an individual industry it fails to deliver value, since it is possible for individual shareholders to achieve the same hedge by diversifying their portfolios at a much lower cost than those associated with a merger.

ii. Overextension: Tend to make the organization fuzzy and unmanageable.

iii. Manager's hubris: Manager's overconfidence about expected synergies from M&A which results in overpayment for the target company.

iv. Empire building: Managers have larger companies to manage and hence more power.

v. Manager's Compensation: In the past, certain executive management teams had their payout based on the total amount of profit of the company, instead of the profit per share, which would give the team a perverse incentive to buy companies to increase the total profit while decreasing the profit per share (which hurts the owners of the company, the shareholders); although some empirical studies show that compensation is rather linked to profitability and not mere profits of the company.

vi. Bootstrapping: Example, how ITT executed its merger.

6) M&A marketplace difficulties

No marketplace currently exists for the mergers and acquisitions of privately owned small to mid-sized companies. Market participants often wish to maintain a level of secrecy about their efforts to buy or sell such companies. Their concern for secrecy usually arises from the possible negative reactions a company's employees, bankers, suppliers, customers and others might have if the effort or interest to seek a transaction were to become known. This need for secrecy has thus far thwarted the emergence of a public forum or marketplace to serve as a clearinghouse for this large volume of business.

At present, the process by which a company is bought or sold can prove difficult, slow and expensive. A transaction typically requires six to nine months and involves many steps. Locating parties with whom to conduct a transaction forms one step in the overall process and perhaps the most difficult one. Qualified and interested buyers of multimillion dollar corporations are hard to find. Even more difficulties attend bringing a number of potential buyers forward simultaneously during negotiations. Potential acquirers in industry simply cannot effectively "monitor" the economy at large for acquisition opportunities even though some may fit well within their company's operations or plans.

An industry of professional "middlemen" (known variously as intermediaries, business brokers, and investment bankers) exists to facilitate M&A transactions. These professionals do not provide their services cheaply and generally resort to previously-established personal contacts, direct-calling campaigns, and placing advertisements in various media. In servicing their clients they attempt to create a one-time market for a one-time transaction. Many but not all transactions use intermediaries on one or both sides. Despite best intentions, intermediaries can operate inefficiently because of the slow and limiting nature of having to rely heavily on telephone communications. Many phone calls fail to contact with the intended party. Busy executives tend to be impatient when dealing with sales calls concerning opportunities in which they have no interest. These marketing problems typify any private negotiated markets.

The market inefficiencies can prove detrimental for this important sector of the economy. Beyond the intermediaries' high fees, the current process for mergers and acquisitions has the effect of causing private companies to initially sell their shares at a significant discount relative to what the same company might sell for were it already publicly traded. An important and large sector of the entire economy is held back by the difficulty in conducting corporate M&A (and also in raising equity or debt capital). Furthermore, it is likely that since privately held companies are so difficult to sell they are not sold as often as they might or should be.

Previous attempts to streamline the M&A process through computers have failed to succeed on a large scale because they have provided mere "bulletin boards" —static information that advertises one firm's opportunities. Users must still seek other sources for opportunities just as if the bulletin board were not electronic. A multiple listings service concept has not been applicable to M&A due to the need for confidentiality. Consequently, there is a need for a method and apparatus for efficiently executing M&A transactions without compromising the confidentiality of parties involved and without the unauthorized release of information. One part of the M&A process which can be improved significantly using networked computers is the improved access to "data rooms" during the due diligence process.

7) The Great Merger Movement

The Great Merger Movement happened from 1895 to 1905. During this time, small firms with little market share consolidated with similar firms to form large, powerful institutions that became even market dominating. The vehicle used were so-called Trusts. To truly understand how large this movement was—in 1900 the value of firms acquired in mergers was 20% of GDP. In 1990 the value was only 3% and from 1998–2000 it was around 10%–11% of GDP. Organizations that commanded the greatest share of the market in 1905 saw that command disintegrate by 1929 as smaller competitors joined forces with each other.

Short-run factors

One of the major short-run factors that sparked The Great Merger Movement was the desire to keep prices high. That is, with many firms in a market, supply of the product remains high. During the panic of 1893, the demand declined. When demand for the good falls, as illustrated by the classic supply and demand model, prices are driven down. To avoid this decline in prices, firms found it profitable to collude and manipulate supply to counter any changes in demand for the good. This type of cooperation led to widespread horizontal integration amongst firms of the era. Horizontal integration is when multiple firms responsible for the same service or production process join together. As a result of merging, this involved mass production of cheap homogeneous output that exploited efficiencies of volume production to earn profits on volume. Focusing on mass production allowed firms to reduce unit costs to a much lower rate. These firms usually were capital-intensive and had high fixed costs. Due to the fact of new machines were mostly financed through bonds, interest payments on bonds were high followed by the panic of 1893, yet no firm was willing to accept quantity reduction during this period.

Long-run factors

In the long-run, due to the desire to keep costs low, it was advantageous for firms to merge and reduce their transportation costs thus producing and transporting from one location rather than various sites of different companies as in the past. This resulted in shipment directly to market from this one location. In addition, technological changes prior to the merger movement within companies increased the efficient size of plants with capital intensive assembly lines allowing for economies of scale. Thus improved technology and transportation were forerunners to the Great Merger Movement. In part due to competitors as mentioned above, and in part due to the government, however, many of these initially successful mergers were eventually dismantled. The government over time grew weary of big businesses merging and created the Sherman Act in 1890, setting rules against price fixing (Section I) and monopolies (Section II). In the modern era, everyone knows of the controversy over Microsoft, but starting in the 1890s with such cases as U.S. versus Addyston Pipe and Steel Co. the courts attacked such companies for strategizing with others or within their own companies to maximize profits. Ironically, such acts against price fixing with competitors created a greater incentive for companies to unite and merge under one name so that they were not competitors anymore and technically not price fixing. The Sherman Act is still under debate to this day, ranging from broad to strict to mixed interpretations. There are many varied opinions on whether it is acceptable to dominate a market based on size and resources, and we must wait and see what the courts of the future will conclusively decide.

Impact of cross-border M&A

In a study conducted in 2000 by Lehman Brothers, it was found that, on average, large M&A deals cause the domestic currency of the target corporation to appreciate by 1% relative to the acquirer's. For every $1 billion deal, the currency of the target corporation increased in value by 0.5%. More specifically, the report found that in the period immediately after the deal is announced, there is generally a strong upward movement in the target corporation's domestic currency (relative to the acquirer's currency). Fifty days after the announcement, the target currency is then, on average, 1% stronger.

Major mergers and acquisitions in the 1990s

Top 10 M&A deals worldwide by value (in mil. USD) from 1990 to 1999:

Rank	Year	Purchaser	Purchased	Transaction value (in mil. USD)
1	1999	Vodafone Airtouch PLC	Mannesmann	183,000
2	1999	Pfizer	Warner-Lambert	90,000
3	1998	Exxon	Mobil	77,200
4	1999	Citicorp	Travelers Group	73,000
5	1999	SBC Communications	Ameritech Corporation	63,000
6	1999	Vodafone Group	AirTouch Communications	60,000
7	1998	Bell Atlantic	GTE	53,360
8	1998	BP	Amoco	53,000
9	1999	US WEST	Qwest Communications	48,000
10	1997	Worldcom	MCI Communications	42,000

Major mergers and acquisitions from 2000 to present

Top 10 M&A deals worldwide by value (in mil. USD) since 2000:[2]

Rank	Year	Purchaser	Purchased	Transaction value (in mil. USD)
1	2000	Fusion: America Online Inc. (AOL)	Time Warner	164,747
2	2007	Schwebend: Barclays Plc	ABN-AMRO Holding NV	90,839
3	2000	Glaxo Wellcome Plc.	SmithKline Beecham Plc.	75,961
4	2004	Royal Dutch Petroleum Co.	Shell Transport & Trading Co	74,559
5	2006	AT&T Inc.	BellSouth Corporation	72,671

Rank	Year	Purchaser	Purchased	Transaction value (in mil. USD)
6	2001	Comcast Corporation	AT&T Broadband & Internet Svcs	72,041
7	2004	Sanofi-Synthelabo SA	Aventis SA	60,243
8	2000	Spin-off: Nortel Networks Corporation		59,974
9	2002	Pfizer Inc.	Pharmacia Corporation	59,515
10	2004	JP Morgan Chase & Co	Bank One Corp	58,761

8. Dilutive effect

Definition and theory

Dilutive effect is the result of a transaction that decreases earnings per common share (EPS).

III. Analyzing the case

1. How is the situation of HFS and CUC before they merged?

By 1996, Silverman was fronting eight national hotel-motel chains. Recorded earnings had spurted from $21 million to $80 million, and Wall Street hailed Hospitality Franchise as a great new growth story. Growth fueled the market price, which made acquisitions cheap; cheap acquisitions helped keep the growth rate up. So the strategy went, propelling Silverman down the diversification path into other fragmented brand-name franchise fields, like real estate brokerage and auto rentals. The purchase, first of Century 21, and then Coldwell Banker, made Silverman a major player in the residential brokerage and relocation business.

Sales between 1985 and 1988 climbed from $87.5 million to $271.8 million. CUC was on its way to becoming the fifth largest holding of the 66 mutual funds specializing in small companies. The multiples generated by its demand made CUC stock a super merger currency.

2. How is the leadership mixed between the two companies?

From the effective date of the merger (December, 1997) to January 1, 2000, Silverman was to be president/CEO, with Forbes as chairman. After that date, the two would switch — Silverman to chairman; Forbes to CEO. The table of organization carried eight vice-chairmen (four from either side) and 28 directors (14 from each side).

3. Why didn't Ernst & Young find out the accounting problem of Cendant earlier?

The culture of the accounting profession itself has undergone a major change. As what used to be the "Big Eight" coalesced into what is now the "Big Five," competition sharpened. One solution was to diversify out of the labor-intensive business of bookkeeping into the much higher margin line of "consulting" on items like management, technology, and recruiting. Consulting has boomed to the point where traditional audit fees now account for only 30 percent of Big Five revenues. Some of the cross-selling is done by regular line bean counters who have no wish to irritate the clients they are hoping to upgrade.

4. How should be investors alert for?

Manipulating merger reserves is a common practice. Investors can detect it by: 1) checking the footnotes in the annual report; 2) being alert for the broadening trend for an acquiring company to take as big a write-off as possible on its new partner's research and development "in progress"; 3) checking out pooling of interest accounting; 4) checking cash flow versus reported earnings; 5) stock buybacks; 6) the impact of management stock options on reported earnings; 7) the dilutive effect; 8) options.

IV. Translation of the Case

如果你是个价值投资者，那么请相信你的直觉。如果某支股票好得让人难以置信，也许其背后真有问题也说不定。尽管有证券交易委员会监督员的监督和花在请会计师上的数十亿美元，但可能还是有人在造假账，如 HFS 和 CUC 国际等令人瞠目结舌的案例。

亨利·R.西尔沃曼和沃尔特·A.福布斯，两位亿万富翁。一位是"神经质的工作狂"，彻头彻尾的"完美主义者"；另一位自由自在，穿着牛仔裤、运动鞋在办公室到处晃荡，以苏打饼干充饥，周末和下属一起打垒球。

但两个人都出售股票，在深入研究了金融工程工具后，两个人亮出他们的报告收益：每年增长 25%，主要是通过买进，受到了华尔街的吹捧。证券分析家和激进合并会计使得西尔沃曼和福布斯这两家公司实现了 50 倍的收益增长。正是因为收购会计中的秘密，西尔沃曼和福布斯才可能将他们的报告收益增长公布得比实际内部增长高了许多。例如，1996 年，西尔沃曼向股东们宣布收益上涨了 75%。但如果你不算当年的买进，就会看清实际收益将近 20%，而这 20% 中的大部分还是来自早前的买进。

西尔沃曼和福布斯把用虚拟的上涨股票货币去购买实实在在的资产的合法技术运用到了极致。正是这种极致将两个人带入到一种超级合并中，又获得了华尔街的更多赞美。但令所有人都没有想到的是，这一强强联合却很快就分崩离析，成为上世纪最大的金融灾难之一，使得不够警惕的投资者们损失惨重。

灾难本来是可以避免的。早就有征兆警告股东们。有些股东意识到了，但多数被会计师和证券分析家们鼓惑而受到了重创。西尔沃曼和福布斯的故事值得细细研究。报告收益往往不是看起来的那样。

截止到 20 世纪 80 年代初期，西尔沃曼一直做融资买进生意。他最具代表性的收购是两度成功收购了 Days 连锁低档宾馆。他的策略是提供一个集中的预约和营销系统，以抵消收入的不足，这一策略用以适应这个具有影响力的收购理念，目的是有利可图，以最少的资本支出来产生足够的现金流量，从而尽快用现金支付买进债务。

截至 1996 年，西尔沃曼已经拥有了八家酒店——汽车旅馆连锁，收益也从 2,100 万美元跃至 8,000 万美元，他的 HFS 公司也被华尔街誉为新的增长奇迹。增长刺激了市场价格，从而买进成本低；而低的买进成本使得增长率持续较高。西尔沃曼开始了多样化经营，进入了其他连锁领域，如房地产经纪业和汽车租赁业。但指导思想没有改变：那就是通过收购连锁产业，保持 HFS 的虚拟公司性质。HFS 先后收购了 21 世纪和科德韦尔银行家，西尔沃曼从而成为住房经纪业和住房置换业的有影响力的经营者。

沃尔特·福布斯是 CUC 国际的主席。他在不到 25 年的时间里将 CUC 从起步阶段发展成为美国最大的折扣会员购物服务承办商，销售额达到了 23 亿美元。1984 年，经过十年多的不懈努力，福布斯似乎离自己建立一个无商店的社会的目标越来越近了。他的策略要求增加更多的折扣服务（餐饮和旅游等等），建立一个广阔的会员基础，从而使他能够进行交叉销售。福布斯的交叉销售与西尔沃曼在 HFS 努力做成的是一致的：酒店连锁向顾客介绍新近收购的 Avis 汽车租赁服务，两家公司再向有购房意向的客户介绍 21 世纪房地产经纪人。

西尔沃曼和福布斯领导的都是虚拟的实体——没有产品目录，无硬资产使用，前景是丰富的现金流量。摩根斯坦利的分析家们认为 CUC 是涌现出的最有前途的公司。CUC 的销售额从 1985 年的 8,750 万美元上升到了 1988 年的 2.718 亿美元。公司正跃升为第五大 66 种共有基金的持有者。由需求而产生的市盈率使得 CUC 股票成为了一支超级合并通货。西尔沃曼和福布斯在战略上非常相像——公司合并等于成长，等于跨国公司，等于合并，还等于……

1996 年，当 CUC 的销售额接近 20 亿美元时，福布斯已经策划了至少 25 次买进。采购会计使 CUC 的账目有些晦涩难懂。没有几位华尔街的分析家思考过这些，但早在 1991 年，福布斯杂志的迈克尔·奥泽南就开始质疑这些推动 CUC 直线上升的账目了。奥泽南发现了一系列早期的警告讯号：

- CUC 越来越难吸引新的会员；
- 差不多三成注册的会员同年年底就注销了会员身份；
- 交叉销售的想法并不成功；
- 营销成本影响现金流量，即被该公司会计信息所掩盖的一个动量。

证券交易委员会对 CUC 会计情况的质疑加深了分析家们的疑虑，但华尔街仍然维持着 CUC 普通股很高的点数以及极具诱惑力的市盈率。也正是这样的市盈率让福布斯可以继续他的收购买进。报告销售额和报告收益继续着有节奏的上涨，并且不可避免地导致一个可能性：如果两大虚拟公司——CUC 和 HFS 联手会怎样呢？福布斯和西尔沃曼互相需要对方。HFS 和 CUC 合并的谈判有了结果的时候，这一超过 110 亿美元的合并案还有很多未解开的问号。其中一个问题就是两位主席迥然不同的个性。

关于领导权：从合并生效日期（1997 年 12 月）到 2000 年 1 月 1 日，西尔沃曼将作为总裁/首席执行官，而福布斯作为主席。2000 年 1 月 1 日以后，两个人岗位对调——西尔沃曼作为主席，而福布斯作为首席执行官。整个上层建筑有 8 位副主席（双方各 4 位），28 名主任（双方各 14 名）。一些主管同新公司有着密切的外部业务关系，从而引出了对他们独立性的质疑。有少数主流分析家甚至暗示了这些明显的障碍。

不管此次合并向股东做出了怎样的长期承诺，高级管理层还是很快就见到了好处。合并之前，福布斯的基本工资稍高于 78 万美元，奖金也是同样的数目。合并后，他的基本工资则是 125 万美元，奖金稍少于基本工资，或是税前收益的 0.75%。

虽然他们的联合被称为平等的合并，但很明显西尔沃曼更平等。他的基本工资是 150 万美元，奖金稍少于基本工资的 150%，或税前收益的 0.75%。除西尔沃曼和福布斯，其他高级管理层也享受到了这种较之合并前更高的工资、更高的奖金、更高的期权和既定享受退休的权利。西尔沃曼和福布斯为互相找到对方而窃喜。

两家公司合并成为 Cendant 公司后,西尔沃曼亲自到 CUC 下属的许多子公司进行了考察。他的审计员仅被给予了有限进入 CUC 非公开档案的权利。CUC 担心泄露了公司重要的信息。西尔沃曼对于不能及时了解 CUC 公司的详细情况感到很急躁。西尔沃曼要求福布斯将原来部门通过 CUC 两步传达报告改为直接向他的总会计负责人斯科特·福布斯(与沃尔特无关)报告。

沃尔特同意了西尔沃曼的要求,但请求延期一个月在第一季度结束后再做调整。西尔沃曼同意了,但急躁的他一个星期后又变卦了。他要求 CUC 立即上交报告。斯科特·福布斯与前 CUC 总裁,也是新任 Cendant 副主席的 E.柯克·希尔顿会面就细节进行研究,同时 CUC 的四名会计主管也出席了会面。

斯科特·福布斯记得希尔顿交给了他一份现金流量数据表,并请他帮助 CUC 在新的财政年度将 1.65 亿美元从合并储备变为收入。交给福布斯的一份日程表显示 CUC 为它几个部门的储备调整安排了总共 2.02 亿美元的预算。这笔现金将来自约 5.5 亿美元的储备金,新公司将以解雇费、诉讼费、工厂倒闭费用及其他重组花费的形式支出。

似乎 CUC 在谈论推动一种具有攻击性的审计标准,也就是在大合并案中很常见的所谓"巨额冲销"会计。将可能是几年的支出变为"一次性支出",而不是按实际支出去记账以保证未来的收益看上去更好。在 CUC(和 HFS)的案例中,两家经营多年的公司的合并使得局外人很难看清营业费用情况。高估合并费用,就能使原本可能突兀的曲线平缓。斯科特·福布斯不喜欢他听到的一切。诚然,自公司于 1983 年上市以来,安永作为全球五大会计事务所一直在对其进行审计,并未产生过任何异议。

CUC 增长的销售额和收益中有多少来自于其经营呢?又有多少被临时项目夸大了而未被 HFS 所察觉呢?了解到 CUC 1997 年的净收入中的 1.44 亿美元来自非营业来源,西尔沃曼勃然大怒。得知 CUC 需要拿出储备中的 2 亿美元来弥补 1998 年的营业预算时,西尔沃曼更为震怒。西尔沃曼跟沃尔特·福布斯说他要副主席希尔顿和财政主管克斯默·柯利亚诺立即从公司消失。但新闻上并没有提到辞退的事情,也没提到公司背后的混乱。

虽然西尔沃曼在电话会议上向华尔街说了很多宽心话,但会计主管斯科特·福布斯在 Cendant 新泽西的总部还是听到了很多议论。为了继续追查,他找到了 CUC 以前的雇员——卡斯帕·萨伯蒂诺。萨伯蒂诺告诉福布斯在 1997 年前三个季度,他对销售额和支出做了一系列"向上的"调整,正是这样的调整使得 CUC 的报告收益上涨了 1.76 亿美元。捏造的数目已经纳入到了公司一级的综合账目中,但没纳入任何经营单位的账目。萨伯蒂诺将细节情况报告给福布斯和财务主管迈克尔·摩纳哥，说他已经从储备中捏造了 9,300 万美元的第四季度收益，但"尚未经证实"。

萨伯蒂诺承认这些数字是公司上层（如已故的财务总监柯利亚诺）杜撰的，以符合承诺给华尔街的收益目标。可以预知的收益增长是大型合并和投资的关键。只要收益是增长的，那么付出什么样的代价都不为过。

萨伯蒂诺之所以向斯科特·福布斯和摩纳哥报告是一种自我保存的表现。柯利亚诺已经离开了公司，福布斯和摩纳哥都不愿承担由柯利亚诺和财务副主席安妮·佩博下令而造假账的责任。各个部门负责会计工作的下级人员也受命进行"调整"，要么帮着登记捏造的"向上的"数目，要么抓牢储备金。这是一种很典型的例子，说明激进会计法出轨是非常容易的。

坏消息很快就上了新闻，并且传到了证券交易委员会和新泽西纽华克的联邦检查官耳朵里。发现的 CUC 会计违法问题可能迫使 Cendant 从其报告的 1997 年利润 8.72 亿美元中砍掉 1 亿到 1.15 亿美元。CUC 可能必须重新申明其报告收益。

华尔街疯狂地作出回应，股票受到重创，几乎急剧下降了 50 点。

针对 Cendant、西尔沃曼和福布斯的 70 多起股票持有人诉讼案中的第一起控告严重违反证券法的案子，当时已经快到法庭审理阶段。原告申诉：福布斯和西尔沃曼在公司会计丑闻败露之前的数月内通过销售 7,000 多万美元股票而获益。

在辩护中，西尔沃曼和福布斯均否认事先对造假账知情。

西尔沃曼将愤怒指向了福布斯。福布斯和希尔顿——更不用说安永的会计师们怎么会没能识别这个骗局呢？一个非常尖锐的问题。西尔沃曼感到被背叛了。福布斯也是。他是事发后五天才知情的。他抱怨道："我应该和西尔沃曼同时了解情况。"西尔沃曼反击说，福布斯不知情是因为自己（西尔沃曼）不知道谁和谁串通一气。正是在这样的气氛中，西尔沃曼开始努力把福布斯排挤出公司。西尔沃曼曾经认可的管理结构——两个公司各占一半的董事会——使他现在束手无策。就像许多大型合并一样，Cendant 也是一座建立在沙滩上的房子。

这种局面不仅反映在 Cendant 依然萎靡的股市上，当亚瑟·安德森的会计师们拿出一份报告说明损失比原来的估计还要严重许多时，这种局面愈加严峻。又有 2,000 万美元的"会计错误"被暴露出来。CUC 至少已经三年伪造账目，而 Cendant 不得不为此将 1997 年的利润砍掉 2,400 万美元——是先前预测的两倍多。新的数据表明 CUC 1997 年报告收益的 1/3 都是虚无缥缈的。

审计师们还发现福布斯 1995 年和 1997 年有大约 200 万美元的开支有疑问，其中包括 100 万美元未经证明的现金垫款和美国快递服务，还有差不多 60 万美元的私人飞机支出。福布斯签署过的飞机支出报告显示从 Cendant 的合并储备中扣除。由此可知 CUC 非常放任的财务管理是由上及下的。

福布斯在被排挤之前，最终选择辞职。他说他的辞职是对所有股东和雇员解决这一难题最有利的办法。

福布斯的辞职是有很大诱因的。从他"无缘由"辞职后，Cendant 不得不按其雇佣合同中所规定的付清解雇费，3,500 万美元现金、2,200 万美元期权和 210 万美元的人寿保险费。

亚瑟·安德森的报告全文已经公布。从 1995 年到 1997 年，"非法"会计使得 CUC 的收益上涨了 5 亿美元；会计"失误"虚报收益 2 亿美元。减掉这些虚数，CUC 现在就象是一艘废船。

报告引述了由上级下令，下级数十名会计人员在收入、支出和合并储备上伪造的数个胜数的条目。由执行副总裁科斯莫·柯利亚诺、CUC 的主管安妮·佩博和会计主管卡斯帕·萨伯蒂诺下令，目的是将季度收益虚增至华尔街对 CUC 收益预测的水平上。报告上说："如果某一季度的实际收入是每股 10 美元，而分析家们的预测是 18 美元，那么就要调整 8 美元来增加收入。"

安永对 CUC 进行了 15 年的审计。他们的工作是怎么做的？至少 4 名 CUC 的高级会计主管，包括柯利亚诺和佩博，在加入 CUC 之前都曾在安永工作过。所以他们对安永的审计方式非常熟悉。亚瑟·安德森的报告称这是"一次计划周密的行动"，其中每个季度的营业、营销和行政支出都煞费苦心地保持一致。

安永在合并前没有资格地签署了 CUC 的账目，像其他牵扯其中的人一样，安永成为几起股票持有人诉讼的被告。Cendant 也加入了攻击。"安永不但没有揭露阴谋，反而选择助纣为虐，收取了几百万美元的费用。"

安永没有承认自己的失误，但却为 Cendant 股票持有人的诉讼支付了 3.35 亿美元。

亚瑟·安德森的报告引述了几个安永本可以发现骗局的迹象，但是报告主要攻击的还是柯利亚诺、佩博和萨伯蒂诺的工作。报告围绕着一个明显的问题：这三个人为什么要承担着刑事处罚的风险去保证 CUC 的收益（和市盈率）保持增长呢？

柯利亚诺持有 80 万股 CUC 的期权。被解雇之前，他每年赚取 30 万美元，包括 10 万美元的奖金，他住在康州郊区，车道上停着几辆丰田车，但他对这种尊贵的生活方式似乎并不满意。柯利亚诺是一个人颠覆了整个会计账目，还是他也和他的部下一样——遵守命令呢？

亚瑟·安德森的报告止步于柯利亚诺和他的属下。被调查的 80 名证人里没有一位直接暗示福布斯或希尔顿。Cendant 审计委员会的负责人向董事会递交的报告中也只是提到福布斯和希尔顿"也应为发生的一切负责"。他们没能"创造一个环境，在这个环境里，是不允许出现不实的会计报告的"。柯利亚诺在新泽西纽华克向联邦法庭坦白犯有共谋和电信欺诈罪。佩博承认犯有共谋罪。萨伯蒂诺犯有协助支持电信欺诈罪。

柯利亚诺坦言"我的上司鼓励我这样做"，CUC 自由宽松的企业文化"已经持续了许多年，是我们的上司使之根深蒂固的"。

不需要一份组织结构表也能知道柯利亚诺的上司只有沃尔特·福布斯和希尔顿。检察官也向新闻界表明他将"继续追查"。西尔沃曼对于证据将最终指向谁一点都不怀疑。他跟记者说："很明显，只有少数人对欺诈知情，而证据最终指向的必然是希尔顿和福布斯。"

陪审团指控福布斯和希尔顿犯有共谋和电信欺诈罪 10 年之久。福布斯和希尔顿否认了指控，但两人还面临着证券交易委员会的民事诉讼，要求他们"交出"阴谋进行时卖出的 CUC 股票所获得的利润。

"CFO"杂志报道，有迹象显示西尔沃曼不去回避风险，反而证明风险是正当的。Cendant 的副主席迈克尔·摩纳哥告诉"CFO"："要想赢，就要承担风险。"西尔沃曼愿意承担风险，因为他需要 CUC 来保证持续增长。这种被预测出来的风险在大型合并案中是非常典型的。这种账面上看起来很好，但是在现实中却难以快速发展的合并案的死亡率是非常高的。推动账目符合华尔街的预测的诱惑是难以抵挡的。Cendant 并不是唯一的例子。

这些高层真的愿意冒着坐牢的风险去铤而走险而达到华尔街预测的水平吗？在 Cendant 的案例中，起初只是为了粉饰某个季度的利润，但到了下个季度又要伪造更多的利润以达到平衡。

当问题越来越严重并最终崩溃时，会计师们在哪里呢？这是证券交易委员会几年来一直在问的问题。会计这个职业本身的文化也在经历巨大的变化。过去的"八大"会计师事务所合并成现在的"五大"时，随之出现的是竞争的愈加激烈。一个解决方法就是由原来的劳动密集型的记账变为利润更高的对管理、技术和招聘等进行的"咨询"。咨询业的发展已使传统审计费如今只占五大会计师事务所收入的 30%。会计师们不愿惹怒他们的客户。当公司高层想要捏造账目，会计师要想做出违背高层意愿的判决会有多么困难呢？华伦·布费在给他 Berkshire Hathaway 的股东的一封信中强调了会计师们面对的这个困境，"许多行政主管对于实实在在报告收益的无视是行业的耻辱。审计在这方面没有做出什么积极的举动。虽然审计师们应该将投资大众当作客户，但他们往往不是这样，而是向那些选择他们并发给他们酬劳的公司经理们磕头"。

证券交易委员会怀疑投资者们作出投资决定所依据的数据的可靠性，因此试图将会计师驱逐出咨询业。一些事务所已经这么做了，但还有一些仍在抗争。

从 Cendant 的失败中能学到什么呢？是不是现在一些非常热的股票都像 CUC 一样具有欺骗性呢？一些看上去有价值的股票会不会只是资产被虚报了而实际上是垃圾股呢？你可以打赌，但考察却不是那么容易的。

内部欺诈不是那些闭门造车的分析家们所能发现的。但正像投资咨询师罗伯特·雷恩克在他对 CUC 早先的不同看法中显示的那样，及早发现激进会计的蛛丝马迹是防卫的基本。他的调查显示，沃尔特·福布斯通过降低他本应为出现取消会员卡资格而建立起来的储备而增加的现金流量。顺着这条线索，雷恩克成为了华尔街为数不多的几位得出福布斯的报告收益全是骗局的结论的分析家之一。

在 CUC 完全失控的激进会计通常是合法的，因为被奉为圣经的公认会计原则中有很多灰色区域，而通常是合法的。就像是圣经一样，公认会计原则需进行阐释。因此就出现了在 CUC 的滥用合并储备循环为收益的情况。

假造合并储备是非常普遍的行为。如何发现呢？查看一下年度报告的脚注。脚注应讲清楚合并储备的规模、储备是如何使用的、其中有多少又变回了收益。储备不会永久存在。举例来说，如果储备占一个公司报告的一股利润 1 美元的一半，并且一股售价 20 美元的话，那么股票并不是按名义上的 20 倍收益来进行交易，而是按 40 倍的收益来交易。但股票真的值那么多吗？

另一个扭曲真正收益的前紧后松的开支安排，是购进公司越来越倾向于在其新伙伴"正在进行的"研发上，进行尽可能大的销账。

原因是这样的：这些正在进行的研发都有可能会成功。在研发上记下多达几十亿的动机是这些钱被一次性销账，从而使得日后的收益相比较看上去更多。研发销账也倾向于减少在"商誉"方面的拖累——购进公司为票面价值所支付的费用。因为商誉被降低并且影响了许多年的收益，所以目的是使其最低化。

另一个要检验的合并方法就是权益结合，其允许双方将资产的票面价值联合起来。这样做消除了降低商誉所带来的问题，并且夸大了未来每一年的收益。进行权益结合的困难很大。权益结合要符合一系列会计标准，但是自从 1990 年牛市开始以来，这样的交易以几何数字增长。权益结合的另一个积极效果是：它使得管理层更容易隐藏为可能不成功的合并所付出的费用。

还有以下要检查的弱点包括：现金流量对报告收益。现金流量（收入减去所有费用）可能是检验一个公司运作如何的最真实的数字了。如果报告收益比现金流量增长得快的话，那么两者之间的增长差就要有个来源。希望来源不是像 CUC 那样"向上的"虚调整。

还有一个潜在危险是股票的买回。从本质上讲，股票的买回没有任何问题。

如果一个公司的股票在市场价格很低，买回股票可能是一种很好的使用多余现金的方法，但要小心负债筹措资金进行买回；这只是一种负债换取股票来刺激收入的方式，从而使公司很难应对其业务或经济上的低靡。这种情况很容易就能检查出来：回顾一下公司最近几年的历史。随着收益的增长，资产中债务的份额增长是不是也伴随着股票份额的增长呢？要对这种增长持怀疑态度，你可以在 Value Line 的行业报告中找到相关历史数据。

同时仔细查看一下报告收益的管理股票期权的影响。虽然广泛认为期权的目的是保持管理上的强权，但实际上期权是一把双刃剑。虽然期权实际上是一种劳动力成本，但并不被称为费用，而是资本化的费用。所以，期权的作用是压低支出费用而虚报收益，通常虚报 30%或更多。

摊薄影响来自已发行股票数的增长——通过除法计算出每股的利润。算术是无情的。如果已发行股票数以 10%增长，而收益却没有相应的增长，那么就是摊薄 10%。在摊薄影响下，利润 20%的增长将得到每股收益只有 9%的增长。期权的影响应被看作是对未来的抵押贷款。在购买股票之前，仔细考虑，并研究一下年度报告的脚注，祝你好运。标准是如此的暧昧，你无法把握两个公司是否按同样的方式评估他们的期权。

期权当然也是 Cendant 引发争议的一个大问题。西尔沃曼和他那丧失了信用的股票又怎样呢？当西尔沃曼正在努力地对公司的损失进行补救的时候，一些持怀疑态度的人又对 Cendant 变为乐观态度。西尔沃曼对记者说："我们需要的不是资金，而是信用。"可是信用，一朝被摧毁，再重新建立，可就不那么容易了。

有这么一个道理，说来容易做来难，那就是：不要认为报告的数目就是票面价值。一定要认真研究数字背后的东西。要记住：如果某支股票好得让人难以置信，也许其背后真有问题也说不定。

Chapter Seven
First Lady on Wall Street —
Muriel Siebert

第七章
华尔街第一女经纪人——穆里尔·希伯特

I. Case Study

In nearly a half-century on Wall Street, Muriel F. Siebert has punched her way through many a glass ceiling. Among her distinguished "firsts": First woman admitted to the New York Stock Exchange, first woman discount broker, and first woman appointed New York State Bank Superintendent. And, to the cheers of feminists, the first U.S. working woman to become a billionaire on her own.

The latter breakthrough unfortunately proved more fleeting than Siebert's other achievements. Online trades are the fastest growing segment of the brokerage firm (Muriel F. Siebert and Company) she started over three decades ago. Spotting this connection early in the Internet craze, Web-happy speculators went wild. In the space of a couple of days, they pushed Siebert's holding company, Siebert Financial Corporation, from a low of $8.50 to a high of $70, giving the boss's 19.8 million shares a market of $1.4 billion. She segued in and out of the Big Rich for a couple of months until reality set in and the stock drifted through $55 on its way back to $13.50. "It's a good thing I didn't try to spend it," laughs Siebert, leaning over her at-the-desk lunch to drop a morsel of chicken to "Monster Lady," her long-haired pet chihuahua.

Almost all Siebert's capital is tied up in her firm (she owns 87 percent of it). From a pocketbook point of view, Siebert remains unfazed by this manic turn in her fortunes. "It's not as if I didn't have enough money to take care of myself," shrugs Siebert, who contributes heavily in energy and cash to such major feminist causes as the International Woman's Forum and the New York Women's Agenda. What really does worry her is the institutional side of the equation—the market dynamics that drove her stock and the way it bucketed all over the quote screen. For volatility and volume it beats anything seen in the Wild West markets of Hetty Green's time. "I hate to see innocent, misguided people get hurt," says Siebert. At its peak, the action was so frenetic there were days when the stock changed hands as many as three times in a single trading session, an incredible display of the bigger-fool theory.

Some people made money on the swing, of course, including Siebert's independently trusted charitable foundation. "They sold a little in the 20s," she grimaces, "but that's not me." One of the reasons for the volatility in the stock is the fact that Siebert has held on to so much of it. Her stash leaves only about two million shares available for public trading, a scarcity value the Securities and Exchange Commission quickly looked into when online chat rooms began slavering all over it. "It's no longer the Lord who gives and takes, it's the day traders," snaps Siebert, banging her cluttered desk for emphasis. "That's the way it is these days."

In truth, of course, Siebert wasn't a billionaires at all. If anything, she and her fellow shareholders were victims of momentum players hipped on the illusion they could outgun the professionals, trading in and out on often grossly unfounded Internet gossip. It wasn't just Siebert Financial. Hundreds of other closely held stocks were on a moving hit list that gulled thousands of naïve investors into paying the price for trades they never should have made.

Thin floats like Siebert's—relatively few shares available for public trading— are easy to manipulate, and thus ready targets for hustlers. Siebert's anger—and the SEC's deep interest—centered on chat room punters zap trading in and out of Siebert Financial on rumors that the firm was a buy-out candidate. Or on the perception that it was a cheaper buy than bigger discounters like Charles Schwab and Company, also in heavy day-trade play. Or there were good auspices like the westerly direction of pigeon flights in Central Park. When online trading turned out to be the hottest business on the World Wide Web, any rationale would do. Probing for clues behind what looked like yet another online pump-and-dump scheme, the

SEC zeroed in on the chat room bouncing to most of the noise. It turned out to be Tradingplaces.net, a Web site run by Chris Rea, 50, a Niles, Illinois-based stock caller. His trademark battle cry: "Let's rumble in the Wall Street jungle."

Self-dubbed "Merlin," Rea in earlier incarnations ran a home business that cranked out mailers for auto dealers. He peddled his electronic services (including day-trading tutorials and broker recommendation) to subscribers at $279.95 a month. The cash brought access to a cyberstorm of advisories, sometimes several a minute, flagging "Monster Buys" and "Trade Alerts." "Value picking up, you chart watchers. When you see the value go up bigger, this gonna explode," went one typical Merlin call. Or, "Pull back alert: I would take profits here." "Ghosts," like Warlock, Wizard, and Stoned, flitted across the screen, blipping encomiums to Rea's trading skills, pumping chatter into a frenzy that quickly radiated to other get-rich-quick sites. Count the footprints in the millions.

So, the SEC questions for Siebert were those directed at dozens of other episodes in which chat room gurus were suspected of trading in front of their own subscribers. Corporate insiders have also been found to dump stock into volcanic chat room moves.

Did Siebert know Rea? Queried the investigators. Did she do business with him? Had she sold any of her stock on his calls? No, no, and no were the answers. The question for shadowy Rea, whose puffed-up resume showed no particular background in U.S. securities, and who is not a registered advisor or broker: Had he been collecting reciprocal fees from the brokers he highlighted for subscribers? Had he traded against or worked outside deals on the stocks that he was touting? Rea denied any wrongdoing, was never charged by the SEC, and Siebert sees no foolproof way to protect traders from their own greed. Siebert has been doing her bit by tightening up margin requirements—the amount of borrowed money punters can trade on—and riding herd on hyperactive accounts. Siebert is also moving her no-frills brokerage firm into the advice and education business. She recently bought for about $2 million two free-standing sites—dollar.com and the women's financial network—and wrapped them into her own Siebert net.

The aim is to enrich her content with nuts-and-bolts pieces on topics the IRA legislation and 401k plans. It's not a purely eleemosynary pursuit. Siebert hopes a strong educational bent will help her broaden her product line beyond the bread-and-butter discount business to include new branded offerings such as mutual funds, money market funds, and insurance. Siebert thinks that putting serious financial information and planning tools into the mix will give her an eyeball edge over the hundreds of other women's sites in the field. "No horoscopes, childrearing, or hobby pieces," she promises. Her hope is the educational tack will generate enough trade to pay for the site. Despite her long commitment to women's groups, men account for the biggest portion of Siebert's commission business, and she is by no means ruling them off the site. But the heart of her new marketing pitch is that divorce, death, and other life changes demand that women "take control of their financial destiny." "We're going to help them do that, have some fun, and maybe make a little money," says Siebert. If it doesn't work? The irrepressible Siebert grins and feeds "Monster Woman" a bit of organic greens. "Hey, if it doesn't work, Uncle Sam is my partner."

There are competitive reasons for going into the advice business even if the expense of doing so cuts into profits. Traditional full-line brokers who have always offered advice of a sort are staling market share from operatives like Siebert.

There is one other reason—self-defense. "A lot of people who have never been in a down market got hurt," says Siebert, "so we got hurt, too. We think people should be reminded of basic values like earnings and cash flow." "I've always been good at numbers," continues Siebert. "They light up the page for me."

That's the conservative analyst side of Siebert speaking. Her business success, though, shows that she is not afraid of taking risks. Siebert's first long shot—the one that took her from the native Cleveland to Wall Street—was a complete leap into the unknown. She had been studying business and accounting at Western Reserve College in her native Cleveland. When her father died of cancer after a long siege, Seibert chucked school and took off for New York. Her assets totaled $500, a beat-up old Studebaker, and about a jillion dollars worth of chutzpah. "If you are going to sit there and wait for other people to do things for you," says Siebert, "you will soon be 80-years-old and look back and say 'Hey, what did I do?'" "My mother," she continues, "had a God-given voice, and she was offered a place on the stage, but nice Jewish girls didn't go on the stage in those days. So, I grew up with a woman who was frustrated her entire life," continues Siebert. "I certainly wasn't going to continue that role. I vowed I would do whatever I wanted to do."

Strong stuff. Siebert first took it to the personnel office at the United Nations and got turned down—no language skills. She then took it to Merrill Lynch and got turned down again—no college degree, and no Wall Street smarts, either. Stocks were not the subject of conversation at the Siebert dinner table. Her only exposure to the stock exchange had been on a visit to New York years before. On to Bache and Company. This time Siebert played up her accounting studies, lied her way into a college degree—and got the job. It was 1954, Siebert was 22, and only Wall Street's big producers were making top dollar. As a $65-a-week analyst trainee on the wire desk, Siebert shared a $120 a month apartment in the East Side enclave of Tudor City, and after six weeks probation got a $5 a week raise. "It was $3.80 net, laughs the numerific Siebert," "so I had an extra 20¢ for lunch." Siebert broke in fielding stock queries from Bache branches and talking over the answers with analysts. She was learning fast. "The accounting back ground helped a lot," recalls Siebert. Soon she was covering industries cast off as less than interesting by senior analysts radio, TV, movies, airlines. Riffling through memory, Siebert fastens on one study that particularly pleased her—a prescient look at the deep-discounted inventory value of Hollywood's old movies.

Siebert was doing well for a kid analyst—well enough to quit sleeping on her roommate's couch and move into her own apartment. But she was not doing so well as male analysts of similar attainment. "I fought like a son of a bitch to get ahead," she recalls. When she told Bache she deserved a raise and was talking to a competitor, Siebert was ordered to clean out her desk—pronto!

She moved to Shields and Company for something like $9,500 a year, definitely a step up the ladder. The quality of her research brought in three institutional customers. Siebert's modest annual bonus was keyed to the commissions they generated. Male brokers who brought in business got a 40 percent cut That rankled. "I didn't create my business simply by pounding on the door and saying 'I'm a woman, I'm entitled,'" Siebert told journalist Beverly Kempton. "I made my success by slugging it out with the boys."

Women were a distinct minority in the upper reaches of Wall Street. Siebert recalls that most of her fellow analysts treated her "like one of the guys," but traditional barriers were slow to come down. At one point between jobs, for example, Siebert circulated a resume with her (Muriel) full name on it and got not a single response. She sent out her next resume with just her initials on it, and got an immediate call back. Further, companies scheduled analysts meetings at luncheon clubs where women were banned or sometimes weren't allowed through the front door (Siebert got in through the kitchen). And then there was the locker room atmosphere of a generally male world. "To me, the sexual stuff was just part of the game," says Siebert. "I remember telling some guys to go do the physically impossible to themselves."

Serious harassment and discrimination cases still pop up on Wall Street, but Siebert thinks "the protective laws have changed a lot of things." "Sometimes women are too sensitive," adds the tough-minded Siebert. "Places like the floor of the New York Stock Exchange are known to be animal farms," she continues. "When people work under a lot of pressure, the language can get rough. I learned all my foul language at the trading post. It doesn't mean a thing to me," she adds, "They're just words."

Siebert's quick adaptive ways are one of the keys to her success. She used to stutter and never thought of herself as a salesperson. But growing confidence in her analytical skills made it easier for her to deal with big institutional clients. She remembers doing a study of NCR, for example, seeing a period of rising earnings ahead because of projected cuts in depreciation charges. When one autocratic fund manager, disenchanted with the company, came in with a sell order on NCR, she persuaded him to hold on to a stock that he subsequently made good money on. "That established another customer," recalls Siebert. "So then I could call him and say, 'Hey, I think you should buy this because…'"

Wall Street research was far more objective in those days. Analysts now increasingly cut the cloth to land investment banking business. Siebert argues that when she was coming up, analysts were free to write buys or sells with little fear of retribution. These days sell recommendations are rare, partly because discounters such as Siebert have changed the way Wall Street makes its money. With tough competitive commission rates the norm, profit margins on that side of the business have been stretched paper thin. The real money is in huge fees thrown off by underwriting and merger and acquisition deals. Instead of being paid on salary and bonus (as Siebert was), compensation now flows mainly from the investment banking side. "We're talking about millions for analysts who get close to a company," says Siebert. "Nothing wrong about millions," she adds, "but the issue of credibility puts the onus on the firm." The incentives almost invariably make for roseate recommendation.

That's one of the reasons why there are so many earnings "surprises," instantly picked by TV's financial commentators and magnified into erratic price swings. *Forbes* columnist David Dreman highlights the phenomenon, citing sell-offs of 50 percent in Intel and Apple Computer last year: when earnings fell below expectation. Dreman raises a critical question: "Wouldn't it be nice to find an analyst who warned you away from Intel and Apple with a sell recommendation?"

Chairman of the Jersey City, New Jersey-based investment advisory firm that bears his name, Dreman reinforces Siebert's view. Analysts looking to investment banking fees, he asserts, "cannot bring themselves to say the word 'sell.'" You have to learn to see through the code words. The closest most analysts come to the dreaded "S" word is to damn with faint praise: "accumulate," "neutral," "hold," or even "long-term buy."

Dreman interprets any such rating as a warning to bail out. These new assessments may seem favorable—a switch, say, from "aggressive buy" to "buy"—but Dreman interprets them as signaling "ditch the dog." His bottom line: "Read the research if you respect the analyst, but tear off the recommendation page and use it for kindling."

So, how is the investor to cope? As is clear from the new education net Siebert has established, she thinks people should be doing their own homework and look at establishment research with a questioning eye.

Siebert is as contentious as her dustmop-size "Monster Lady" who has the run of the office and instantly challenges strangers. She was purged from Shields and Company for entertaining a partnership offer from a rump research group that was about to set up outside the firm. That deal did not gel, but Siebert did hook on as a principal with two small firms before setting her cap for a New York Stock Exchange seat. No major firm had yet taken on a female partner, so Siebert figured her only next step up was to crash the barrier of the totally male Exchange establishment and become a member. Nothing in the by-laws said she couldn't, but nobody made it easy either, says Siebert. Nine of the first ten members she asked to sponsor her turned her down flat.

Siebert by then had put together a thick book of institutional clients and was earning what the *New York Times* estimated to be "a half-million dollars a year." That cut no ice with the banks. The Exchange demanded that she get a guaranteed loan for $300,000 of the $445,000 the seat would cost her. No bank would come up with the money until the Exchange formally agreed to admit Siebert. It was months before she was able to resolve this Catch-22, and become the first woman allowed to buy into the 1,366 member sanctum. So intimidating were the bars that she was the first woman even to apply in the Big Board's them 175-year history.

Siebert was taking on considerable personal exposure. A booming stock market had pushed seat prices to the highest level in 37 years. Siebert thanks to the publicity her breakthrough fanned, women looking for jobs or advice came by in droves. "They didn't have to look too far to find me," recalls Siebert. "The office was so tiny that all they had to do was open the door, and there I was." Siebert rarely worked the floor, spending most of her time, "upstairs," doing research and landing new clients. Siebert took a lot of kidding about the availability of plumbing when she did get to the trading posts. It was two years, she says, before anyone told her there actually was a lady's room tucked away in a corner of the Exchange floor.

Opportunistic as ever, Siebert again kicked up a ruckus when she became one of the Exchange's first member to plunge into the discount business. "May Day" 1975 brought the end of the fixed commission, pushed through by big institutional investors and the SEC. With negotiated rates now the rule, competition had come to Wall Street. It was a dramatic shift from the cozy way of doing business that dated all the way back to the Exchange's founding. Old, established, full-line brokers saw in this sea change severe damage to their profit margins and looked daggers at upstarts like Muriel F. Siebert and Company. When it comes to establishment slights, Siebert has a long memory. Wall Street's reaction to her discount initiative, says her Web site biography, was "quick and hostile." Her long-time clearing house dropped her and her firm faced SEC expulsion in 60 days if she could not find another house to clear her trades.

Though among the first out of the discount blocks, Siebert is these days dwarfed by such top dogs as Charles Schwab and Company and the Fidelity Management Group. The advent of electronic trading has sharpened price competition and at the same time fostered the opening of some 18 million Internet brokerage accounts. Despite the sell-off in high-tech stocks, some 35 percent of all trades generated by individual investors are made online, with bigger numbers still to come. The advantages: Trading is cheap ("no fee" brokers abound), convenient (trade from anywhere anytime), and offers ready-access to resources like instant stock quotes, initial public offering dates, and corporate earnings estimates.

Amid a blizzard of competing claims, Siebert notes that her firm has placed first or second ("That's not too shabby, is it?") among discounters rated annually by such consumer-oriented publications as *Smart Money* and *Kiplinger's Personal Finance Magazine*.

How to go about making a choice? Although increasingly rare as the industry grows through adolescence, Web site crashes and long telephone delays are still not uncommon, particularly on big volume trading days. One test: Call a couple of brokers several times over a couple of days and see how quickly you get picked up. Anything much over eight seconds (Siebert average) is below par. See what kind of answer you get to a question like this Kiplinger sample: "Are margin rates different in IRAs than regular accounts?" (Answer: IRAs can't be margined.)

Check aneillary service such as getting the year-end cost basis on your holdings, particularly stocks you have sold. Make sure you get real-time rather than delayed quotes. You want the stock price on your screen to be as close to the market as you can get it. Online trades, contrary to the advertising blarney, are not executed the second you tap the "Enter" key. Your order has to be routed through your broker to wherever it is being filled (floor trader, electronic market system), and may be executed away from the price you are expecting. One way to save yourself disappointment is to put in a limit order specifying the price at which you want to trade. Most discounters charge more (typically $5) to handle limit orders.

Some other threshold questions. Can your broker get you a meaningful crack at initial public offerings? (Don't count on getting a moon shot in any drop-dead amount.) What about inactivity fees if you don't trade? What does it cost to open and close an IRA, and what's the annual maintenance fee? As Siebert explains, advertised commission rates may seem low, but many discounters try to get some of their cost back by "tacking on a lot of fees." "They tack on postage," she says, "or they tack on the statement charges or charge you if you want to transfer and ship a security to a relative. You have to look at all the fees."

Siebert also suggests a check on the standard of the financial information you can access. Probably no more than a dozen discounters offer institutional-quality research, often only to high net worth customers. Remember that commission rates are not all. Cheapest is not necessarily best. A low-ball broker may be fattening his profit margins with "payment for order flow"—typically a rebate of $2 or more a trade from the market maker to whom he has routed the order. This perfectly legal kickback may mean that you're getting lousy execution—unwittingly compensating the market maker by paying fractionally more on a buy and receiving fractionally less on a sell. Put those fractions together and you're paying a lot more than just the commission.

One way to check on the quality of an execution is to ask for the exact time of your trade. Punch in a one-minute intra-day reading on a Web site such as Bigcharts.com. If your price is worse than the trades grouped around the same time, take it up with your broker. Limit trades typically don't throw off order flow payments and thus are more likely to produce tighter trades. Though little known to investors, payments for cash flow are the mother's milk of the business, particularly for "no fee" discounters. "It's a rip-off," says Muriel Siebert, who claims to have "reduced payments to nothing."

Along with other discounters. Siebert thrived on the heavy trading volume of the bull market. Her prosperity represents a long gritty comeback. The business nearly foundered after she put it in a blind trust to take on a new challenge as New York State Bank Superintendent. It was no political plum. The portfolio included oversight of some 500 banking institutions with more than $400 billion in assets, and over 1,000 small loan companies, check cashers, and sales finance companies— all licensed by the state. For anyone with less drive than Siebert, taking on the assignment would have seemed quixotic. Siebert's newly formed brokerage firm, only two years into the business, was just finding its feet. The capital in the firm was mortgaged to the money she had to borrow to buy her exchange seat, and the market was still in shock from the great sell-off of 1973—1974. "How could I refuse?" chuckles Siebert. "For a kid from Cleveland, it was a real challenge."

She was in the right place at the right time. Then Governor Hugh L. Carey was determined to put a woman in the job. Siebert's name kept coming up, making her a rare Republican ("social liberal, fiscal conservative") in a Democratic administration. It didn't hurt that Siebert had made some good Democratic connections through her work in women's organizations.

Siebert recalls her confirmation hearings with a triumphant laugh. The only written objection to her appointment came from a prominent financial journalist. How come? Asked the head of the state senate banking committee. Siebert recounted how the journalist had breached a confidence, directly attributing to her sensitive background information she had given him on a brokerage deal. So? Asked the banking committee chairman. "Well, I think he felt hurt when I called him up and told him he was a no good goddamn son of a bitch," answered Siebert, bringing down the house.

She was confirmed unanimously, just in time in 1977 to deal with New York City's failing Municipal Credit Union. Its total assets—$130 million—were much bigger than the insurance fund of the back-up government agency, the National Credit Union Administration. Siebert responded by taking over the MCU and running it.

It was a bad time for savings institutions of every kind, all too easily reminiscent of the bank runs of the Depression. Historic institutions like the Greenwich Savings Bank, chartered in 1833, were being drained by a mismatch in runaway interest rates. Forced to pay as much as 15 percent to hang on to deposits, Greenwich was stuck with about $1 billion in mortgages long on the books at about 8.5 percent. It was a desperate situation, mirrored in at least four other similarly stricken savings banks. With earnings registering zero, the Greenwich and its mates were heading for what would have been the first mutual savings bank insolvencies ever.

Billions in deposits were at risk. "I could cover one bank, but a whole industry?" asks Siebert, her voice trailing off. She fought commercial bank efforts to cherry-pick the mutuals and lobbied the Federal Deposit Insurance Corp. for an orderly bailout. I buried four of them, recalls Siebert, ticking off the stronger thrifts into which she merged the sick banks. "We managed to do it with only modest cost to the FDIC and no losses to depositors."

At odds with the Carey administration on such touchy subjects as foreign takeovers of local banks (she was against), Siebert quit after five years, deciding the job had become one "for watchdogs, not creators." She went out on a high note, resigning to take a stab at the Republican nomination for U.S. Senator. Siebert finished third in a three-way race. She financed her campaign with $250,000 of her own money, leaving in the archives lasting images of her determination. There she is, in stocking feet, standing on an up-ended milk crate, peering over a lectern, exhorting a group of female supporters.

Siebert's sabbatical was over. She had learned a lot, picked up visibility, projected herself as a role model—and very nearly lost her business. It had done badly under a caretaker management during the five years she was grappling with the banks. There were some easy choices. Siebert could have sold her firm at a decent profit, and latched on to one of the several high-powered jobs she was offered. Being ("I am a fighter") Siebert, she of course forged on. She succeeded in rehabbing her firm into a nimble boutique. She has done all the right things—brought in experienced management, kept up with technology (although at a somewhat slower pace than some of her competitors) and pulled off a couple of useful acquisitions, with the usual contention along the way.

Siebert took a lot of flack from competitors, for example, over the shrewd unorthodox way she eased her firm into a public listing five years ago. In a typical opportunistic move, Siebert merged into J. Michaels, Incorporated, a down-at-the-heels inner-city furniture retailer that had run out of options. It liquidated paying $17 a share to its principals, and on the exchange wound up with a 2.5 percent piece of what instantly morphed into Siebert Financial Corporation. Siebert made no bones about her objective. She needed the currency of a publicly owned stock, however obscure, to reward employees with options, and to engineer the acquisitions she needed to spur growth. A clueless *New York Times* reporter, chin wagged that role model Siebert had shamelessly "decided to go public in a back-door way usually reserved for shadowy penny stocks," thereby opening the door to cheap shots from competitors. One of them harrumphed that hidden balance sheet problems no doubt explained why Siebert did not go public with a conventional direct sale and raise some capital.

Siebert didn't need capital because she was financing the firm mainly out of her own pocket. It's also likely that she shied away from a broader public offering because she didn't want to let too many outsiders into her own good thing. Siebert is her own best steward. She collects a modest salary of $150,000 a year (no bonuses, no options), and does not take down the 16¢ a share in dividends she is entitled to, thereby saving Siebert Financial $3.1 million a year.

It's the Siebert savvy at work. Dividends keep minority holders happy, but would be punitively taxable to her—a non-starter. The tax return she handed out to reporters during her Senate primary run showed that Siebert, like any sensible feminist, would rather augment her capital than share it with the Internal Revenue Service. Her earnings at the time were buffered by no less than 18 legitimate audit-proof shelters. Close attention to cash flow has enabled Siebert to bankroll her firm out of her own pocket. She has financed expansion with direct loans and by putting up her stock as collateral against bank loans.

Siebert is now in her late 60s and the time when she can continue to play one-woman band may be coming to an end. Competitive pressures are so intense and technology-driven capital needs so high, Siebert will either have to take on outside partners or merge into some larger organization.

Siebert says she has gotten offers and "might" sell out "if the price was right." This is a painful dilemma for Siebert at a late stage in her life. The firm is basically an extension of herself, a bully-pulpit that has given resonance to her fight for women's rights. It is also the prime source of municipal underwriting fees she has split with local charities and the cash she has put into projects such as small loans to female start-ups. "You've got to give back to the system," says Siebert with a conviction that underscores a troublesome question. Who could ever truly succeed the feisty Muriel Siebert? She has not married, has no family in the business, and has learned first-hand that a caretaker management is a sure ticket to oblivion. What to do? For the moment Siebert says only, "I expect to be around for a good while."

Siebert's quandary is endemic to most entrepreneurs running a personal business never quite permitted to become institutionalized. The lone hand approach is becoming untenable in the face of the changes sweeping the business. Traditional middle-tier discounters like Siebert, offering low rates and a modicum of service, long had the field to themselves. Then came the huge upsurge in bull market volume and the advent of online trading. Heavy volume is catnip for discount profit margins, but the increasing amount of it done on the Internet skewed the mix. Wiring the house raised capital costs, but improved efficiencies set off a rate war. Pure online brokers emerged, forcing hybrids like Siebert into the double bind of coming down on price and upgrading service.

Talking about the cost of installing new touches like a voice-recognition order system while shaving prices to $14.95 per trade, Siebert frets over where the price-cutting will end. "The online firms have been offering too much to get new accounts," she complains. "Seventy-five free trades if you open a new account? That's really saying we'll almost pay you to bring your account to us." "We don't make much at $14.95," continues Siebert. "Would I go to $8.00 to build more customers? No, I could not give them service."

So, the rope frays while yet another new force exerts its pull. Deep-pocket traditional brokers like Merrill Lynch, anchored to an expensively built sales and distribution system, have begun to change their look. Offering competitive discount packages with advisory hand-holding, the old-line firms have already bitten off almost 30 percent of total online assets traded. As online trading goes mainstream, moving from hotshot day traders to older, more conservative investors wanting advice, the onslaught will continue to build. Some of the expected growth (online traders are likely to triple to 14 million in the next couple of years) will be cannibalized from existing accounts, but the old-lone brokers are on the move.

Bigger discounters have countered by backing into traditional portfolio management preserves via mergers like Charles Schwabs' combination with U.S. Trust Corporation. This potent blend of price and service is changing the contours of the business, hence Siebert's acquisition of the women's financial network and her dollar.com Web sites. Though limited by comparison with, says, E*trade's link to accounting firm Ernst & Young financial planners, the new outlets will offer the kind of unvarnished counsel that is a Siebert specialty.

Drawing on almost a half-century of experience on Wall Street, Siebert offers a sampler of advice: Forget about chasing hot stocks, however tempting they may seem. "I tell people, stick to your guns," says Siebert. "You will make money eventually. There is really no substitute for picking a company that your own research shows is going to increase its earnings and has a good outlook."

Discount brokers don't necessarily do it all. Siebert says her clients pay 6¢ a share for a round-trip buy-and-sell, while the same trade at a full-service broker may amount to as much as 50¢ a share, each way. But, "If that broker is giving you top-quality research," notes Siebert, "it's worth it." Her thought: Save money by voting a split ticket. "We have some accounts using full-service brokers who will trade some with them and some with us."

Straighten out your feeling about risk. If you're comfortable with risk, pick the best stocks in a "vibrant group with lots of momentum," says Siebert, but if "they are just today's game, watch them closely." For balance, throw in some companies you know are "not going out of business"—drug companies such as Merck and Bristol-Myers, for example.

Knowing when to sell is a lot tougher decision than what to buy. "If you find the reasons you like the stock in the first place are still there, you can be conservative and sell half to get your cost out," advises Siebert. "Or, if you expect a slow-up in earning, sell more."

Siebert's personal investment program, of course, still consists of putting every last nickel back into her own business. "I'm still fighting like a son of a bitch," she laughs. Fighting to be what she has been from the start—an independent woman.

Key Words and Expressions:

ancillary	adj. 辅助的，副的
archive	n. 存档，档案文件
auspice	n. 预兆，前兆，吉兆
autocratic	adj. 独裁的，专制的
bailout	n. 跳伞，将优先股发给股东作为红利之行为
blarney	n. 谄媚，奉承话
blip	n. 雷达上显示的点
blizzard	n. 大风雪
boutique	n. 专卖流行衣服的小商店
brokerage	n. 经纪人之业务，回扣
catnip	n. 猫薄荷
charitable	adj. 仁慈的，慈善事业的，宽恕的
chihuahua	n. 吉娃娃（一种产于墨西哥的狗）
chutzpah	n. 放肆
clutter	n. 混乱
columnist	n. 专栏作家
cut into	侵犯，打断
depreciation	n. 贬值，减价，跌落
disenchanted	adj. 不再着迷的
eleemosynary	adj. 施舍的，接受救济的，慈善的
enclave	n. 被包围的领土
encomium	n. 赞辞，赞美，称赞
endemic	n. 地方病
erratic	adj. 无确定路线，不稳定的
fleeting	adj. 飞逝的，短暂的
foolproof	adj. 十分简单的，十分安全的，极坚固的
fractionally	adv. 极少地，微小地
free-standing	adj. 自立的，不需依靠支撑物的
frenetic	adj. 发狂的，狂热的
grimace	v. 扮鬼脸，做苦相

grossly	adv. 非常，很
gull	v. 欺诈，骗，使上当
guru	n. 宗教导师，领袖
hipped	adj. 着迷的，忧郁的
horoscope	n. 占星，诞生时的星位
hustler	n. 皮条客，骗徒，催促者
hyperactive	adj. 活动过度的，极度活跃的
incarnation	n. 赋予肉体, 具人形, 化身
insolvency	n. 无力偿还，破产
intimidate	v. 胁迫
irrepressible	adj. 镇压不住的，抑制不住的
jillion	adj. 很多的，大量的
manic	adj. 狂躁的
manipulate	v. （熟练地）操作，巧妙地处理
non-starter	n. 弃权出赛的马，早就无成功希望的人
nuts-and-bolts	具体细节
old-line	adj. 历史悠久的，保守的
onus	n. 责任，负担
pronto	adv. 很快地，急速地
pump-and-dump	拉高出货
punter	n. 下赌注的人，用篙撑船的人，船夫
quixotic	adj. 堂吉诃德式的，狂想家的
rationale	n. 基本原理
roseate	adj. 玫瑰色的，红润的，容光焕发的
round trip	往返旅行
ruckus	n. 喧闹，骚动
rule off	划线隔开
rump	n. 尾部，臀部，残余
sanctum	n. 圣地，密室，书房
scarcity	n. 缺乏，不足
shy away from	躲避，离开，羞于
slow-up	放慢速度
stash	n. 隐藏处
subscriber	n. 订户，签署者，捐献者

top dog	胜利者
tutorial	n. 指南
unanimously	adv. 全体一致地，无异议地
unfounded	adj. 没有理由的，毫无根据的
volatility	n. 挥发性
vow	n. 誓约，宣誓

Notes:

1. Muriel Siebert 穆里尔·希伯特

1967 年 12 月 28 日，三十多岁的穆里尔·希伯特成为现代纽约股票交易所第一位女性成员。她以性格坚韧、雄心勃勃又和蔼可亲而著称。她曾在数家经纪公司当过股票推销员，后来自立门户，成为人数不多、却为争取重要地位而奋斗的华尔街著名女性经纪商之一。

2. Merrill Lynch 美林证券公司

美林证券公司是世界领先的金融管理与咨询公司之一，在 36 个国家建立了分支机构，管理的资产达 1.1 万亿美元。作为投资银行，它是全球领先的债务和股权证券保险商，并为世界范围内的企业、政府、公共机构以及个人提供战略咨询服务。美林的投资经理人带领公司成为世界最大的金融资产管理人之一。

3. Charles Schwab and Company 美国嘉信理财公司

美国嘉信理财公司是为个人投资者、投资管理人、退休计划、以及机构投资者提供一系列的投资理财服务的企业。名列史坦普 500 大企业 (S&P500) 的嘉信理财以完善与有价值的服务著称。公司总裁 Charles R. Schwab 先生于 1974 年创立公司时，立志提供"全世界最有用、最诚实的证券服务"。多年来，这个理念依然没有改变。嘉信理财的发展带动了美国证券界的许多改革。从 1989 年推出的电话下单系统、到 1991 年推出的"共同基金超级市场"，嘉信理财的一系列"全美首创"都已经成为证券界的基本服务。

4. E*Trade 亿创理财公司

亿创理财公司为零售、企业及机构客户提供环球理财服务，并以网上投资为基础，推广业务至零售客户，为他们提供一站式个人的投资、银行、借贷策划及顾问等服务。在美国，亿创理财公司为企业提供员工持股计划等不同服务，以及协助证券公司提升和促进交易，更为国际机构提供一系列证券交易产品和服务，例如机构性买卖交易等。亿创的营商宗旨是利用我们的专业知识和技术，通过互联网为客户提供综合、个人及增值的理财服务。

5. Merck 美国默克制药公司

世界制药企业的领先者，总部设于美国新泽西州，是一家以科研为本，致力于研究、开发和销售创新医药产品的跨国制药企业。1889 年，乔治·默克接管德国默克在美国纽约的分公司并创立美国默克，即默沙东。根据德国默克与默沙东(美国默克)协议，默沙东公司只可在北美地区使用"默克"之名。美国默克不同于德国默克：由于在美国出口业务的成功开展，默克公司于 1887 年在纽约成立了一个分公司。1889 年，由 Heinrich Emanuel Merck 的孙子乔治·默克接手经营。1891 年，默克美国分公司 Merck & Co. 成立。第一次世界大战期间默克丧失了很多海外子公司，其中便包括 Merck & Co.。如今这两家公司除了共同的名字"默克"之外，已经没有任何联系。应商业需要，双方一致同意，在美国和加拿大，"默克"归 Merck & Co. 独家使用，而在欧洲和世界其他各地，"默克"则由德国默克公司独家使用。与之相对应的，Merck & Co. 在北美之外的业务经营，须以 Merck Sharp & Dohme 或 MSD Sharp & Dohme（默沙东）的名义进行。而默克股份两合公司在北美的业务则要以 EMD （Emanuel Merck, Darmstadt 首字母缩写）的名义开展。

6. Bristol-Myers Squibb Company 百时美施贵宝公司

百时美施贵宝公司是一家以"延长人类寿命，提高生活质量"为使命的全球性医药及相关保健产品公司。在过去的 118 年里，百时美施贵宝致力于新药和营养品的研发，并在治疗癌症、心血管、代谢类综合症及传染病等领域享誉盛名。1887 年，两位美国青年，威廉·麦克拉伦·布利斯特（Bristol）和约翰·瑞普·麦尔斯（Myers），带着梦想创建了一家直接向医生销售药品的公司。19 世纪后期，爱德华·罗宾森·施贵宝（Squibb）成立了一家以自己名字命名的制药公司。1989 年两家公司合并为百时美施贵宝公司，成为当时世界上第二大制药公司。

II. Knowledge Points

1. SEC〈Scurities and Exchange Commission〉

The US regulatory body responsible for overseeing and administering rules associated with all sectors of the securities industry. Its main aim is to protect investors and maintain the integrity of the markets by full public disclosure.

2. Penny Stock

1）Definition

A type of ordinary share which is currently of negligible value, but may prove to be a good speculative investment. In the US these shares are priced at less than one dollar. In the UK they cost less than one pound.

In the U.S. financial markets, the term penny stock commonly refers to any stock trading outside one of the major exchanges (NYSE, NASDAQ, or AMEX), and is often considered pejorative. However, the official SEC definition of a penny stock is a low-priced, speculative security of a very small company, regardless of market capitalization or whether it trades on a securitized exchange (like NYSE or NASDAQ) or an "over the counter" listing service, such as the OTCBB or Pink Sheets. The terms penny stocks, microcap stocks, small caps, and nano caps are also all sometimes used interchangeably, however per the SEC definition, penny stock status is determined by share price, not market capitalization or listing service.

In the UK markets, penny stocks, or penny shares as they are more commonly called, generally refer to stocks and shares in small cap companies, defined as being companies with a market capitalization of less than £100 million and/or a share price of less than £1 with a bid/offer spread greater than 10%... In the UK Penny Shares are covered by a standard regulatory risk warning issued by the Financial Services Authority (FSA).

In France, penny stocks generally refer to risky stocks with a price of less than 1 euro.

Penny stocks generally have market caps under $500M and are considered extremely speculative, particularly those that trade on low volumes over the counter. The Securities and Exchange commission warns that, "Penny stocks may trade infrequently, which means that it may be difficult to sell penny stock shares once you own them. Because it may be difficult to find quotations for certain penny stocks, they may be impossible to accurately price. Investors in penny stocks should be prepared for the possibility that they may lose their whole investment."

2) High-Risk Investments

Many new investors are lured to the appeal of penny stocks due to the low price and potential for rapid growth which may be as high as several hundred dollars in a few days. Similarly, severe loss can occur and many penny stocks lose all of their value in the long term. Accordingly, the SEC warns that penny stocks are high risk investments and new investors should be aware of the risks involved. These risks include limited liquidity, lack of financial reporting, and fraud.

Since a penny stock has fewer shareholders, it is less "liquid", meaning it will not trade as many shares per day as a larger company. Any sudden change in demand or supply of stock can lead to a lot of volatility in the stock price. This lack of liquidity can send a stock price soaring up quickly or crashing down quickly. Lack of liquidity and volatility also makes penny stocks much more vulnerable to manipulation by management, market makers, or third parties. A lack of liquidity can also make it extremely difficult to sell a stock, particularly if there are no buyers that day. This can also make the stocks extremely difficult to short.

Secondly, unlike NASDAQ or the NYSE, there are only minimal listing requirements for a stock to remain on the OTCBB, namely that they make their filings with the SEC on time. In fact, companies that fail to meet minimum standards on one of the broader exchanges and are delisted often relist on the OTCBB or the Pink Sheets.

Furthermore, stocks trading on the Pink Sheets (recognizable with a .PK suffix) have little to no regulatory or listing requirements whatsoever, at least compared to major markets. There are no minimum accounting standards, change in notification of ownership of shares, and reported other material changes affecting the financial viability of a company, all of which are designed to protect shareholders.

The SEC notes most the same about Internet message boards, where fraudsters claiming to be unbiased investors who've carefully done their due diligence may in fact be company insiders, and that a single person or a small team can create the appearance of a huge interest in a stock simply by creating a huge number of aliases, while banning the most vocal or perceptive critics of these offerings.

3) Penny Stock Fraud

Microcap stock fraud

The reason for all this relentless promotion of penny stocks is because of the profits to be made through illegal pump and dump schemes. The SEC explains how it works:

"A company's web site may feature a glowing press release about its financial health or some new product or innovation. Newsletters that purport to offer unbiased recommendations may suddenly tout the company as the latest 'hot' stock. Messages in chat rooms and bulletin board postings may urge you to buy the stock quickly or to sell before the price goes down. Or you may even hear the company mentioned by a radio or TV analyst. Unwitting investors then purchase the stock in droves, creating high demand and pumping up the price. But when the fraudsters behind the scheme sell their shares at the peak and stop hyping the stock, the price plummets, and investors lose their money. Fraudsters frequently use this ploy with small, thinly traded companies because it's easier to manipulate a stock when there's little or no information available about the company."

There are all sorts of variations of the classic pump and dump, from short-and-distort to selling chop stocks—the last being a scam in which shares are acquired for pennies under Regulation S and then illegally sold to overseas or domestic retail investors. Other features of the typical penny stock scam include spam e-mails and junk faxes that tout ludicrous and fraudulent claims, crooked newsletter writers who promote a stock for a fee, message boards swarming with "buy now!!!" postings about a stock from anonymous, paid posters, fake or misleading press releases issued by the company, or boiler rooms full of cold-callers targeting naive, elderly, or foreign buyers all in attempt to drive up the share price while the insiders sell.

A more recent outbreak of penny stock fraud is far more brazen, and is based mostly overseas. Organized crime gangs in Eastern Europe and Asia will acquire a large number of shares of a moribund penny stock. Then, using passwords and logins to electronic brokerages, such as E*Trade, stolen at public computer terminals in hotels and elsewhere, they will then use the hijacked customer accounts to buy up shares, while at the same time selling their own shares, draining the customer accounts and leaving their victims holding thousands of shares of worthless penny stocks.

While not all stocks listed on the Pink Sheets or the OTCBB are fraudulent, one Business Week article estimated that chop stocks alone "make up perhaps half the 85 million-share daily volume of the OTC Bulletin Board."

Internet spams

Almost any Internet user with an e-mail address will have been exposed to penny stock promotions through e-mail spam. Approximately fifty-five billion unsolicited "spam" e-mail messages are sent each day, a significant proportion of which tout penny stocks, usually as part of a pump and dump scheme. According to a study conducted at Oxford, 15% of all spam was related to penny stock fraud. According to the study, "People who respond to the 'pump and dump' scam can lose 8% of their investment in two days. Conversely, the spammers who buy low-priced stock before sending the e-mails, typically see a return of between 4.9% and 6% when they sell."

3. Market trends

1) Definition and theory

Market trends reflect the general direction of prices or rates in financial markets. Participants in a given market use price charts to observe these trends, and to identify investment and trading opportunities.

That market prices do move in trends is one of the major premises of technical analysis, though the description of market trends is common to Wall Street, the economics profession, and the Federal Reserve.

Market trends unfold in periods when bulls (buyers) consistently outnumber bears (sellers), or vice versa. A bull or bear market describes the trend and sentiment driving it, but can also refer to specific securities and sectors ("bullish on IBM", "bullish on technology stocks," or "bearish on gold", etc.).

2) Primary market trends

Bull market

A bull market tends to be associated with increasing investor confidence, motivating investors to buy in anticipation of further capital gains. The longest and most famous bull market was in the 1990s when the U.S. and many other global financial markets grew at their fastest pace ever.

In describing financial market behavior, the largest group of market participants is often referred to, metaphorically, as a herd. This is especially relevant to participants in bull markets since bulls are herding animals. A bull market is also described as a bull run. Dow Theory attempts to describe the character of these market movements.

Bear market

A bear market tends to be accompanied by widespread pessimism. Investors anticipating further losses are motivated to sell, with negative sentiment feeding on itself in a vicious circle. The most famous bear market in history was 1930 to 1932, marking the start of the Great Depression.

Prices fluctuate constantly on the open market; a bear market is not a simple decline, but a substantial drop in the prices of a range of issues over a defined period of time. By one common definition, a bear market is marked by a price decline of 20% or more in a key stock market index from a recent peak over at least a two-month period. However, no consensual definition of a bear market exists to clearly differentiate a primary market trend from a secondary market trend.

3) Secondary market trends

A secondary trend is a temporary change in price within a primary trend. These usually last a few weeks to a few months. A temporary decrease during a bull market is called a correction; a temporary increase during a bear market is called a bear market rally.

Whether a change is a correction or rally can be determined only with hindsight. When trends begin to appear, market analysts debate whether it is a correction/rally or a new bull/bear market, but it is difficult to tell. A correction sometimes foreshadows a bear market.

Correction

A market correction is sometimes defined as a drop of at least 10%, but not more than 20% (25% on intraday trading).

Major disasters or negative geopolitical events can spark a correction. One example is the performance of the stock markets just before and after the September 11, 2001 attacks. On September 7, 2001, the Dow fell 234.99 points to 9,605.85, thoroughly pushing the Dow into a correction. On September 17, 2001, the first day of trading after the attacks, the Dow Jones Industrial Average plunged 684.81 points to 8,920.70. That loss officially pushed the Dow, not just even further into a correction, but into a bear market. (Although unless investors had prior knowledge of the events of September 11, 2001, it would be impossible for the attacks to have had an effect on the markets ahead of time.)

Because of depressed prices and valuation, market corrections can be a good opportunity for value-strategy investors. If one buys stocks when everyone else is selling, the prices fall and therefore the P/E ratio goes down. In addition, one is able to purchase undervalued stocks with a highly probable upside potential.

Bear market rally

A bear market rally is sometimes defined as an increase of at least 10%, but no more than 20%.

Notable bear market rallies occurred in the Dow Jones index after the 1929 stock market crash leading down to the market bottom in 1932, as well as throughout the late 1960s and early 1970s. The Japanese Nikkei stock average has been typified by a number of bear market rallies since the late 1980s while experiencing an overall downward trend.

4. Initial public offering

1) Definition and theory

An initial public offering (IPO) is the first sale of a corporation's common shares to investors on a public stock exchange. The main purpose of an IPO is to raise capital for the corporation. While IPOs are effective at raising capital, being listed on a stock exchange imposes heavy regulatory compliance and reporting requirements. The term only refers to the first public issuance of a company's shares. If a company later sells newly issued shares (again) to the market, it is called a "Seasoned Equity Offering". When a shareholder sells shares it is called a "secondary offering" and the shareholder, not the company who originally issued the shares, retains the proceeds of the offering. These terms are often confused. In distinguishing them, it is important to remember that only a company which issues shares can make a "primary offering". Secondary offerings occur on the "secondary market", where shareholders (not the issuing company) buy and sell shares with each other.

The majority of IPOs could be found on the Nasdaq stock exchange, which lists companies related to computer and information technology. Similarly, the Over The Counter Bulletin Board Exchange (OTCBB) lists companies related to computer and information technologies as well, with stock prices typically much lower and affordable than those of companies listed on one of the major stock exchanges.

2) Reasons for listing

When a company lists its shares on a public exchange it will almost invariably look to issue additional new shares in order to raise extra capital at the same time. The money paid by investors for the newly-issued shares goes directly to the company (in contrast to a later trade of shares on the exchange, where the money passes between investors). An IPO therefore allows a company to tap a wide pool of stock market investors to provide it with large volumes of capital for future growth. The company is never required to repay the capital, but instead the new shareholders have a right to future profits distributed by the company.

The existing shareholders will see their shareholdings diluted as a proportion of the company's shares. However, they hope that the capital investment will make their shareholdings more valuable in absolute terms.

In addition, once a company is listed it will be able to issue further shares via a rights issue, thereby again providing itself with capital for expansion without incurring any debt. This regular ability to raise large amounts of capital from the general market, rather than having to seek and negotiate with individual investors, is a key incentive for many companies seeking to list.

3) Procedure

IPOs generally involve one or more investment banks as "underwriters." The company offering its shares, called the "issuer," enters a contract with a lead underwriter to sell its shares to the public. The underwriter then approaches investors with offers to sell these shares.

The sale (that is, the allocation and pricing) of shares in an IPO may take several forms. Common methods include:

—Dutch auction

—Firm commitment

—Best efforts

—Bought deal

—Self Distribution of Stock

A large IPO is usually underwritten by a "syndicate" of investment banks led by one or more major investment banks (lead underwriter). Upon selling the shares, the underwriters keep a commission based on a percentage of the value of the shares sold. Usually, the lead underwriters, i.e. the underwriters selling the largest proportions of the IPO, take the highest commissions—up to 8% in some cases. Multinational IPOs may have as many as three syndicates to deal with differing legal requirements in both the issuer's domestic market and other regions. (e.g., an issuer based in the E.U. may be represented by the main selling syndicate in its domestic market, Europe, in addition to separate syndicates or selling groups for US/Canada and for Asia. Usually the lead underwriter in the main selling group is also the lead bank in the other selling groups.)

Because of the wide array of legal requirements, IPOs typically involve one or more law firms with major practices in securities law, such as the Magic Circle firms of London and the white shoe firms of New York City.

Usually the offering will include the issuance of new shares, intended to raise new capital, as well the secondary sale of existing shares. However, certain regulatory restrictions and restrictions imposed by the lead underwriter are often placed on the sale of existing shares.

Public offerings are primarily sold to institutional investors, but some shares are also allocated to the underwriters' retail investors. A broker selling shares of a public offering to his clients is paid through a sales credit instead of a commission. The client pays no commission to purchase the shares of a public offering, the purchase price simply includes the built in sales credit.

The issuer usually allows the underwriters an option to increase the size of the offering by up to 15% under certain circumstance known as the greenshoe or over-allotment option.

5. Blance Sheet

Definition

An accounting statement of a company's assets and liabilities, provided for the benefit of shareholders and regulators. It gives a snapshot, at a specific point of time, of the assets that the company holds and how the assets have been financed.

6. Market Maker

Definition and theory

A market maker is an individual or a firm who quotes both a buy and a sell price in a financial instrument or commodity, hoping to make a profit on the turn or the bid/offer spread. Market makers usually hold an inventory of the securities in which they make markets.

In foreign exchange trading, where most deals are conducted OTC, and are therefore completely virtual, the market maker sells to and buys from its clients. Hence, the client's loss is the company's profit and vice versa. Most foreign exchange trading firms are market makers and so are many banks, although not in all currency markets.

Most stock exchanges operate on a matched bargain or order driven basis. In such a system there are no designated or official market makers but market makers nevertheless exist. When a buyer's bid meets a seller's offer (or vice versa) the stock exchange's matching system will decide that a deal has been executed.

In the United States, the New York Stock Exchange (NYSE) and American Stock Exchange (AMEX), among others, have a single exchange member, known as the "specialist," that acts as the official market maker for a given security. In return for providing a required amount of liquidity to the security's market, being on the other side of trades when there are short-term buy-and-sell-side imbalances in customer orders, and attempting to prevent excess volatility, the specialist is granted various informational and trade execution advantages.

Other U.S. exchanges, most prominently the NASDAQ Stock Exchange, employ several competing official market makers in a security. These market makers are required to maintain two-sided markets during exchange hours and are obligated to buy and sell at their displayed bids and offers. They typically do not receive the trading advantages a specialist does, but they do get some, such as the ability to naked short a stock, i.e. selling it without a borrow. In most situations only official market makers are permitted to engage in naked shorting.

On the London Stock Exchange (LSE) there are official market makers for many securities (but not for shares in the largest and most heavily traded companies, which instead use an automated system, SETS). SETS is scheduled to be replaced by TradElect on 18th June 2007. Some of the LSE's member firms take on the obligation of always making a two way price in each of the stocks in which they make markets. It is their prices which are displayed on the Stock Exchange Automated Quotation system, and it is with them that ordinary stockbrokers generally have to deal when buying or selling stock on behalf of their clients.

Proponents of the official market making system claim market makers add to the liquidity and depth of the market by taking a short or long position for a time, thus assuming some risk, in return for hopefully making a small profit. On the LSE one can always buy and sell stock: each stock always has at least two market makers and they are obliged to deal.

This contrasts with some of the smaller order driven markets. On the Johannesburg Securities Exchange, for example, it can be very difficult to determine at what price one would be able to buy or sell even a small block of any of the many illiquid stocks because there are often no buyers or sellers on the order board. However, there is no doubting the liquidity of the big order driven markets in the

U.S.

Unofficial market makers are free to operate on order driven markets or, indeed, on the LSE. They do not have the obligation to always be making a two way price but they do not have the advantage that everyone must deal with them either.

7. Mismatch

1) Definition and theory

Mismatch is the difference between the length of time for which money is borrowed and the length of time for which it is invested, or the difference between the maturities of borrowing and investments. One example is when a bank borrows money for a C1125 short time but lends it for a longer period, so there is a mismatch between its source and use of funds.

2) Asset liability mismatch

In finance, and particularly banking, an asset-liability mismatch occurs when the financial terms of the assets and liabilities do not correspond. For example, a bank that chose to borrow entirely in U.S. dollars and lend in Russian rubles would have a significant mismatch: if the value of the ruble were to fall dramatically, the bank would lose money. In extreme cases, such movements in the value of the assets and liabilities could lead to bankruptcy or liquidity problems.

Asset-liability mismatches can occur in several different areas. A bank could have substantial long-term assets (such as fixed rate mortgages) but short-term liabilities, such as deposits. Alternatively, a bank could have all of its liabilities as floating interest rate bonds, but assets in fixed rate instruments.

Asset-liability mismatches are also important to insurance companies and various pension plans, which may have long-term liabilities (promises to pay the insured or pension plan participants) that must be backed by assets.

Few companies or financial institutions have perfect matches between their assets and liabilities. Financial institutions in particular specialise in "controlled" mismatches, such as between short-term deposits and somewhat longer term loans to customers.

III. Analyzing the case

1. Why did Siebert suggest a check on the standard of the financial information you can access?

Because that commission rates are not all. Cheapest is not necessarily best. A low-ball broker may be fattening his profit margins with "payment for order flow". You are unwittingly compensating the market maker by paying fractionally more on a buy and receiving fractionally less on a sell. Put those fractions together and you're paying a lot more than just the commission.

2. What was the way you check on the quality of an execution?

The way is to ask for the exact time of your trade. Punch in a one-minute intra-day reading on a Web site such as Bigcharts.com. If your price is worse than the trades grouped around the same time, take it up with your broker. Limit trades typically don't throw off order flow payments and thus are more likely to produce tighter trades.

3. Which way did Siebert choose in order to against bank loans?

Siebert has financed expansion with direct loans and by putting up her stocks as collateral against bank loans.

4. In your opinion, why Siebert can make herself a success?

Siebert's bussness success, though, shows that she is not afraid of taking risks. She has "fought like a son of bitch to get ahead" in a male world and punched her way through many a glass ceiling. Siebert is also her own best steward. She collects a modest salary of $150,000 a year (no bonuses, no options), and dose not take down the 16¢. a share in dividends she is entitled to, thereby saving Siebert Financial $3.1 million a year. It's the Siebert savvy at success.

IV. Translation of the Case

在近半个世纪的华尔街上，穆里尔·希伯特在自己的人生道路上冲破了层层限制女性在职场发展的"玻璃天花板"，创造了多个卓著的"第一"：第一位拥有纽约证券交易所席位的女性；第一位创办提供佣金折扣经纪公司的女性；第一位出任纽约州银行监察官的女性。并且，作为倡导男女平等主义的佼佼者，她还是第一位靠自己奋斗成为亿万富翁的在职女性。

后面的突破不幸证明了比前面的成就都要来得迅速。网上交易是她三十年前创办的经纪公司（穆里尔·F. 希伯特公司）发展最快的部分。看到了互联网的发展，网上投机者变得很狂热。在几天的时间内，他们推动希伯特的控股公司——希伯特财政公司从每股最低的 8.5 美元涨到最高的 70 美元,给老板 1,980 万股份一个 14 亿美元的市场。她继续出入于大户室几个月，直到股票从 55 美元回落到 13.5 美元。"我没有试图花掉它真是一件好事。"希伯特一边笑着说，一边倚着她吃午饭的桌子把一口鸡肉喂给了她的长毛吉娃娃犬"怪夫人"。

几乎希伯特所有的资金都投资在她的公司里（她占有 87%的股份）。从小处看，希伯特对于她财富的骤变保持得很冷静。"我好像不是没有钱来照顾自己。"她说话时耸了耸肩，她把精力和金钱都贡献给了女性的事业，如国际女性论坛和纽约妇女会议。使她担心的是习以为常的均衡观点——市场的动力驱动她的股票以及大盘顷刻间直线而下。波动性和成交量对诸事的打击仿佛把人们带到了海蒂·格林时代美国西部拓荒前的蛮荒市场。"我不愿意看到那些无辜的、被误导的人们受到伤害。"希伯特说。在最严重的时候，反应相当剧烈，以至于在一段时间，在一个交易期股票就会转手三次，真是一个令人难以置信的傻瓜理论的体现。

一些人时而赚钱，时而赔钱。当然也包括希伯特独自委托的慈善机构。"他们在 20 年代只卖出了一点儿，"她做了个鬼脸说，"但那不是我。"股票不稳定的原因之一是希伯特过于坚持。她只留下约 200 万股份作为可用的公众交易，当网上聊天室开始到处垂涎欲滴的时候，安全和交易委员会很快对缺乏评估做了相关调查。"不再是上帝来安排给或是拿，而是每天交易的人们，"希伯特厉声说，拍着杂乱的桌子强调，"如今的方式就是这样。"

事实上，希伯特当然不是亿万富翁。如果有什么的话，她和其他股东成了因熟知那些假象而更有优势的动态投资者的受害者，根据网上流传的毫无根据的传言买进或者卖出。不光是希伯特财政公司，数以百计的其他证券公司也在受打击的名单中，他们欺骗数以千计的天真投资者，使他们付出了本不该付出的钱。

像希伯特这样相对公众交易份额很少的低流量股份很容易处理，因此就迅速成为了骗徒的靶子。希伯特的愤怒——证券交易委员会浓厚的兴趣——集中在聊天室，希伯特财政公司被下注者低价买入和卖出使得有谣言说公司要买下股份。或者被理解成是与像嘉信理财这样更大的折扣商交易相比，纵然是在日交易量庞大的时候也是一个更廉价的买入。又或者有一些吉兆就如鸽子朝西飞往中央公园。当网上交易成为环球网最火的交易时，任何有理智的人都会加入。在看上去像是另一个在线拉高出货骗局的背后探查线索，证券交易委员会把矛头对准了噪音最大的聊天室。Tradingplaces.net 这个网站被关闭了，这是由一个叫克里斯·瑞尔的人经营的，此人 50 岁，奈尔斯市人，伊利诺斯州股市的召集员。他的标志性语言是："让我们在华尔街的丛林里搏击吧！"

自封为"终极魔法师"的瑞尔最早经营的家族产业是为汽车经销商制造包装邮件用的箱子。他宣扬他的电子服务（包括每日交易指南，经纪人推荐）给客户，价格为每月 279.95 美元。金钱带来了计算机咨询风暴，有时在几分钟内就会发生"魔鬼买家"和"贸易警报"。"学会估价吧，你这个只看走势图的人。当你们看到价格上扬过快时，就接近崩盘了。"这真是典型的终极魔法师的提示。或者是"快收警告：我们要收获利益。""魔鬼们，"像 Warlock、Wizard 和 Stoned，都从屏幕上一闪而过，一时间对瑞尔交易技巧的集中推崇，从默默无闻，迅速被传播成为了另一个使人迅速致富的网址，看看数百万的足迹吧。

因此，证券交易委员会询问希伯特的原因是，数十件诸如聊天室头目被怀疑在他们自己的客户面前交易等一系列不着边际的事情。公司内部人员也被发现有把股票倾入火爆聊天室的行为。

希伯特认识瑞尔吗？很多研究者质问。她和他有过交易吗？她是否在他的指导下买过股票？没有，没有，没有是唯一的答案。对于这个不太被人了解的瑞尔而言，他自己夸张的简历显示他没有特殊的美国安全部门的背景，也不是注册的咨询人或经纪人。问题是他收取他客户费用吗？对于那些他曾经非常看好的股票,他自己是已经进行了交易还是正在寻求交易?瑞尔否认做错过什么，证券交易委员会从不收费，希伯特也没有办法保护那些自身贪婪的交易者。希伯特能做的是加强差额的盈利——下注者可利用的借款数目——以及依靠大众极度的活跃账户。她还把她的经纪公司做成指导性和教育性的产业。她最近花200 万美元买了两个独立的网站—dollar.com 和女性金融网，这两个网站都可以连入她自己的 Siebert.net。

她的目的是丰富其内容，如个人退休账户立法及 401K 计划等话题。这不是一个纯粹的慈善事业。希伯特希望这种强烈的教育倾向能帮助她拓宽她的业务范围，而不仅仅是刚刚能谋生的佣金折扣事业。还要发展一些新的服务，如互惠基金、货币市场基金和保险业。希伯特认为把严肃的金融信息和计划编制工具植入其中会吸引数百个不同于这个领域的其他妇女网站的眼球。"没有星占术，没有育儿学或者其他的业余爱好板块。"她承诺。她的希望是她的教育方针能够使人花钱来访问她的网站。尽管她只对妇女群体做了担保，但男性客户还是占了希伯特客户的最大一部分，她决不可能把他们排除在外。但是她的新的市场核心是离婚、死亡和其他生活中的变故需要妇女们"掌握自己的经济命运"。"我们要帮助她们做这件事，使他们获得乐趣，并且尽可能赚到一些钱。"希伯特说。如果做不到呢？希伯特情不自禁地一边咧嘴笑着一边喂给"怪夫人"一些有机绿色食品。"嘿，如果不行，山姆大叔就是我们的搭档。"

即使做这行盈利不多，但依旧有很多竞争理由让人从事这一咨询商业。传统的全职经纪人提供的咨询都是从像希伯特这样的人创造的市场份额中窃取而来的。

还有另外一个原因——自我防御。"许多从没经历过股市低迷的人受到了伤害，"希伯特说，"所以我们也受到了伤害。我们认为应该给这些人做最基本的提醒，如收入和资金的流转。""我一向擅长数字，"她继续说，"它们点燃了我的生活。"

从她的这些话中可以看出她是一个保守的分析师。但是她事业的成功又表明她不害怕谈及冒险。希伯特的第一次风险大的赌注——从克里夫兰来到华尔街——是进入未知世界的一次飞跃。她曾在家乡克里夫兰的西瑞瑟福大学学习商业和会计。在她父亲经过一段长期努力的医治却最终难逃死于癌症后，她辍学来到纽约。她当时的全部财产只有 500 美元，那些钱旧得甚至还散发着烤面包的味道,但是对她来说已经很多了,足以去挥霍一下。"如果你想坐在那等着其他人为你服务，"希伯特说，"那你很快到了 80 岁，回头再看你会问：'我都做了些什么？'""我的母亲，"她继续说，"有上帝赋予的好嗓子，她本可以在舞台上演出，但那个年代，美丽的犹太女孩子是不能上舞台的。所以，我是伴着妈妈一生的郁闷成长起来的，"希伯特接着说道，"我当然不愿意走她走过的路，我声明我要做自己想做的事情。"

坚韧不拔。希伯特找的第一份工作是联合国的人事部，但她被拒绝了，原因是她没有语言技能。然后她找到了美林公司，却再次遭到了拒绝，因为她没有大学文凭，也就没有华尔街人应有的智慧。股市不是在希伯特餐桌前对话那么简单的事情。她唯一一次到证券交易所是几年前拜访纽约的时候。之后她又到了巴奇公司。这次她发挥她学习会计的特长，撒谎说她有大学文凭，于是她得到了这份工作。那是 1954 年，希伯特 22 岁，而那时在华尔街只有大股东才能赚大钱。身为一个坐在桌子后面听电话、一周 65 美元薪水的分析师培训人，希伯特在都铎城的东部和人同租一间一月 120 美元租金的公寓，六周试用期过后她就获得了一周 5 美元的加薪。"净赚 3.8 美元，"她笑着说，"这样一来我每天可以多 20 美分花费在吃午餐上。"希伯特从巴奇分公司进入股市领域和分析师们交流，她学得很快。"以前学过的会计帮了我很多。"她回忆说。很快，她的业务开始涉及那些高级分析师不太感兴趣的行业，如广播，电视，电影和航空行业。记忆泛起波澜，一件特别的事令希伯特记忆很深——投资好莱坞的老电影。

作为一个初级分析师，希伯特做得很成功，以至于她离开了原来的合租公寓搬进了自己的公寓。但是在同等的业绩下，她的收入却不如其他的男分析师。"我像个狗娘养的一样为了成功拼搏着。"她回忆说。当她和巴奇公司提出加薪并和她的竞争者交涉时，他们让她立刻收拾东西走人。

希伯特来到了希尔德公司，年薪 9,500 美元，完全上了一个台阶。她的调查研究质量给她带来了三个机构客户。她每年的分红是她事业成功的见证。男经纪人可以得到 40% 的提成，这让她不满。"我不能把我的事业做成仅仅通过敲门然后说：我是一个女人，我有资格。"希伯特告诉记者贝弗莉·科普顿说，"我的成功是在男人堆里摸爬滚打出来的。"

女性在华尔街上流层是明显的极少数。希伯特回忆到，大多数的分析师都把她当作"他们中的一分子"对待，但传统的观念障碍还是渐渐地显示出来。比如在各行业中都有体现的一点：如果希伯特在简历里写出了她的全名（穆里尔），她就不会被录用，如果只写她的姓她就会立刻收到答复。另外，公司分析师每次聚会的午餐俱乐部也不让女人参加，或者不能从前门进入（希伯特从厨房进入）。整个屋子里的气氛也是被男人世界所主导。"对于我，性别是我事业中很重要的一件事，"希伯特说，"我记得我告诉过许多人去做他们性别不允许做的事情。"

严重的困扰和歧视事件仍旧出现在华尔街，但是希伯特认为"保护法已经改变了许多事情"。"有时候女性太过于感性，"意志坚定的希伯特补充说，"像纽约交易所这样的地方以像动物农场而著名，"她继续说，"当人们在诸多压力下工作，语言就会变得粗俗。我学会了在交易所说的所有脏话。它对我并不代表什么。"她补充道，"他们只是些词汇而已。"

希伯特很强的适应性是她成功的秘诀之一。她过去常常口吃，从来没想过自己能成为销售人员。但是在她分析技能中不断增长的自信使她很容易地应付那些习以为常的大机构客户。她记得研究过纽约证券交易所的股票，例如：看到一个阶段赚的钱不断攀升，因为计划削减贬值费用。当一个一意孤行的投资经理，对公司不再抱有希望，要求卖掉纽约证券交易所的股票时，她劝说他坚持买这个他一直都赚钱的股票。"那样又和另一个客户建立了联系，"希伯特回忆说，"所以我能给他们打电话说：'嗨，我认为你应该买这个，因为……'"

在那些日子里，华尔街的调研是很客观的。分析师们如今不断地削减土地投资银行商业。希伯特辩论说，当她工作时，分析师们可以自由地写下该买的和该卖的，没有任何担心被报复的恐惧感。现在出售建议越来越少了，部分是因为像希伯特这样的折扣商改变了华尔街的赚钱方式。随着激烈竞争的委托利率标准化，这种业务的差额利润越来越少。真正的利润是不包括保险业、合并和收购交易的巨额酬金。不再靠工资和分红（像希伯特），补偿主要来自投资银行一边。"我们所谈论的是，那些和公司关系密切的分析师可以赚上几百万。"希伯特说，"这并没有错，"她补充道，"但是可信度问题增加了公司的负担。"这个动机几乎总是导致乐观的建议。

这是为什么这么多收入令人惊异的原因之一，立刻引起电视财经评论员的关注，并且夸大了股市价格飘忽不定的事实。《福布斯》财富专栏作家大卫•卓曼阐述了这种现象，引证了去年奔腾和苹果公司的证券跌价 50%的例子：当赚钱比预想的少时怎么办。卓曼提出了一个尖锐的问题："找一个分析师提醒你，给你做一个以卖掉股票来远离奔腾和苹果公司这样的推荐难道不是件好事吗？"

作为泽西市的主席，新泽西名下的投资顾问公司负责人卓曼支持希伯特的观点。分析师们指望着投资银行业的费用，他断言，"不会让他们自己说出'卖掉'这个词。"你必须学会看透其中的奥妙。大多数分析师说到了那个可怕的"S"就会用像"积聚"、"中性"、"持股观望"，或者甚至"做长线"等轻微的赞美话来名褒实贬。

卓曼把所有类似的责骂解释成一个摆脱危险的警告。这些新的估价似乎是讨人喜欢的，据说是从"积极买入"到"买入"的转变，但是卓曼将其解释为食之无味，弃之可惜。他的底线是：如果你尊重分析师就读读他们的报告，但是撕掉推荐的那页，用它来烧火。

那么，投资者应怎么做？从希伯特新建立的 education.net 上看，她认为人们应该自己做足功课，用带着问题的眼睛来对待那些报告。

希伯特和与她拖把大小的"怪夫人"一样好争吵，会在办公室里跑来跑去并会随时向陌生人挑战。她被从希尔德公司辞掉，由于她款待了一家合伙企业集团，此集团正打算在公司外设立一个分支调研机构。这笔交易没有成功，但在希伯特获得纽约证券交易所席位前，她把与两家小公司的合作看得很重要。在这以前没有大的公司接受过女合伙人，所以希伯特的下一步计划是打破男士一统交易所的常规，并成为其中一员。法律没有说她不能，但是也不是一件容易事，希伯特说，最初十个人里有九个会拒绝她。

希伯特那时的机构客户可以整理成厚厚的一本书，收入也像《纽约时报》预测的一样"一年能赚 50 万"。那对银行毫无影响。交易所要求她获得 44.5 万美元中的 30 万美元担保借款来确保她的席位。在交易所正式同意接纳希伯特之前没有一家银行同意借给她钱。几个月后她解决了这第 22 条军规，变成第一个可以买进 1,366 席位的女人。她也是有着 175 年历史的纽约证券交易所批准的女性第一人。

希伯特具有相当大的个人影响力。股票市场的急速发展使交易席位的价格达到了 37 年来的最高点。穆里尔·F. 希伯特公司开始建在百老汇街 120 号的一间小办公室里。由于她公开的煽动，那些找她找工作或寻求建议的妇女络绎不绝。"她们用不着站在远处寻找我，"希伯特回忆说，"我的办公室很小，她们推开门就能看见我。"希伯特很少在楼下工作，大多数时候都在"楼上"，做调查研究和登记新客户。当希伯特确实来到交易所时，她对水管装修业的实用性开了许多玩笑。两年后，她说，在交易厅的角落里居然才修了一个女卫生间。

　　像往常一样抱着机会主义思想，当希伯特成为交易所最先发起折扣商务的一员时，她再次引发了一场骚乱。1975 年的国际劳动节带来了固定佣金时代的结束，由大的制度投资者和证券交易委员会完成。根据议定的比率，现在，制度和竞争都来到了华尔街。这是一个从制定好一切方法的安逸交易方式退回到交易所成立的戏剧性转折。过去已经成立的全线经纪人看到在这次转变的潮流里，他们的经济利益受到重挫，并且看到了像穆里尔·F. 希伯特公司这样的暴发户们手中拿着的匕首。当想起成立时的脆弱，希伯特有一段长长的记忆。华尔街对她主动折扣做出反应，说她的网站传记是"快速的和敌对的"。长期与她做结算的公司断绝了与她的业务往来，在 60 天内她如果不能再找到一家结算公司的话，她将面临被证券交易委员会逐出交易所的窘境。

　　虽说身为跳出折扣风波的先行者，但这些日子希伯特在像嘉信理财和富达管理集团这样的胜利者面前显得很渺小。电子商务时代的到来一方面削尖了价格竞争，同时也孕育了约 1,800 万因特网佣金账目的开放。尽管高科技股走跌，但伴随数目的持续变大，全部交易额的近 35% 来自个体交易者的在线交易。其有利条件是：交易是廉价的（免酬金经纪人大量存在）、方便的（随时随地都可以交易），并提供资源即时准入，比如即时股票报价、初始的公共资料提供以及全体收入评估。

　　在竞争需求的大风雪中，希伯特在那些具有消费导向的出版物上，诸如"Smart Money"和"Kiplinger's Personal Finance Magazine"上，记录了她的公司每年在贴现率行业名列第一或第二名的骄人业绩（"那还算不赖，是吧？"）。

　　如何去着手创造机会呢？虽然在工业增长蒸蒸日上的时期已日益罕见，但网站破产和电话长时间延续依旧屡屡发生，特别是在大流量交易日。我们来做一项测试：连续几天给几个经纪人打若干个电话，看你多长时间能够得到理睬。任何事超过 8 秒钟（希伯特的平均数）都不符合标准。看看像吉普林的例子中那样的问题会得到一个怎样的答复吧："个人退休账户的保证金率与正常账户不同吗？"（回答：个人退休账户没有保证金。）

　　检查一下辅助服务，就像得到基于你所持有股份的年终成本，特别是你已卖掉的股票。实时确认你的所得胜于延期报价。你想要让股票的价格显示在屏幕上，与市场动态尽可能地接近。在线交易与虚假的广告词一样，不会在你敲下回车键那一秒就实行。你的指令不得不通过你的经纪人被发送到无论哪个执行者那里（场内交易人、电子市场系统），并可能以一个与你期望值相差甚远的价格成交。把你从自己的失望中挽救出来的一条路，就是在你想要交易的时候输入一条限制性的指令来指定价格。大多数折扣商要加收（以 5 美元为代表性的）费用来执行限制性指令。

还有一些其他的先决问题。你的经纪人能在首次公开发行股票时为你找到一个意味深长的商机吗？（别指望在一些倒闭的数量里找到什么奇迹。）如果你不交易，那么不活跃账户管理费会是多少呢？开户或注销一个个人账户的费用是多少呢？每年的年费又是多少呢？希伯特解释说，广告佣金率仿佛微不足道，但许多折扣商试图通过"附加诸多费用"来收回一些他们的成本。"他们增加邮资，"她说，"他们要么附加金融分析费，要么当你想把证券转送时额外收费。你不得不过目所有费用。"

希伯特还倡议在你能接近的财政信息标准中做核对。大概只有不超过十几家折扣商肯提供制度质量调研，通常还仅仅是在网络高消费人群中展开。记住：佣金比率不是全部。最廉价的并不是最需要的。一位开出虚低价的经纪人也许正以"为委托单流量所支付的成本"为名义来填肥他自己的腰包。做市商与他发送指令的人做的每笔交易中那份 2 美元或者更多一些的折扣就是很典型的例子。这种完美的合法回扣或许意味着你正遭到无情的掠夺。因为在你买入时多付的那一点点钱和在你卖出时少赚的那一点点钱已经在你毫不知情的情况下装进了做市商的口袋中。把那些小钱汇总起来要比你所支付的佣金多得多。

一种检查你每笔交易质量的办法就是去找到你交易的准确时间。每天用一分钟时间在像 Bigcharts.com 这样的网站上阅读。如果你的报价在同一时间低于周围的交易者，就去责问你的经纪人吧。限价交易是典型的不能抛开流量指令支付的交易，因此更可能产生紧缩交易。虽然投资者很少知情，但现金支付流量是供商业存活的母乳，特别是对于"免费"折扣们。"这是一种偷窃，"主张"任何支付也没有减少"的穆里尔·希伯特说。

同其他折扣商一起，希伯特靠着牛市庞大的交易量得以发达。她的繁荣代表了一个长期坚忍不拔的复兴。她将公司保密委托，这样使她得以承担起担任纽约州银行监察官这项新的挑战，在这之后商业几近崩溃。没有行政上的扶植。约有 500 家左右的银行机构超过 4 千亿美元的资产，以及 1,000 多家由政府许可开办的小型贷款公司、检查出纳机构和销售融资公司进行了资产组合。对于任何比希伯特缺乏干劲的人来讲，承担这项任务就犹如是堂吉诃德式的狂想。希伯特新近成立的经纪人佣金公司，仅从商两年的时间就找到了立足之地。她的公司的资产被当成了她购买交易所席位所需资金的贷款抵押，而市场从 1973 年到 1974 年跌价大抛售以来还始终处于震荡不稳的状态。"我怎能拒绝？"希伯特吃吃地笑着说："对于一个从克里夫兰来的小孩来说，这的确是个挑战。"

她在恰当的时间出现在了恰当的地点。当时的纽约州州长休·L. 凯利决定增加一名女性官员。对希伯特的提名持续上升，使她成为一名民主党行政部门里稀有的共和党人（"社会自由主义者、财政的保守派"）。这对希伯特来说无关痛痒，她通过自己在妇女组织中的工作与民主党建立了许多良好的关系。

希伯特回忆起她确认听证时脸上带着洋洋得意的笑容。对她就职的唯一书面反对意见来自一位卓越的金融业新闻记者。怎么会这样呢？州参议院银行业委员会的首脑提出这样的质疑。希伯特叙述了那位新闻记者如此费尽心机，直接归因于她在一次经纪人佣金交易中曾经给过他的敏感的背景信息。那又怎样呢？银行业委员会主席问道。"好吧，我想是当我打电话给他并告诉他，他是一个下贱狗娘养的时候使他受到了伤害。"希伯特的回答语惊四座。

她被全体一致通过了，不偏不倚正好在 1977 年与纽约市失败的城市信用合作社做生意时。其总资产 1.3 亿美元，比后备政府代理——国家信用管理局的保险基金还要庞大得多。希伯特负责接管城市信用合作社并运转它。

这是个对于各类储蓄机构都不幸的时代，一切都那么容易让人回忆起经济大萧条时期的银行管理运作方式。像格林威治银行这样的历史上著名的金融机构，该银行成立于 1833 年，却被大萧条时期失控的利率政策所拖垮。面临要支付 15%保证金的压力，格林威治银行用账本上近 8.5%的 10 亿美元做抵押。这是一个令人绝望的局面，映射着至少四家有类似遭遇的其他银行。随着收入的零寄存，格林威治银行和其难兄难弟们，动身去寻找第一个共有的曾经无力偿还贷款的储蓄银行。

拿 10 亿美元做保证金是在冒险。"我能保护一个银行，但整个工业怎么办？"希伯特问道，她的声音减弱了。她对抗商业银行以谋求努力摘樱桃式的共同发展，并为了能有秩序地将优先股给股东作为红利而去游说美国联邦存款保险公司。"我埋葬了他们其中的四家。"希伯特回忆道，简单描述了她廉价合并的那几家有问题的银行。"我设法只给美国联邦存款保险公司适度成本来完成这件事，并力图使保证金无损失。"

与凯利行政部门争执诸如地方银行境外接管（她持反对意见）这类令人难以处理的问题，希伯特 5 年后辞职，决定这项工作开始变成"为了监管人员的工作，而不是为了创建者的工作"。她高调退出，辞职后试图竞选共和党议员提名。希伯特最终在一场三权分立的斗争中名列第三。她用自己的钱为竞选筹措了 25 万美元，成了留在她心灵深处的永恒记忆。这就是她，穿着长裤，站在一个倒扣着的板条牛奶箱上,凝视着诵经台下一群女性支持者发表着劝诫的女人。

　　希伯特的假日结束了。她学到了很多,收获显著,计划使自己成为一个行为榜样,却几乎险些丢掉了她的生意。在她与银行打交道的 5 年里,她的公司被员工经营得一团糟。还有些轻松容易的抉择。希伯特本来可以以正当的利益卖掉她的公司,并可以在多个她熟悉的高性能行业里立足。作为 ("我是一名战士") 希伯特,她当然已千锤百炼。她成功地使她的公司重整旗鼓,成为一家敏捷的专卖流行衣服的小商店。她做了所有该做的事情——引进经验管理、紧跟技术潮流(虽然步伐比她的某些竞争对手稍微慢了一些)、赢得几个有用的收购,伴随着纷纷的争论一路向前。

　　希伯特从竞争对手那儿挖来许多宣传员,比如:通过精明的非正常途径,她在 5 年前灵活地使自己的公司成为公开上市公司。在一次典型的机会主义的运作中,希伯特合并了 J.麦克斯公司,那是一家位于市中心的潦倒的家具零售商,且没有任何股权。她清算支付每股 17 美元的本金,并在为交易中瞬间转入希伯特财务公司 2.5%的资金而激动不已。希伯特对自己的目标毫不犹豫。虽说很渺茫,但她需要公开持有股的流通,用期权去酬劳雇员,用她需要的刺激增长收购给她的工程师。一名无能的《纽约时报》记者,颐指气使地指责希伯特这位行为楷模,曾不知羞耻地 "决定为其储备的有阴影的低价股票能公开认证而利用走后门这样的秘密途径",因此公然对竞争对手使用卑鄙下流的手段。他们中的一个人表示不赞同:藏匿资产负债表的问题无疑诠释了为什么希伯特不以常规的直接出售和提升部分资本来公开认证。

　　希伯特不需要资本,因为她经营公司的钱主要不是从自己口袋里掏出来的。也可能她躲避一个更明朗的公开报价,因为她不想让过多无取胜希望的人搅和了她的好事。希伯特是她自己最好的雇员。她为自己每年搜集恰如其分的15 万美元薪水(没有奖金、没有期权),并且不拿走本应属于她的股权下每股16 美分的分红,这样一来,她每年为希伯特财务公司省下了 310 万美元。

　　这是希伯特对工作的悟性。股息令少数持股者保持开心,但会为她,这样一个早就无成功希望的人,招来庞大的应征税。她参加参议院最初竞选阶段把赋税利润分发给记者的行为,说明她与那些明智的男女平等主义者一样,宁可加大她的资本也不愿意将其与美国国税局分享。她在那个时期的收入被正如 18 项合法审计证据所庇护。对现金流量的紧密关注使希伯特能够为她的公司提供资金,且不从自己的口袋里掏钱。她靠利用她的股票做担保来获取直接贷款,负担起了经济膨胀的经费,从而抵制银行贷款。

　　希伯特现如今已近 70 岁了,或许她能继续扮演独奏女乐队的时代已接近了尾声。竞争压力如此剧烈,科技驱动又需要大量的资本,希伯特既要不得不雇佣外界合作伙伴，又要与一些大的组织进行融合。

希伯特说她已经得到股权并"可能"在"价格正好的时候"卖出。在希伯特此生晚年的舞台上，这对于她来说是个让人痛苦的进退两难的局面。公司基本上是她自我的延续，一个为她的女权事业战斗给予共鸣的天字第一号讲坛，也是从地方慈善机构分离出的城市保险业经费的主要来源，还是她诸如女性小额贷款等项目启动资金的来源。"你不得不恢复到原先的系统，"希伯特用深信不疑的语气强调着这个麻烦的问题。究竟谁能真正成为活跃的穆里尔·希伯特的后继者呢？她在商海里沉浮，没有结婚，没有家庭，并且切身地体会到，一个过渡时期的管理者绝对难逃被人遗忘的命运。将来要做些什么呢？只在希伯特说话的这一刻："我期望能经常被采访。"

希伯特的窘境是大多数自主经营自己买卖的企业家的通病，他们是从来不会被充分允许形成制度化的。单枪匹马的干法正渐渐地不能在大规模变化的商业场面维持。像希伯特一样传统的中间层折扣商，提供低利率和少量服务，长期占据着他们自己的领域。之后出现了牛市交易量巨潮，在线交易也随之而来。庞大的交易量是贴水利润的猫薄荷，但在因特网上持续增长的成交量也混合了进来。网络交易提升了资产资本，但效率的提升引起了一场利率之战。纯粹的在线经纪人的出现，促使希伯特们陷入了既要约束价格下降又要提升服务质量的双重困境。

当提起安装像声音识别指令系统的花费会使每笔交易削价 14.95 美元的时候，希伯特为削价到什么程度才是个头而苦恼。"在线公司曾贡献得太多，以至于得不到新的利益了。"她抱怨道。"我们不要太过于重视 14.95 美元，"希伯特回答道。"我会用 8 美元去打造更多的顾客吗？不，我不会给他们提供服务。"

因此，当另外一个新的力量发力时绳索就会磨损。像美林公司一样的传统资产经纪人，锚定一项高价的建筑销售及分配系统，使他们的眼光开始转变。当在线交易成为主流，从快车式的日交易到日趋成熟，更多保守的投资者缺乏忠告，冲击会继续不断地形成。一些预期增长（在线交易者的数量在未来几年之内可能会三倍于 1,400 万人）将会从现存的账目中被调拨，但资深经纪人们正蠢蠢欲动。

更大的折扣商已经通过合并退回到了传统的资产组合式的计量管理，就像嘉信理财与美国信托的合并。价格和服务的有力结合正改变着商业的轮廓，也同样适用于希伯特的妇女财经网络和其 dollar.com 网的收购。尽管受比较所限，据亿创的链接账目公司安永公司金融计划者透露，新的出路将提供质朴的商议形式，那是一个希伯特专业。

吸收了在华尔街近半个世纪的经验，希伯特提出一个建议样本：忘掉追赶热门股吧，无论他们看上去多么诱人。"我和人说，握紧你的枪，"希伯特说，"你最终将会挣到钱。那的确没有为了挑选一个经你自己的调查研究显示其收入将要增长，并会有一个好的前景的公司的替代品。"

折扣经纪人没必要什么都做。希伯特说她的客户为往返行程的经销每股支付 6 美分，而同样的交易在一个全服务经纪人那里也许要差不多每股 50 美分，两面取佣金。但是，"如果那个经纪人正在给你提供最高品质的调查研究，"希伯特指出，"那么就值得。"她认为：通过给不同党派候选人投票来存钱。"我们有一些账户使用全服务经纪人，他们既能与他们之间的一些人交易，又能与我们之间的一些人交易。"

消除你的冒险感。如果你与冒险打交道觉得很舒服，那么就从一个"有诸多动力的振动团体"里挑选最好的股票。希伯特说，但是如果"他们只是昙花一现，那就近近地观望着他们"。为了资产均衡，抛掉一些你了解的公司"不是歇业"——比如，像默克和百时美施贵宝这样的制药公司。

知道什么时候卖出要比知道买进什么难下决定得多。"如果你发现你喜欢股票的首要原因如今还在，你可以做个保守派，并且卖掉一半股票来抽出你的成本，"希伯特建议说，"否则，如果你期望放慢赚钱速度就再多卖掉一些。"

至于希伯特个人的投资计划，诚然，她仍旧继续将每一个五分硬币都投放到她自己的公司中，"我仍旧拼命战斗着，"她笑着说。就像她刚开始的时候一样，作为一个独立自主的女人战斗着。

Chapter Eight
The Venture Capital's Capitalist—
Georges Doriot

第八章
风险投资家——乔治斯·多利特

I. Case Study

As the man who institutionalized venture capital, General Georges F. Doriot performed brilliantly by following a deceptively simple formula: Bet the jockey not the horse.

For openers, the business plan could not have been more amateurish. It was four typewritten pages, reproduced on contact paper, so that it read a funky white on black. The two engineers, both in their thirties, had labored over it during many a lunch hour snatched in the reading room of the Lexington, Massachusetts Public Library. They lifted the format from a "How to Start A Business" section of an economics text. It was molded on a case study of a made-up company called Pepto-Glitter Toothpaste.

Sweating in their Sunday best, anxious over the pitch for $100,000 in start-up money they were about to make to a venture capital board packed with prestigious names, the engineers tried to absorb some last-minute coaching. The venture staff, sold by their own rigorous study of the engineers' potential, wanted the deal to fly. Look, they counselled, to convince the board, you've got to talk around the business plan:

• Don't use the word computer. Computers are losing money. The board will never believe that two engineers out of the MIT labs are going to beat IBM. Tell them you're going to make printed circuit modules.

• Don't tell them you're going to net five percent. Why would anyone invest in you for five percent? Tell them 10 percent; you have to show a better return then RCA.

• Tell them you're going to make a quick profit. Forget about the four-year projections. Most of the board is over 80 and they are not looking for long-term returns.

Improvising on their Pepto-Glitter script as they went, the engineers won a tentative okay: $70,000 in cash instead of $100,000, but with a $30,000 loan to follow if the front money produced results. Because the Boston-based American Research and Development Company (ARD) was taking all the risks, pronounced the board, it was only fair that the venture firm get a whacking 70 percent of the equity in the new company. It was understood, of course, that the two would plunge immediately into making digital logic boards. The strategy was to get up and running and generate the cash flow needed to support a more sophisticated product line further down the line. And by the way, get that word "computer" out of the company name. Let's call it the Digital Equipment Company (DEC).

This was 1957 and the beginning of one of the most fruitful collaborations ever in venture capital lore. In time, American Research shareholders cashed that $70,000 investment into more than $400 million worth of Digital Equipment stock.

ARD staffers were by no means certain that the DEC technology would fly, but they got the most important thing right—the brilliant engineering skills and work ethic of the two founders, Harlan Anderson and Kenneth Olsen. The decision embodied the philosophy of Georges F. Doriot, for 26 years the driving force behind ARD, the United State's first publicly owned venture firm, and chief architect of organized venture capital as we know it.

Although the French-born Doriot died at age 87 in 1987, the unique stamp is as high profile as ever. Consider:

• Executives Doriot trained at ARD—many of them prized students went on to establish or to help run a number of top venture firms on their own. Among them: Greylock Management, Fidelity Ventures, Limited, the Palmer Organization, the Old Boston Capital Corporation, and the former Morgan Holland Partners. In the same ameboid fashion, these lineal descendants went on to finance a treasury of recent start-ups such as, Doubleclick, Incorporated, Copper Mountain Networks, and Preview Systems.

• Many of the 7,000 students brought Doriot's philosophy to the top of many of the United States' biggest corporations. Among them: James D. Robinson III, former chairman of American Express; William McGowan, founder of MCI; and Philip Caldwell, former chairman of the Ford Motor Company.

Thus, when Doriot needed a director to reinforce the board at DEC, he could simply call talent like Philip Caldwell. Doriot's Rolodex was "one of the best networking tools in the business," recalls a former ARD executive. "It brought us deals and if we had a marketing or technology problem with one of our companies, we could tap some of the best brains in the country."

The success of Doriot's start-ups, based partly on his ability to capitalize on the resources of major corporations, along with those of MIT and Harvard, contributed mightily to the lower New England economy. The evolution of Boston's famed Route 128 as a high-tech hotbed was an early model for Sand Hill Road and Silicon Valley.

Bet the jockey, not the horse. That was the precept—along with rigorous preinvestment research and unstinting follow-up counseling—behind Doriot's launch of more than 200 start-ups. They were winnowed from more than 5,000 proposals. "When someone comes in with an idea that's never been tried," Doriot told *Forbes*, "the only way you can judge it is by the kind of man you're dealing with."

Some of the companies Doriot backed were losers in a high-risk business, where five out of every six start-ups do not make it past year five. Several million dollars, for example, evaporated in an early cast at processing frozen apple juice and deveined shrimp. DEC was a once-in-a-lifetime hit, but Doriot brought in other storied high-tech winners such as Transitron, Tracer Lab, High Voltage Engineering, and Ionics, Incorporated.

The quality of Doriot's judgement shows in ARD's numbers. It was put together in 1946 with the help of such institutional backers as Merrill T. Griswold of the Massachusetts Investors Trust and Karl T. Compton, president of MIT.

The handfuls of other venture pools around then were all privately run for the benefit of families like the Rockefellers, Phippses, and Whitneys. Thus, ARD was unique in its identity as a publicly owned closed-end investment company. It offered two great advantages: Outside investors of modest means for the first time could take a crack at the potentially high rewards of venture capital, but without running the risk of illiquidity, common to private venture deals.

ARD was formed in 1939 on the night that Germany invaded Poland. It grew out of a meeting between Doriot and ARD's backers. The consensus was that venture capital was too critical an element to be left in private hands. It should be institutionalized by putting money and advice together on a sustained, organized basis. The plan was pigeonholed by the outbreak of World War II.

Doriot came back to Cambridge and his lecture hall in 1940 after having been brevetted a Brigadier General as Director of Military Planning for the Army Quartermaster Corps, and Deputy Director of Research and Development for the War Department. Part of Doriot's assignment was to see that war material was produced and shipped to the right place at the right time. Getting the job done included helping establish new companies to get rolling on specialty high-tech items.

With Doriot at its head, ARD started life with a public offering of $5 million. When ARD closed its books a quarter of century later, the capital account stood at better than $400 million—not including generous pay-outs in portfolio stocks like High Voltage Engineering along the way.

Doriot was a lot more than just a brilliant portfolio manager. Money was less important than the social and economic impact of nursing new technology to maturity. Support talented people long term, build a company, and "the rewards will come," he insisted.

Sustained effort was very much part of the Doriot heritage. His father, an engineer, designed the first Peugeot automobile. He passed on the work ethic to young Georges with considerable force: If Doriot dropped below first in his lycee class, he got spanked. Young Doriot subsequently made it through the University of Paris and Harvard, but little wonder that in later years he almost always used a father-child analogy to describe his ties to his start-ups. He thought of them as his "progeny." Sometimes criticized for staying too long with losers Doriot would retort: "If a child is sick with a 102-degree fever, do you set him?"

Doriot carried the same fatherly feel into his classrooms, teaching an eclectic and wildly popular course at the Harvard Business School called simply

"Manufacturing." It was about anything but man facturing. The course centered mainly on Doriot's high ideals of how businessmen should behave and his humanistic views of solving such workday problems as how to structure a board of directors or what to do with a good early stage promoter who has no head for later stage operations.

Doriot was a commanding figure in class. He rarely took questions. He told his students that he would talk and that they would listen. He urged them to write down what they thought about his talks in the "Manufacturing" notebooks he asked them to keep. "Learn how to test yourself now," he told his students. "There will be no examinations when you leave school, and you'll miss them."

In his search for perfection, Doriot challenged everything. He pooh-poohed Harvard's famed case study approach, and regularly farmed out his students for on-the-job training. "Experience is the best teacher," said the General. Doriot was suspicious of numbers, warning students they could be manipulated to prove anything.

He inculcated in his students his own questing mind-set. Corporate guest lecturers were severely cross-examined. Disappointed that his students had not been tough enough on a visiting president of U.S. Steel doesn't understand what business they are in," he told the class. "They are in the materials business, not the steel business. They are completely ignorant of aluminum and plastics." As one devoted student later told *Forbes*, "Doriot was the first person to think in these terms. He had more influence on what happened in American business than the whole rest of the Harvard faculty put together."

Prize students like James Morgan, who became a senior vice president at ARD and went on to open his own venture shop, remembers the classload putting a heavy burden on married students. It was only theoretically leavened by the General's views on such outside topics as how to choose a wife, and his annual lecture cueing the women themselves on how to deal with the corporate culture.

The General's ideas on the subject, laughs Morgan, "would curl the hair of feminists." The ideal wife would clip newspapers and magazines for ideas her husband should be aware of, pack his bag for him on business trips and, in general, provide "unlimited support." The General himself could not have been more uxorious. He wrote innumerable love poems to his wife Edna. She, in turn, would slip notes into his pajama pockets as she—following the job description, of course—

obligingly packed his bag for the road.

Jim Morgan nonetheless remembers anticipation of the wives' lecture as stirring almost as much anxiety as the bloodletting that took place when the General tore apart a business proposal. "My wife has a fiery temper," says Morgan. "She was pregnant. I'd been promising her I'd be home more, and here I was spending more time than ever in the library. I was afraid she was going to have it out with the General."

Morgan underestimated the General's charm. Morgan's wife Maureen came home dazzled. "What a wonderful man! The first thing the General told us to tell you is, 'you've got to work harder,'" she said approvingly. It was yet another example of the General's fondness for indirection, teasing ideas out of students and ARD's professionals in Socratic dialogue.

Charles Coulter, for instance, a retired ARD president, recalls biking over to the General's home in Boston's Back Bay to clear up some business one rainy Saturday afternoon.

As many of his old colleagues do when reminiscing about the General Coulter slips into a French accent. Opening the door to Coulter's ring, Doriot asked "Sharlie, the bicycle when it rains, is it not dangerous?" "Yes," agreed Coulter, "the tires lose traction." "So," asked the General, "is it not possible to improve the bite of the tires? One could perhaps improve the traction with a new grade of rubber. Could not the gearing be improved? And as to the distribution of the rider's weight, could not the frame be altered?" "I know this sounds silly," laughs Coulter. "I'm standing there in the rain. The General is sheltered in the doorway and he's building a new high-tech bicycle company while I get wet."

Though not a technician, Doriot had what Jim Morgan calls a "philosopher's approach to science." "It was all in the questioning of that great inquisitive mind. The General would bore in like this," recalls Morgan, making a tight corkscrew motion with his right hand.

The General dug for detail. Morgan recalls one ARD associate who spent long hours sitting up with a sick electric motor company. The motors just weren't up to quality standards. The associate was flabbergasted when the General asked him what seemed to be a simple but germane question: "What about the bearings? Were they roller or ball bearings?" The MIT graduate and crack analyst had to confess he didn't know. Red-faced with embarrassment, the ARD associate "sat there in front of the General feeling about this big," says Morgan, holding out thumb and index finger a millimeter apart.

The General had a gift for aphorism that sometimes sounded sententious, but always stuck in the mind. Talking with *Forbes* on one occasion, for example, Doriot ticked off a number of convictions that are as valid today as they were in that interview 35 years ago.

• On careers: "There are three ways a man can go; to success, mediocrity, or oblivion. Of these, mediocrity is the most dangerous because it is enjoyable."

• On creativity: "A creative man merely has ideas; a resourceful man makes them practical. I look for the resourceful man. The man I want knows what to do with liabilities."

• Of trouble in small companies: "I like to see trouble come early in our little companies. Unless there is trouble, I worry. I want to know early how a man will behave under adversity."

• On hazards in small companies: "A little success makes some people get conceited. You can't run a small company on a 40-hour week."

• On capital gains: "I view capital gains as a reward for a job well done, not as a goal. The interesting ideas are research, development, production, distribution, and sales. If one can finance, produce, distribute, and sell right, he will get his reward."

The General's pursuit of the long term was thoroughly organized. From Wednesday to Saturday, he was all ARD; from Sunday to Tuesday, he was all Harvard. It wasn't as easy as he made it seem. He never made an evening business appointment or ate dinner the night before his classes, once confiding to an associate that even after 40 years, he felt nauseous before facing his students.

Few students sensed this vulnerability in the General. If they had, it might even have deepened their devotion. Aging alumni regularly turned out by the hundreds for major birthday and anniversary celebrations, still showing what Charles Waite, one of ARD's Old Boys, calls the "missionary zeal" of Doriot's philosophy. "We believed we were doing something for the greater good, making America a better place," says Waite, who moved on from ARD to help found Greylock Management.

A sense of commitment was partly a response to the easy leap that the Doriot philosophy made from campus to start-ups. As late as 1960, Waite recollects in the book *Done Deals*, venture capital was "still an academic experiment in some ways, because Doriot was head of it, and he was more than anything else a teacher." "He was in business to test a thesis," continues Waite, "Money really wasn't a very high objective."

Doriot's missioners trolled MIT and Harvard's labs, making converts among scientists working on technology initially related to defense or the space effort. Backed by modest research contracts from Washington, they needed the additional capital it took to bend spaceware applications to commercial use. One such find was Tracer Labs, a maker of analytical instruments, and a prime example of how a single ARD investment might generate dozens of others. As Charles Waite recalls, many Tracer Lab operatives came up with new applications their bosses wouldn't buy, so they'd "leave and come to us, or others, and get financing" to start their own companies.

Semiconductor producers such as Transitron, yet another ARD winner, showed the same branching phenomenon. "People poured out of Transitron, starting little companies, either in California or Boston," says Waite. "And if they weren't coming out of these companies," continues Waite, "there would be professors at MIT or Harvard, or elsewhere, that read the stock sheets and could see that there might be opportunities."

The ferment added significantly to the economic gains ARD's founders helped to bring about in the Boston area. One sure sign of that showed in the way that empty mill space, a relic of New England's dead textile industry, was filling up. The space—plentiful and cheap—was itself a catalyst to development. Ken Olsen and his partner, Harlan Anderson, for example, squeezing every last nickel out of their 870,000 ARD advance, headed straight for an old woolen mill in Maynard Massachusetts. A double football-field-sized 9,000 square feet, cost them only 25¢ a square foot, including watchman service and heat. Thanks in part to its low overhead, DEC, much to the relief of ARD's older directors, managed to eke out a profit in its first year. Doriot, ever worried about flash-in-the pan triumphs, had a typical response. "I'm sorry to see this," he said, "no one has ever succeeded this soon and ever survived." The General did not want his children to leave the nest too soon.

When people talked of ARD, they thought of its most visible presence, the General. Doriot wasn't all business. He contributed generously to and helped run Boston's French Library.

Then there was the annual black-tie New Year's Eve party in the Doriot home. After dinner, the General would give a humorous talk, once mock-complaining that as a naturalized citizen, he could not become president of the United States. His only route to power, he said, would be as head of a union of computer programmers that would enable him to shut down Wall Street at will.

This was a whimsical turn for the General, who often used his sense of humor to diffuse ARD's internal tensions. Wall Street could not have been more generous to ARD. Its stock typically traded at a premium, partly because investors saw it as a cheap call on ARD's huge hoard of DEC. DEC's breakthrough success with the interactive minicomputer made it one of the fastest growing companies in the country. Reflected celebrity drew new venture proposals by the hundreds across the General's desk. Those that made the cut got a lot of handholding, often by the General himself. Denzil Doyle, former president of Digital Equipment of Canada, now long a venture capitalist himself, recalls the influence that Doriot's caring had on him. "I saw how the mentorship with Ken Olsen worked, and I got really intrigued by its role in managing a company," says Doyle.

Of course, he was experiencing what the General's hard-working staffers had known all along. Doriot tried to reward them with the same incentive that drove ARD's entrepreneurs—options—but was frustrated by government fiat. As investment company employees, the staffers were forbidden the incentives of options in either their own company, DEC, or any other portfolio company. Some staffers, not including the General, did get a chance to buy into the DEC shares Harlan Anderson sold after a quarrel that ended his partnership with Ken Olsen. That left a few ARD senior people sitting comfortably on what turned out to be $50 million or more, while the rank-and-file worked long hours at low pay making millions for the managers of portfolio companies.

The General, focusing on the investment side of the business, pretty much left the day-to-day detail to others. That worked well enough—for a while. Charles Waite recalls having "good times," and felt he was "making the contribution that the great man wanted me to make." Then along came Optical Scanning Corporation. It was in deep trouble. Some ARD staffers wanted to pull the plug, but Optical Scanning was another child Doriot did not want to sacrifice. Acting with customary indirection, Doriot put a "still pretty green" Charles Waite on the board and let him advance the money that kept Optical alive for the next couple of years. Doriot did not "want to write the checks himself," recalls Waite. Searching for a consensus, the General wanted his senior staff "to want him to write the checks."

Set up as a kind of fall guy, Waite worked hard with the entrepreneur ("something the other guys didn't do") and finally got Optical in shape for a public offering. It was a very nice turnaround. ARD's potential loss of $3 million turned into a $20 million profit; the entrepreneur's net worth went from zero to $10 million. Waite's reward: a $2,000 raise. He agonized over that, loved what he was doing, but decided he should be "somewhere where he was compensated adequately." He followed his buddy Bill Elfers, who had been the Number 2 man behind the General for years, to help set up Greylock Management.

Given ARD's unrewarding regulatory structure and the entrepreneurial climate the General had helped to create, defections were inevitable. Doriot had put venture capital on the map, but in the 1960s it was still a very comfortable mainly East Coast business. There were probably no more than 50 principals involved in what was still very much a gentleman's game. Everyone knew everybody else, there was no direct competition, and plenty of sharing of deals. There was also plenty of time—time to check out the business on the ground; time to study the potential market and competition; time to follow the prime Doriot precept of digging into character. "There wasn't much hurry to do the deal." One result was fewer mistakes than now and far more credible merchandise coming to the end-game of the new issues market.

ARD, always abundantly stocked with talent from the deep reserves of Doriot's Harvard classes, continued to thrive by nurturing good investments that also carried the kicker of economic good. One example: Ionics, Incorporated, another find culled from the chemical engineering labs of MIT. Its low-cost ion separation technology was a whole new look, with wide application, on desalting sea water. On ARD books at a cost of around $400,000, Ionics was by the early 1970s worth some $2 million. It was one of 45 stocks in a portfolio carrying 50 companies that had not yet gone public holding only three losers. One of the losers was a stylistic low-tech tic—a $500,000 investment in a chain of convalescent homes written down to a notional $1.

The long string of successes raised ARD's net asset value from $5 to a high of $90 a share (after a four for one split), not including earlier distributions of a number of portfolio stocks. Better yet, ARD stock often as not traded at premiums of 80 percent or more, partly because investors saw it as a cheap way of hopping on the DEC bandwagon. On the books at $61,400, with a market value of $354 million,

DEC by the early 1970s had ballooned to more than 75 percent of ARD's assets.

Though not yet a director himself, the General worked tirelessly behind the scenes, helping Olsen over crises like the breakup with partner Harlan Anderson. "My job," the General liked to say, "is to watch, pray, and spread happiness."

Olsen's biggest problem was the double-edged sword of managing growth. DEC had gone public in 1966 at $22 a share, giving ARD in just nine years a return of more than 50 times its money. The number continued to multiply as DEC quickly capitalized on a technology that made its refrigerator-sized mini-computers cheaper, faster, and less complicated than IBM's room-sized main frames. DEC was fast outgrowing its old Maynard mill, creating new jobs in the area by thousands, and increasing revenues by 30 percent to 50 percent a year. Paradoxically, ARD was trapped in the dilemma of DEC's success. As the steward of both companies, the General was too sage a manager not to realize that he had a succession problem on his hands—his own. He was 72 and mortal. If he were to die without a successor, there was a chance that ARD's 65 percent control of DEC might fall into hostile hands.

Inextricably linked to the question of succession was how to sterilize the huge block of control stock that could destabilize both the market and DEC's management. Over brandy with a couple of ARD directors, the General explored the options. One was merger with another venture capital firm molded in the ARD style. That didn't work. Another was to lure one of Doriot's Old Boys from a different top venture firm. That didn't work either. Another suggestion did. Doriot and Bill Miller, President of Textron, Incorporated, long diversified out of textiles into conglomerate deal making, were good friends. The General sat on the Textron board; Miller on the ARD board. Thus, Miller was a known quantity thoroughly familiar with the General's style. A Textron buyout of ARD would close all the right circuits; it would reinforce Textron's deal-making capacities; perpetuate the ARD name as a division; and keep the General on as chairman, with a mutually agreed upon venture executive as president and heir-apparent.

Equally elegant was the disposition of the DEC stock. It would be spun off, premerger, to ARD shareholders, who would also get a modest piece of Textron as part of the purchase package. However carefully structured, the Textron deal rankled some of Doriot's Old Boys. Who had been better trained than they to take on the succession? What's more, the DEC stock could have been spun off to shareholders at any time before. The General's strategy was to hang on to the crown jewels. They were, in effect, an advertisement for himself. DEC kept Doriot's reputation green, and the deals coming in the door.

Whether the General sensed it or not (as T. Rowe Price did), a runaway market was soon to go over the cliff. Thus, the spin-off had the timely advantage of upstaging a killer sell-off. The General's posting to Textron, on the other hand, was a less than happy event. Doriot was in good health, still full of zest for the job, but quickly decided that his agreed upon back-up—and designated successor—did not understand venture as he did. The two just did not click.

It was originally planned that Doriot could stay on as long as he liked. Caught in the impasse between Doriot and his presumed successor, Textron offered both a package. The General took his (there had been no pension at his frugally run ADR), worrying how his company, now a step-child, would fare under the new regime.

In fact, it grew awkwardly and far less spiritedly in the conglomerate milieu than it might have in its natural habitat. Under the presidency of Charles Coulton, ARD made a lot of money for Textron, but the fit was never quite right. Ultimately, ARD was surrendered to the General's surviving Old Boys in a leveraged buyout.

The General kept himself busy as ever and spending much of his time helping Ken Olsen bypass the minefields of runaway growth. He counseled patience over severe organizational problems, and talked up Olsen every chance he got. Introducing the DEC chief at a Newcomen Society meeting marking the company's 25th anniversary, for example, the General told the group it was a good thing that Olsen had not been around in 1712. That was when British innovator Thomas Newcomen began making the improved steam engines that ushered in the industrial revolution. "Newcomen was a lucky man," Doriot told the group. "If Ken Olsen had been alive then, he would have designed a better engine, and today this would be called the Olsen Society."

So strong was the attachment that Olsen held several board meetings at Doriot's home while the General lay dying of lung cancer in 1987, at age 87. It was a generous gesture, and the General's pragmatic spirit lingered long over his most rewarding progeny. Years later, when DEC itself fell before the onslaught of the microprocessor, it was Doriot-trained director Philip Caldwell who forced Ken Olsen to resign.

The Doriot influence continued well beyond the grave. Thanks partly to the critical mass formed by his Old Boys, the number of venture capital funds in the field now has multiplied to more than 7,000. The amount of money flooding into them over the last decade, mainly from institutional investors, is up tenfold to $30 billion. The eye-popping incentive of big wins like ARD's early DEC investment is still at the heart of the game. So is risk. Unwary investors following the rainbow of venture got clipped for billions in the recent implosion of dot com new issues, just as they had in earlier fads like biotechs.

Doriot saw change coming, lamenting that too many new venture firms were bent on building stocks rather than sustainable companies. His style of venture capital, time-intensive—makes sure as best we can this company is viable—is being edged out by quick-hit operators, more interested in profitable exit strategies than building great companies. We've got a hot idea here, get it into the new issues market, quick! Doriot, a year or two before he died, summed up the trend:

He said he had just finished one of his stump speeches on the need for venture capital to create lasting companies when an enthusiastic young man approached and congratulated him on his talk. His own new company, backed by a brilliant business plan, the young man said, was already doing exactly as Doriot urged.

"Really," beamed the General, "what do you make?"

"Oh, about $1.32 a share," was the response.

Old Boys like Frank Hughes, a former president of ARD, chuckle sardonically over this tale. Many of them, edging toward retirement, have tried to instill the Doriot doctrine in the next generation, but find it an uphill fight against incalculable economic and cultural change. "Many young people do not much care about building substance, something that will stick in the fabric of the economy," argues Frank Hughes. "It's the way we are now," he adds. "Instead of being a by-product of work, cash has become an end in itself. It's the way people keep score."

What used to be a collegial environment is now big business. Huge pools of capital can no longer be profitably deployed into small startups. ARD style hands-on mentoring is vanishing, too. "You see it in these so-called skyrockets," Hughes continues. "Venture capital people work to make a quick killing on an IPO and then move on. Six to eight months later, the company is bankrupt."

How many of the more recent crop of start-up entrepreneurs would fit the General's description of the young Ken Olsen. "He was perceptive, he had managed people, he saw the relationship between production and distribution, he had a full understanding of the market two to three years out, and his ideas were not so far advanced as to be dangerous." Doriot may have over-praised Ken Olsen, but the job specifications could not be more sound.

In the end, DEC had a great run for many years, but failed to mature into a lasting company. Happily for the General, the downfall came after his death. But if Georges Doriot leaves behind him no corporate monument, his legacy is perhaps prouder than that of those who did. He not only invented venture capital, he showed how it ought to be done. And that is a mighty contribution to American capitalism.

Key Words and Expressions:

alumni	n. 毕业生，男校友
confide	v. 吐露，倾吐(秘密)
eclectic	adj. 不拘一格的，兼收并蓄的
equity	n. 股票，股本
fall guy	替罪羊，替死鬼
farm out	分派
ferment	n. 酵素，蓬勃发展
flabber-gasted	目瞪口呆的
handholding	n. 关怀备至，手把手的指导
illiquidity	n. （企业等）缺少流动资金
incentive	n. 鼓励，奖励
inculcate	v. 谆谆教诲，反复灌输
institutionalize	v. 使制度化
jockey	n. 职业赛马骑师
leverage	n. 举债经营
liabilities	n. 不利条件，各种可能性
lycee	n. 法国公立中学
naturalize	v. 加入国籍
option	n. 购买权,期权
pay-outs	花费，支出
pigeonhole	v. 把……束之高阁
pooh-pooh	v. 贬低，对……嗤之以鼻
pools	n. 联营，联合基金

portfolio	n. 投资组合，有价证券财产目录
posting	n. 过账
premium	n. 贴现率
printed circuit	印刷电路
promoter	n. 赞助人，出资人
rank-and-file	n. 普通员工
sententious	adj. 说教的，言简意赅的
spin-off	资产分派，让产易股
sterilize	v. 冻结，封存
traction	n. 附着，牵引，摩擦力
troll	v. 唱歌庆祝
turnaround	n. 彻底改变，好转
uxorious	adj. 溺爱妻子的

Notes:

1．Equity 股本

指股东在公司中所占的权益，多用于指股票。英文 equity market 是指股票市场，即股票发行与交易的市场。

2．Venture capital 风险投资

风险投资是指由职业金融家投入到新兴的、迅速发展的、有巨大竞争潜力的企业中的一种权益资本。

3．ARD 美国研究与开发公司

1946 年 ARD 公司的成立标志着现代风险投资的开端。1946 年，世界上第一家风险投资公司——美国研究与开发公司（ARD）宣告成立，这是世界风险投资史上的里程碑，从此风险投资开始了专业化和制度化的发展历程。

1946 年，哈佛大学商学院教授乔治斯·多利特（Georges Doriot）与麻省理工学院校长卡尔·坎普敦（Karl Canpton）联合波士顿的一些商业人士创建了"美国研究与开发公司"（ARD）。该公司是第一家公开交易的封闭型投资公司，由职业金融家管理，主要为新成立的快速成长中的创业企业提供权益性融资。ARD 在成立初期由于本身以及所投资的企业缺乏赢利能力和流动性，所以出现了负现金流，不仅没有获得预期的资本收益，也没有能力支付股东红利，其股票因此大打折扣，进一步筹资也遇到了很大的困难。

然而，1957 年 ARD 对数字设备公司（Digital Equipment Corporation，DEC）的投资获得了巨大的成功，不仅成为 ARD 公司成长的重要转折点，同时也预示了风险投资事业的美好前景。

4．Georges Doriot 乔治斯·多利特

1946 年，美国哈佛大学经济学教授多利特（Georges Doriot）在波士顿创建了别名为"美国研究与发展"（ARD，American Reasearch and Development Corporation）的风险投资公司，拉开了现代风险投资业的序幕。

5．Closed-end investment company 资本额固定的投资公司

资本额固定的投资公司是一种股数固定、股票只在股票交易所或其他认可的市场上出售的投资公司。

6．DEC 数字设备公司

DEC 曾经是世界上最成功的电脑厂商之一。虽然它有过 40 多年的辉煌，但就像电脑业中许多公司那样，DEC 公司在激烈的竞争中历经磨难，一度走上成功的颠峰，最终还是被人兼并，走完了作为一家独立电脑企业的创新历程，给业界留下深深的遗憾和长久的思索。

DEC 公司的创建，与麻省理工学院（MIT）林肯实验室有天然的联系，也可以说，它是高等学府科研人员"下海"办公司，把科技成果转化为商品的典范。

7．Ken Olsen 肯·奥尔森

1926 年 2 月出生在康涅狄格州。父亲是一位没有大学学历的机械工程师，拥有几项发明专利，十分注意培养他的孩子在机械和电子学方面的爱好，三个儿子后来都子承父业做了工程师。奥尔森从小就脚踏实地，干什么都不会让人失望。麻省理工学院的毕业生都把冯·诺依曼和杰·弗雷斯特当做心中的偶像，希望成为电脑科学家。然而，他却偏要"下海"经商办企业，一心想把类似于 TX-0 那样的电脑推向社会。由于职务的关系，奥尔森一度充当 MIT 和 IBM 之间的联络员。完成任务后，他清醒地认识到——他要研制计算机，并相信自己比 IBM 做得更好。1957 年 8 月，"数字设备公司"在马萨诸塞州梅纳德（Maynard）镇，一家 19 世纪的毛纺厂 8,500 平方英尺厂房里挂牌，企业名称的英文缩写是"DEC"。1992 年，奥尔森原来的副手罗伯特·帕尔默（B. Palmer）接任总裁，后又被选为 DEC 公司董事长。

8．ARD 高压电工程公司

ARD 最终于 1946 年宣告成立,成立之初仅筹集资金 350 万美元,其第一笔投资是麻省理工学院 5 个物理学家和工程师创办的高压电工程公司(High

Voltage Engineering Corporation,HVE),并帮助使它成为首批在纽约股票交易所上市的具有风险投资背景的高技术公司。

II. Knowledge Points

1. Venture Capitalist

1) Definition and theory

Venture capital is a type of private equity capital typically provided by professional outside investors to new, growth businesses. Generally made as cash in exchange for shares in the invested company, venture capital investments are usually high risk, but offer the potential for above-average returns. A Venture Capitalist (VC) is a person who makes such investments. A venture capital fund is a pooled investment vehicle (often a limited partnership) that primarily invests the financial capital of third-party investors in enterprises that are too risky for the standard capital markets or bank loans. Venture capital can also include managerial and technical expertise. Most venture capital comes from a group of wealthy investors, investment banks and other financial institutions that pool such investments or partnerships. This form of raising capital is popular among new companies, or ventures, with limited operating history, who cannot raise funds through a debt issue. The downside for entrepreneurs is that venture capitalists usually get a say in company decisions, in addition to a portion of the equity.

2) Venture capital fund operations

Roles within a VC firm

Venture capital general partners (also known in this case as "venture capitalists" or "VCs") are the executives in the firm, in other words the investment professionals. Typical career backgrounds vary, but many are former chief executives at firms similar to those which the partnership finances and other senior executives in technology companies.

Investors in venture capital funds are known as limited partners. This constituency comprises both high net worth individuals and institutions with large amounts of available capital, such as state and private pension funds, university financial endowments, foundations, insurance companies, and pooled investment vehicles, called fund of funds.

Other positions at venture capital firms include venture partners and entrepreneur-in-residence (EIR). Venture partners "bring in deals" and receive income only on deals they work on (as opposed to general partners who receive income on all deals). EIRs are experts in a particular domain and perform due diligence on potential deals. EIRs are engaged by VC firms temporarily (6 to 18 months) and are expected to develop and pitch startup ideas to their host firm (although neither party is bound to work with each other). Some EIR's move on to roles such as Chief Technology Officer (CTO) at a portfolio company.

Structure of the funds

Most venture capital funds have a fixed life of 10 years, with the possibility of a few years of extensions to allow for private companies still seeking liquidity. The investing cycle for most funds is generally three to five years, after which the focus is managing and making follow-on investments in an existing portfolio. This model was pioneered by successful funds in Silicon Valley through the 1980s to invest in technological trends broadly but only during their period of ascendance, and to cut exposure to management and marketing risks of any individual firm or its product.

In such a fund, the investors have a fixed commitment to the fund that is "called down" by the VCs over time as the fund makes its investments. There are substantial penalities for a Limited Partner (or investor) that fails to participate in a capital call.

Compensation

In a typical venture capital fund, the general partners receive an annual management fee equal to 2% of the committed capital to the fund and 20% of the net profits (also known as "carried interest") of the fund; a so-called "two and 20" arrangement, comparable to the compensation arrangements for many hedge funds. Strong Limited Partner interest in top-tier venture firms has led to a general trend toward terms more favorable to the venture partnership, and many groups now have carried interest of 25%~30% on their funds. Because a fund may run out of capital prior to the end of its life, larger VCs usually have several overlapping funds at the same time; this lets the larger firm keep specialists in all stages of the development of firms almost constantly engaged. Smaller firms tend to thrive or fail with their initial industry contacts; by the time the fund cashes out, an entirely — new generation of technologies and people is ascending, whom the general partners may not know well, and so it is prudent to reassess and shift industries or personnel rather than attempt to simply invest more in the industry or people the partners already know.

3) Raising substantial venture capital

Venture capital is not generally suitable for all entrepreneurs. Venture capitalists are typically very selective in deciding what to invest in; as a rule of thumb, a fund may invest in as few as one in four hundred opportunities presented to it. Funds are most interested in ventures with exceptionally high growth potential, as only such opportunities are likely capable of providing the financial returns and successful exit event within the required timeframe (typically $3\sim7$ years) that venture capitalists expect.

This need for high returns makes venture funding an expensive capital source for companies, and most suitable for businesses having large up-front capital requirements which cannot be financed by cheaper alternatives such as debt. That is most commonly the case for intangible assets such as software, and other intellectual property, whose value is unproven. In turn this explains why venture capital is most prevalent in the fast-growing technology and life sciences or biotechnology fields.

If a company does have the qualities venture capitalists seek such as a solid business plan, a good management team, investment and passion from the founders, a good potential to exit the investment before the end of their funding cycle, and target minimum returns in excess of 40% per year, it will find it easier to raise venture capital.

4) Main alternatives to venture capital

Because of the strict requirements venture capitalists have for potential investments, many entrepreneurs seek initial funding from angel investors, who may be more willing to invest in highly speculative opportunities, or may have a prior relationship with the entrepreneur.

Furthermore, many venture capital firms will only seriously evaluate an investment in a start-up otherwise unknown to them if the company can prove at least some of its claims about the technology and/or market potential for its product or services. To achieve this, or even just to avoid the dilutive effects of receiving funding before such claims are proven, many start-ups seek to self-finance until they reach a point where they can credibly approach outside capital providers such as VCs or angels. This practice is called "bootstrapping".

There has been some debate since the dot com boom that a "funding gap" has developed between the friends and family investments typically in the $0 to

$250,000 range and the amounts that most Venture Capital Funds prefer to invest between $1 to $2m. This funding gap may be accentuated by the fact that some successful Venture Capital funds have been drawn to raise ever-larger funds, requiring them to search for correspondingly larger investment opportunities. This "gap" is often filled by angel investors as well as equity investment companies who specialize in investments in startups from the range of $250,000 to $1m. The National Venture Capital association estimates that the latter now invest more than $30 billion a year in the USA in contrast to the $20 billion a year invested by organized Venture Capital funds.

In industries where assets can be securitized effectively because they reliably generate future revenue streams or have a good potential for resale in case of foreclosure, businesses may more cheaply be able to raise debt to finance their growth. Good examples would include asset-intensive extractive industries such as mining, or manufacturing industries. Offshore funding is provided via specialist venture capital trusts which seek to utilise securitization in structuring hybrid multi market transactions via an SPV (special purpose vehicle): a corporate entity that is designed solely for the purpose of the financing.

5) Venture capital and development

Venture capital can be used as a financial tool for development, within the range of SME finance, by playing a key role in business start-ups, existing small and medium enterprises (SME) and overall growth in developing economies. Venture capital acts most directly by being a source of job creation, facilitating access to finance for small and growing companies which otherwise would not qualify for receiving loans in a bank, and improving the corporate governance and accounting standards of the companies.

Venture capital is used as a tool for economic development in areas such as Latin America and the Caribbean.

2. Closed-End Investment

Definition and theory

When an investment company issues a fixed number of shares in an actively managed portfolio of securities, the shares are traded in the market just like common stock. Most mutual funds are open-end funds, not closed-end. The main difference with closed-end funds is that market price of the shares is determined by supply and demand and not by net-asset value (NAV).

3. Digital Equipment Corporation (DEC)

Definition

Digital Equipment Corporation was a pioneering American company in the computer industry. It is often referred to within the computing industry as DEC. (This acronym was once officially used by Digital itself, but the official name was always DIGITAL.) Its PDP and VAX products were arguably the most popular minicomputers for the scientific and engineering communities during the 1970s and 1980s. DEC was acquired by Compaq in June 1998, which subsequently merged with Hewlett-Packard in May 2002. As of 2006 its product lines were still produced under the HP name. From 1957 until 1992 its headquarters was in an old woolen mill in Maynard, Massachusetts.

Digital Equipment Corporation should not be confused with Digital Research; the two were unrelated, separate entities; or with Western Digital (despite the fact that they made the LSI-11 chipsets used in Digital Equipment Corporation's low end PDP-11/03 computers). Note, however, that there were Digital Research Laboratories where DEC did its corporate research.

4. The United States Army Quartermaster Corps

1) Definition and theory

The United States Army Quartermaster Corps is a combat service support (CSS) branch of the United States Army. It is also one of three U.S. Army logistics branches, the others being the Transportation Corps and the Ordnance Corps.

2) History

The Quartermaster Corps is the U.S. Army's oldest logistics branch, established 16 June 1775. On that date the Second Continental Congress passed a resolution providing for "one Quartermaster General of the grand army and a deputy, under him, for the separate army." From 1775 to 1912 this organization was known as the Quartermaster Department. In 1912, Congress consolidated the former Subsistence, Pay, and Quartermaster Departments to create the Quartermaster Corps. Quartermaster units and soldiers have served in every U.S. military operation from the Revolutionary War to current operations in Iraq (Operation Iraqi Freedom) and Afghanistan (Operation Enduring Freedom).

3) Functions

The function of the Quartermaster Corps is to provide the following support to the Army:

—general supply (except for ammunition and medical supplies)

—mortuary affairs (formerly graves registration)

—subsistence (food service)

—petroleum & water

—field services: aerial delivery (parachute packing, air item maintenance, aerial delivery, rigging and sling loading)

—shower, laundry, fabric/light textile repair

—material and distribution management

4) Former functions

Former functions and missions of the Quartermaster Corps were:

i.   military transportation (given to the newly established Transportation Corps in 1942)

ii. military construction (given to the Engineer Corps in the early 1940s)

iii. military heraldry (given to the Adjutant General's Corps in 1962)

iv. remount / war dogs

v.   clothing

5. War Department, United States

Definition

Federal executive department organized (1789) to administer the military establishment. It was reconstituted (1947) as the Dept. of the Army when the military administration was reorganized. During the American Revolution, military affairs were largely supervised by the Continental Congress, and under the Articles of Confederation a secretary of war was put in charge of defense matters. In Aug., 1789, the U.S. War Dept., headed by the Secretary of War with cabinet rank, was created to organize and maintain the U.S. army—under the command of the President in time of peace and war. Subsequent legislation expanded the department's organization, and until 1903 the commanding General of the Army and various staff departments aided the Secretary in guiding the military establishment. Its supervision of naval affairs was soon transferred (Apr., 1798) to the U.S. Dept. of the Navy. At times the War Dept. supervised quasimilitary matters—e.g., the distribution of bounty lands, pensions and the Reconstruction of the South after the Civil War, but by the 20th cent. the only such responsibilities that remained were the construction of public works in connection with rivers and harbors and the maintenance and operation of the Panama Canal. Meanwhile, the purely military functions of the department were vastly expanded in war periods, and after the Spanish-American War the War Dept. was thoroughly reorganized (1903). The office of the commanding General of the Army was abolished, and the general staff corps was established to coordinate the army under the direction of the chief of staff, who was charged with supervising the planning of national defense and with the mobilization of the military forces. Thereafter the War Dept. absorbed several new functions; it was given supervision over the newly created National Guard and under the National Defense Act of 1916 the officers' reserve corps was created within the department's organization. This act also established the office of Assistant Secretary of War to coordinate the procurement of munitions. After World War I the War Dept. was again revamped (1922). Its scope of military activities, however, remained wide, stretching from the supervision of the U.S. Military Academy (West Point) to the guidance of insular affairs and occupied territories and to the intricate organization of defense. In World War II plans were laid to coordinate the activities of the armed services and with the creation (1947) of the National Military Establishment—which later became (1949) the U.S. Dept. of Defense—the War Dept. was reconstituted as the Dept. of the Army, which became a division of the Dept. of Defense. The Secretary of War, holding a post with high cabinet rank, became the Secretary of the Army, an office without cabinet rank, and several of the department's functions, notably those connected with the air arm, were transferred.

6. A portfolio company

Definition

A portfolio company is a company or entity in which a venture capital firm or buyout firm invests. All of the companies currently backed by a private equity firm can be spoken of as the firm's portfolio.

7. Old boys

Definition

At most public schools and a few universities in the UK, and to a lesser extent in Australia and Canada, the phrases old boy and old girl are traditionally used for former school pupils, and old member for former university students. The term is often mistakenly thought of as synonymous with "graduate" because it is most commonly used as such, even though it is not literally correct. Sometimes used in informal settings are the forms alum or alumn as is the gender-neutral plural equivalent alums. Although many coeducational institutions usually use the term "alumni" to refer to graduates of both sexes, those who object to masculine forms in such instances may prefer the phrase alumni and alumnae or the form alumnae/i. This has become the choice of many women's colleges that have started to admit men.　Alumni reunions are popular events at many institutions. They are usually organized by alumni associations and are often social occasions for fundraising. Recently, the definition of "alumni" has expanded to include people who have departed from any kind of organization or program. As such, one can potentially be a "corporate alum" of XYZ Company, or an alum of a military branch, non-profit organization, fraternities and sororities, or training process.

III. Analyzing the case

1. What's the suggestion of ARD to Ken Olsen and Harlan Anderson to start a business?

• Don't use the word computer. Computers are losing money. The board will never believe that two engineers out of the MIT labs are going to beat IBM. Tell them you're going to make printed circuit modules.

• Don't tell them you're going to net five percent. They wound not invest in you for five percent. Tell them 10%, you have to show a better return than RCA.

• Tell them you're going to make a quick profit. Forget about the four-year projections. Most of the board is over 80 and they are not looking for long-term returns.

2. What made ARD decide to invest in DEC?

ARD staffers were by no means certain that the DEC technology would fly, but they got the most important thing right—the brilliant engineering skills and work ethic of the two founders, Ken Olsen and Harlan Anderson. The decision to go with what was mainly a bet on the character of the two embodied the philosophy of Georges Doriot,　for 26 years the driving force behind ARD, who performed brilliantly by following a deceptively simple formula: Bet the jockey, not the horse.

3. What's the purchase package between ARD and Textron?

A Textron buyout of ARD would close all the right circuits: it would reinforce Textron's deal-making capacities; perpetuate the ARD name as a division; and keep the General on as chairman, with a mutually agreed upon venture executive as president and heir-apparent. Equally elegant was the disposition of the DEC stock. It would be spun off, premerger, to ARD shareholders, who would also get a modest piece of Textron as part of the purchase package.

4. Why was it hard to instill the Doriot doctrine in the next generation? And by what was it replaced?

It was hard to fight against incalculable economic and cultural change. Many young people do not much care about building substance, something that will stick in the fabric of the economy. Instead of being a by-product of work, cash has become an end in itself. His style of venture capital, time-intensive—make sure as best they can the company is viable—is being edged out by quick-hit operators, more interested in profitable exit strategies than building great companies.

5. What was Doriot's job specifications?

He should be perceptive, he should be good at managing people, he should see the relationship between production and distribution, he should have a full understanding of the market two to three years out, and his ideas should not be so far advanced as to be dangerous.

IV. Translation of the Case

乔治斯·多利特在风险投资制度化方面做得非常出色,他遵循了一个极为简单但又容易造成假象的原则:把赌注押在赛马骑师身上,而不是赛马身上。

对于初创公司者而言,商务计划制定得非常外行,只有四页打印纸,复写在接触印相纸上,在黑色底子上字迹非常白。两个三十来岁的工程师,利用很多午餐时间,抽空跑到马萨诸塞公立图书馆的来克星顿阅览室辛苦地写着商务计划。他们从一本经济学教科书里的"如何创办公司"中套用了这一商务计划制定格式。这建立在对一家名为 Pepto-Glitter 的虚构的牙膏公司进行的案例分析的基础之上。

穿着最讲究的衣服却紧张地出着汗,焦虑着要从满是威名显赫的大人物的风险投资董事会那里得到十万美元的启动资金,这两个工程师竭力吸纳最后这一紧急关头的指导。风险投资公司的全体成员,对这两个工程师的潜在能力进行了缜密的分析之后，想达成这一交易。他们交换着意见：瞧，要想说服董事会，你们在谈论商务计划时得让人不得要领。

• 不要使用计算机这个词，计算机不会让人赚钱。董事会决不会相信这两个麻省理工学院实验室的工程师会打败 IBM 公司。告诉董事会你们要生产的是印刷电路组件。

• 不要告诉董事会你们会净赚 5%。如果只赚 5%，为什么要投资给你们？告诉他们会赚 10%，你们必须显示比 RCA 公司更高的回报率。

• 告诉董事会你们会很快获利。忘记为期四年的规划远景。董事会大部分成员都 80 多岁了，他们等不了长期回报。

这两个工程师按照 Pepto-Glitter 牙膏的计划方案进行了即席准备，从董事会获得了 7 万美元而不是 10 万美元现金的承诺，但如果前期投资取得了效果，随后会有 3 万美元的贷款。董事会宣称，因为以波士顿为总部的美国研究与发展公司（ARD）承担了所有的风险，风险公司分得新公司 70% 的股份是很公平的。当然了，两个工程师立即着手成立数字逻辑董事会是可以充分理解的。这一策略就是要使新公司运转起来，并且产生所需的资金流以进一步支持一个更为复杂的产品生产线。顺便提一句，公司名中不要用计算机这个词。就称做数字设备公司（DEC）。

这是 1957 年，是风险投资领域最富有成效的合作的开端。最后，美国公司的股东们把 7 万美元的投资兑现为价值 4 亿美元的数字设备公司的股票。

美国研究与发展公司（ARD）的职员决非肯定 DEC 技术会上涨，但他们却做出了最正确的选择：即数字设备公司（DEC）的缔造者哈兰·安德森和肯尼斯·奥尔森出色的工程技术及工作理念。决定把赌注押在这两个工程师的个性上，这体现了乔治斯·多利特的哲学理念，26 年来，他一直是美国研究与发展公司（ARD），即美国第一家国有风险公司的幕后决策者，也是我们所熟知的有组织的风险投资的缔造者。

生于法国的 87 岁的乔治斯·多利特死于 1987 年，但他给风险投资打下的独特印记却始终鲜明。想象一下：

• 多利特在美国研究与发展公司（ARD）所训练出来的经理人员，他们之中很多人都是获得奖学金的学生，他们不断独立创办或帮助经营风险公司。他们当中包括：Greylock 管理公司，Fidelity 风险有限公司，Palmer 组织公司，老波士顿资本公司，以及原 Morgan Holland 合伙公司。公司名称虽然经常有变化，但他们的线性后代公司却不断为近来新创办的一些基金提供资助，比如 Doubleclick 股份公司、铜山网络公司、前景系统公司。

• 多利特在哈佛所教授的 7000 名学生当中的很多人把多利特的哲学理念

带入了美国许多一流企业的高层。他们当中有：James D. Robinson 三世，美国快递公司前主席；William McGowan，MCI 公司的创始人；以及 Philip Caldwell，福特汽车公司前主席。

因此，当多利特需要一个经理来强化数字设备公司（DEC）的董事会时，他只需给像 Philip Caldwell 这样的天才管理者打个电话。美国研究与发展公司（ARD）前经理回忆说，"多利特成立的 Rolodex 是一个巨大的商业网络，它促使我们达成了很多交易，并且假如我们的任何一家公司遇到营销或技术问题，我们都可以连线美国最优秀的人才加以解决。"

多利特帮助创办的诸多起步公司的成功，一部分原因就在于利用了各大公司以及麻省理工学院和哈佛的人力资源，这极大地促进了新英格兰较为低迷的经济状况。波士顿有名的 128 号路演变成高科技发展中心，是沙山和硅谷高新园区发展的初步模式。

把赌注押在赛马骑师身上，而不是赛马身上，这同严格的投资前调查及随后无数次的交换看法，是多利特创办的 200 多家起步公司的原则。它们从 5,000 多个提案中筛选出来。多利特告诉《福布斯》杂志："当有人怀揣着一个从未尝试过的想法走进来的时候，你可以对这一想法做出评判的唯一办法就是根据跟你打交道的这个人。"

多利特支持创办的一些公司是高风险商业投资中的失败者，其中，六家公司当中有五家的维持时间不超过五年。比如说，凭空损失了早期投资的用于加工处理冷冻苹果汁及去壳虾的数百万美元。虽然数字设备公司（DEC）是一生中机会唯一的巨大成功，但多利特也成功创办了其他一些史有记载的公司，比如，Transitron 公司、Tracer 实验室、高压电工程公司，以及 Ionics 股份公司。

多利特的评判能力也显示在美国研究与发展公司（ARD）的成员身上。ARD 是于 1946 年，在一些公共机构的支持者的帮助之下建立的，比如马萨诸塞投资者信托公司的 Merrill T. Griswold 以及麻省理工学院校长 Karl T. Compton。

那时候，少数其他风险联营基金都是由私人为了家族利益创办的。因此，ARD 是一家身份独特的、公有的、封闭型的投资公司。它有两大优势：诚实经营的局外投资者首次可以尝试具有潜在的高额回报的风险投资，但又不用承担常见于私人风险公司交易中缺少流动资金的风险。

ARD 于 1939 年德国入侵波兰之夜成形，它脱胎于多利特和 ARD 支持者之间的一次会议。大家一致的意见认为，风险投资是非常关键的因素，决不能落入私人手中。应该持续地有组织地把资金和建议融为一体，使风险投资制度化。但计划因为二战的爆发而被搁置一旁。

多利特作为陆军军需兵军事计划署主任以及战争研究与发展部门副主任

被晋升为陆军准将名誉军衔之后，于1946年重回剑桥和他的讲堂。多利特的部分职责就是确保战争物资的生产，并在正确的时间运送到正确的地点。完成这一工作就涉及帮助建立新公司以生产高科技产品。

以多利特为首的ARD以政府提供的500万美元起步，到25年后ARD停止记账，资金账户达到4亿美元，其中还不包括购买比如高压电（High Voltage）工程公司有价证券股票的大笔支出。

多利特不仅仅是一名出色的投资公司管理者。金钱的重要性远不如培育成熟的新技术所带来的社会和经济的影响。长期支持有才干的人，创建公司，那么，他坚持认为：一切终会有回报。

努力坚持是多利特从父亲那里继承下来的部分品质。他的父亲是一名工程师，设计了首辆Pengeot汽车。他用了相当大的力量把工作理念传给年幼的多利特：如果多利特在法国公立中学的成绩下降到第二名，就会受到严厉地斥责。年轻的多利特随后完成了巴黎大学和哈佛大学的学业，毫无疑问在以后的岁月里，他总是用父亲与孩子的关系来比喻他与初创公司间的关系。他认为那些公司都是他的子女。有时因为支持失败者时间太久而受到指责，多利特会反驳说："如果一个孩子生病了，发烧华氏102度，你会卖掉他吗？"

多利特同样也把这种父亲般的感情带到了课堂上，他在哈佛商学院教授的是一门称为"制造学"的课程，这门课兼收并蓄，不拘一格，极受欢迎。这门课会涉及制造之外的很多话题，这门课的中心思想是多利特关于商人行为规范的思想，以及他对解决一些日常问题的人文主义看法，这些日常问题涉及如何构建董事会，如何跟一个早期阶段出资而又不懂得随后阶段经营的人打交道，这样的多来特是课堂上的掌控者，他几乎不接受提问，他告诉学生他讲他们听。他敦促学生在"制造"课的笔记本上记下他们对他讲课的想法。他告诉学生："现在要学习如何检测自己，你们离校后，不会再有考试了，但你们会怀念考试的。"

多利特追求完美，挑战一切。他对哈佛著名的案例分析嗤之以鼻，他通常把学生分派出去进行工作培训，他说，"经验是最好的老师"。多利特对数字持有疑问，他警告学生，人为操纵数字可以用来证明一切东西。

他谆谆教诲学生要有探求的心态，来自公司的客座演讲者应受到严格追问。他对学生未能锲而不舍地追问前来访问的美国钢铁公司总裁而感到失望，他告诉学生，他们忽略了一个显而易见的重点："美国钢铁公司并不了解他们所从事的生意，他们干的是材料买卖，而不是钢铁买卖。他们对铝和塑料完全无知。"他的忠实的学生随后告诉《福布斯》杂志，"多利特是第一个以这种方式思考的人，他对美国企业的影响比哈佛其他教员加在一起还要大。"

曾获奖学金的学生，比如，詹姆斯·摩根，他成为 ARD 的副总裁，还创办了自己的风险公司，他记得大学课业给许多已婚者带来了沉重的负担，只有陆军准将的一些关于如何挑选妻子的话题，以及提示女性如何应付企业文化的讲座会活跃沉闷的课堂环境。

将军对这些话题的看法，摩根大笑着说道："会吓死女权主义者。"理想的妻子会把丈夫需要了解的观点展示出来，用回形针把报纸和杂志中的内容夹住，也会在丈夫有商务行程时为他整理行装，总之，要为丈夫提供无限的支持。将军本人也极为溺爱妻子，他给妻子爱德纳写了无数的情诗，而她反过来也会在他的睡衣口袋里偷偷塞入便条。当然了，她也会按照工作安排，为他体贴地整理行装。

吉姆·摩根还记得对关于妻子内容讲座的期待，以及当将军扯碎了他的一份商业提案时所引发的焦虑和不安。摩根说："我妻子脾气易躁，她有孕在身，我一直对她承诺会更多呆在家里陪她，然而我却将更多的时间花费在图书馆里。我想她是打算和将军开诚布公地谈谈，以解决此事。"

摩根低估了将军的魅力，摩根的妻子毛瑞一脸迷惑地回到家里。"多么出色的男人，将军让我们告诉你们的第一件事就是：你们必须更加努力地工作。"她赞同地说道。还有另外一个例子也说明将军喜欢迂回战术，以苏格拉底式的对话从他的学生以及 ARD 专家口中获得观点。

举例来说，查尔斯·库特，退休的 ARD 总裁，回忆自己在一个下雨的周六下午，骑车去将军在波士顿百克湾的家，想要澄清某个商业问题。

像很多老同事在回忆将军时一样，库特用了法国腔英语。库特按门铃，多利特问道："查理，下雨天骑车不危险吗？"库特表示赞同："是，轮胎没有附着力。"将军问："是否有可能改变轮胎的咬合力?有人也许会用高级橡胶来提高附着力，能不能改进齿轮装置？关于骑车人身体重量的分布，能不能改变车的框架？"库特大笑着说："我知道这听起来很愚蠢，但我就站在雨里，将军站在门口避开了雨。我浑身湿透，而他却在构建一个新的高科技自行车公司。"

尽管多利特不是技术人员，但却具有吉姆·摩根所说的哲学家对待科学的态度。"他那个极爱钻研的大脑就好提问。将军会像这样子钻进去"，摩根回忆说，用右手作了一个月瓶塞钻钻东西的动作。

将军善于挖掘细节。摩根回忆起一个 ARD 同事花了很长时间扶持一个衰败的电动机公司。电动机总运不到质量标准。将军问了他一个看似简单却非常恰当的问题："轴承怎么样？它们是滚柱轴承还是球形轴承？"这一问题问得这位同事目瞪口呆。这位麻省理工学院的研究生、一流的分析专家不得不承认他不知道。因为困窘而满脸通红，这位 ARD 同事"坐在将军面前，感受到细节上存在这么大的差距"，说着，摩根伸出拇指和食指，比划出一毫米的距离。

将军善于说警句，听起来言简意赅，却总会深深刻在心里。举例来说，35年前，多利特在一次接受福布斯采访时，列出了很多至今仍然非常有效的信条。

·关于事业："一个人有三条路可走：迈向成功，成为庸人或被人遗忘。这三者当中，成为庸人是最危险的，因为这会让人感到快乐。"

·关于创造："一个有创造力的人只需具有想法，一个机变的人会使这些想法变为事实。我需要的是机变的人，我需要的人必须知道如何应对各种可能性。"

·关于小公司遇到的问题："我希望早点看到小公司的问题，我担心的是没有问题。我想早点知道一个人在逆境中的表现。"

·关于小公司的危险："小小的成就会让一些人自负。你不能靠一周40小时来经营一家小公司。"

·关于资金收益："我把资金收益看作是干好工作的回报，而不是干好工作的目标。有意思的想法在于研究、开发、生产、分配和销售。如果一个人能正确地进行筹资、生产、分配和销售，那么他就会获得回报。"

长期以来，将军的工作安排非常有序。从周三到周六，他完全属于 ARD，从周日到周二，他完全属于哈佛，但事情并非看起来那么容易。他在上课前一夜，从不安排商务预约或吃晚宴。他曾向一位同事吐露：甚至经过了40多年，他在面对学生时仍会因为紧张而感到恶心。

几乎没有学生感到将军身上的软弱。即使有，也只会使他们加深对他的忠诚。数百名上了年岁的老校友，经常定期聚会，举行重大生日或周年的庆祝活动，正如同 ARD 公司的一位老校友查尔斯·威特所说的，这显示出了对多利特哲学思想的传教士般的热情。"我们相信，我们正为更大的利益而作一些事情，这会使美国成为一个更加美好的国家。"威特说这番话时已离开 ARD 公司，去帮助创建 Greylock 管理公司。

献身热情部分地反映了多利特哲学思想从校园到新创办的公司的一种轻而易举的飞跃。1960 年，威特在《完成的交易》一书中指出，风险投资"从某个方面来说仍只是以多利特为首所进行的一种学术尝试，他不仅仅是一名老师，他在商务活动中检测论点，赚钱并非一种至上的目标"。

多利特哲学思想的传播者们欢庆麻省理工学院实验室和哈佛实验室的落成，这使原来从事国防和航天技术的科学家们出现了转变。他们在与华盛顿达成的研究合约的支持下，需要额外资金使航天技术应用转变为商用。制造分析仪的 Tracer 实验室首先发现了这一转变，它也是 ARD 公司由单一投资产生多元投资的实例之一。据查尔斯·威特回忆，许多 Tracer 实验室的技术人员偶然发现他们的老板不想购买新的应用技术，都会离开那里到我们公司或其他公司，寻求资金援助以创办自己的公司。

　　Transitron 是一家半导体生产商，也是另一个 ARD 的成功者，同样显示出了分支现象。威特说："人们涌出 Transitron 公司，在加利福尼亚或波士顿创办小公司，如果不是他们从这些公司中出来创业，也会有麻省理工学院或哈佛的教授们出来创业：因为他们看了股票杂志，并看到了商机。"

　　公司蓬勃发展极大地增加了由 ARD 的缔造者们帮助产生的波士顿地区的经济效益。一个确实的证据就是一座空置的毛纺厂，它是一处新英格兰纺织业的遗址，又重新恢复了生机。大量便宜的空地，其本身就是发展的催化剂。肯·奥尔森和他的合作伙伴哈兰·安德森尽量节省 87 万美元的 ARD 发展金，径直来到马萨诸塞州梅纳德的一个古老的毛纺厂，以每平方英尺 25 美分的价格购买了两倍于足球场大小的 9,000 平方英尺土地，其中还包括了值夜人员服务费和供暖费。部分原因多亏了低廉的管理费用，DEC 在第一年就获得了利润，这令 ARD 的经理们感到很欣慰。多利特担心企业只会获得一时的成功，他说道："我很担心这样迅速的成功不能维持下去。"将军不想让他的孩子们太早地离开巢穴。

　　人们一谈到 ARD，就会想到将军，他是 ARD 的灵魂人物。多利特并非一切都为了生意。他慷慨捐助并帮助创办了波士顿法语图书馆。

　　每年新年前夜，在多利特家里都会举办需正式着装的宴会。吃过晚宴，将军会发表幽默的讲话，并曾嘲讽地抱怨：他虽然加入了美国籍，却不能成为美国总统。他说，他通往权力的唯一之路就是成为计算机程序员联盟领袖，这使他可以随意关闭整个华尔街。

　　这种场合对将军而言，是个神奇的转变场所，他经常用他的幽默感化解 ARD 内部的紧张。华尔街对 ARD 的回报也非常慷慨。ARD 股票交易价格通常很高，有了 ARD 的巨大宝藏 DEC，投资者会把 ARD 股票看作是看涨期权，DEC 凭借具有人机交互功能的小型计算机取得了突破性成功，这使 DEC 成为美国发展最快的公司之一。

　　当初仰仗多利特成为名人的那些人提出了数以百计的风险投资建议，让多利特审查过目。筛选后的那些提议得到了将军本人手把手的指导。丹兹·多尔，加拿大数字设备公司前总裁，他本人早已成为风险投资家，回忆起多利特的关心扶持给予他的影响，"我看到多利特对肯·奥尔森的指导非常奏效，我确实对（他）在指导管理公司方面所发挥的作用有极大兴趣"。

　　当然，多尔只是经历了将军手下那些辛苦工作的员工所一直知道的情况。多利特力图以激励 ARD 企业家的相同的奖励回报员工，即股票购买权，但却因为政府规定而感到失望。作为投资公司雇员，这些员工被禁止作为奖励购买自己 ARD 公司，或 DEC 公司，或其他所投资的任何公司的股票。有些员工，不包括将军本人，确曾有机会买入 DEC 股票。那时，哈兰·安德森与肯·奥尔森发生争执而终止了合作关系，哈兰因此出售了自己在 DEC 的股份。这使得 ARD 少数几个资深员工可以舒服地坐等股票升值为五千多万美元，而普通员工一天要工作很长时间，得到很低的报酬，却为所投资的公司的经理们赚得数百万美元。

将军把精力都放在了商业投资方面，而把许多日常的细节工作交给他人去做。这在一段时间里取得了很好的效果。查尔斯·威特回忆起这段幸福时光，感到自己"做出了这个大人物想让我作出的贡献"。然后光扫描公司来了，公司处境艰难。有些 ARD 员工想弃之不顾，但光扫描公司是多利特舍不得丢弃的另外一个孩子。以惯常的迂回策略，多利特把资历尚浅的查尔斯·威特放进了董事会，让他在随后的几年内向光扫描公司提供资金以维持它的生存。威特回忆说：多利特不想自己开支票。为了寻求一致的意见，将军想让他的资深员工迫使他开支票。

威特当了替罪羊，他与光扫描公司的总裁共同努力，最终靠政府提供的资金使这家公司具备了一定规模，公司状况彻底好转。ARD 潜在的 300 万美元的损失变成了 2,000 万美元的盈利，公司老板的净资产从零变为 1,000 万美元。威特得到的回报是工资涨了 2,000 美元。他因此极度痛苦，虽然热爱他的工作，但还是决定另谋他就以得到足够的回报。他随自己的朋友比尔·埃尔法斯去帮助创建 Greylock 管理公司，比尔·埃尔法斯多年来一直是将军背后的二号人物。

鉴于 ARD 毫无报偿的管理结构以及将军帮助创建的企业文化，ARD 的弊端难以避免。多利特使风险投资声名赫赫，但在 20 世纪 60 年代它还主要是涉及东海岸的企业。大概仅有 50 名负责人从事着这一绅士般的游戏。大家彼此认识，没有直接竞争，共享交易。他们也有大量时间在实际情况下检查企业，研究潜在的市场和竞争，并且按照多利特的主要原则挖掘性格。没有必要太仓促达成交易。这样做的结果就是出错比现在少，并且很多可信赖的产品走到了新发行市场的最后阶段。

ARD 总是储备着大量人才，他们来自于多利特所教授的哈佛班，所以 ARD 能通过培育良好的投资而持续兴盛。当然其中也有给 ARD 造成损失者，举例来说，Ionics 股份有限公司从麻省理工学院的化学工程实验室挑选的，该公司低成本的离子分离技术是一项应用广泛，从海水中脱盐的全新技术。在 ARD 账目中，投资成本约 40 万美元，但到了 20 世纪 70 年代初，Ionics 公司价值约

200 万美元。它是所投资的尚未知名的 50 家公司的 45 种股票之一，只有三家未获成功。其中一家失败的公司具有典型的低技术特征，投资 50 万美元建立的康复之家连锁店，最后的账面价值降低到 1 美元。

一长串的成功使 ARD 的净资产从一股 5 美元提高到一股 90 美元，还不包括早前配给的很多有价证券。ARD 股票通常不是在 80% 或更高贴现率时交易，部分原因在于投资者认为跳上 DEC 这辆马车很合算。账目上 61,400 美元，市值 3.54 亿美元，20 世纪 70 年代初 DEC 占 ARD 资产额的 75% 以上。

尽管还不是经理，但将军不知疲倦地在幕后工作，帮助奥尔森在与哈兰·安德森合伙关系决裂后度过了危机。将军常说："我的职责就是关注，祈祷并传播幸福。"

奥尔森最大的问题就是管理规模扩大这柄双刃剑。DEC 在 1966 年以每股 22 美元成为知名公司，在仅仅 9 年时间里给予 ARD 的资金回报超过当初的 50 多倍。这一数字持续增长，因为 DEC 快速利用新技术，这使得它的冰箱大小的微型计算机比 IBM 的房间大小的主机更为便宜、快捷、易于操作。DEC 的发展迅速超过了原买的每纳德毛纺厂，创造了数以千计的新的工作机会，每年以 30% 到 50% 的收益增长。令人矛盾的是，ARD 也陷入了 DEC 成功的困境，作为两家公司的管家，将军是一个非常睿智的管事人，他意识到他面临着找人接替他的继承问题。他 72 岁了，终有一死，如果他未找到接班人就死了，很有可能 ARD 对 DEC 65% 的控股权会落入敌对者手中。

与接班问题密不可分的是如何冻结大量控制股，它可能破坏市场和 DEC 管理的稳定。跟几个 ARD 经理喝着白兰地，将军研究着选择办法。一个办法是，跟另一家 ARD 模式的风险公司合并，但这不能奏效。另一个办法是，从另一家风险公司高层管理者中吸纳过来一个多利特的老校友，但这也不能奏效。而另一个建议很奏效。多利特和比尔·米勒是好朋友，米勒是 Textron 股份有限公司的总裁，长期以来，在纺织业以外兼营大型联合企业交易。将军是 Textron 董事会成员，米勒是 ARD 董事会成员。因此，可以预见米勒的行事原则，他也极其了解将军的行事风格。Textron 全部收购 ARD 将会结束所有 ARD 业务，强化 Textron 的交易能力，使 ARD 作为一个分支公司保留名称，将军继续担任主席，选一个双方同意的擅长风险投资管理的人作为总裁和当然的接班人。

DEC 股份的处置也同样简要明确，股票会分配给母公司的股东，即提前并给 ARD 股东，作为一揽子交易的一部分，ARD 股东也可以得到适当的 Textron 股份。尽管作了谨慎的安排，Textron 交易却使得多利特的老校友感到痛心。谁能比他们受过更好的培训，可以成为接班人？此外，DEC 股票本可以在此前任何时候分配给母公司的股东，将军的策略就是要保留王冠上的宝石，这实际上是为宣扬自己。DEC 使多利特声望长存，交易会自行上门。

不管将军能否预知，发展过于迅猛的市场会很快掉落悬崖。让产易股及时避免了绩优股价格暴跌。将军把公司过账给 Textron，也不是尽如人意。多利特健康状况很好，仍旧充满工作热情，他很快断定他的指定接班人并不像他一样了解风险投资，这两个人根本合不来。

原计划多利特愿意留任多久就多久。Textron 在多利特与他的指定接班人之间进退两难，向双方提供了一揽子交易。将军同意拿退休金离开，担心自己沦为继子身份的公司在新的管理制度下如何生存。

事实上，公司发展困难，在大型联合企业的环境中远不如在原来的环境中那么生气勃勃。在查尔斯·库顿担任总裁期间，ARD 为 Textron 赚了很多钱，但一阵子赚钱是不利于公司发展的。最终，ARD 拱手让给了将军那些从困境中挺过来的老校友，他们举债经营，全部买下了 ARD。

将军还像以前一样忙碌，大部分时间帮助肯·奥尔森避过发展失控时的危险形势，他建议对严峻的组织机构问题要冷静，利用每一次机会劝说奥尔森。在为庆祝 DEC 公司 25 周年而举行的纽克曼社团会议上，将军在介绍 DEC 当家人时说，幸亏奥尔森没有生活在 1712 年。那一年正是英国革新家托马斯·纽克曼改进蒸汽机，开创工业革命的年头。多利特告诉社团成员，"纽克曼是个幸运的人，如果奥尔森生活在那个时候，他会设计出更好的发动机，那么今天，这个社团就会称为奥尔森社团了。"

对多利特怀有真挚的情感，奥尔森有几次在多利特家里召开了董事会，那是 1987 年，将军 87 岁了，因患肺癌而濒于死亡，奥尔森作出了这一慷慨的姿态。将军的务实精神历久犹存，对他培养的后辈有莫大的益处。多年后，DEC 因为微处理器的攻击而衰败，正是多利特培训出来的经理菲利普·凯德威尔迫使肯·奥尔森辞职。

多利特死后影响仍在。多亏了他的老校友所发挥的关键作用，风险基金的数目增至 7000 多家。过去十年中洪水般涌入风险基金的，主要来自公共机构投资者的资金数额增长了 10 倍，共有 300 亿美元资金。ARD 早期投资 DEC 获得了巨大成功，这样令人振奋的激励因素仍然是商业游戏的核心，但同样也存在风险。追求五花八门的风险投资而又掉以轻心的投资者在近来集中投资网络这一新兴事物时，损失了数十亿美元，正如他们早前风行投资生物技术一样。

多利特看到了变革来临，悲叹有太多的风险投资公司一心想扩大股票交易，而非建立可持续发展的公司。他进行风险投资的风格，即集中时间尽最大可能确保公司能独立发展，已被希望快速命中目标的经营者所取代，他们对盈利后退出策略更感兴趣，而非建立大公司。我们有了一个新想法，就要使它尽快进入新发行市场，要央！多利特在他去世前一两年，总结了这一趋势。

他说他刚完成一次巡回演讲，内容涉及需要风险资金开创可持续发展公司，一个热情的年轻人走过来祝贺他演讲成功，他说他的新公司，靠着出色的商务计划获得了资金支持，正如多利特所鼓励的那样运作良好。

"真的吗？"多利特欣喜地问道，"你达到了什么程度？"

"哦，一股约 1.32 美元。"年轻人回答道。

ARD 前总裁弗兰克·休吉这样的老校友讥笑着这一趣事。他们很多人都接近退休，力图向下一代灌输多利特的信条，但却发现难以抵挡不可预料的经济和文化变革。休吉说："很多年轻人不太关心建立实在的东西，而这是在经济结构中得以维持的根本。这已经成为现今行事的方式。金钱不再是工作的副产品，而成为工作的目标，这是人们在比赛中记分的办法。"

大学校园的氛围如今成了大企业环境。资本联合不再可能去创办极为盈利的小的起步公司。ARD 亲自指导的风格不复存在。休吉接着说道："你们在冲天火箭中见到过下面类似的情况，风险投资者努力使风险企业公开上市，大获成功，维持了六到八个月后，这家公司破产了。"

刚创办公司的企业家中，有多少人身上具备的素质能适合将军所描述的年轻时的肯·奥尔森呢？"他反应敏锐，善于管理员工，明白生产和分配间的关系，充分了解未来两至三年的市场，他的观点不会太前瞻而造成危害。"多利特也许过分赞扬了肯·奥尔森，但他对工作的说明却非常正确。

最终，DEC 良性运转多年，却也未能成为一家可持续发展的公司。对将军来说，值得庆幸的是，DEC 的衰败是在他死后。如果多利特身后未留下丰碑式的风险投资模式，那么，他的遗产也许比很多人留下的遗产都更值得夸耀。他不仅创造了风险投资，也指出了如何去运作它。他对美国资本主义做出了巨大的贡献。

Chapter Nine
Angel Investing—
Paul Bandrowski

第九章
天使投资——保罗·班祖斯基

I. Case Study

At age 38, Buffalo-Based business angel Paul Bandrowski is something of an early start-up himself. Along with an informal band of fellow angels—family, friends, business associates—Bandrowski has helped to finance maybe a dozen new high tech companies. He has become rich in the process but traces one of the most important lessons he learned about bootstrapping capital to fifth grade elementary school. "It's very simple," laughs Bandrowski. "You can get your business model right, your pricing right, your suppliers right, and then—wham—you get decked by the unpredictable."

Bandrowski is talking about more than just the cinnamon sticks he put up in his mother's kitchen and hawked at school for 10¢ a pack. He caught a sweet-tooth fad and rode it to the point where he was grossing $300 a month. Business was so good Bandrowski had to add his kid brother to the work force. That's when he was decked by the unforeseen.

It materialized in the form of a suddenly intolerant regulatory authority. "The principal suspended me for three days for neglecting my schoolwork," groans Bandrowski. Call it the parable of the cinnamon stick. The scourge of the unpredictable is all too common in what has become a full-time pursuit for Bandrowski—assaying small companies, helping to shape them, and rounding up the angel capital needed to get them off the ground.

Bandrowski and his fellow angels, cloaked in the Broadwayese for financial backers, are a new manifestation of private investing. Working outside the strictures of formal venture capital partnerships, they are freelancers, often operating in loose consort. By some estimates, there are more than two million angels in America. Many, like Bandrowski, are entrepreneurs who cashed in on early business success, now reinventing themselves by channeling smarts and capital into fledgling companies.

The risks, lurking in X-factors such as product failure or skewed market analysis, are high. The Small Business Administration figures that five out of every six of the kind of early-stage ventures Bandrowski midwifes never make it beyond year five. Bandrowski thinks the odds are somewhat better than the SBA makes them. He puts the rate of attrition at one out of every two—still high, but not prohibitive matched against what the enthusiastic Bandrowski calls "Big hits that can bring 75 to 100 times your money."

The big hit potential led hundreds of freelance angel bands like Bandrowski's to pump perhaps as much as $60 billion into 50,000 or more start-ups last year. By some estimates that is more than 30 times the capital mustered by deep-pocket professional venture firms, which typically focus on lower-risk efforts higher up the development chain.

A huge speculative wave builds ever higher, pushing venture tech companies to absurd levels; and then recedes piling them up on the rocks. These cycles have savaged whole industry segments like biotech, and now dot coms. That's when shrewd investors like Bandrowski start picking up salvage cheap.

He's typical of the many entrepreneurs who cash out of early success to put money and skills to work in loose alliance with other private investors. They start ahead of the game. The arrangement is cheap—no front-end costs or profit sharing with managing partners, as is the case in formal venture capital deals. Coinvesting also makes diversification easy in a high-risk business by pooling comparatively small pieces of individual money ($50,000 to $100,000) over a number of deals. Typically, each of the pooled investments runs to $1 million or so, centered mainly on start-ups with revenues of well under $10 million. Most such companies have not yet developed to a point where they can attract venture capital—too risky, proportionately too small, and too costly to monitor closely.

Bandrowski, for example, sits as vice-chairman of Sun Hawk, incorporated into which he recently combined a fledgling start-up. The Seattle-based digital publishing company gave him a solid minority holding in a listed stock. Bandrowski plans to help reinforce the combination with an infusion of badly needed new capital. That doesn't mean he intends to run Sun Hawk. "It's very satisfying," says Bandrowski. "I get to help these guys I may not know the technology and I'm not going to get in anybody's way, but entrepreneurs are surprised when I show them how pricing models work across different industries, and what it takes to get a banker to answer your phone calls."

Looking to squeeze more value out of the Buffalobased affiliate, Schreiber and Bandrowski hit on the idea of spinning off some of the technology into encryption software designed to keep Internet intellectual property rights from getting ripped off. Competitors were already in the field, but there was clearly a fast-growing market in movie, publishing, and software companies deeply worried about protecting digital copyrights from hackers and pirates.

Schreiber and Bandrowski managed to sell the concept to Softbank, but burned up a $500,000 advance in less than six months. When the two went back for more, they were told the cupboard was bare. With a modest equity of their own riding on the outcome, Schreiber and Bandrowski started tapping on venture capital doors and came up empty. "Nobody understood what we were trying to do," recalls Bandrowski. "They said, 'Digital rights? What are they?'" "Also," adds Bandrowski, "at some level they figured we were just a couple of guys from Buffalo. Maybe we could do steel mills, but what did we know about the Internet?"

So, Schreiber and Bandrowski turned with fading hope to a band of local angels. They, in fact, had never done a tech deal, cautiously sticking to what they knew best —Buffalo's traditional industrial and metal-bending skills. The narrowness of that focus kept Schreiber and Bandrowski on tenterhooks as they auditioned. Were the angels, taking a cue from Warren Buffett, going to shy from tech propositions they wouldn't try to understand? Schreiber and Brandrowski worked their way through two breakfast meetings at the Buffalo Club. The lead angel was Ross Kenzie. "A rough, gruff military man turned banker," says Bandrowski, "who asked really tough questions." As Bandrowski anticipated, the romance of tech investing did not go down easily with Kenzie, who had done well in some 30 deals over the years, most of them hard asset buyouts. "What do you mean, you're not going to make money in the first 12 months?" demanded the burly Kenzie. Bandrowski and Schreiber eased the group slowly through the crypto technology and realized they were home free when one angel piped up with an epiphany: "Last time I read, Yahoo was not a bad early buy." With members of the group chipping in $50,000 to $100,000 each for a total of $3 million, Bandrowski and Schreiber were off to the races.

Their start-up, Reciprocal, Incorporated is a prime example of how angels network—one deal leading to another—and how angel money gets leveraged into bigger dollops of financing. Softbank's capital begat the Kenzie capital, getting Reciprocal to a working stage where Bandrowski and Schreiber could do missionary work on deeper pockets. This time around, venture capital firms realized they were looking at something more substantive than just two guys from Buffalo. So did Microsoft, hot on the kind of crypto it takes to prevent repetitions of the massive computer break-in it suffered last year. Put it all together and you've got the $75 million in additional capital it took to make Reciprocal a going concern now employing some 200 and conservatively worth several hundred million dollars. At this writing, Reciprocal has not yet gone public, another big multiplier Kenzie's angels can look to down the road. Though they could have cashed out handsomely at several points along the line, Kenzie's angels still hold an extremely cheap slice of Reciprocal in what has become a transforming experience. Bandrowski says the group, having finally taken the plunge, has now gone in to invest in a number of high-tech deals with him. One of them is a tenstrike called OpenSite Technologies, a Research Triangle Park, North Carolina-based developer of online auction software.

While running Reciprocal as Chief Executive Officer, Bandrowski was giving a helping hand—as well as cash—to Michael Brader-Araje, OpenSite's founder. "When I first started talking to Michael," laughs Bandrowski, "he told me he didn't know a capitalization table from a billiard table." Brader-Araje learned quickly, but not without pain. As OpenSite developed, still hungry for capital, Brader-Araje, Bandrowski, and the Kenzie angels looked to a public offering. Ready to fly in the summer of 1999, they scrubbed because of a downdraft in the market. Early last year, they were poised for another try, but market turbulence again forced them to abort. "It was not exactly a happy experience," founder Brader-Araje told *Forbes*.

It's easy to tell where the separate paths these two long-time partners have chosen diverge. Angels tend to be unstructured free spirits. Their ranks are populated with definitely hands-on types. Some are retired executives, determined not to spend their days yukking it up at the 19th hole. The younger contingent tends to be 40-ish, with leisure and money enough to be nearly full-time investors. Both commodities are spiked with the conviction that it's time to do something new. Paul Bandrowski is typical of this restless breed. "I knew I'd never be good at running a big company," he says. "Once you get it together, it's time to move on. My personal exit strategy is when you get to have 25 to 40 people on the payroll. That's when I'm out of there."

Thus, a critical distinction: Some 400,000 active angels (those who do three or more deals a year), in the main, are entrepreneurial-manager types who, so to speak, have got their hands dirty on the shop floor. Venture capital on the other hand tends to be staffed by financial-investor types with comparatively little direct business experience. The difference shows in the angel's willingness to take on higher risks and stick with them longer. They can be more patient because they don't have to kowtow to limited partners demanding quick returns or measure up to performance yardsticks to keep their jobs.

Logically, in terms of time and risk, angeldom should generate higher rewards. Winners like OpenSite get a lot of ink and certainly whet the appetite. Angels think big. They go in, according to a University of New Hampshire Venture Research Center survey, with the hope of quintupling their money in five years. That's the expectation. The reality may be quite different. Actual returns, spread over the spectrum from groups like the Nashua, New Hampshire Breakfast Club to the Silicon Valley angels, are hard to get at. The odds are they come in at no worse than the long-term 15 percent to 20 percent notched by the venture industry, and possibly higher.

That's better than the long-term stock market return, and of course there's always the hope of a big hit. Two things are certain: Storming in where most venture capital firms fear to tread, angels finance some 75 percent of the nation's start-ups. That makes angeldom a huge social and economic phenomenon that has to be treated with respect. It's hard to see dilettantism in the mighty contribution angels make to job creation and the boost they give to the United States lead in world technology.

Angels have a long and honored history. Well before they picked up the vogue

Broadway descriptive, they were known as private investors and helped to bankroll such groundbreakers as Alexander Graham Bell and Henry Ford.

Another certainty: Angels have more fun.

Much of the reward tends to be psychic—the buzz angels like Paul Bandrowski get from rolling up their sleeves and pitching in. There are social rewards too—bragging rights when a winner like OpenSite is booted home. The entry cost is not insuperable. "Accredited" investors, by Securities and Exchange Commission fiat, must be able to show a minimum worth of $1 million (including primary residence) or annual income thresholds of $200,000 ($300,000 joint). Angels come in all shapes and sizes. Some may chip in to only one or two deals; others may diversify across a number. Many are passive, quite willing to hand their proxies to the Paul Bandrowskis of the universe. Some, mainly cashed-out entrepreneurs with deep pockets, fly solo; most band together in more than 100 affinity groups like Ross Kenzie's Buffalo crowd. As Zina Moukheiber reported in Forbes, the syndication approach had been popularized by some of the big names surfacing at the top of many successful investments. Capital Investors of Washington, D.C., for example, includes such star quality as MCI World Com vice-chairman John Sidgmore.

The name are hotly pursued by promising entrepreneurs on the make. Group power means collectively bigger investments spread over more possibilities. It also makes for better networking, as in the cross-pollination that projected the Kenzie group out of its preoccupation with old economy buyouts into high-tech growth. Some groups, in the each-one reach-one fashion typical of angels, have recruited a 100 or more members. Others (Bandrowski, for me) keep it small. Inner-directed lead angels often just don't want to deal with too many other egos.

Most groups meet regularly to check out potential deals. It's often a bar and buffet scene, as was a recent monthly confab of the Texas Angels in the ballroom of Austin's Four Seasons Hotel. Some 90 members of the group have turned out for this $100 a head bash. After swapping business cards and high-tech tales, juggling drinks and hor d'oeuvres at the warmup reception, they get down to the serious stuff of the audition. The three start-ups pitching the crowd tonight have already survived two cuts.

They're among the half-dozen possibilities winnowed from more than 30 business plan summaries submitted to the group's steering committee. The first pass, aimed at picking three finalists who will do ten-minute standups before the crowd tonight, took place a week ago in the University of Texas auditorium before a five-person selection committee. It was by no means the hammer and tong inquisition nervous entrepreneurs clearly feared. They got encouragement and criticism in equal amounts. "You are lecturing and investors hate to be lectured," one entrepreneur was told. "We just want to know what the deal is." Yet another suppliant, deep into the innovations of his software package, was told to lighten up. "When you have a really technical product like yours, you have to discuss its benefits in layman's terms," was the instruction. "I hope this discussion will help you do that."

For the three who survived this cut, the preliminary offered useful cues as to how to package their ten-minute spiels for the formal presentation at the Four Seasons. The questions there also tended to center on technological feasibility, a crucial consideration for angels trying to figure out which horse they want to bet. There are some things the start-ups don't like to give away. "We'll have to plead the Fifth on that," was the response to one pointed query." "It's key intellectual property, and we can't reveal it right now." The topic was aired more openly in private discussion over coffee and dessert after the formal Q&A. Angels interested in follow-up booked additional time with the entrepreneurs. There would be weeks of continuing research before anyone started talking money. It was a satisfied group that headed to the elevators. "The social stuff is fun," smiled one angel. "But as you can see, it's also very, very professional."

The social side is definitely part of the appeal. What can be so wrong in a mix where you can make some money, perhaps big money, and give a budding business a lift, all in the company of kindred souls? Ideally, nothing. The threshold question is: Have you got the real angel stuff? The answer is partly a function of where else you've invested your money and how tolerant you are of risk. Seasoned hands like Paul Bandrowski can afford to put a big chunk of assets into private investing and expect to do well. If you've got some extra casino money that you can afford to lose, go for it! But only if you've got a balanced portfolio of other investments that will see you through the five to seven years it might take for a start-up to work out. The old venture capital wheeze applies here: Lemons ripen before plums. Thus, you should have enough free cash to diversify over a number of deals, and a reserve to put into follow-up financing.

If your hope is to add sweat equity to the cash, be realistic about the amount of free time you can spare. Equally important, check your temperament. If you're a Charlie-take-charge guy, you can be sure that any entrepreneur worth his salt will tell you to stuff it. If you do want to put energy into a deal, you'll likely be better off angeling with a couple of friends or in a small group.

The other side of the coin is, how comfortable do you feel about delegating big decisions to someone else? The point here is the difference between loose and organized groups. Both put on regular dog-and-pony shows for members. In the informal groups, individuals structure their own deals, taking on the whole burden of research, legal work and negotiations. Formal groups like the Washington D.C.-based Womanangels net invest as a unit. Each of its members has agreed to chip in a minimum of $75,000 over three years, with the right to ante up more on the side if they so choose. This band of professional women, age range 30s to 60s, is fronted by a managing partner who takes on all the details. Typically, managers work for modest pay against a 15 percent cut of the profits. That's a lot cheaper than the 20 percent to 30 percent of the profit (plus two percent annual fees) imposed by the professionals in venture capital firms.

Formal or informal, many groups are often led to invest in a particular industry by common expertise. Paul Bandrowski's success with Reciprocal, for example, has nudged him into focusing on encryption technology. Investing in what you know is one way to reduce risk, and carve out a niche where you might be helpful. At the same time, be sure you're not investing in too specialized a property. If one product doesn't work out, is there a fallback application that might?

Finding a group that fits is all part of the networking process. Chat up professionals who might be plugged in: bankers, lawyers, accountants, university entrepreneur programs, investment bankers. Take a look at matching services that put angels and entrepreneurs together. There are probably 100 or so such outlets, many of them nonprofit or university affiliated. Most of them stage face-to-face venture forums, or tie capital and business together with the help of newsletters and the Internet.

Most angel groups screen potential members (if only to make sure that they meet the SEC's "accredited investor criteria")—a useful process that enables would-be members to ask questions, too. That's the time to look into items such as a group's risk tolerance, investment criteria, exit strategies management, and success ratio. Ask for brochures, annual reports, details on presenter forums. You are investing in a group as well as a portfolio, so talk to as many members as you can. It's nice to know you're among friends. If you don't seriously exercise this sort of due diligence, you may find yourself akin to Grouch Marx, who deadpanned that he would never join a group that was willing to let him in.

Part of the self-selection process—will this group and I get along?—turns on whether you are searching for the same kind of deals. Risk levels, the amount of money involved, the price of a venture all vary with the stage of development. The stages shake down like this:

Seed financing usually involves only modest amounts of outside financing, but lots of sweat equity on the part of the founder. Typically, the cash goes to a product that looks good on paper, but has not yet been developed. At this stage of the game, for example, Amazon founder Jeff Bezos had put $10,000 of his own cash into Amazon com and borrowed $40,000. Van Osnabrugge and Robinson, authors of Angel Investing, put the adjusted price of his stock at 001 a share.

Start-up financing is ticketed to companies rounding out development and market studies, but not yet a truly commercial operation. It was at this level that Bezos's mother and father tucked a total of $240,000 into Amazon. Their price: 1717 a share.

First (early) stage companies have burned up development capital and need another jolt of cash to set up full-scale manufacturing and sales. This is when two angels invested a combined $54,408 into Amazon. Their cost: 3333 a share. They were followed by a 20-angel syndicate that put up a little less than $100,000. Their cost was also 3333 a share.

Second (later) stage companies are generating revenues (but not necessarily profits), have a solid management crew in place, and need money for expansion. Two venture capital firms invested a total of $8 million in Amazon at this point. Their cost: $2.34 a share.

In its first public offering, not quite three years after Bezos put up his $10,000. Amazon com raised $49 million at a price of $18 a share. That cheered the 3333 cents-a-share angels no end. In the early stages, Bezos, his family—and the angels—were taking most of the risk, so they got in cheap. They also harvested the biggest rewards. The later arriving venture capitalist firms, investing in what was a going concern, paid considerably more for a still handsome but lesser return. It's a classic demonstration of risk-reward ratios and how each layer of financing builds a base for the next.

The risks and rewards vary so that you should be sure that any angel band you might want to join is in sync on the stage that suits you best. Further, if you hope to help the entrepreneurial launch, is there room for you to do so? Other points to explore: industry concentration (typically high-tech), minimum investments, and overhead costs like the manager's cut—if any.

Networking puts angels together; networking brings them the deals they invest in. Computerized matching services do this out of a confidential database submitted by both sides. Some screen start-ups for minimal standards before putting them on the date list; others do not.

All matching services fade out after making the introduction. Angels do a lot of prospecting on their own—Ross Kenzie and the Buffalo Angels' willingness to talk to Paul Bandrowski, for example, even though he came from the Ultima Thule of technology. The early filtering process is important in the way that time is important. In angeldom, as elsewhere, you have to kiss a lot of frogs before you find a prince. So, one threshold question, always, is a cautious "who brought this deal in?" Finders are not always objective; they are often selling.

There is almost always a certain amount of judicious exaggeration in such presentations. In their pitch to the Buffalo Angels, Bandrowski and Schreiber leaned heavily on Yahoo! And the financial rewards that high-tech investment can bring. That certainly caught the group's attention. What really clinched the deal, though, was Bandrwoski and Schreiber's demonstrated management skills, and a detailed explanation of the market they were shooting for. Anyone can cobble together a glitzy business plan. The dot coms that destructed like a string of Chinese firecrackers were all plausible enough to find backers. The angel's imperative is to cut through the paper and ballyhoo to the reality (if any) behind the business plan. Thus, Bandrowski says Ross Kenzie "checked all of our references and talked to everyone to learn the technology." "It was one of the most painstaking pieces of due diligences I have ever seen," adds Bandrowski.

So, Kenzie did not permit the Bandrowski-Schreiber charm offensive to distract him. That puts him one up on the general run of angel. University of New Hampshire research suggests that entrepreneurial enthusiasm and personality weigh heavily in angel investment decisions. Good vibes are nice, particularly if you hope to work directly with the entrepreneur. But the higher virtues lie in demonstrated expertise and some concrete display of management skills, not always easy to find anywhere, let alone in a largely untried start-up.

One measure of those qualities is how sedulously the founder bootstrapped his firm before looking to outside help. Basically, how much hustle has he shown? Is he logging the requisite 80 to 100 hours a week? How much of his own money is at risk? Is he leveraging—and regularly paying off—credit card and home equity debt to keep himself afloat? Is he working out of his garage, or in rented space that eats up capital? Is he working out of his garage, or in rented space that eats up capital? Is he working with used or leased equipment rather than splashing out for new? Why not insist on dedicated frugality and fully utilized sweat glands in a wanna-be you're going to give your money to?

Think of Pual Bandrowski's background as a model for the kind of entrepreneur you want on your side. Put temporarily out of business by regulatory authority—the principal in his fifth grade elementary school venture—Bandrowski tried again two years later. No cinnamon sticks this time. "I talked to my dad about wholesale margins on candy bars—he was always in business—and the markups looked good," recalls Bandrowski. Using some of the capital from his cinnamon stick gig, Bandrowski bought $200 worth of Snickers and Milky Ways at a discount outlet for 12¢ each. He sold them for 30¢ each (a nickel over then retail) during the lunch hour through a gang of 20 kids, splitting with them the 18¢ markup. "It was a good business plan," laughs Bandrowski. "There was immediate cash flow and the marketing costs were quite low."

Bandrowski spent almost all his subsequent school years in one business or another, including a software company he put together with a group of fellow students at Central Michigan University. "That's where we did have marketing problems," says Bandrowski. "Nobody wanted to buy from us because they thought we were just a couple of college kids." They persuaded an angel—one of his friends' fathers—to put some cash into the venture and handle the marketing. The switch worked. "We wound up selling out to another group and actually made some money," recalls Bandrowski.

Central Michigan was one of the six colleges Bandrowski attended and left. "I was always arguing with my professors," he says. The last of those arguments erupted at the University of Chicago, where Bandrowski took exception to a case his professor was presenting. "You think it actually works that way?" queried

Bandrowski. When the academician insisted it did, Bandrowski asked him if he'd ever been in business. "No. What difference does that make?" came the answer. "I walked out and never looked back," says Bandrowski. Eight ventures later, Bandrowski had enough cash to reinvent himself as an angel.

A probing mind and a precocious interest in business are typical of many top entrepreneurial names; something to look for in your search for talent. Take Amar Bose, whose experiments on loudspeaker design led to the founding of Bose Corporation, a state-of-the-art audio products company. He set up a home radio repair shop in Philadelphia at age 13 during World War II when his father's import business faltered. At that time, almost everyone who could repair radios was in the military. Soon Bose's shop (employing seven other students at 50¢ an hour) was one of the biggest in town.

Similarly, as a 14-year-old during the German occupation of Greece, George Hatsopoulos, founder of Thermo Electron, built radios on the sly and sold them mainly to the Underground. He filled a notebook with inventions, hoping he could one day build a business around them. That's precisely what Hatsopoulos did. An inspiration on how thermionic emissions could be harnessed to convert heat into electricity with no moving parts became the core of his Thermo Electron empire.

Granted those are exceptional talents, but the early commitment to business is not. Such predictive experience is one of the first things to look for in a prospective entrepreneur. Passive angels often don't make a point of sitting in on early talent interviews. That's a mistake. In early-stage companies, you're investing first in people, then in a product. One common angel regret is failure to truly size-up a founder. Will he stand up when things go wrong, as they invariably do? Can he put a real management team together, or does he feel comfortable only with yes-men?

Feeling and intuition frequently control how angels invest. Often there is very little else to go on. Financials aren't very much help in assessing a company with very little history, but they should nonetheless be challenged. Business plans should be screened as part of the early due diligence, too. Treat them as sales documents. Take no entrepreneurial projections for granted. What you're looking for is a unique product in a fast-growing market that will preempt the competition. The search should be focused. Your group should be playing to its own industry strengths, with savvy lead angels running an independent check on market potential.

You can hire outside experts to do the grunt work, but that adds to the cost of what is by definition already an expensive, time-consuming process. Preliminary screening should be rigorous enough to allow only the very best bets to get to the formal due-diligence stage Once you get there, take a cold look at traditional items such as cash flow and potential rate of return. Do they look promising enough to make this investment worthwhile? Angels often do not do as much deep research as they should—one of the reasons why they make decisions far more quickly than venture capitalists and, as a result, get to repent at leisure.

Without deep thought, it's hard to resolve one of the toughest questions in venture finance: Could this company work out and how big a piece of it are you entitled to for taking on most of the risk? It's important to hammer out those issues in the precontract bargaining. Since they intend to live with the entrepreneur for half a decade or more few angels haggle to the last for an extra two percentage points of equity. But who gets what for how much can become an everlasting bone of contention, even in such great success stories as the creation of Digital Equipment Company. Friends say that Kenneth Olsen, founder of the computer maker (now part of Compaq Computer) to this day feels that he gave up too much of his company for too little—70 percent of it for a $70,000 seed investment that ultimately netted shareholders of Georges Doriot's American Research and Development Company more than $400 million.

Business angels often feel that they've been taken too, regretting that they didn't push for better terms. You don't want to be too aggressive. But don't settle for less than a meaningful minority position (20 to 30 percent), and maybe a seat on the board like Paul Bandrowski's vice-chair position at Sun Hawk.

A grab for control is a no-no. Why strip a fledgling company of what may be its most valuable asset—the entrepreneur's incentive to build? And why worry about equity anyway? Convertible debt is probably a better option. If things do go badly, debt will give you at least a claim on assets. Other considerations before you go to contract: Illiquidity is one of the great drawbacks of investing in start-ups. How do you get your money out? In an outright failure, you might be able to salvage something from the bankruptcy court. If the business merely bumps along at subsistence levels, the customary escape routes are trade sales, management buyouts or mergers (like Paul Bandrowski's combining his start-up into Sun Hawk). Cashing in through the new issues market is every angel's dream exit, but a long shot. In effect, angels run a farm system, happy to get from semipro to the minor leagues, knowing only that exceptional talent will make the leap to big time.

Careful monitoring is the best way to help your entry move up in class. Make sure that you're getting maximum mileage out of every new dollar in capital you put up. Keep pay scales tight, and make stock a major element in compensation packages. Doing so saves start-up cash and pushes incentive from the top right on down through to the mail room. Fight any temptation to hire expensive management from the outside. Cultivating talent in-house is bootstrapping by other means and part of the satisfaction of plunging into venture investing.

There are other ways to do so, of course. You can invest—passively—in publicly traded incubators such as Safe Guard Scientifics or Soft Bank Ventures—both selling for a lot less now than a year ago. You can invest in publicly traded business development companies, or even in venture-oriented mutual funds. You can do that, but you'll never feel the creative buzz that Paul Bandrowski talks about. "Angeling sure beats working," he says.

Key Words and Expressions:

ante up	[美俚]（不得已而）付账，付钱；提出
bankroll	vt. 提供资金
bone of contention	争论的焦点，争端
cloak	n. 斗蓬，宽大外衣，掩护
	vt. 用外衣遮蔽，披斗篷
chat up	用与人闲聊来获得对方的好感,搭讪
cobble together	胡乱拼凑，粗制滥造
confabulation	n. 会议　　v. 会谈
dilettantism	n. 业余的艺术爱好，浅涉文艺，浅薄涉猎
hammer out	锤成，苦心想出，推敲出
hawk	vt. 兜售，（沿街）叫卖
groan	vt. 呻吟着说
limited partner	有限责任股东，有限责任合伙人
lurk	vi. 潜藏，潜伏，埋伏
make for	（尤指匆匆地）走向，有利于，倾向于，导致，向前进
no end	非常

on the make	在制作中，野心勃勃
on the sly	秘密地
overhead cost	间接费用，管理费用，间接成本，营业成本，总开支
public offering	公开销售证券
put out of business	使无法进行，使停业，使破产
pitch in	努力投入
roll up one's sleeve	卷起袖子，准备行动
scourge	n. 鞭，笞，苦难的根源，灾祸 vt. 鞭打，痛斥，蹂躏
seasoned hand	老手，得力人手
shop floor	n. 车间；工场
splash out	[口] 随意花钱，大肆挥霍
stock swap	证券交易
syndication	n. 企业联合组织
take the plunge	冒险尝试
Ultima Thule	天涯海角，最远点
winnow	vt. 簸，扬（谷），吹开糠皮, 吹掉, 精选
worth one's salt	称职，胜任

Notes:

1. Angels 天使人

"天使人"（angels）是指既富有雄厚的资金实力，又富有管理经验的个人。他们看准了投资机会后，就用自己的钱，加上自己的管理经营经验，参加企业的整个从小到大的成长过程。他们所投资金在 5 万到 150 万美元之间。他们往往作为董事会的成员直接参与所投企业生产与发展。据统计，20 世纪 90 年代初，美国大约有 200 万这种天使人。他们之中绝大部分是靠自己发家的第一代百万富翁。这个比例正在上升。1984 年，《福布斯》杂志评出的全美 400 名最富有的个人中 40% 是自己起家的。到了 1994 年，这个比例达到 80%。微软公司的比尔·盖茨名列榜首。他本人曾在生物工程界多次从事创业投资，以扶持新兴企业。

2. boot strap investment "布罗波投资"或"鞋带投资"

"布罗波投资"或"鞋带投资"（boot strap investment）是指那些在企业

的最初发展阶段所作的投资。这种投资或以私人直接投资的形式，或以放弃工资的形式实现的。后者也叫做"血汗资本"。

3．Nashua 纳舒厄

　　纳舒厄：曼彻斯特南部梅里马克河畔新罕布什尔南部的一个城市。建立于公元 1655 年，在 19 世纪早期成为一个纺织中心，人口 79,662。

4．Alexander Graham Bell 亚历山大·格雷厄姆·贝尔

　　电话发明家亚历山大·格雷厄姆·贝尔，1847 年生于苏格兰爱丁堡市。虽然他只在学校念了几年书，但是通过家庭的熏陶和自学却受到了良好的教育。贝尔对语音复制感兴趣是很自然的，因为他父亲是语言生理、语言矫正和聋哑教学方面的专家。

　　1871 年贝尔移居马萨诸塞州波士顿市。在那里于 1875 年他有了导致发明电话的一些发现。1876 年 2 月他申请电话发明的专利权，几个星期之后就获得了该项发明的专利权。有趣的是，还有一名叫伊茉沙·格雷的人申请类似装置的专利权的报告与贝尔的同一天到达，但只是晚到了一个多小时的时间。

　　贝尔获得专利权不久就在费拉德尔菲亚市百年纪念展览馆展出了他的电话。他的发明引起了观众的极大兴趣，并且获了奖。但是东方联合电报公司花 10 万美元获得了该项发明权，拒不购买贝尔的电话。因此贝尔及其同事一起于 1877 年 7 月成立了一家公司，即今日美国电话电报公司的祖先。电话在金融上一举获得巨大的成功，美国电话电报公司现在是世界上最大的私人企业公司。

5．Henry Ford 亨利·福特

　　亨利·福特（1863～1947），是美国福特汽车公司的创始人，出生在美国密歇根州底特律市几英里外的迪尔伯恩村。他的祖父约翰·福特是爱尔兰移民。亨利·福特儿时的梦想是做一个钟表匠，他在机械方面的天赋和对它的痴迷，成就了他一生的事业。16 岁那年，他独自一人来到底特律，开始了他发明家、创造者、汽车大亨的辉煌生涯。A 型车、T 型车的接连成功，使亨利体味到巨大的成功喜悦。但他并没有止步不前，福特生产线是 20 世纪初革命性的创举，流水线的生产方式整整影响了美国乃至全世界大半个世纪，这种生产方式被称为福特主义。亨利·福特一直工作到 1945 年 9 月 20 日。这一天，28 岁的孙子亨利二世从他手中接过了亨利王国的最高权力。

6．George Hatsopoulos 乔治·海佐波勒斯

　　美国热电公司（Thermo Electron）的创始人和董事长，该公司位于马萨

诸塞州的沃尔瑟姆市（Waltham）。47 年前，一个富于创业精神的希腊移民乔治·海佐泼勒斯（George Hatsopoulos）在美国创办了热电集团，他是麻省理工学院的一名工程系学生，后来成为学院的机械工程系教师。他是一名非常优秀的技术人才和发明家，也是一位创业者，这一点对于理解热电集团的发展至关重要。

7．SBA 小企业管理局

SBA 的职能是：尽可能地扶持、帮助和保护小企业的利益，以及对小企业提供顾问咨询服务。SBA 直接对小企业提供贷款，以及为小企业向银行作担保，使小企业能从银行获得贷款，同时为小企业在获得政府采购订单以及在管理和技术方面提供帮助和培训等。自 1953 年创业以来到目前为止，SBA 已为 1,280 万家小企业提供直接和间接的帮助，目前 SBA 向小企业发放的贷款总额达 250 亿美元。1958 年，通过了投资法案创建了小企业投资公司（SBIC）计划。在 SBA 的许可证下，SBIC 可以是一个私人的风险投资公司，通过享受政府的优惠政策，为小企业提供长期贷款和在高风险的小企业进行权益性投资。现在 SBIC 成为美国风险投资公司家族中的重要一员。

8．Georges Doriot 乔治斯·多利特

乔治斯·多利特（Georges Doriot）是美国早期杰出的风险资本家，他为美国的风险投资的创立、专业化运作和产业化作出了巨大的贡献。

9．RTP (Research Triangle Park) 三角研究园

Research Triangle Park，美国北卡罗莱纳州的三角研究园是世界上最大的研究园，毗邻北卡罗莱纳州的罗利（Raleigh）、达勒姆（Durham）和教堂山（Chapel Hill），1969 年由企业界、学术界和工业界的领袖共同倡导举办，规划面积约 7,000 英亩，因园址恰好选在以三座城市中三所大学（达勒姆市的杜克大学、罗利市的北卡罗莱纳州立大学和查佩尔希尔市的北卡罗莱纳大学）为顶点构成的三角形地带的中央，故得名。其南北长 9.6 公里，东西宽 3.2 公里。经过四十多年的建设，已经开发了大约 86% 的规划面积，园内共有公司和各类组织 140 个，其中有 106 个是研发机构，孕育了一批像 IBM、思科、索尼、爱立信和北电网络等国际高新技术研究领域的巨人，是美国最大也是最成功的高科技园区之一。

10．SafeGuard Scientifics

是一家通过为其购得的科技类的公司提供高级经营和管理的支持服务，以增加这些公司的长期价值的公司。该公司主要并购和开发三种公司：商业和信息技术、软件和新兴技术。

II. Knowledge Points

1. SBA (Small Business Administration)

1) Definition and theory

The Small Business Administration (SBA) is a United States government agency that provides support to small businesses.

2) Mission

According to the agency, the mission of the Small Business Administration (SBA) is "to maintain and strengthen the Nation's economy by aiding, counseling, assisting, and protecting the interests of small businesses and by helping businesses and families recover from economic and other disasters."

The agency is also responsible for providing loans to homeowners and renters that have been victims of presidentially declared disasters. Presidential declarations automatically make disaster assistance available to victims if they meet qualifications. The Department of Agriculture and state governors also have the authority to request declarations on areas affected by disasters in their jurisdictions. Over 80% of the loans processed by the agency are for home owners and renters.

3) Structure

The SBA is an independent agency that operates under the authority of the Small Business Act of 1953. The secretary of commerce delegates small business responsibilities to the SBA. The organization and management of the SBA consists of an administrator and deputy administrator, who are appointed by the president and approved by Congress; field office directors; and administrators for the various program areas. The SBA also has associate administrators for the following offices: Disaster Assistance; Field Operations; Public Communications, Marketing, and Customer Service; Congressional and Legislative Affairs; Equal Employment Opportunity and Civil Rights Compliance; Hearings and Appeals; and Management and Administration.

There are also associate administrators for Investment; Small Business Development Centers; Surety Guarantees; regular Government Contracting; and Minority Enterprise Development. Assistant administrators handle International Trade; Native American Affairs; Veterans Affairs; Women's Business Ownership;

and Size Standards, and Technology. There is an associate deputy administrator for Government Contracting and Minority Enterprise Development. These offices are then the backup and resource for over 68 field offices that administer the programs and monitor loans. The Inspector General Office audits and maintains the integrity of the loans and the SBA programs.

4) History

The SBA was established on July 30, 1953, by the United States Congress with the passage of the Small Business Act. Its function was to "aid, counsel, assist and protect, insofar as is possible, the interests of small business concerns." Also stipulated was that the SBA should ensure a "fair proportion" of government contracts and sales of surplus property to small business. This was accomplished primarily through the Small Business Innovative Research program and government "set-asides."

The SBA also makes loans directly to businesses and acts as a guarantor on bank loans. In some circumstances it also makes loans to victims of natural disasters, works to get government procurement contracts for small businesses, and assists businesses with management, technical and training issues.

The SBA has directly or indirectly helped nearly 20 million businesses and currently holds a portfolio of roughly 219,000 loans worth more than $45 billion making it the largest single financial backer of businesses in the United States.

The SBA has survived a number of threats to its existence. In 1996 the then newly Republican-controlled House of Representatives planned to eliminate the agency. It survived and went on to receive a record high budget in 2000. Renewed efforts by the Bush Administration to end the SBA loan program have met congressional resistance, although the SBA's budget has been repeatedly cut, and in 2004 certain expenditures were frozen.

5) SBA Loan programs

The most visible elements of the administration are the loan programs it administers. The SBA itself does not grant loans. Instead, the SBA guarantees against default certain portions of business loans made by banks and other lenders that conform to its guidelines.

Contrary to popular belief, these programs are not generally for persons with bad credit who can't get bank loans, nor are they primarily used for startup funding; rather, the primary use of the programs are to make loans for longer repayment periods and with looser affordability requirements than normal commercial business loans. Also, a business can qualify for the loan even if the yearly payment would be the same as the previous year's profit, whereas most banks would want payment for a loan to be no more than two-thirds (2/3) of the prior year's profits for a business. The lower payments, longer terms and looser affordability calculations allow some businesses to borrow more money than they could otherwise.

One of the most popular uses of SBA loans is for commercial mortgages on buildings occupied by a small business. These programs are chosen because most bank programs, while having similar payments and rates, require borrowers to refinance every five years.

Types of Business Loans Include:

i. Loan Guarantee Program: The 7(a) Loan Guarantee Program are designed to help small entrepreneurs start or expand their businesses. The program makes capital available to small businesses through bank and non-bank lending institutions.

ii. 504 Fixed Asset Financing Program: The 504 Fixed Asset Financing Program is administered through non-profit Certified Development Companies throughout the country. This program provides funding for purchasing land or construction. Of the total project costs, a lender must provide 50% of the financing, a Certified Development Company provides up to 40% of the financing through a 100% SBA guaranteed debenture, and the applicant provides approximately 10% of the financing.

iii. MicroLoan Program: Available for up to $35,000 through non-profit, micro loan intermediaries, to small businesses considered unbankable in the traditional banking industry.

iv. Economic Development Program: SBA partners such as SCORE and the Small Business Development Centers (SCDC's), operating in each state provide free and confidential counseling and low-cost training to small businesses.

v. Business Development Program: Assists in the development of small businesses owned and operated by individuals who are socially and economically disadvantaged.

6) SBA Loan Industry

The SBA loan industry can be divided into distinct categories:

i. The largest United States Banks, such as Bank of America and Wells Fargo, generate the bulk of their SBA loan volume by the loans, especially the express loan and line of credit, being offered to those who would be declined for a normal bank loan due to factors such as length of time in business or slightly stricter affordability factors. These banks have sophisticated computer systems that generally makes this process seamless, and are quite different from other financial institutions who utilize SBA lending for separate and distinct purposes.

ii. SBA loans are used heavily by banks of all sizes to finance the purchase or construction of business owner occupied real estate (i.e. real estate purchased by a business). Many banks only offer SBA loans for this purpose. In particular, they are using to finance properties that the bank would consider too risky to finance on their own, due to them being of a special or environmentally risky nature that can make their resale value limited; these properties include Motels, Gas Stations, and Car Washes.

iii. SBA loans are also used to allow individuals to buy existing businesses. Since, unlike in real estate transactions, commercial lenders are allowed to pay a referral fee to business brokers who help people buy and sell businesses, this segment of the industry is dominated by smaller banks and stand alone finance companies who engage in this practice.

2. Development capital

Later stage finance for more established companies which are profitable or nearly profitable. Generally less risky than early stage finance.

3. Risk-reward ratio

Often imprecise analysis tool that measures the potential risks of a course of action against the potential rewards. It is imprecise if it is not possible to obtain comprehensive information about the potential risks and rewards. In the case of investment analysis the potential upside and possible risks to the company invested in cannot be quantified with any certainty.

4. Going concern

1) Definition and theory

A going concern describes a business that functions without the intention or threat of liquidation for the foreseeable future, say at least within 12 months.

2) Application

Use in Accounting

In accounting, "going concern" refers to a company's ability to continue functioning as a business entity. Accountants and auditors may be required to evaluate and disclose in the notes to the financial statements whether a company is no longer a going concern, or is at risk of ceasing to be one.

Financial statements are prepared on the assumption that the entity is a going concern, meaning it will continue in operation for the foreseeable future and will be able to realize assets and discharge liabilities in the normal course of operations. Different bases of measurement may be appropriate when the entity is not expected to continue in operation for the foreseeable future.

Use in Risk Management

If a public company reports that its auditors have doubts about its ability to continue as a going concern, investors are likely to take that as a sign of increased risk. Some fund managers may be required to sell the stock to maintain an appropriate level of risk in their portfolios. A negative judgment may also result in the breach of bank loan covenants.

5. Industry concentration

1) Definition and theory

In economics, market concentration is a function of the number of firms and their respective shares of the total production (alternatively, total capacity or total reserves) in a market. Alternative terms are Industry concentration and Seller concentration.

Market concentration is related to the concept of industrial concentration, which concerns the distribution of production within an industry, as opposed to a market.

2) Desirable properties

To be practically useful, a market concentration measure should be decreasing in the number of firms in the market. Additionally, it should also be decreasing (or at least nonincreasing) with the degree of symmetry between the firms' shares.

3) Examples

Commonly used market concentration measures are the Herfindahl index (HHI or simply H) and the concentration ratio (CR). The Hannah-Kay (1971) index has the general form

$$HK_\alpha(x) = \begin{cases} (\sum s_i^\alpha)^{\frac{1}{\alpha-1}} & \text{if } \alpha > 0, \alpha \neq 1 \\ \prod s_i^{s_i} & \text{if } \alpha = 1 \end{cases}$$

Note, $\prod s_i^{s_i} = \exp(\sum s_i \log(s_i))$, which is the exponential index.

4) Uses

When antitrust agencies are evaluating a potential violation of competition laws, they will typically make a determination of the relevant market and attempt to measure market concentration within the relevant market.

5) Motivation

As an economic tool market concentration is useful because it reflects the degree of competition in the market. Tirole (1988, p. 247) notes that:

Bain's (1956) original concern with market concentration was based on an intuitive relationship between high concentration and collusion.

There are game theoretic models of market interaction (e.g. among oligopolists) that predict that an increase in market concentration will result in higher prices and lower consumer welfare even when collusion in the sense of cartelization (i.e. explicit collusion) is absent. Examples are Cournot oligopoly, and Bertrand oligopoly for differentiated products.

6) Empirical tests

Empirical studies that are designed to test the relationship between market concentration and prices are collectively known as price-concentration studies; see Weiss (1989).

Typically, any study that claims to test the relationship between price and the level of market concentration is also (jointly, that is, simultaneously) testing whether the market definition (according to which market concentration is being calculated) is relevant; that is, whether the boundaries of each market is not being determined either too narrowly or too broadly so as to make the defined "market" meaningless from the point of the competitive interactions of the firms that it includes (or is made of).

7) Alternative definition

In economics, market concentration is a criterion that can be used to rank order various distributions of firms' shares of the total production (alternatively, total capacity or total reserves) in a market.

III. Analyzing the Case

1. How many financing stages are divided for a company development?

Seed financing, Start-up financing, Early stage financing, Later stage financing, IPO (initial public offering).

2. What is the critical distinction between angeldom and venture capital?

Some 400,000 active angels, in the main, are entrepreneurial-manager types who, so to speak, have got their hands dirty on the shop floor. Venture capital on the other hand tends to be staffed by financial investor types with comparatively little direct business experience. The difference shows in the angel's willingness to take on higher risks and stick with them longer. They can be more patient because they do not have to kowtow to limited partners demanding quick returns or measure up to performance yardsticks to keep their jobs.

3. What are typical of many top entrepreneurial names?

Probing mind and a precocious interest in business are typical of many top entrepreneurial names.

4. Why do feeling and intuition frequently control how angels invest?

Often there is very little else to go on. Financials are not very much help in assessing a company with very little history. Take no entrepreneurial projections for granted.

IV. Translation of the Case

　　38 岁的商业天使人保罗·班祖斯基在布法罗(美国纽约州西部一城市)开始了自己早期的创业。他同家人、朋友和商业伙伴一起组成了天使基金成员，共同出资成立了 12 家新型的高科技公司。在此过程中，他不仅积累了资金，还懂得了重要的经验教训，明白了血汗资本的含义。班祖斯基笑着说："其实这一切都很简单，只要商业模式正确，商品价格合理，供应商合适，那么出乎意料的事情就会发生。"

　　班祖斯基不只是在谈论从母亲的厨房里取走桂皮枝，在学校里以每包 10 美分的价格售出的事情。他开始有一帮追随者，随后发展至他每个月就可以挣 300 美元。生意很好，于是他弟弟就加入到了他的队伍里来，也就是在这个时候，上帝垂青了他。

　　突然事情发生了变化。班祖斯基痛苦地说："校长因为我忽视功课，而停了我三天课。"这可以称为桂皮枝事件吧。在班祖斯基全职经营生意——要分析鉴定小公司，帮助他们成型，并集拢天使资金使公司运转时，出乎意料的噩运是常有的事。

班祖斯基和他的天使成员展现了一种新的私人投资形式。他们不受正式风险投资机构的束缚，是自由职业者，常常以一种松散的模式进行运作。据估计，在美国有两百多万这样的天使投资人。其中很多人，像班祖斯基一样是曾经的创业者，而现在重新投资到一些新型企业。

失败的风险很高，其中受很多种因素的影响，比如：产品失败、市场分析不当等。小公司管理口心数据显示，在班祖斯基资助的初创小公司中，六个中有五个都经营不到五㕒。班祖斯基认为成功的可能性总比受小公司管理局管理的比率要大。他认为 50% 的消耗率太高，不能同狂热的班祖斯基说的"能使你的钱翻 75 到 100 倍的好机遇"相匹配。

许多像班祖斯基这样的自由天使投资组织意识到了潜在的好机遇，去年就向 50,000 多小型初创企业大约投资了 600 亿美元。具有充足财力的专业风险投资公司主要针对那些风险低、高回报的企业，然而据估计，天使基金组织投资金额是其金额的 30 多倍。

巨大的投机浪潮愈演愈烈，把投资高科技公司的投资机构推向了荒谬的程度，然后退潮时，却在石头上撞毁。这种循环已经摧毁了工业的某些板块，像生物工艺，而现在却要摧毁网络公司（dot.coms）。 正是在这个时候，像班祖斯基这样精明的投资者开始收集便宜的打捞物。

班祖斯基像很多典型的企业家一样，同其他个人投资人一起组成松散的形式，将自己早期的成功赚取的金钱及经验都投进去。他们走在游戏的前面，操作简单便宜，没有前后期的开销或者也不需要与管理者分红利润。与前面讲的风险投资案例不太一样。共同投资也可以在投资高风险行业时候做出多种选择，把相对一小部分个人资金(50,C00 美元到 100,000 美元)投资到多种交易中，从而规避风险。特别是，每次共同投资金额达到 100 万美元左右，主要集中在收入不到 1,000 万的小型初创企业上。风险投资多不会关注这些公司，因为风险太高，规模太小，并且监控起来花费太高。

例如，班祖斯基合并了一个初创型高新企业成立了 Sun Hawk 公司，并任其副总裁。西雅图总部的电子出版公司让他持有上市股票的一部分股票。班祖斯基计划投入急需的新的资本来帮助合并。但这并不意味着他有意要经营 Sun Hawk 公司。班祖斯基说："这很过瘾，我想要帮助这些人。 我可能不懂技术，也不想妨碍任何人，但是我告斥他们价格模型如何在不同的行业里运转，如何让一个银行家接电话等，这让所有的企业家都很惊讶。"

　　想从布法罗联营公司中赚取更多的利润，施瑞博尔和班祖斯基想到一个好主意，可以利用高科技发展开发加密软件来保护网络知识产权不受侵害。虽然此领域已有人开发，但是市场前景很好，很多电影制造商、出版商、软件开发公司都十分担心自己的电子产权被黑客或者盗版商所侵害。

　　施瑞博尔和班祖斯基想要把这种想法卖给日本的软件销售商，但是在还不到六个月的时间里就把贷款的 500,000 美元花个精光。他们还想去销售商处多贷些时，被告知是不可能的。自己的为数不多资产在等待回报时，他们只能去找风险投资商们，但是未果。班祖斯基回想当时说："没有人能明白我们想要做什么，他们总是在问数字产权？什么是数字产权？并且，从某种意义上来说，他们总是认为我们只是来自布法罗的两个家伙而已。或许我们只能做些钢铁生意，但是我们对因特网知道些什么呢？"

　　因此，施瑞博尔和班祖斯基灰心失望，转向了成立一个地方的天使投资队伍。其实他们从来都没有涉足过高科技行业，一直都坚守在自己所熟知的领域——布法罗的传统工业以及金属弯曲工艺。这种局限性使得施瑞博尔和班祖斯基只能集中在帐篷钩的生产上。如果是天使投资人，则就应该跟沃伦巴菲特学习，应该远离他们不懂的高科技行业？施瑞博尔和班祖斯基在布法罗投资俱乐部谈论了两个早晨终于达成协议。总天使人是罗斯肯兹。班祖斯基说："一个粗鲁的退役军人变成了一个银行家，"正如班祖斯基预期的一样，"谁也没有质疑。"肯兹德高科技投资没有像过去的几年中大约 30 笔交易一样顺利地进行下去，以往都是买下所有的产品。魁梧的肯兹质疑道："你什么意思?难道你在开始的 12 个月不打算挣钱？"施瑞博尔和班祖斯基利用加密技术慢慢地说服了团队，并开始意识到有一位天使人投入时，他们就稳操胜券遥遥领先了，"上次我看的时候，雅虎还很便宜"。每个成员投资 50,000 到 100,000 美元，共 300 万美元，施瑞博尔和班祖斯基就可以高枕无忧了。

　　他们成了互惠的初创小型高科技公司能很好地说明天使投资网络，一个交易带来另一个交易，这也正是天使人怎么使融资变成更大的资金团。软件银行的资金带来了肯兹资金，使得公司可以运转，施瑞博尔和班祖斯基可以做更深层次的工作了。这一次，风险投资公司意识到，他们看到的不只是来自布法罗的两个家伙，而是能够带来巨额利润的财神了。虽然微软为避免再次像去年那样遭受大量计算机入侵，对加密技术十分苛刻，但也同意这种看法。都加起来，一共有 7,500 万美元，可以雇佣大约 200 名员工，使公司持续经营，保守估计价值几亿美元，当时，公司还没有上市，另一个肯兹天使投资人却能够预测未来。尽管他们在发展过程中可以在需要时拿出大笔资金，这些天使投资人依旧只拥有公司的小部分，这已经成了一种转换经验。班祖斯基说，最后已经冒险投资的投资团，现在已经同他一起投资了很多初创高科技公司。其中一个很成功的投资的公司是 OpenSite 技术公司，是三角研究园的一家公司，总部在北卡罗莱纳州的在线拍卖软件的开发商。

班祖斯基在作为行政总监经营着自己的公司的同时，还向 OpenSite 公司成立者迈克尔·布莱德-阿拉日（Michael Brader-Araje）提供帮助，并予以投资。班祖斯基笑着说：“我第一次找迈克尔谈话时，他跟我说他弄不清楚台球台与股份表的区别（table）。”布莱德-阿拉日学得很快，也下了一番功夫。随着 OpenSite 的发展，资金依旧短缺，布莱德-阿拉日、班祖斯基和肯兹天使投资人开始通过公开销售证券来寻求资金。在 1999 年夏天准备开始时，市场的滑坡使得他们不得不放弃。去年年初，他们准备再来一次，但是市场动荡使他们又被迫中止。奠基人布莱德-阿拉日告诉福布斯记者说：“这实在是一次伤心的经历啊。”

两个长期以来的合作伙伴选择了不同的道路。天使人趋向于无组织的自由派，他们等级属于绝对的干涉型，其中一些是退休的主管人员，不想浪费他们的余生。年轻的成功人士，多在 40 岁左右，有充足的时间与金钱成为一个专业投资人。生活的富足使得他们深信，应该做点什么了。保罗·班祖斯基就是这样一个典型的不安分的人。他说：“我知道我从来都不擅长经营一个大的公司。一旦公司运作起来了，你就必须开始新的项目了。我个人的撤离策略是，在有 25 到 40 个员工的时候，我就要撤离此处了。”

因此，主要的区别是：大约 400,000 个活跃的天使投资人（一般一年做 3 到 4 个单子），主要是企业家、经理类型的，因此他们多会参与到公司的管理中来。而风险投资主要是金融投资人类型的，相对来说，直接的经营经验少一些。由这种区别可以看出，天使投资人自愿承担较高的风险，并且会坚持较长时间经营公司。他们不必担心有限责任股东要求尽快带来利益回报，或者达到要求的成绩标准来保持住自己的工作，因此可以更加从容。

从逻辑上来讲，不管是从时间还是风险上来看，天使投资都应该有更加丰厚的回报。像 OpenSite 这样的成功者可以获得丰厚的回报，肯定刺激着他们的欲望，天使们想要得更多。据新罕布什尔州大学风险研究中心调查数据显示，他们怀着五年让资本翻五番的希望投资。这是他们的期望，实际情况则可能是大相径庭。实际的回报由于分散在像纳舒厄、新罕布什尔州的早餐俱乐部以及硅谷天使人中，是很难能够拿到手的。最多也就是风险行业漏掉的长期的 15% 到 20%，也许会更高些。

那也要比长期股票市场回报高些，当然还有可能一举大胜呢！有两件肯定的事情：天使投资人常常投资到风险投资公司不敢涉足的领域里，已为全国 70% 的初创型高科技企业融资。这让天使投资成为一个巨大的社会经济现象，而不容忽视。天使人对创造工作，推进美国在世界技术领域的领先地位做出了不可估量的贡献。

天使投资历史悠久，受人尊敬。在百老汇描述之前，大家众所周知，天使人就是私人投资者，帮助像亚历山大·格雷厄姆·贝尔和亨利·福特这样的惊人的发明家，向他们提供资金。

另外一件可以肯定的事是：天使投资人有更多的乐趣。

天使人得到更多的精神回报，像保罗·班祖斯基这样的天使投资人积极做准备并投入资本。同时也有社会回报，像 OpenSite 那样的成功情况，就有了鼓吹的资本了。报名费不是问题，由证券交易管理处批准的公认投资人必须拥有至少 100 万美元的净资产（包括初次注册费）或者年收入达 20 万美元的佳绩，（联合合计年收入 30 万美元）。天使人形式多样，规模不一。有的仅仅投资了一两笔交易，而有些则可能有很多投资项目。很多人都很被动，乐意让保罗·班祖斯基来做他们的代理。一些有钱的企业家们往往自己单独行动，多数还是联合起来，成立 100 多个联合组，就像罗斯·肯兹的布法罗团队一样来运作。像吉纳·穆克黑伯（Zina Moukheiber）在《福布斯》中报道的一样，成功的投资人很喜欢用企业联合组织的方法。比如，华盛顿的投资人就有这样的明星：微波-世界通讯公司（MCI World Com）的副总裁约翰·斯德莫尔。

野心勃勃的企业家们都大有前途，正激烈地追逐着这些有名气的投资人。团队的力量可以筹集更多的投资，成功的可能性就大大地提高。同时也有利于更好的网络经营，像异花授粉一样，让肯兹集团摆脱了旧经济的困扰，发展起高科技产业。一些投资集团是一对一的经营模式，一般都已经招募了 100，或者更多的成员。其他的投资人一般还是小规模运作(例如班祖斯基)。内部主导的天使人不想过多地干涉到别人。

多数的团队会定期聚到一起，讨论一些潜在的交易。常常聚在酒吧、餐馆等，就像最近的一次得克萨斯州的天使投资人聚在奥斯丁的四季酒店宴会厅里谈论一样。此团队共 90 人。在开始的招待会上，天使人交换名片和高科技信息，在开始痛饮以及享用精美冷盘后，开始认真考虑严肃的问题，认真聆听宣讲。今天晚上的三个初创公司已经成功了两个。

这两个是从递交给团队领导委员会的 30 个经营计划中胜出的 6 个中脱颖而出的。第一个通过的是，一周前五个小组的委员会在得克萨斯州大学的礼堂里进行的，今天晚上主要是通过 10 分钟的面谈挑出最终三名来。这绝对不是紧张的企业家们所害怕的法庭审判。既有表扬也有批评。"你是在说教，而投资人最讨厌说教了，我们只是想知道投资的企业是做什么的。"其中一个企业家被告知。另一个对自己的软件包的创新太过投入，就建议他放松一些，"有了像你这

样的技术产品，就应该使用一些通俗的语言来谈一下产品的优势。我希望这次会谈能让你明白这一点。'

对于胜出的三位来说，准备会对于如何在四季酒店里的 10 分钟的正式面谈提供有效的演练，在此的问题也主要是围绕技术可行性展开，这也是天使人做出决定时要考虑的关键性问题。同时也有一些问题，是初创公司不愿意透露的。对于提出的问题，答案是："我们对此要保持沉默，这是重要的知识产权，我们现在不方便告知。"在正式的问答过后，在咖啡屋的个人谈话话题要自由很多，有兴趣的天使人可以接着与企业家们预定另外的时间。在谈及金钱之前，可能会有长达几周的继续调研。成功的则就继续了。一位天使人笑着说："社会材料很有意思，但是你看，也相当专业呢。"

社会因素确实是吸引人的一方面。你可以赚钱，也许是一大笔钱，同时又可以助新生公司一臂之力，这怎么会有错呢?原则上来讲，是没有错的。首要问题是:你是否真的拥有了天使人的材料?此问题的答案能部分回答你把资金投资到其他地方，以及你承受风险的能力。像班祖斯基这样的老手就可以把大笔资产投入到私人投资中来，并期待带来丰厚的回报。如果你拥有一些额外的闲钱，并且不在乎输赢，那就投资进来。对于一个新型公司，大概要 5 到 7 年的时间才能看出你是否有一个平衡的证券投资。老的风险资本谚语也适用于此:"柠檬早熟于李子。"(指好的投资还没有赢利，而糟糕的投资就开始赔钱了。)因此你需要有足够的资金来分散在不同的投资项目中，预留一部分后续投入资金。

如果你想投入一些精力来赚取更多，那就要考虑到你的实际空闲时间。同样，最好看一下你的脾气禀性是否适合。如果你是一位可以放手干的人，任何一个称职的企业家都会让你忙得不可开交。如你真的想投入精力，最好同朋友一起，或者加入到一个小团队中来，情况会更好些。

另一方面就是你委托别人给你做决定是否舒服。这里所谈的问题是指有组织的与松散的团队之间的区别。两者都会定期组织一些活动。但是在非正式的团队中，个人自己组织自己的投资项目，所有的调研、法律程序、谈判等都由个人来完成。而像以华盛顿为总部的 Womanangels.net 这样的正式团体总是以一个整体在投资，每个成员要在三年中至少投资 75,000 美元，也有可能更多。其专业成员大多是年龄在 30 到 60 岁的女士，他们会选一个管理人员来处理这一切事宜。多数情况下，管理人会至少拿走利润的 15%作为工资，相比较风险投资公司，专业投资人收取利润的 20%到 30%(再加上 2%的年费)，这已经很低了。

不管正式还是非正式团队都会在专业人士的建议下投资到某一个领域，例如，班祖斯基投资 Reciprocal 成功了，这使他主要集中在加密技术领域投资。

投资自己所熟悉的行业是一种降低风险的方法,开拓出自己有用武之地的企业。同时,不要投资太专业的领域。如果一项产品失败了,是否还有什么退路可以挽救?

找到适合的团队就是加入天使网络的过程,同一些有可能加进来的专业人士多聊一聊,例如:银行家、律师、会计、大学的企业项目、投资银行家等。留意一下天使人与企业家的匹配服务,大约有 100 个这样的服务场所,多数是免费的,或者大学附属的。这些服务机构会举办一些面对面的投资论坛,或者利用信件和网络把资金与投资项目联系起来。

多数天使团队要对潜在的成员进行筛选(确保他们符合证券交易委员会的公认投资人的标准),同时也是准成员对团队提出自己问题的过程。这时可以问清楚团队的风险承受力、投资标准、退出策略管理,以及胜算比率等问题。尽量索要一些小册子、年度报告、推荐论坛的详细信息。你是在以团队投资,也是在投资证券,尽可能地多与其他成员进行交流,让自己融入其中。如你未能这样做,就会发现你跟格鲁楚·马克斯(Groucho Marx)很相近,他拒绝加入任何团队。

自我选择的过程(我是否适合这个团队?)依赖于你是否在寻找同类的投资交易,不同的发展阶段、风险水平、投资金额,以及投资价格都会随着变化。公司发展阶段如下:

种子投资,一般只需要少量的外部资金,但是公司的奠基人要投入大量的人力,一般是资金投入到一个理论上看来很好的但是还未曾开发的产品中,例如:在此阶段,亚马逊的奠基人杰夫·贝祖把自己的 1 万美元投资亚马逊公司(Amazon.com)的建设中,又从《天使投资》的作者范·奥斯纳伯鲁格(Van Osnabrugge)和罗宾逊(Robinson)那里借了 4 万美元,把股票的价格调整到每股 0.001 美元。

初创阶段的投资是指对于处在发展与市场研究阶段,但还未真正的进行商务运转。就是在此阶段,贝祖的父母向亚马逊公司投资 24 万美元,他们的股价是每股 0.1717 美元。

初期的公司已经启动发展资本,并需要另一轮的资金投入开始全面的投产与销售。这时,两位天使投资人一共向亚马逊公司投资 54,408 美元,他们的成本价是每股 0.3333 美元,随后又有 20 位天使人联合起来共投资不到 10 万美元,他们的成本价依然是每股 0.3333 美元。

第二阶段公司开始有了收入,(但严格来讲并不是利润),拥有实力雄厚的管理人员,急需资金来扩大生产。此时,两家投资公司共向亚马逊公司投资 800 万美元,他们的成本价是每股 2.34 美元。

在贝祖投资自己的 1 万美元后不到三年的时间，公司就开始首次公开销售证券，亚马逊公司以每股 18 美元的价格共筹集资金 49,000,000 美元，这对于以每股 0.3333 美元买到的天使投资人来说无疑是十分高兴的事情。公司初期，贝祖、他的家人，以及天使投资人承担着很高的风险，很便宜地购进，当然也赚取了最丰厚的利润。后期投资的风险资金公司是对一个正常经营的企业投资，所以相对来说投资资金多，而回报相对少些，这就是典型的风险收益比率，并且表明了资金如何为下一步做准备。

风险与回报都在不断变化着，因此应该确保加入的天使团处于你所适合的阶段。再者，如你想要进行早期的启动投资，也要看一下是否有发展的空间。另外还应该注意：行业集中度、最少投资额、总开支，如果有管理人员的提成，也要包括在内。

网络投资把天使人联系起来，让他们一起讨论投资项目。许多网络提供的匹配服务都是从双方提供的保密数据库来进行搜集匹配的。一些按照最低投资额筛选掉某些初创企业，而有的则不会这样。

把双方联系起来后，所有的匹配服务机构就会自动退出。天使人自己要做很多工作来作出决定，例如，尽管保罗·班祖斯基只是一个来自遥远地区的天使人，罗斯肯兹和布法罗的天使人都很主动地同他联系，早期的筛选过程就时间来讲很重要。天使投资，跟其他事情是一样的，在成功之前要付出很多。因此，首要问题就是要十分小心，"谁发现的这项交易？"项目的发现人并不都是投资的目标，他们常常是售卖方。

在此演讲中总是有一定量的夸张。在布法罗的天使人演讲时，他们更多地是利用 yahoo 以及高科技行业的投资所能带来的经济回报在说服。这当然会抓住投资团队的注意力。然而真正导致此交易成功的因素是班祖斯基和施瑞博尔所展示出来的管理能力，以及他们对未来市场的认真全面的剖析。任何一个人都可以胡乱拼凑一份华丽的经营计划，就像网络公司表面上看来是切实可行的，是能够找到投资人的。但是却像一串爆竹一样消失了。天使人的使命就是越过纸张，透过现象找到经营计划的本质，因此，班祖斯基说，罗斯·肯兹"检查了我们所有的资料，并且与每个人交谈来掌握科技的动态。这真是我所见过的比较艰苦的事情。"

因此，肯兹不会让班祖斯基的诱人进攻影响到自己的决定。正是这一点使肯兹比较成功地经营着天使投资。美国新罕布什尔州大学研究中心表明，企业家的热情与人格直接决定着天使人的投资。有激情很好，特别是你想要直接同企业家们工作在一起时。但是更大的优点是证实专门技术和管理技能的运用，这些都是很难发现的，更别说是在一个还未经实验的初创企业里。

　　衡量这些品质的一个标准是看初创者在寻求外界帮助前是如何努力筹集资金的。基本上指，他做了多少工作？是否一周必须的 80 到 100 小时都做了详细的记录？他有多少钱在危险中？他是否在举债经营，不断地还清债务，投入资金与努力使企业正常运转？他是在自己的车库还是在花费很多钱租来的地方工作？他是在使用二手或者租来的设备还是大肆挥霍买来新的使用？为何不充分发挥节俭精神，自力更生呢？

　　以保罗·班祖斯基的背景作为一个你想要与其投资的例子，管理机构(投资学校的校长)暂时使其停业，两年后，他再次开始投资。这次跟桂皮枝没有任何关系。"我跟父亲谈到了糖果的零售差额（我爸爸常做生意），涨价幅度还不错。"班祖斯基回忆到。班祖斯基利用自己从桂皮生意中赚取的资金，以每块 12 美分的价格购进价值 200 美元的士力架（Snicker）和牛奶糖（Milky Ways），然后在午饭时候，20 个同学一起以每块 30 美分卖出，(零售每块赚 5 美分)，大家平分所得的利润。班祖斯基笑着说，"这是一个很好的商业计划，很快就有资金流入，并且销售成本十分低廉。"

　　在随后的学习时间里，班祖斯基总是在不断地做各种各样的小生意，其中包括他在密歇根中心大学与同学们一起成立了一个软件公司。他说，"我们那个公司存在销售问题，大家都认为我们只不过是一群大学生，没有人买我们的产品。"其中一个朋友的父亲是一位天使投资人，他们就游说天使人投资，并管理公司的市场问题。奇迹出现了。班祖斯基回忆道："最后公司卖给了另一个集团，实际上我们还赚了一笔钱呢。"

　　班祖斯基共上了 6 所大学，都未曾毕业，密歇根中心大学就是其中之一。他说，"我经常跟教授们争论。"最后一次争论发生在芝加哥大学。班祖斯基对老师给的案例持有不同观点，于是他就质疑："你真的认为实际中会是那样的吗？"教授坚持如此，班祖斯基就怀疑老师是否真的曾经做过生意，得到的答案是："没有做过，这难道有什么区别吗？"班祖斯基说："我走出去后，就从不回头。"班祖斯基经过 8 次风险投资后，就拥有了足够的资金来作为天使投资人再次投资。

　　许多成功的企业家们都有一个探索的头脑和对商业提早的兴趣，具有天才的潜质。拿阿玛尔·博士作为一个例子，他对扩音器设计的试验是最终博士公司建立的开始。博士公司是一家生产具有艺术特性的音响设备公司。二战期间，他父亲的进口生意开始滑落时，13 岁的博士就在费城建了一个半导体修理铺，当时会修理半导体的人几乎都参军了，博士店以每小时 50 美分的价格雇佣了 7 名学生，很快，博士店铺就成为费城最大的店铺之一了。

　　无独有偶，在德国占领希腊期间，14 岁的乔治·海佐波勒斯秘密地制造半导体，主要在地铁上售卖，后来建立了热电集团。他有一个笔记本，记录了一些创新思想，希望有一天可以围绕这些思想建立一家公司。他最后实现了自己的愿望，建立了热电集团。热电子发射产生的能量可以转化成电力成了热电集团的核心。

假如说这都是一些例外的天才，早期对商业的执著却是一致的。未来的企业家应该首先具备这种前瞻性。被动的天使投资人常常不会重视参加这种早期的人才会谈。这其实是一个错误。对于刚起步的公司，首先决定投资的是人，然后才是产品。天使人一般最害怕的事情是未能正确估量一个初创人。他是否可以像多数人那样在出现问题时经受得住考验？他是否真的能够组织好一个管理团队？他是否只有跟随声附和的人一起工作才会感到舒服？

天使投资人常常依赖于情绪和直觉。很少其他的东西来参考。经济状况对于评价一个刚刚起步的公司是没有用的，但是常常会对此作出挑战。经营计划应该作为早期筛选的一项指标，把其看作销售文件，不要把企业家们的预测当作真理。你在寻找的是一个在快速发展的市场中能够快速胜出的特殊产品。调查应该聚焦到一起。你的团队应该发挥起自身的行业实力，机智的天使人应对市场潜能做一个独立的审查。

也可以从外面雇佣专家来做这些事情，但是这样就会对本来就已经很昂贵、耗时的过程增加成本。早期的筛选应该是很严格的，只有很不错的机会才能过渡到要进行正式认真筛选的阶段。一旦过了前期的筛选，就要冷静地看一下传统指标，比如现金流、潜在的回报率。他们是否很有希望，而值得做这个投资？天使人们常常不会做如此深入细致的调查，这也正是他们为何比风险资本人作出的决定要快得多的原因之一，结果，也常常会在闲暇时悔悟一番。

没有深入的考虑，就很难解决风险基金的难题：这个公司能否成功，承担大部分风险后，能拥有公司多少股份？在预约的议价中就要弄清楚这些事情。由于天使人们想要与企业家一起共事 5 年，甚至更长的时间，很少有人会为了再多 2 个百分点而争论到最后。但是谁付出多少，得到多少是永久争论的焦点。即使是在像创立数码器材公司这样成功的案例中亦如此。朋友们说计算机制造者（现在是康柏电脑(Compaq Computer)的一部分）的创造人，肯尼夫·奥尔林，直到今天都还认为他放弃的太多，而得到的太少，放弃了公司 70%的股份换来了 7 万美元的种子投资，最后网络了乔治斯·多利特的美国风险投资公司研发公司 4,000 多万美元的投资。

天使人也常常觉得自己被欺骗了，后悔他们没有奋力争取更好的条件。不要太咄咄逼人了，但是至少不要只满足于只占少数股份，或者董事会的一个职位，就像班祖斯基在 Sun Hawk 中的副总裁一职。

争夺控制权是一大禁忌。企业家的动力应该是刚起步企业最为珍贵的资产，为何要剥夺这最有价值的东西呢？为何要担心资产净值呢？可转换债券是一个较好的选择，至少如果企业真的破产了，债券还可以保证对资产进行索赔。签合同前还应该考虑到资金的非流动性是对起步公司投资的一大缺点。你如何撤资？如公司彻底破产，估计还能从破产法庭上打捞回点东西，但是如果公司处在半死不活的边缘，常用的撤资途径是同行拍卖，买断管理经营权，或者是合并（就像保罗·班祖斯基把自己的小公司同 Sun Hawk 合并起来）。在新的证券发行市场获得回报是每个天使人梦想的撤资途径，但是却是承担了更大的风险。天使人在经营着一个农场系统，从半专业成为一个小联盟的成员就会很高兴，只有特殊的才能才能使其成为一流的投资者。

认真监控才能使你的投资获得好的回报。要确定你的资本获得最大的收益，薪资标准要压低。补偿项目中，股票是很重要的一个指标。这样就可以节省企业的现金，给公司从上到下注入活力。抵制从外面雇用昂贵的管理人员的诱惑。内部培养人员是筹资的另一种方法，同时也是满意于投入风险投资的一部分。

当然还有很多种其他的方法。可以投资到公开的企业孵化器中，像安保科技公司（Safe Guard Scientifics）或者软银风险投资公司（Soft Bank Ventures），都比去年价格要低得多。你可以投资到公开交易的商业发展公司，或者是风险共同基金中。可以这么做，但是永远也不会感受到班祖斯基所讲的创造性的话语。他说："天使投资不仅仅是工作。"

附录

Vocabulary

A

aerospace industry	航空航天工业
accountability	n. 责任，义务
acquiring company	购入其他公司股权的公司
acquisition	n. 收购
aggressive conservative investor	积极和谨慎的投资商
air reduction	空气还原
alumni	n. 毕业生，男校友
America online (AOL)	美国在线服务公司
ancillary	adj. 辅助的，副的
angularity	n. 有角的部分
ante up	v. [美俚]（不得已而）付账，付钱，提出
archive	n. 存档，档案文件
as buy-and-hold investor	作为买入并持有的投资者
as vulture investor	作为秃鹰投资商
at the peril of	冒……的危险
auspice	n. 预兆，前兆，吉兆
autocratic	adj. 独裁的，专制的
aviation industry	航空工业

B

back office	内勤工作
bailout	n. 跳伞，将优先股发给股东作为红利之行为
balance sheet	资产负债表
ballast	n. 压舱物，稳定力量
bankroll	vt. 提供资金
bank run	银行挤兑
bankruptcy	n. 破产
bankruptcy trustee	破产管财人
base pay	基本工资
bear market	熊市
Berkshire Hathaway	伯克希尔·哈撒韦公司
blarney	n. 谄媚，奉承话
blip	n. 雷达上显示的点
blizzard	n. 大风雪
board of trade	同业公会，经济部
bond yield	债券市场利息率
book value	账面价值
bounced check	空头支票
boutique	n. 专卖流行衣服的小商店
bow out	退休，告老，辞职，不做（某事）
brevet	vt. 使名誉晋升
brokerage	经纪人之业务，回扣
bull market	牛市

C

cash advance	现金垫款
catnip	n. 猫薄荷
caveat	n. 中止诉讼手续的申请
chat up	用与人闲聊来获得对方的好感，搭讪
charitable	adj. 仁慈的，慈善事业的，宽恕的

cheap and safe investment	廉价安全的投资
cheap and safe investment philosophy	廉价和安全的投资原则
chew out sb.	严厉责备某人
Chicago Board of Trade	（美）芝加哥交易所
chihuahua	n. 吉娃娃（一种产于墨西哥的狗）
chivvy	v. （使）烦扰，耍花招
christen	vt. 命名
chutzpah	n. 放肆
Citicorp	西特公司
civil suit	民事诉讼
cloak	n. 斗篷，宽大外衣，掩护
	vt. 用外衣遮蔽，披斗篷
clunker	n. 不值一文的东西
clutter	n. 混乱
cobble together	胡乱拼凑，粗制滥造
collateralize	v. 以……作抵押
columnist	n. 专栏作家
cop a plea	避重就轻地认罪
confide	v. 吐露，倾吐（秘密）
come up the hard way	通过艰苦努力而达到目前的地位
commodity futures	期货交易
Commodities Futures Exchange	商品期货交易所
confabulation	n. 会议
	v. 会谈
cook the books	伪造或窜改财务报表，造假账
creditor	n. 债权人
credit report	信用报告
criminal contempt	n. [法] 严重之藐视法庭行为
custodian	n. 管理人
custody	v. 收容
cut into	侵犯，打断
Curb Market	股票证券场外交易市场
current ratio	流动比率

D

debacle	n. 崩溃
deflationary	adj. 通货紧缩的
depreciation	n. 贬值，减价，跌落
depressed stock prices	低迷的股票价格
dilettantism	n. 业余的艺术爱好，浅涉文艺，浅薄涉猎
disenchanted	adj. 不再着迷的
diversification	n. 分散风险
divestiture	n. 财产权等的剥夺
dividend	n. 股息，红利
dividend payout	派息
dividend yield	股息生息率
dogma	n. 教条
dog and pony show	盛大表演
dot-com	n. 网络公司
down payment	预付定金
downplay	vt. 贬低，低估
due from	应收

E

earnings yield	收益率
eclectic	adj. 不拘一格的，兼收并蓄的
effective market theory	有效市场理论
egregiously	adv. 惊人地，无比地，异乎寻常地
eleemosynary	adj. 施舍的，接受接济的，慈善的
Electroglas	伊智公司
enclave	v. 被包围的领土
encomium	v. 赞辞，赞美，称赞
endemic	n. 地方病
energy industry	能源工业
equity	n. 股票，股本
erratic	adj. 无确定路线，不稳定的

expostulate	vi. 劝诫，忠告
expiration	n. 终结；期满
exponential	adj. 指数的

F

fall guy	替罪羊，替死鬼
farm out	分派
feisty	adj. 好争吵的，活跃的
ferment	v. 酵素，蓬勃发展
field trip	（学生）实地考察旅行
fifth amendment	[法] 第五条修正案
financials	n. 财政
flabber-gasted	adj. 目瞪口呆的
fleeting	adj. 飞逝的，短暂的
foolproof	adj. 十分简单的，十分安全的，极坚固的
forest products industry	林产品业
fractionally	adv. 极少地，微小地
franchise	n. 特权
free cash flow	自由现金流
free-standing	adj. 自立的，不需依靠支撑物的
frenetic	adj. 发狂的，狂热的
front for	主办
Futures Exchange	期货交易所
futures trading	期货交易

G

GEICO	政府雇员保险公司
General Electric	（美）通用电气
gloss over	辩解；掩饰
greenhorn	n. 生手，缺乏经验的人
grimace	v. 扮鬼脸，做苦相
groan	vt. 呻吟着说

grossly	adv. 非常，很
growth stocks	成长股
Guggenheim Exploration Company	（美）古干海姆探测公司
gull	v. 欺诈，骗，使上当
guru	n. 宗教老师，领袖

H

handholding	n. 关怀备至，手把手的指导
hang paper	[美俚] 假造支票
hatch cover	装货仓盖
hawk	vt. 兜售，（沿街）叫卖
heavy selling	抛售
hipped	adj. 着迷的，忧郁的
hitch	v. 延迟
hit the roof	勃然大怒
horoscope	n. 占星，诞生时的星位
hustler	n. 皮条客，骗徒，催促者
hype	n. 大肆宣传，炒作
hyperactive	adj. 活动过度的，极度活跃的
hyperbole	n. 夸张法

I

idle capacity	闲置生产能力，空闲容量
illiquidity	n. （企业等）缺少流动资金
incarnation	n. 赋予肉体，具人形，化身
incentive	n. 鼓励，奖励
inculcate	v. 谆谆教诲，反复灌输
in hock	在典当中，在坐牢，负债
Interstate Commerce Commission	州际商务协会
interest coverage	利息保障倍数
intrinsic value	内在价值
insolvency	n. 无力偿还，破产

insomniac	n. 不眠症患者
institutionalize	v. 使制度化
intimidate	v. 胁迫
inventory	n. 详细目录，存货，财产清册，总量
IPO	n. 首次公开募股
irrepressible	adj. 镇压不住的，抑制不住的

J

Japanese market	日本市场
jillion	adj. 很多的，大量的
jockey	n. 职业赛马骑师

L

leverage	n. 举债经营
leveraged buyout	融通债务
liabilities	n. 不利条件，各种可能性
limited liability	有限债务责任
limited partner	有限责任股东，有限责任合伙人
liquidate	v. 清算
liquidation	n. 清算
liquidity	n. 流动性，偿债能力
litigation	n. 诉讼
locked-in	adj. 牢固的，不上市证券的
Longleaf Funds	长叶基金
lurk	vi. 潜藏，潜伏，埋伏
lycee	n. 法国公立中学

M

malaise	n. 不舒服；抑郁；心神不安
manic	adj. 狂躁的
manipulate	v. （熟练地）操作，巧妙地处理

margin of safety	安全边际
margin of safety investment rule	安全系数投资规则
market risk	市场风险
member firm	美国证券交易所的成员行号
Minerva	n. 密涅瓦，智慧、技术及工艺之神
Ministry of supply	n. 陆军供应部
molybdenum	n. [化] 钼（金属元素，符号 Mo，原子序号 42）
multiple	n. 市盈率

N

Nabors Industries	石油钻探公司
nativist	n. 先天论者，本土主义者
naturalize	v. 加入国籍
net current asset	流动资产净额
net quick liquidation	净清算价值
net working capital	净运营资本
New York Produces Exchange	纽约物品交易所
no end	非常
no-load	n. 资产净值
non-starter	n. 弃权出赛的马，早就无成功希望的人
nuclear power industry	核能公司
numbered account	账号
nuts-and-bolts	具体细节

O

obligations	n. 待付款
old-line	adj. 历史悠久的，保守的
on margin	凭保证金额购买证券
on tap	可随时使用
on the make	在制作中，野心勃勃
on the sly	秘密地

onus	n. 责任，负担
open-end	n. 开放基金
option	n. 购买权，期权
overhead cost	间接费用，间接成本，营业成本，总开支

P

pan out	成功
pandemonium	n. 喧嚣；大混乱；大吵大闹
pay-outs	n. 花费，支出
Penn Central Railroad bonds	佩恩中央铁路债券
Pepperell Manufacturing	佩博雷尔制造
personal guarantee	个人担保
Phi Beta Kappa	美国大学优等生之荣誉学会
pick up the pieces	（跌倒后）重新爬起来（对小孩讲的）
pick up the tab	替人付账
pigeonhole	把……束之高阁
piggybacking	n. 载搭，捎带，指借助别人的道路进入的行为
pinpoint	v. 查明
pitch in	努力投入
pooh-pooh	v. 贬低，对……嗤之以鼻
pools	n. 联营，联合基金
portfolio	n. 投资组合，有价证券财产目录
posting	n. 过账
power and light companies	能源和照明公司
premium	n. 贴现率
price / earning ratio	市盈率
price-to-book value	股价与股票账面值的比率
pricing of companies	公司的定价
printed circuit	印刷电路
produce exchange	物产交易所
progenitor	n. 先辈
promoter	n. 赞助人，出资人

pronto	adv. 很快地，急速地
proviso	n. 限制性条款，附文，附带条件
public offering	公开销售证券
Public Service Company of New Hampshire	美国新罕布什尔州公用事业公司
pump-and-dump	v. 拉高出货
punter	n. 下赌注的人，用篙撑船的人，船夫
purveyor	n. 承办商
put out of business	使无法进行，使停业，使破产

Q

quixotic	adj. 堂吉诃德式的，狂想家的

R

rank-and-file	n. 普通员工
rationale	n. 基本原理
real estate	房地产
receivership	n. 破产管理，破产清算
reorganization strategy	重组策略
repository	n. 贮藏室，智囊团，知识库，仓库，储存库
resource conversion	资源转换
retail industry	n.零售业
risk limiting	风险限制
roll up one's sleeve	卷起袖子，准备行动
round trip	n. 往返旅行
roseate	n. 玫瑰色的，红润的，容光焕发的
Rosenwald Foundation	（美）洛克菲勒基金会
Rubaiyat	《鲁拜集》
ruckus	n. 喧闹，骚动
rule off	划线隔开
rump	n. 尾部，臀部，残余

runaway market   失去控制的市场

s

sanctum	n. 圣地，密室，书房
savings and loan industry	储蓄和贷款业
scarcity	n. 缺乏，不足
scourge	n. 鞭，笞，苦难的根源，灾祸
	vt. 鞭打，痛斥，蹂躏
seasoned hand	老手，得力人手
serendipitous	adj. 善于作意外发现的；侥幸得到的
selling of investments	投资出售
semiconductor equipment manufacturers	半导体设备制造商
semiconductor equipment	半导体设备
senior mortgage	优先抵押债务
sententious	adj. 说教的，言简意赅的
settlement price	结算价
sequester	adv. 幽静的，隐蔽的
	vt. 使隐退，使隔绝，扣押，没收
severance payment	解雇费
shop floor	车间；工场
short-term earning	短期收益
shy away from	躲避，离开，羞于
slow-up	n. 放慢速度
speculator	n. 投机者
spiel	n. 招揽生意的言辞
spin-off	n. 资产分派，让产易股
splash out	[口] 随意花钱，大肆挥霍
standby	n. 可以信任的人，使船待命的信息，备用
stash	n. 隐藏处
sterilize	v. 冻结，封存
stock swap	证券交易
stopgap	adj. 暂时的，权宜之计的
subscriber	n. 订户，签署者，捐献者

sustainable	adj. 可持续的
Swiss Bank Corporation	瑞士银行有限公司
syndication	n. 企业联合组织

T

take the plunge	冒险尝试
tenure	n. 占有期；任期；占有条件
the underlying value of a business	潜在的商业价值
Third Avenue Value Fund	第三大道基金公司
Tokyo Marine & Fire Insurance	东京海运和火灾保险
top dog	胜利者
traction	n. 附着，牵引，摩擦力
trajectory	n. [数] 轨线；常角轨道
troll	n. 唱歌庆祝
turnaround	v. 彻底改变，好转
tutorial	n. 指南

U

UCLA	（美）加州大学洛杉矶分校
Ultima Thule	天涯海角，最远点
unanimously	adv. 全体一致地，无异议地
underling	n. 部下
underscore	vt. 强调
undervalued assets	低估资产
unfounded	adj. 没有理由的，毫无根据的
unload	v. 抛售
uxorious	adj. 溺爱妻子的

V

| value investing | 价值投资 |
| value stocks | 价值股 |

value strategy	价值策略
virtuosity	n. 精湛技巧，高超
volatility	n. 挥发性，反复无常
vow	v. 誓约，宣誓

W

weather eye	密切注视，保持警惕
Whitman Martin J.	马丁·J. 惠特曼
Whitman's investments	惠特曼的投资
whopping	adj. 巨大的，庞大的
	adv. 非常地，异常地
winnow	vt. 簸，扬（谷），吹开糠皮，吹掉，精选
wiped out	精疲力竭的，资产被耗尽的，破产的
worth one's salt	称职，胜任
wringer	n. 敲诈者
write-off	n. 销账，勾销，账面价值的削减

X

x out	清除，取消，删除

参考文献

Bernsten, Richard. *Navigate the Noise: Investing in the New Age of Media and Hype*. John Wiley & Sons, Inc. 2005.

Bodie, Z. A. Kare & A. J. Marcus. *Investments*. 机械工业出版社. 2007.

Brennan, Jack. *Straight Talk on Investing: What You Need to Know*. John Wiley & Sons, Inc. 2004.

Luenberger, David G. *Investment Science*. 中国人民大学出版社. 2004.

Osnabrugge, Mark Van. *Angel Investing: Marching Startup Funds*. Jossey-Bass. 2000.

Phalon, Richard *Greatest Investing Stories*. John Wiley & Sons, Inc. 2001.

Whitman, Martin J. & Martin Shubik. *The Aggressive Conservative Investor*. John Wiley & Sons, Inc. 2005.